SOCIOLOGY

Class, Consciousness, and Contradictions

Albert J. Szymanski
University of Oregon

Ted George Goertzel
Rutgers University at Camden

D. VAN NOSTRAND COMPANY
New York • Cincinnati • Toronto • London • Melbourne

GIFT

13302

D. Van Nostrand Company Regional Offices:
New York   Cincinnati

D. Van Nostrand Company International Offices:
London   Toronto   Melbourne

Library of Congress Catalog Card Number: 78-62187
ISBN: 0-442-27879-9

Published by D. Van Nostrand Company
135 West 50th Street, New York, N.Y. 10020

10 9 8 7 6 5 4 3 2 1

Preface

SOCIOLOGY: CLASS, CONSCIOUSNESS, AND CONTRADICTIONS offers a comprehensive and systematic introduction to sociology. Its goal is to introduce students to sociology as the critical study of society, for a better understanding of the social world and a greater ability to act as members of that world. We believe that a systematic sociology can be developed only within the confines of a consistent paradigm. We present an overview of sociology from a Marxist perspective. This perspective is made explicit in the first chapter.

Chapter 1 acquaints the student with the sociology of knowledge (which is needed in order to make sense of the alternative models in sociology) and discusses the major approaches to the study of sociology. The remainder of the book is a theoretical and methodological presentation of the Marxist perspective in sociology. We show how the sociological theories we present can be used to explain the historical development of human societies and how they enable us to analyze the structure of contemporary American society. We apply the theories to the full range of topics usually treated in sociology, including the individual, culture, racism, and sexism.

The book can be used in a variety of ways. Instructors who wish to challenge students with a new perspective may use the book alone or as a core text. Others who prefer to present a multiple-paradigm course may supplement the text with contrasting readings.

Each chapter has materials that will help extend the student's understanding of the concepts presented in the chapter. These materials include a summary, review questions, suggestions for further study, and an extensive bibliography. The suggestions for further study emphasize ways in which the themes of the chapter can be related to the student's own experiences and interests. While a few of the projects may require guidance from the instructor, students can do most of the projects independently. An *Instructor's Manual* is available.

This book is a true collaborative effort. Albert Szymanski wrote the first draft of the manuscript. Ted Goertzel revised and rewrote each chapter, added additional material, and edited the illustrations. Drew Humphries wrote Chapter 9 on Crime and the State especially for this volume.

We are indebted, as with any textbook, to the works of others who wrote the literature on which it is based or who helped us as teachers or friends. We must mention especially C. Wright Mills and Paul Sweezy, who were key precursors to the radical sociology movement of the 1960s. Mills was truly the "father" of radical sociology. We have both been influenced by the work of G. William Domhoff, Paul Baran, André Gunder Frank, James O'Connor, Herbert Marcuse, Nicos Poulantzas, and others whose work is cited in the references to each chapter.

Ralph England and Juan Long have contributed to the intellectual development of Albert Szymanski. Joseph Kahl and Irving L. Horowitz were equally important to Ted Goertzel. Susan Jacobs Szymanski, Jerry Neilson, Joe Schoenfeld, Harry Humphries, Steve Johnson, and Jerry Lembcke are among those at the University of Oregon who were important to both of us during our time there. Other Oregonians who contributed their criticism of many of our ideas are Richard Pozzuto, David Wellman, and the members of the Feminist Theory Collective.

The Union of Marxist Social Scientists, the Insurgent Sociologist, and the East Coast Conference of Socialist Sociologists have given us much intellectual and personal support. Maria Brown, Donald Wallace, Drew Humphries, and other members of the Philadelphia Socialist Sociology Group have been invaluable resources for Ted Goertzel during the last few years. Albert Szymanski would especially like to thank Terry Hopkins, who introduced him to so many ideas, taught him the methods of comparative crossnational analysis, and was so generous with his time and energy during his years at Columbia University.

Thanks are due Jean Darian, who helped substantially with the chapter on ecology and population, and to Jeff Schevitz, who critiqued the first draft. We wish to express our sincere appreciation to the following people who provided constructive criticisms and suggestions in the development of this text: Professor Gene Grabiner, SUNY at Buffalo; Professor Henry Etzkowitz, SUNY at Purchase; Professor Martin Oppenheimer, Livingston College, Rutgers University; and Professor J. W. Freiberg, Boston University. Our publisher, Judith Joseph, and our editor, Cheryl Trobiani, made many valuable suggestions. Doris Boylan and Theresa Peretta did consistently excellent work in typing the manuscripts.

                                                          Albert J. Szymanski
                                                          Ted George Goertzel

Contents

10 Imperialism and Development   242

Mechanisms of Control / Causes of Imperialism / Role of
Imperialism in the U.S. Economy / Effects of Imperialism on Third
World Countries / Conclusions / Summary / Review Questions /
Suggestions for Further Study / Selected Readings

11 Racism and Capitalism   268

Functions of Racism / Development of Race Relations in the U.S. /
South Americans: the New Cheap Labor / Effect of Economic
Discrimination on White Workers / Summary / Review Questions /
Suggestions for Further Study / Selected Readings

12 Family, Sex, and Society   285

Origins of Sexism / Transformation of Housework / Women in the
Labor Force / Sexism and Women's Work / Class and Women's Oppression / Class and Political Divisions / Summary / Review Questions / Suggestions for Further Study / Selected Readings

13 Ecology and Population   305

Destruction of the Environment / The Environment and the Profit
System / Population and Economic Growth / Summary / Review
Questions / Suggestions for Further Study / Selected Readings

14 Social Movements and Revolution   314

The Nature of Social Movements / Types of Social Movements /
Conditions for the Success of Social Movements / Looking Toward
the Future / Conclusions / Summary / Review Questions /
Suggestions for Further Study / Selected Readings

Chapter 1

An Insider's Guide to Sociology: Radical and Otherwise

"When *I* use a word," Humpty Dumpty said, in a rather scornful tone, "it means just what I choose it to mean—neither more nor less."

"The question is," said Alice, "whether you *can* make words mean so many different things."

"The question is," said Humpty Dumpty, "which is to be master—that's all."

Lewis Carroll
Alice's Adventures in Wonderland

The student who embarks on the study of sociology may feel that she or he has stumbled into a strange new world, less entertaining than Alice's perhaps, but no less confusing. Sociologists claim to be scientific, or at least most of them do, but the word seems to have a very different meaning than in the physical or biological sciences. The sociologists often seem unable to agree about the most basic assumptions or findings of their discipline. In a science like astronomy, questions such as whether the earth revolves around the sun, or vice versa, may generate tremendous controversy, but eventually they are resolved and scientific work moves on to other questions. Social scientists, on the other hand, frequently reopen the most basic issues, rejecting the work of their predecessors rather than building upon it.

Of course, any field of study becomes problematic when you study it closely.

1

Thomas Kuhn has shown that even such venerable sciences as physics and chemistry have had their periods of revolutionary upheaval, when supporters of one approach within the discipline rise up and overthrow the defenders of the old assumptions. These revolutions in the physical sciences are few and far between, however, while the social sciences seem to be in a state of permanent revolution, with adherents of different points of view within the field constantly attacking each other.

Why are the social sciences filled with conflict and controversy over basic issues? We believe it is because social science is inherently and necessarily political as well as scientific. While social scientists can use scientific methods of research, gathering empirical data to test their hypotheses, the questions they ask, the concepts they use, the theories and hypotheses they advance cannot help but have an effect on the society they study. Social science is a part of society, in a way in which physics and biology are not part of the physical or biological world. Social scientists cannot be arbitrarily split off from the social and political conflicts that are a central part of the societies they study. For this reason, it makes sense to speak of a radical sociology or a conservative sociology, while there is no clear and direct way in which such ideological categories can be applied to different approaches within such sciences as physics or chemistry.

This political dimension in sociology is not undesirable. Indeed, the fact that sociological findings have political and ideological relevance makes them more interesting and important. Unfortunately, many sociologists have felt bad about the political nature of their discipline, and have tried to convince themselves that there is no difference between their work and that of a physical scientist. Often they have argued that their own work is scientific and "unbiased" while the work of others with whom they disagree is "biased" and hence unscientific. In their attempt to make their work look nonpolitical, they have often used obscure and technical language, even when ordinary, everyday words could be used to express the same ideas. Students often complain that sociologists take commonplace ideas and express them in such a way that they are difficult to understand. We believe this is at least in part a consequence of taking ideas that have political implications and attempting to make them sound neutral and "objective."

This book presents an introduction to sociology from a radical perspective. While we believe our work to be scientific and based on objective evidence, we also recognize that it is guided by radical assumptions. It would be possible for us to ignore or disguise this fact in writing our book, as authors of many liberal and conservative textbooks have done, but this would only make the book less interesting and more difficult to read. The reader would have to read our abstract concepts, and infer from them what our underlying perspective was, in order to really understand what the book is about. This would be asking our readers to do a job that is really the responsibility of the authors, and would be less than completely honest.

We do not intend to give equal weight to liberal and conservative sociology. There are other books for that, and most students growing up in America have had more than adequate exposure to these ideologies even if they have not yet examined the sociological data that has been produced by their supporters. Radical sociology is, however, in many ways a response to liberal and conservative sociology. In most of the chapters of this book we will be carrying on an explicit or implicit debate with the alternative approaches to the problems discussed. Consequently, in this first chapter we will discuss conservative and liberal sociology, and make explicit how it differs from radical sociology. This will give us an opportunity to discuss the logical nature of sociology, and its historical and social origins.

PARADIGMS IN SCIENTIFIC DISCIPLINES

Recent studies in the history of science have highlighted the fact that research cannot be conducted without prior assumptions that structure and organize thought. Thomas Kuhn has used the concept of *paradigm* to refer to models of inquiry that guide scientific work. Paradigms provide a conceptual structure, a framework, for understanding the phenomena studied by a given science. They indicate the types of questions that should be asked, and the kinds of evidence that can be used in answering questions. In the physical sciences, usually one paradigm governs the entire field for a long period of time. Eventually, work within the limits of a paradigm reaches a dead end, when significant problems emerge that cannot be answered without going outside the paradigm. This leads to a period of crisis, followed by a scientific revolution. Most frequently, this revolution is led by a great thinker whose work provides a concrete example of how to do work within the new paradigm. A well-known example is Albert Einstein, whose work on relativity established a new paradigm in physics, replacing the paradigm advanced by Isaac Newton over two hundred years earlier (although many of Newton's findings could be incorporated into the new paradigm). Another is the replacement of the *phlogiston* theory in chemistry with a new paradigm that completely denied the existence of phlogiston.

Sociology differs from physics and chemistry in that there are a number of paradigms competing at any one time. Consequently, struggles between adherents of different paradigms have been very important in sociology, and an understanding of the nature of paradigms is the key to understanding society from the inside. Each sociological paradigm provides a set of categories with which to comprehend the social world. These categories are the mental units by which social reality is perceived. Each paradigm represents an *alternative* way of looking at the social world, which, at least in the first instance, appears to be as scientific or correct as any other. Because each poses its own key problems and specifies the methods it will accept, it is not at all easy to confront adherents of a paradigm with evidence that refutes it. Almost any phenomena can be interpreted in the terms of a given paradigm. Therefore, paradigms can and do compete with each other for dominance over extended periods of time. The adherents of a competing approach are very difficult to convince of the validity of the objections of others because each paradigm itself establishes the criteria by which to evaluate others.

People who adhere to a specific paradigm tend to use various arguments to avoid considering problems posed by other paradigms. They may simply deny that the problems are of any importance, or that they exist at all. For example, most liberal and conservative sociologists believe that the Marxist problems of false-consciousness and class interest are false problems that have no meaning. Adherents of a paradigm may simply argue that supporters of another paradigm need not be taken seriously because they are naive, unscientific, ignorant, ideological, or biased.

If this method of ignoring adherents of another paradigm does not work, the next step is often to simply classify their work as belonging to some other academic discipline. Thus, rather than denying the existence or importance of problems raised by Marxists, conservative or liberal sociologists may say, "that's a problem for the economists, not for us." Many sociologists argue that certain problems that they cannot explain well within their favorite paradigm are really problems for the economist, psychologist, philosopher, or political scientist.

If issues cannot be ignored or consigned to another discipline, adherents of a paradigm will generally try to incorporate them into their own paradigm. This usually involves redefining what members of another paradigm are "really" saying. By focusing on selected parts of their argument, and considering only part of their evidence, it is usually possible to account for contradictory evidence or to consider it as a special case of one's own paradigm. This is how liberals and conservatives often deal with Marxist arguments. Liberal sociologist Robert Merton, for example, argues that Marx was really a functionalist, while conservative sociologist Talcott Parsons redefines Marx's concepts in order to fit them into his system, meanwhile emptying them of their original content.

Paradigms have significant consequences for the work that sociologists do. Sometimes, sociologists devote considerable energy to these debates and arguments with supporters of other paradigms. Often, these struggles involve concrete material issues, such as jobs and promotions. Within particular sociology departments, there are often struggles over what kind of sociologist should be hired for a vacancy, or over whether or not a particular sociologist's work is good enough to justify promoting him or her to a permanent, tenured, position. While these decisions are supposed to be made by hiring or promoting people whose work is of high quality, evaluations of the quality of work are naturally influenced by opinions of the paradigm that the sociologist in question uses.

For a scientific discipline to progress, it is necessary to do a great deal of work within the limits of a specific paradigm, without taking time or energy to defend every assumption against attack from people who do not accept the paradigm. Kuhn referred to *normal science* as this sort of work done within a paradigm. A paradigm specifies many things that are needed to do scientific work. It specifies basic assumptions about the nature of the subject matter to be studied, and basic concepts to be used in studying it. It specifies the range of phenomena to be considered, the central problems to be studied, and specific theories composed of laws and hypotheses about the phenomena. It also specifies the research methods to be used in proving hypotheses, and the basic values that guide inquiry. Of all these things, the basic assumptions and concepts are the most central, since these tend to shape everything else.

While paradigms cause a great deal of controversy and conflict, they must not be seen as troublesome or unnecessary philosophies that "bias" scientific work. Without paradigms to guide their work, scientists would not be able to work together on common problems. They would have to begin at the beginning each time they did a project, as do poets or artists or other workers in nonscientific fields. While their work might be interesting, it would not build into a cumulative body of scientific knowledge that could be relied upon by others interested in the same area.

Components of Paradigms

Since paradigms are so important, understanding them is fundamental for the student of any scientific field. Before we go on to discuss the paradigms in sociology, therefore, we will take the time to discuss on a more abstract level the seven basic components of a paradigm. These components can be found in paradigms in any scientific discipline, whether in the social, biological, or natural sciences, although we will use examples from sociology.

The first element to be considered is the *basic assumptions.* These are more or less taken-for-granted or "common-sense" orientations toward the phenomena being studied. For example, some sociologists believe that people are inherently competitive and aggressive, others that they are inherently cooperative and loving. Some feel authority is necessary for social life to be possible; others feel that authority always benefits some at the expense of others. Some see all social behavior as an exchange among individuals or groups; others see social behavior as an acting out of the inherent value system of a society, and still others view social phenomena as the rational pursuit of interests. All such orientations are really prior to the development and testing of specific theories about social relations and are virtually impossible to refute to the satisfaction of those who believe in them.

Concepts are the categories used to describe aspects of social phenomena. Concepts are the smallest units of a paradigmatic definition of social reality. They specify what entities the social world does and does not contain. They further implicitly suggest the interrelationships among concepts, that is, the concepts themselves suggest specific theories. For example, the concept of *class* within the Marxist paradigm not only categorizes people in terms of class but also suggests that the divergent interests of classes can be used to explain social and political phenomena. Likewise, the liberal sociological concept of *value* or *norm* not only categorizes ideas in these terms but also suggests that values and norms determine other aspects of social reality.

By the *range of phenomena* considered significant is meant the area of social phenomena that a paradigm defines as important, in other words, those places that it suggests one should look for data. Some paradigms insist that the relevant data for sociological research should come from interactions of individuals in small group situations, others that it should come from observing whole societies.

A specific *theory* is either a statement relating two or more concepts or a set of such statements. It is theories in this sense that are normally tested in research, or through political or economic practice. *Problems* are those issues that the overall paradigm indicates are important questions but that the paradigmatic system has not yet adequately explained in its own terms. Different paradigms have different theories and pose different problems. For example, radicals have normally considered a central problem to be the presence or absence of class consciousness within a class. They have constructed many theories to account for its presence or absence. A central problem for the sociological liberal is the problem of deviance. Many theories attempting to explain deviance have been developed. Neither overall paradigm subscribed to by each group specifies the problem that the other views as centrally important as a significant problem. As a consequence neither bothers to put forth a theory to explain what the other considers to be a central problem.

Every paradigm also has its favored *methods for testing* its theories. This is the case because certain methods are naturally suited to solving particular kinds of problems. Any tradition of normal science assumes a commitment to similar rules and standards of research procedure. The commitment to employ a particular method and to use it in a particular way naturally carries with it an assurance that only certain sorts of things can be studied. For example, the mandate to use only experimental methods means that whole societies and long-term change cannot be considered, because there is no way for sociologists to experiment with whole societies. Similarly, commitment to employ only survey methods means that attitudes necessarily become central explanatory concepts.

Every sociological paradigm contains implicit *values* (feelings that things are either good or bad). These values are generally either conservative (supportive of the legitimacy of the status quo) or radical (undermining of the legitimacy of the status quo) or liberal (accepting the basic limits of the status quo, but encouraging limited changes). Sociology, by the very nature of its subject matter, cannot avoid becoming committed to one side or another in political controversies. Sociological paradigms cannot retreat from political commitments even though they may claim to be value-free and independent of partisanship. In fact this is always a myth. It is logically impossible to separate the analysis of social relations from the evaluation of social relationships. This is so because values are an inherent part of social relationships, which scientific analyses can logically only support or contradict.

The nature of sociology as the study of social relations dictates that it is political. The real question is not whether it is "value-free," but rather "what are its values?" For example, popular mythology in the United States claims that the U.S. is a democratic society. If political sociology comes up with research that supports this claim, then it is liberal; on the other hand, if it finds evidence that the society is not democratic, then it is radical. There is no way that a study of political decision-making could avoid supporting one or the other political ideology. Likewise, a study of the dynamic behind U.S. foreign policy must either support the prevailing legitimation that it is motivated by altruistic concerns or the radical ideology that it is motivated by the search for profits. Inevitably, a sociological study or theory will come down on one side or the other.

There is an integral relation between all ideas about a society and the various vested interests within that society. The social sciences are inherently tied up with the system of social relations by the very nature of their subject matter. Thus, their results (or nonresults) are inevitably tied up with the interests of classes, institutions, and total societies. Any talk about the autonomy of social science must be dismissed as a nonsense notion of only ideological use.

The question of the values implicit in sociological ideas is logically distinct from the question of the truth or falsity of such ideas. Because ideas are conservative or radical does not mean they are necessarily true or false. A sociological statement can be true and conservative (that is, fundamentally supportive of the status quo), true and radical (that is, fundamentally delegitimizing of the status quo), false and conservative, or false and radical. A simplistic classification of sociological ideas as either "scientific" or "value-laden" bears no relation to the real world. The real problem is rather one of determining which "value-laden" ideas are scientifically true and which false. Such a determination, of course, also indicates what values and interests are most consistent with scientific truth.

HISTORICAL DEVELOPMENT OF SCIENCE

Science has progressed with incredible rapidity during certain periods in history. During other periods progress has been slow or nonexistent. There is nothing in the inherent nature of science that explains these trends; science progresses steadily during any historical period only if encouraged to do so by society. Rather, it is social forces that encourage or permit the development of science. True science, the objective search for understanding of the real nature of empirical reality, emerges when powerful interests in society have a need for such knowledge. Generally, this occurs when a powerful social class is attempting to change society to better suit its interests. During periods of social stagnation, such as the Middle Ages in Europe, elite groups generally find that religion or other forms of mysticism better suit their needs for intellectual doctrine. These doctrines tend to legitimize the status quo, to make it seem inevitable and impossible to change, even if it displays certain unpleasant qualities.

The physical sciences grew up with the rise of commercialism in Europe in the seventeenth, eighteenth, and nineteenth centuries. Science developed in exactly those areas where the commercial revolution was concentrated: first in Italy, a little later in western Germany and the Low Countries, still later in England. The physical sciences reached maturity with the demand of developing industrial capitalism for hard information on the behavior of chemicals, machines, heat, lenses, etc. This information was necessary for the advance of industry, and for the development of military technology that made it possible for the European capitalist nations to dominate the earth. For example, Boyle's law of gases, a classic scientific theory, was developed because there was a need to understand what happens inside a gun when a bullet is fired.

While the development of the sciences was a product of the practical needs of developing capitalism, it was opposed by the vested interests of feudal society. The development of physical science was opposed by the Church and by feudal interests who were afraid of being economically and morally undermined by the new capitalism and its advance. Christianity was the key to the legitimacy of the feudalistic system of social relations. Everything in feudal society was conceived of in terms of *hierarchy* and *place*. The position of everyone was justified by the Bible. Women should be subordinate to men, children to parents, peasants to landlords, apprentices to masters, and subjects to their kings, all because it was God's will as revealed in the Bible and interpreted by the Church. The Bible as the ultimate source of our knowledge of God's will became a document whose integrity was absolutely essential to defend. Since there is a passage in the Bible stating that God commanded the sun to stand still, it must follow that the sun revolves around the earth. Consequently, Bruno, Copernicus, et al., must have been wrong. Any other conclusion would undermine the legitimacy of the entire Bible, and hence the entire system of religious justifications for the structure of social relations of feudal society.

Because of such factors, it was inevitable that the physical sciences could develop only because of a long and successful struggle between the rising capitalist forces, with their demand for practical information and their desire to destroy the legitimacy of feudal social relationships, and the declining feudal forces, interested primarily in continued obscurantism and the preservation of their privileges. The victory of the natural sciences over medieval scholasticism is a direct product of the victory of capitalism over feudalism.

The resistance of aristocratic groups to science continued for a very long time. The teaching of science until very recently has been opposed by lay and clerical intellectuals concerned with the education of pupils for state service or elite life. The teaching of the sciences began very late at Oxford, Cambridge, Harvard, Yale, and other elite schools, which have traditionally favored "classical" over scientific education. As a result, until very recently, most of the major innovations in the physical and biological sciences did not take place in universities (which were closely tied to the most reactionary forces in society) but rather were made by individuals most closely tied either directly or indirectly to capitalist interests (that is, either employed by capitalists or enveloped in intellectual circles inspired by industrial capitalism, rather than cloistered in scholastic institutions).

Although the biological sciences have fared well in their partnership with developing capitalism, they have not fared as well as the physical sciences. First, the demand for practical biological knowledge and the consequent rewards from the dominant class structure for producing that kind of knowledge have not been as great as for knowledge in the physical sciences. The exception is the demand for practical knowledge in the areas of agriculture and medicine. Second, the results of the biological sciences have had a more direct bearing on social relations, and hence on the legitimation or delegitimation of dominant interests, than have those of the physical sciences. The most sensitive areas of biology are its studies of the innate potentialities, needs, instincts, and adaptability of people (genetics, biopsychology) and the study of the evolution of the human species. Thus, not only did the Church oppose Darwinianism until quite recently (some sects, of course, still oppose it) but biological research was suppressed or distorted in both Nazi Germany and the Soviet Union to suit the ends of the dominant ideologies and interests.

For the most part, today, the actual results of the natural sciences are no longer as significantly distorted as they have been in the past in order to meet the demands of the dominant interest structure of society. Rather, the influence of the prevailing interests is exerted mainly by selective support. That is, those aspects of physics, chemistry, and biology that appear to be the most useful to the dominant groups are supported the heaviest, while those that don't appear as useful are supported lightly, if at all.

The lesson to be learned from this is that the natural sciences became "objective" only after a great struggle, and only because the practical results of such objectivity proved to be highly beneficial to the dominant interests. The needs of the dominant groups for legitimation were a constant obstacle to the development of the scientific method.

History of Social Science

The social sciences emerged as a consequence of the development of industrial capitalist society. Many acute social problems were created by the change from an agrarian to an industrial society. In order to free themselves from the traditional constraints imposed by the feudal aristocracy, the industrial upper class had destroyed many of the old political and economic structures. These changes were resisted by many people both from the old ruling classes and from the peasant class, since the peasants were being forced to abandon their old way of life and move into urban factories.

The capitalist class required two things from the social scientists. First, they needed social doctrines to legitimate and justify the new social conditions. They particularly wanted to counter demands for further social changes in the interests of the middle and working classes. Second, they needed objective information about how industrial societies functioned and how they could be made to function more smoothly.

Economics as a scientific discipline developed during this period. The *laissez-faire* school of economics, led by Adam Smith and David Ricardo, legitimated the new market economy. It argued that the market functioned like an "invisible hand" assuring that all decisions were made in such a way as to insure the ultimate good of the society. Their economic paradigm also made it possible to do scientific research about how to maximize profits and expand production within a capitalist system. Economic theories of this period tended to emphasize concepts such as prices, credits, interest, exchange rates, and the like, while obscuring the fact that these factors resulted from relationships between human beings—relationships that were often cruelly exploitative.

A revolution in economics occurred as a consequence of the economic crash in 1929. The classical paradigm was challenged by a new paradigm based on the work of John M. Keynes, which abandoned the idea that market forces should always be allowed free play. Keynesian economics stressed government intervention in the economy to control business cycles, generate demand, control unemployment, and maximize growth. This new theory represented the interests of a more liberal sector of the upper class, which recognized the need to reform the system in order to prevent more radical changes being forced by the working classes.

HISTORY OF SOCIOLOGY

Sociology is also closely tied with vested interests, and plays the same two functions as economics: legitimation of the system and provision of practical information about social problems. The demand for objective intervention about social problems seems to be less than that for economic information, however. Conservative sociology tends to play almost entirely a legitimizing role, while liberal sociology has a somewhat greater scientific emphasis.

The term "sociology" was first used in France in the early nineteenth century by a group of philosophers who were in principle opposed to the French Revolution, and who in any event wanted to make sure revolutionary principles were not extended to the working class. They realized that it was impossible to return to the old discredited myths of feudal society, so they proposed to replace them with a new doctrine that would justify itself by appealing to science. Auguste Comte is the best-known proponent of this reactionary and more or less religious cult, which called themselves "sociologists." In spite of their attempt to claim the legitimacy of science, this group of "sociologists" degenerated into the same kind of shallow thinking and apologetics that characterized most of their predecessors. Despite their lack of important scientific findings, they filled a need felt by the ruling groups in the Western European societies of the time for a new conservative doctrine to replace the old doctrines of feudalism and royal power. Their conservative paradigm thus received support from the government first in France in the latter part of the nineteenth century and soon after in other Western European countries. University professorships in sociology were established at this time, one of the first of which went to Émile Durkheim, whose conservative approach to the study of society soon became predominant in European academic circles. (England was an exception to this trend, probably because traditional feudal political institutions were retained at least as figureheads. In any event, English universities stressed traditional classical education and did not include sociology in their curricula until recent times.) The Durkheimian system stressed order, the contribution that each institution makes to the preservation of order, and the importance of shared ideology in preventing discontent.

The early development of sociology in the United States was largely independent of its development in Europe. From its founding around the 1880s until the 1930s, American sociology and social work were more or less united. The central concerns of American sociologists were crime, immigration, and urban problems. Sociologists were trying to find solutions to these social problems within the existing social, economic, and political framework of society. They were guided largely by a liberal paradigm that argued that social reform was necessary to meet the demands of various groups, such as the farmers and workers, who might otherwise become threats to the system.

Marxist thought also developed during the nineteenth century, supported by the growing labor and socialist movements. Marxist and other radical thinkers, however, were rarely if ever able to obtain university appointments. Karl Marx himself never had a university teaching job, despite his eminent qualifications. Consequently, Marxism influenced the academic sociology of this period largely as an unseen enemy. Conservative and liberal sociologists often worked to counter Marxist ideas, but they rarely explicitly considered Marxism because they wanted to avoid giving it academic respectability or tainting themselves with exposure to it.

During the depression years of the 1930s, however, Marxism became much more influential among intellectuals and students in the United States (and elsewhere). Pressure from the left during this period led to an almost total transformation in American sociology. The old social-problems approach of the liberals seemed inadequate to explain the crisis of the system, and demand for a new conservative paradigm grew. In order to combat the systematic approach of Marxism as an alternative paradigm promising to explain the crisis of the system, American sociology turned to the conservative sociological paradigm that had been developed in Europe. The whole range of sophisticated and systematic European conservative social thinkers were translated into English and pushed in American universities. The old social-work orientation was downgraded with the establishment of Durkheim, Vilfredo Pareto, and Max Weber as the chief sources of ideas within American sociology. This paradigmatic revolution was not without its traumas, such as the creation of a new official journal, the *American Sociological Review,* and the change of name of the leading professional association from the American Sociological Society to the American Sociological Association.

At the same time that systematic conservative theory was institutionalized, liberal sociological researchers changed the focus of their research from urban problems to the more general needs of corporate capitalism. In the late 1920s and 1930s sociologists began to be hired by the corporations to do research on how to get their workers to produce more while causing less trouble, and on how to sell more of their products. Industrial sociology and market research thus became two of the most important areas within sociology. It was the concern with consumer attitudes and their manipulation (to increase demand for corporate products) that produced the hegemony of survey research during this period. Participant observation, a technique suited to the study of urban social problems, went out of favor, while comparative and historical methodology continued to be undeveloped.

One of the major influences on sociology around the 1930s was the demand of the corporations for industrial sociologists who would provide them with information on how to better manipulate and control their work force in order to increase their profits. A whole new subfield of sociology—industrial sociology—developed in response to this need of the corporations. Elton Mayo became the founding father of this field. Mayo conducted a long series of very useful experiments on workers at the Western Electric Hawthorne plant to uncover the causes of greater work efficiency or productivity. After varying such things as the light, heat, music, rest breaks, and the reward systems of the production units he was studying, Mayo finally discovered that it was the treatment of the workers as human beings that had the greatest effect on production. It was his discovery of the techniques of social manipulation of workers that gave financing to a whole generation of industrial sociologists who happily did the dirty work of the corporations until they finally mastered the necessary techniques themselves.

Sociological research, especially survey research, came into its own during World War II with the military's discovery of its usefulness in increasing fire power and kill efficiency. Sociologists were employed during, and immediately after, the war to study such problems as the conditions under which soldiers were most likely to have high morale and fire their weapons at the enemy instead of firing them into the air, the social and psychological characteristics of good pilots, the techniques of effective propaganda, and the effectiveness of strategic bombing. The great influx of military and corporate money into sociology during this period led to the institutionalization of survey methods as *the* technique of sociological research, and the concern with the bureaucratic problem of social control as *the* central orientation of research sociologists.

Alternative Perspectives in American Sociology

The dual demands on sociology—the demand for a sophisticated and conservative ideological alternative to Marxism on the one hand and the demand for practical in-

C. Wright Mills

Courtesy Columbia University

formation for purposes of manipulation and control on the other—led to the development of two sociological paradigms. The first demand produced a synthesis and systematization of the conservative European social theorists. The chief spokesman for this approach was Harvard sociologist Talcott Parsons. The second demand led to the development of practical methods of social research, particularly survey research designed to obtain information about the attitudes and beliefs of large numbers of people. The chief spokesman for this approach was Columbia sociologist Robert K. Merton. There has been relatively little conflict between these two paradigms, largely because each tends to do a different kind of work. Conservative sociologists tend to concentrate on abstract theoretical work, with little attempt to gather empirical data. Liberal sociologists disdain abstract theorizing and tend to focus on practical problems. They tend to develop only limited theories—Merton referred to "middle-range" theories—covering particular practical problems. Although there has been much more or less hidden contempt on the part of the adherents of both tendencies for the other, this has pretty much stayed beneath the surface, primarily because the liberals are reluctant to deal with the types of broad societal issues raised by the conservatives. Radical sociologists, on the other hand, have attacked both groups. The most brilliant radical attack was that of C. Wright Mills, who referred to the first tendency as "grand theory" and to the second as "abstracted empiricism."

Mills was an isolated maverick figure, writing during the 1950s when McCarthyism had a chilling effect on American academia. His work had a great influence, however, among students who were studying sociology in the 1960s. His critique of the conservative and liberal paradigms in sociology made sense to students who also felt the inadequacy of these approaches to deal with issues raised by the emerging civil rights and antiwar movements. His critique of the American power structure, in *The Power Elite*, offered an example of a more relevant sociology. With the growth of the student movement in the 1960s, many radicals entered sociology as a profession (including the two authors of this book). Radical activism broke out at annual meetings of the American Sociological Association in the late 1960s and *The Insurgent Sociologist* began publication as the journal of the radical movement in sociology. While the sociological radicals were inspired by the example of C. Wright Mills (who died in 1962 at the age of forty-five) and received the support of older radicals who had survived the McCarthy period, no single figure emerged as the primary spokesperson of sociological radicalism. Instead, radicals turned to the European socialist tradition for paradigmatic guidance, and most particularly to the works of Karl Marx.

At the present time, we can isolate three major paradigms in American sociology: the liberal, conservative, and radical paradigms. We prefer to use ordinary political terms to describe these paradigms, not merely in the interest of simplicity in language but because we wish to emphasize the political and ideological relevance of each paradigm. Not all sociologists would agree with dividing sociology into these three paradigms, although none would have difficulty in recognizing the three groups we have described.[1]

These three paradigms coincide with the three major political ideologies in the United States, and they draw major elements from these ideologies. Conservatives generally support the existing social order, and believe dissenters should be made to conform to it. Radicals oppose the dominant institutional structure and propose major systematic change. Liberals try to maintain a position in between, not wanting to challenge the system as a whole but still hoping to remedy specific problems within it. Liberalism is the most ambivalent ideology, and liberals tend to swing from one side to another depending on the conditions at a given point in time. Since most sociologists are liberals, it is not surprising that much sociological writing has an ambivalent, indecisive character. It is particularly unfortunate, therefore, when some liberal sociology textbooks present liberal sociology as if it were the only paradigm in the discipline, or when it is presented as the only alternative to conservative sociology. The remainder of this chapter will be devoted to a discussion of the three paradigms.

---

1. Since theory and methodology are often not closely related in American sociology, it is possible to define paradigms in terms of methods, as one author (Ritzer) has done. This author, however, is forced to recognize that all great sociologists worked within more than one of his paradigms. Others tend to see only two paradigms in sociology, generally called the "order" and "conflict" paradigms, although one author (Friedrichs) prefers to call them "priestly" and "prophetic." These authors generally have a good understanding of what we call conservative sociology, but fail to distinguish between liberal and radical sociology.

PARADIGMS IN CONTEMPORARY SOCIOLOGY

In this section we shall examine each of the three paradigms in detail, outlining their basic assumptions, concepts, ranges of phenomena considered, central problems, specific theories, research methods used, and value resonances. Of course, we must present a somewhat simplified version of each paradigm, since there are many variations within each and some sociologists attempt to incorporate elements from more than one paradigm in their work. To simplify our analysis, we have concentrated on the work of three prominent writers whose work tends to serve as an exemplar or model for other work within the paradigm. The three writers are Talcott Parsons (conservative), Robert K. Merton (liberal), and Karl Marx (radical). Later on, we will comment on the work of other sociologists who do not quite follow the models set by these three writers.

THE CONSERVATIVE SOCIOLOGY OF TALCOTT PARSONS

Perhaps the most basic assumption in conservative sociology is that society is an essentially orderly and harmonious entity, a single organism. While the conservative sociologists recognize that there are many diverse individuals and groups in a society, their main concern is how these can be made to fit together in a smoothly operating social system. While some conservatives assume that people are basically evil for biological reasons, Parsons and most sociological conservatives tend to view people as receptive to whatever influences society places upon them. Parsons' most central assumption is that the system of values or beliefs holds societies together. The nature of a society, and any problems that occur within it, are to be explained in terms of values held by the people in the society. Growth in a society means the development of values that better enable the society to adapt to its environment.

In viewing the various aspects of a society, conservative sociologists tend to focus on their contribution to maintaining social order. Parsons, for example, feels that deviant behavior is caused by people not being taught the correct values (not being adequately "socialized"), that inequality is necessary because it motivates people to work better for the good of society, that the state or government is good because it works to help society attain its common goals, that our economic system is organized primarily to help society as a whole meet its needs.

The concepts that Parsons uses tend to focus on the question of order. Parsonian terminology is, however, extremely difficult to use or understand because Parsons generally makes up his own words to convey his central ideas rather than using ordinary everyday words. Many sociologists fall into this trap, in part because concepts are such an important part of sociological paradigms and only by using unique words can a sociologist seem to be saying something distinctive. Parsons, however,

Talcott Parsons

Courtesy Harvard News Office

carries this tendency to an extreme bordering on that of Humpty Dumpty in the
quote from Lewis Carroll at the beginning of this chapter. Since this is a book on radical sociology, we will not burden the reader with a list of Parsonian concepts. In his
book *The Sociological Imagination*, however, C. Wright Mills performed an invaluable service by translating several passages from Parson-ese into straight English. We
can do no better than repeat one of his examples here, both to show the nature of
Parsons's use of concepts, and also the very simple nature of the underlying ideas.
Parsons writes that

> An element of a shared symbolic system which serves as a criterion or stan-
> dard for selection among the alternatives of orientation which are intrinsically
> open in a situation may be called a value. . . . But from this motivational orien-
> tation aspect of the totality of action it is, in view of the role of symbolic systems,
> necessary to distinguish a "value-orientation" aspect. This aspect concerns, not
> the meaning of the expected state of affairs to the actor in terms of his gratifica-
> tion/deprivation balance but the content of the selective standards themselves.
> The concept of value-orientation in this sense is thus the logical device for
> formulating one central aspect of the articulation of cultural traditions into the
> action system.
>   It follows from the derivation of normative orientation and the role of values
> in action as stated above, that all values involve what may be called a social refer-

ence . . . It is inherent in an action system that action is, to use one phrase, "normatively oriented." This follows, as was shown, from the concept of expectations and its place in action theory, especially in the "active" phase in which the actor pursues goals. Expectations then, in combination with the "double contingency" of the process of interaction as it has been called, create a crucially imperative problem of order. Two aspects of this problem of order may in turn be distinguished, order in the symbolic systems which make communication possible, and order in the mutuality of motivational orientation to the normative aspect of expectations, the "Hobbesian" problem of order.

The problem of order, and thus of the nature of the integration of stable systems of social interaction, that is, of social structure, thus focuses on the integration of the motivation of actors with the normative cultural standards which integrate the action system, in our context interpersonally. These standards are, in the terms used in the preceding chapter, patterns of value-orientation, and as such are a particularly crucial part of the cultural tradition of the social system.

C. Wright Mills translates the passage from Parsons into straight English as follows:

People often share standards and expect one another to stick to them. Insofar as they do, their society may be orderly.

Of course, Mills recognized that any book can be condensed into a few sentences and even did so for two books of his own. However, he felt that little would be gained by translating Parsons' book into more than four paragraphs, and invited his readers to turn to the original book to see if they could find more of value. It seems unlikely that many took up the invitation.

After reading Mills' translation of Parsons, the reader may conclude that the emperor has no clothes. It may seem unlikely that Parsons' paradigm will offer anything of value. In fact, the conceptual structure is the most impressive part of the Parsonian paradigm. Parsons' paradigm claims to cover a very wide range of phenomena, including all social systems everywhere and at all times. In practice, however, he generally focuses on contemporary middle-class America, and views other societies in terms of how closely they succeed in approximating the American ideal. The problems that Parsons addresses generally involve the role of values in some situation. For example, Parsons develops a theory of the function of values in the doctor-patient relationship or of the relationship of Calvinist religious ideas in the origin of capitalism, or of how inadequate socialization into dominant values leads to deviant or criminal behavior.

As for methods, Parsons himself generally relies on secondary sources (reinterpretation of the work of others) and on common sense to give illustration to the models he develops. The Parsonian conservative paradigm is, however, quite consistent with the use of standard sociological research methods, such as social surveys (to acquire information on beliefs and values), small group experiments (to get data on how groups adapt and how they maintain order within themselves), or even historical analysis (to illustrate the idea that societies are slowly evolving toward a society like that in America).

Basic Ideas of Conservative Sociology

The conservative paradigm is more concerned with legitimation than it is with actual scientific research. Parsons' basic theory is really quite simple. Its basic points can be reduced to the following propositions:

1. People must be socialized into the prevailing value system in order to preserve the dominant system of order.
2. Those for whom this process of social manipulation does not adequately work must be subject to "second-line defense mechanisms," such as social ostracism and police control, to keep them from disrupting the prevailing system.
3. The "core value system" is the fundamental determinant of the organization and change of social systems.
4. Each major institution (family, religion, the state, the economy) functions to advance the system as a whole. Thus, the function of the government is attainment of the society's goals, not the pursuit of the interests of a dominant group or class. The function of economic institutions is the adaptation of the society to the environment, and not self-serving profit-making.
5. All history reveals the gradual development of the values of a society based on norms and values that apply equally to all people, which provide specific functions for people to perform in different contexts, and which stress the growth of law, equality, democracy, and freedom. Societies become increasingly adapted, integrated, specialized, and rich until all these tendencies are realized, as in the contemporary United States of America.

Parsonian sociology does provide a comprehensive paradigm for viewing society. It is a paradigm that is highly conservative in its value implications. The highly abstract terminology used by Parsons generally makes the paradigm seem more objective and scientific than it really is. Use of this terminology makes it difficult to deal with issues such as basic conflicts of interests between groups in society, since the very terminology would lead one to think of these conflicts in terms of mere differences in values. It is thus important to reduce the Parsonian paradigm to ordinary English so that it can be seen as one limited and politically biased perspective on society, rather than as a highly abstract and scientific theory.

THE LIBERAL SOCIOLOGY OF ROBERT K. MERTON

Liberal sociology differs from conservative sociology in its political implications, but this difference is not obvious or straightforward. Liberal sociologists do not generally offer a liberal model of how societies function that could be compared with the models offered by conservative or radical sociology. Rather, they tend to avoid the question of the larger structure of society, focusing instead on limited problems within one particular part of society. Or, frequently, they focus on social-psychological problems that can be dealt with on the level of individual interactions without examining how these personal problems fit into a larger societal context.

Liberal sociologists tend to be more empirical than theoretical; that is, they are more concerned with doing actual studies of specific phenomena than with speculating about how the broader system works. Robert K. Merton is the best-known theorist of liberal sociology, but he limited himself to developing theories of what he called "the middle range." These are theories that deal with some limited problem, for example, the way people manage the different roles they must play, or how they are influenced by groups they belong to or wish they belonged to.

Liberal sociologists generally take the larger structure of society for granted, and work on resolving specific problems or answering specific questions within it. This approach fits into liberalism as a political ideology. Liberals generally do not question the basic organization of American society, but they do work to reform specific aspects of it. Thus, liberals have been concerned with problems such as racial and sexual discrimination, the pollution of the environment, or the war in Vietnam. But they have assumed that these problems can be resolved without questioning the basic economic or social structure of the United States. When problems such as crime in the streets or worker dissatisfaction with their jobs or working conditions occur, liberals generally assume they can be resolved without major changes in the society or without compromising the interests of either group in the dispute. Liberal sociologists often work in institutions such as Robert Merton's Bureau of Applied Social Research at Columbia University, which help to gather information intended to aid in resolving these problems. Liberal sociology is often much more attractive to undergraduate students than Parsonian conservative sociology, since students often tend to be attracted to sociology because they have an interest in helping to resolve these same problems.

Merton's most basic assumptions differ from those of Parsons largely in terms of the level of analysis they focus on. Merton assumes that society is composed of relatively autonomous units that may or may not be in conflict. His paradigm focuses on the network of socially structured relations between individuals. While Parsons assumes that values held by members of society are essential to hold it together, Merton simply denies that there is any overall principle that holds society together. Thus, the major problem for Parsons, how to hold society together as a unified whole, is not considered important by Merton.

Liberal sociology is well suited to American academic institutions, which tend to divide knowledge of society into distinct disciplines—economics, political science, anthropology, sociology, psychology—since their paradigm leads them to believe that the more specialized one becomes the more likely one is to be able to learn something. Conservatives and radicals, on the other hand, believe that the most important phenomena are characteristics of the system as a whole.

Central Concepts of Liberal Sociology

The most central concept in the Mertonian paradigm is the "role," which means pretty much what it means in everyday English—roles are positions in the social structure that people play, such as teacher, student, wife, policeman, worker, etc. In the past, a distinction was often drawn between "status" (the position) and "role" (the behavior expected of a person in a given position). However, in practice it is difficult to define a position except in terms of what people in that position are expected to do, so that distinction is generally overlooked today. Considerable emphasis is placed on "role strain," that is, on problems people have in fitting into role expectations (generally because of conflicts between the expectations of different roles that they occupy).

Other concepts that are widely used by Merton are "anomie" (a situation where the norms or expectations are inadequate or are conflicting), "reference group" (a group with which a person identifies and takes role expectation), and "manifest function" (the purpose for which something is done) and "latent function" (the actual consequence of some behavior, when this is not what was intended). "Positive functions" are consequences that tend to support the system; "negative" ones tend to undermine the system. Merton is concerned with values and goals, but tends to see these as characteristics of specific roles or groups, not as dominant themes within the society as a whole. The social structure as a whole is nothing more than the summation of individual roles.

Liberal sociology does not place equal emphasis on all parts of society. Merton, for example, has no theory of the state or of the economy. Economic phenomena are generally seen as belonging to a different discipline—economics—and thus need not be dealt with. Political phenomena, similarly, can often be left to the political scientists. If this is not enough, liberal sociologists generally follow the lead of liberal political scientists and view the government as merely reacting to pressures from other groups in society (this is known as "pluralist theory"). Great emphasis is placed on deviant behavior, which is seen as the outcome of people being socialized into deviant roles. In general, liberal sociologists focus on problems that can be studied in terms of their effects on specific individuals. Thus, political phenomena are studied in terms of the attitudes and preferences of individual voters; labor-management problems are studied in terms of the discontents of specific workers.

Robert K. Merton

Courtesy Columbia University

The types of problems that liberal sociologists address are often quite amenable to empirical research. Questions that Merton deals with, for example, are, Why does a group choose a particular response to anomie (normlessness)? Why does an individual choose a given reference group? What are the latent positive functions of an element of society? What is the cause of deviance? What is the source of influence? Or, for some more specific examples, Why do liberals accommodate to bureaucracies? What is the function of the political machine? What is the cause of racial discrimination? Why was morale higher in some army units than in others?

There is a variety of specific theories within the liberal paradigm. Some of them focus on a specific concept; for example, "role theory" deals with how people adjust to social roles, while "symbolic interactionism" focuses on the symbolic systems that people use to influence each other's behavior. Others deal with a specific problem; Merton's theory of deviant behavior, for instance, explains deviancy as resulting from a lack of fit between what society expects people to achieve financially and the opportunities that objectively exist for financial success within the system.

Liberal Model of Bureaucracy

One concept about which liberal sociologists have done considerable theorizing is that of bureaucracy. German liberal sociologist Max Weber observed that as capitalist societies developed they increasingly used organizational forms in which business is conducted according to regular procedures and legal rules and officials occupy clearly defined positions within a hierarchy of authority. In a bureaucracy, according to Weber, officials hold their positions because of their expertise, not because of inheritance or political connections.

Weber presented an idealized picture of bureaucracies, portraying them as highly rational and efficient. He felt that bureaucracies would come to predominate in the modern world because of their superiority to other forms of organization, which were less effective. Liberal sociologists have done considerable research on bureaucracies, often attempting to test Weber's idealized model. Not surprisingly, they have usually found that bureaucracies were not so orderly or efficient as Weber expected. They found that people systematically evaded and twisted the rules, using informal networks of communication to advance their own interests. They found that bureaucratic organizations are often characterized by power struggles between those on the bottom and those on the top, or between different factions within the leadership.

While the liberals have sometimes been insightful in their observations of daily life in bureaucratic settings, the limitations of their paradigm have prevented them from understanding the role of bureaucratic organization in contemporary American society. They have focused on case studies of single organizations, or even of work groups within those organizations, without analyzing the role of those organizations in maintaining class inequality or manipulating social conflicts. Bureaucracy, after all, is hardly a new phenomenon. Elites in Oriental despotic societies, such as ancient China, were highly adept at the use of bureaucratic organization as a means of sustaining their power. Bureaucratic organization is also used by contemporary state socialist societies in order to control and coordinate social production.

Bureaucratic organizaton can be used in an attempt to increase efficiency, but it also may be used as a means of dominating and controlling a large number of people—whether those people be in a factory, an army, or a university. By stifling the creativity and initiative of workers, bureaucratic forms may lessen rather than increase productivity. Liberal sociology, by focusing on bureaucracy as an abstract concept isolated from a larger social context, cannot offer an adequate explanation of the differing ways in which bureaucratic forms of organization are used in various parts of a particular society.

Liberal Development of Research Methodology

While liberal sociology is weak in social theory, it is much stronger in its emphasis on research methodology. Indeed, liberal sociologists are often accused of stressing methods at the expense of theory or even of empirical description. Research methods also are a focus of considerable controversy within liberal sociology. There are three main methodological traditions within the liberal paradigm.

The first is the *experimental* method. By experimentation is meant a method in which the researcher actively manipulates people in order to control the variables he is studying. Most frequently, this is done with small groups in a laboratory situation. A number of subjects, usually college students, are brought into the laboratory and placed into groups. They are given a task to perform, and the researcher evaluates the process by which they perform the task. The laboratory situation is inherently artificial, and there is considerable controversy about how much behavior in the laboratory is actually the same as behavior in the real world. Also, in order to control the situation the researcher almost inevitably uses some sort of deception (often in the form of phony subjects who actually behave according to instructions from the researcher), and there is controversy both over the ethics of this and over its realism. For example, considerable publicity was given recently to a study in which subjects supposedly administered torture to a respondent who seemed to be screaming for mercy. This was interpreted as showing that the respondents would follow orders, no matter how immoral, if they come from a respectable source such as a university. In a sense, however, the respondents had the last laugh since they assumed that nothing done in a research laboratory could really be wrong, and they were correct. In fact no one was being tortured; they were listening to a tape-recorded simulation.

The second method, which has been developed into a fine art by liberal sociologists, is the *sample survey*. This method involves sending out interviewers to a scientifically selected sample of respondents and asking all of them the same questions. In some cases, the questions are structured like multiple-choice tests and the respondents choose among a limited number of responses. In others, the questions are open-ended and the respondent answers in his or her own words, and coders are hired to classify the responses into categories after the interviews are completed. Once the data are in, they are generally punched on I.B.M. cards and analyzed with statistical methods on a computer. It is thus possible to make generalizations about groups; for example, 23 percent of the white respondents classified themselves as liberal versus 53 percent of the nonwhites, or 58 percent of the wealthy respondents voted for Nixon as compared to 28 percent of the poor ones. It is possible to do very complicated statistical manipulations of the data in an attempt to explain variations in a certain variable, or even to draw some implications about the causal effect of one variable on another.

There are significant advantages to the survey method. It is fairly objective, in the sense that any two researchers who ask the same questions to samples selected in the same way should get approximately the same results. It makes it possible to study large segments of the population fairly economically. It has obvious commercial applications, especially in marketing, where surveys are used to determine consumer attitudes about specific products. It is limited, however, to studying phenomena that are formed in the conscious minds of respondents and that they are willing and able to tell the interviewer about. It is difficult to use surveys to study historical change since one cannot go back into history and ask survey questions (although one can sometimes find relevant surveys done by someone else in the past). The survey method is highly appropriate for answering questions raised by the Mertonian paradigm, particularly questions about the behavior of people in particular social roles or about what happens when people occupy conflicting roles. One simply needs to isolate the individuals in the sample who occupy a given role position and study their responses to questions about the topic at hand.

The third method often used by liberal sociologists is to simply *observe* group life. Sometimes the sociologist participates as a member of a group and writes about his or her observations and experiences (this is known as "participant observation"). In other cases, he or she may attempt to be a neutral observer. The sociologists who use this method tend to be a distinct group from the survey and experimental researchers. They tend to be more philosophically inclined, and generally argue that little meaning can be ascribed to statistics as a summary of human attitudes or behaviors. Some of them consider themselves to be radicals, although not in the sense that radicalism is used in this book, and adhere to theories that place great emphasis on people's subjective feelings and ideas about what they are doing. They believe that social reality is essentially a result of people's ideas about it, that the world is what we believe it to be. (These approaches will be discussed later in this chapter, under the category *critical idealism*.)

Observational methods have certain advantages. They enable the sociologist to get close to social life and perhaps to observe things that he or she did not anticipate and thus could not have put into a survey or questionnaire. They often generate colorful anecdotal material that makes for interesting reading (an advantage that is frequently lost when the writer becomes embroiled in vague, quasi-philosophical language). The disadvantage is that observational methods are very restricted in scope. Only relatively small groups can be observed directly, and there is no guarantee that what one observes in a given group is the same as what happens in other groups. Furthermore, not all groups are accessible to observation, and observational sociologists tend to emphasize groups that are deviant or interesting in some way. They rarely if ever study powerful groups, although these groups actually have a much greater ability to shape social reality than the more ordinary groups that are available for study.

Liberal sociologists differ greatly in the methods they use, and it might be possible to divide them into a number of subparadigms if one placed great emphasis on methodology. They are much more alike, however, in their basic assumptions and in the range of phenomena they consider. Through limitations in assumptions about what is important, liberal sociologists generally avoid serious or fundamental analysis of larger societal issues, focusing instead on smaller questions that can be dealt with within the confines of the existing social system.

THE RADICAL SOCIOLOGY OF KARL MARX

Karl Marx was not strictly speaking a sociologist. If he were to be assigned to a particular academic discipline, it would be political economy. His writings, however, cover
the broad range of history, sociology, economics, and political science. This is in
keeping with a basic tenent of the Marxist paradigm: societies must be studied as
whole units, or even as parts of worldwide systems. In this assumption, Marxism is
similar to Parsonian conservatism. The Marxist paradigm differs, however, in its assumptions about the basic factors that hold societies together. While Parsons felt that
values played this central role, Marxism places central importance on economic processes as the dominant force in all societies where structured economic inequality is
present. Rather than seeing societies as stable and integrated, Marxism sees societies
as divided into social classes that have conflicting economic interests. It assumes that
the dominant classes use both persuasion and coercion to dominate the lower classes
and that the conflict growing out of exploitative relations eventually leads to
revolutionary change in the social system.

The concepts used by Marxist sociology naturally draw attention to different phenomena, or interpret phenomena in different ways, than do those of liberal or conservative sociology. For example, Marx has no concept of deviance. The notion of
deviance implies a concept of system, equilibrium, or of common goals that is alien to
Marxism. The behavior referred to as deviant in the other paradigms is explained in
terms of class, interest, and power, just as other behaviors are explained. For another
example, while both Marxism and Parsonianism have a theory of the state, Parsons
sees it as advancing the good of society as a whole, while Marx sees the state as an
oppressive instrument serving the interests of the ruling class.

Levels of Analysis in Marxism

The Marxist mode of conceptualization is more refined than either the Parsonian or
the Mertonian. Like them, it has a set of universal and abstract concepts meant to
apply to all societies at all times, such as "forces of production," "relations of production," "use value." These refer to universal aspects of human societies; all societies
must in some way organize themselves to produce useful material goods if their
members are to survive. In addition to these general concepts, however, Marxism
has a second set of more specific concepts meant to apply only to societies that
have distinct classes with different relationships to the means of production,—
"private property," "alienation," "exchange value." And further, Marxism provides a
still more specified set of concepts for each type of class society with which it deals.
For capitalist societies, for example, the following terms apply: "capital," "free labor,"
"organic composition of capital." The Parsonian and Mertonian paradigms are capable
of observing and analyzing phenomena either on a highly abstract level or on a

Karl Marx

concrete empirical level. This leads to a large gap between "theory" and "research" among adherents of these paradigms. The Marxist paradigm, however, provides intermediate levels of observation and analysis, thus permitting a greater degree of refinement.

We will not attempt to define the central Marxist concepts in this chapter. Marxist concepts are less accessible than those of liberal sociology, since liberal sociology deals largely with phenomena on the level of individual behavior that are familiar to most people. Marxist concepts are useful only when one recognizes the necessity of understanding the dynamics of social systems as a whole. We will consequently introduce them as we proceed through the book.

The problems that are important for Marxist sociology are naturally different from those raised by liberals or conservatives. For Marxists, some of the most important problems are: What are the laws accounting for the transformation of class societies? What is the relation between a given ideology and social structural interests? How does an underclass develop class consciousness? What is the origin of alienation? Some more specific problems that Marxists have addressed include: Why isn't the working class in the United States class conscious? Why does capitalism seem to have stabilized itself in the wealthier countries? What was the source of primitive accumulation that made class societies possible? Why didn't capitalism develop in China or India prior to European colonization? What are the laws that govern the accumulation of capital? What are the causes of crises, unemployment, and wage fluctuations?

The Marxist paradigm thus generates a wide range of problems that can be studied empirically. In this way, it differs from the Parsonian paradigm, which seems to generate fewer relatively specific (and hence empirically testable problems) than do either the Mertonian or the Marxist paradigms. The Mertonian paradigm does generate large numbers of empirically testable problems, but these tend to be less systematically related than the hypotheses generated by the other two paradigms.

The Marxist paradigm encompasses all societies at all times, but most of Marx's work deals with capitalist societies. Much more than the other two paradigms, the Marxist paradigm is comparative and historical. In his own work, Marx focused on England for the study of economic phenomena, on France for the study of political phenomena, and on Germany for the study of ideological phenomena. This was because he felt that each of these countries was most advanced in its development of one specific aspect of capitalist society. Marxists since Lenin have expanded the range of the paradigm to include the developing countries of the Third World as well as the advanced capitalist countries. There has also been some attempt to apply the Marxist paradigm to the state socialist countries, although this remains highly controversial among Marxists.

Theory and Practice in Marxist Sociology

There is much controversy over specific theories within the Marxist paradigm. Nothing could be further from the truth than a view of Marxism as a conclusive set of doctrines that provides a single answer to all problems. Marxism is a paradigm, a frame of reference within which to study societies and how they can be changed. Within the Marxist paradigm, there are many specific theories about specific questions, such as the rise of the bourgeoisie, the development of proletarian class consciousness, the nature of crises, imperialism, and monopoly. Often there are contradictory theories, all within the limits of the paradigm. Certain theories advanced within the Marxist paradigm have been proven wrong, including some advanced by Marx himself, such as the law of the falling rate of profit or the iron law of wages.

Different theories within the Marxist paradigm are not of merely academic interest. One of the central tenets of Marxism is that theories are important insofar as they provide a guide to action. Political parties and groups that accept a general Marxist approach differ on questions of tactics, strategy, and policy. They each advance theories and attempt to prove them both by research and by practical action. Without an understanding of the Marxist paradigm, it would be impossible to understand the arguments between factions in China, between Soviet and Chinese interpretations of Marxism, or between reformist and revolutionary Marxist groups in Western Europe.

Of all the major countries, the United States has probably been least influenced by Marxist thought. This is due to the historical nature of the United States as a frontier society whose capitalist economy was long dependent on immigrant workers, and to its leading role in the world capitalist system. However, as the United States is losing its hegemony in the world and as the contradictions inherent within its social structure mature, Marxist thought is becoming more and more influential. For these reasons, it is important even for students who are not politically inclined towards Marxism to have a good understanding of the Marxist paradigm and the ways in which it is used to analyze contemporary social problems.

Marxists use a fairly wide range of methods to answer questions raised by their theories. Since Marxism stresses historical changes on the societal level, historical methods of research are often used. Marx himself relied upon government documents for much of his data, particularly for statistical information on economic trends. Marxists can also learn from participation in social activities and movements, and from interviews with informed participants in political struggles. Survey methods are also amenable to answering some of the questions raised by Marxists, especially questions about consciousness or political ideologies. However, survey methods are limited in their ability to tap highly controversial opinions and attitudes that interest Marxists, and they play a much less central role than in liberal sociology. Experimental methods are of almost no use to Marxists since it is not possible to test theories about societal change in a small group laboratory. There have, however, been some attempts to use simulation game techniques to illustrate Marxist ideas for teaching purposes.

RADICAL SOCIOLOGY TODAY

The hegemony, or intellectual dominance, of liberal and conservative sociology broke down during the 1960s. This was a period of tremendous activitism from the antiwar, student, youth, black, and women's movements, and sociology students were often among the most militant members of these movements. Some of these students went on to graduate school and became professional sociologists. The radical sociology movement today is in many ways a legacy of that era, although today the roles have been somewhat reversed, with the young professors often tending to be the radicals and the students often being less active.

Critical Idealism

The tendencies that exist within radical sociology today very much reflect different perspectives that developed during the sixties. One important trend during that period was the "hippie," or counterculture, movement. This movement stressed personal rebellion, alternative life styles, altered states of consciousness, and other types of change that could be instituted on an individual basis. In sociology, this perspective is expressed in a group of theories that can be called "critical idealism." Critical idealism draws some inspiration from the more philosophical writings of Karl Marx, particularly those he developed as a young man. It does not, however, operate within the full range of the Marxist paradigm since it generally ignores the larger societal questions that were the primary focus of Marx's work. Critical idealists generally draw more support from theories such as "symbolic interactionism," "ethnomethodology," and "phenomenology," which are essentially liberal in that they do not question the social system as a whole.

The basic principle of critical idealism is that human behavior is governed by how people think about things. People's thoughts about the world arise in interaction between people, with each member of an interaction attempting to define things for the other. Critical idealism tends to stress people's ability to rationally manipulate situations, to change other people's behavior simply by confronting them with new ideas or behavior patterns.

In many ways, critical idealism suffers from limitations present within the whole "hippie" movement. It is true that some people seem to have the freedom and resources to escape from the limitations of the dominant society, say, by moving to a commune in the woods, but for most people separation from society simply is not a real option. Furthermore, it does not seem to be true that people are as rational in their behavior as the critical idealists assume. A more adequate psychological theory, including an analysis of unconscious as well as conscious processes, is needed to explain the way in which individuals function within capitalist societies. At best, critical idealism offers some insight into how individuals survive and find niches for themselves within the confines of an oppressive social system. As such it probably has more to offer to psychology than to sociology, and indeed there is a burgeoning humanistic psychology movement that attempts to give people some help in dealing with these problems. At worst, the critical idealist approach tends to draw attention away from the basic social problems that must be the focus of any radical sociology.

Structuralist Marxism

While critical idealism had a brief period of popularity among radicals in the early 1970s, the large majority of radical sociologists remain committed to working within broader and more systematic perspectives such as the Marxist paradigm as outlined earlier in this chapter. They tend consequently to be concerned with understanding the capitalist system as a whole, and with finding strategies for changing it and transforming it into a socialist system that can truly meet people's needs. There are many differences and disagreements within this group, but they are not so much over paradigmatic issues as over theoretical and political issues within the framework of more or less shared paradigms.

Some radical sociologists place the greatest emphasis on the international nature of the capitalist system. Some of these, known as "dependency theorists," tend to see the focus of revolution and change in the poor nations of the Third World. This corresponds to a political tendency that emerged during the 1960s which tended to see countries such as Cuba, Vietnam, China, Mozambique, and Algeria as the most advanced in terms of revolutionary politics even though they are not advanced economically. Others also focus on the international nature of capitalism but argue that only when capitalism spreads throughout the world as a whole can socialism emerge on a worldwide basis.

Some radical sociologists argue that the way in which the economic and social structure of a particular country is organized is the most important thing shaping the lives of people in that country. Within this more *orthodox structuralist Marxist* group, the major area of difference tends to be along strategic lines. The more orthodox Marxists believe that the best prospect for change is to build a *revolutionary* movement of working people along the lines Lenin followed in Russia or Mao followed in China. Other Socialists incline towards *reformist* politics, favoring a compromise with the more progressive liberal elements in an attempt to move gradually toward a socialist system. These more moderate radical sociologists look more to Scandinavia and Western Europe for models that radicals in the United States could follow. These alternative political strategies are based on different analyses of the nature of contemporary capitalist society and these issues will be discussed at length throughout the remainder of this book. Ultimately, however, no one can be certain about how change will come in the future, so no matter how rational the platforms put out by different political groups may seem, no one can be certain about their political strategy.[2] One makes the best choice possible, after getting as much information as is available, and constantly reevaluates the decision on the basis of actual political experience. A truly radical sociology, however, makes no sense without being grounded in political struggle.

Summary

Sociologists use scientific methods to study societies and the groups that are parts of societies. Despite their commitment to scientific methods, sociologists frequently differ about basic questions such as the essential nature of societies, how they remain orderly, and how they change. They also differ with regard to the social phenomena they study and the methods they use. These differences can be explained as resulting from the fact that sociologists, in common with other scientists, use paradigms as guides to their work. These paradigms specify the concepts that are

---

2. The two authors of this book differ in their political perspectives, with Szymanski taking a more revolutionary stance and Goertzel tending toward reformist politics. Both have written books exploring this issue in more detail (see Selected Readings for Chapter 8).

used to analyze the social world, the kinds of problems that are to be studied, and the methods that are to be used in answering the problems.

While some disciplines in the physical and biological sciences tend to rely on a single paradigm for long periods of time, sociology and other social sciences tend to be characterized by conflict between supporters of different paradigms. This is because the social sciences are inherently ideological as well as scientific. The social sciences are part of the social world, and differences among social scientists parallel the major social divisions within the societies of which they are a part.

There are three main paradigms in sociology: the conservative, liberal, and radical paradigms. The conservative paradigm sees societies as orderly and integrated, largely through the mechanism of common values held by most members of the society. The liberal paradigm does not offer a comprehensive model of societies as a whole, but focuses on limited, "middle-range" problems. The radical paradigm views societies as characterized by instability and change caused by conflict between dominant and oppressed classes.

Review Questions

1. What are the basic elements that compose a paradigm?
2. How are the paradigms in sociology related to political perspectives?
3. Why are concepts so important in sociology?
4. Why did science flower in Europe in the seventeenth, eighteenth, and nineteenth centuries?
5. How did the emergence of economics as a discipline reflect the growth of capitalist market economies?
6. In what ways were the sociologies of Comte and Durkheim conservative?
7. Why did early American sociology differ from early European sociology?
8. When and why was conservative European sociology introduced into America?
9. Which of the three sociological paradigms tends to have the most limited scope of analysis? Why?
10. Why are experimental methods not very useful for radical sociologists?
11. What, according to Talcott Parsons, is the basic element that holds societies together?
12. Which sociological paradigm is most likely to use survey methods? Why?
13. What did liberal sociologists find when they tested Max Weber's theory of bureaucracy?
14. Why does the Marxist paradigm permit a close link between theory and research?

15.   What types of sociology are most closely related to the "hippie," or countercul-
      ture, movement? Why?

Suggestions for Further Study

1.   The concept "paradigm" was first developed by Kuhn in his study of the physical
      sciences. Choose one of the physical or biological sciences that you have studied
      and find out how the concept of paradigm can be applied to that field. Do
      conflicting paradigms exist at the same time, or is one dominant for a long period
      of time? Outline at least two differing paradigms in that field, specifying their
      basic assumptions, concepts, theories, central problems, methods used, and
      value resonances.

2.   Choose three different columns or articles on the same topic from newspapers or
      news magazines. Make sure that one column represents a conservative view-
      point, one a liberal viewpoint, and one a radical viewpoint. You may have to con-
      sult a radical newspaper or magazine for the radical viewpoint as these are rarely
      presented in the mass circulation journals. Show how the basic assumptions and
      concepts used by each writer reflect his or her ideological orientation.

3.   Most people find it easier to detect "biases" or differing ideological perspectives
      in other people than to recognize the basic assumptions that shape their own
      thought. One way to become aware of the roots of your own thinking is to begin
      with your opinions about a given social issue such as race relations, poverty, so-
      cialism versus capitalism, the role of women in society, etc. Write an essay
      defining your opinions, specifying the reasons why you believe them to be cor-
      rect. Specify the evidence or "facts" on which you base your opinion. If your
      opinions have largely been derived from other people who are influential in your
      life, such as your parents, you can ask them to help in elaborating the reasons.
      Once you have finished, you may find it instructive to debate your opinions with
      another student who had taken a different view.

4.   Choose a social problem that concerns you, such as racism, sexism, environ-
      mental pollution, inflation, unemployment, juvenile delinquency, crime, over-
      population, war, poverty, underdevelopment, etc. Construct an analysis of the
      causes and possible cures for this problem from the viewpoint of each of the
      three paradigms discussed in this chapter. Indicate how each of the three para-
      digms would lead to different conclusions about how the problems should be
      handled. If you find it too difficult to construct the arguments yourself, you can
      find conservative, liberal, and radical arguments on the issue in the library.

5.   Together with a group of students from your class, draw a representative sample
      of articles from the sociological journals in your college library. Have each stu-

dent read five articles and determine whether each of them falls within a conservative, liberal, or radical paradigm, on the basis of the questions it discusses, the assumptions it makes, and the concepts it uses. Total up your results to find out which paradigms are predominant in the field as a whole, or in each of the the specific journals found in your library.

6. Write a review of any significant sociological book, taken from the selected readings for any chapter of this book or recommended by your instructor. In your review, specify the basic assumptions that the author makes, the central concepts that are used, the range of phenomena considered, the problems addressed, the theories and methods used, and the values that are implicit in the work.

Selected Readings

Bandyopadhyaj, Pradeep. "One Sociology or Many: Some Issues in Radical Sociology." *Science and Society* 35:1 (Spring 1971).

Baritz, Loren. *The Servants of Power: A History of the Use of Social Science in American Industry.* Middletown, Conn.: Wesleyan U. Press, 1960.

Blackburn, Robin (ed.). *Ideology in Social Science.* New York: Vintage, 1973.

Colfax, David, and Roach, Jack (ed.). *Radical Sociology.* New York: Basic Books, 1971.

Cornforth, Maurice. *The Theory of Knowledge.* New York: International 1971 (1963).

Coser, Lewis. "The Function of Small Group Research." *Social Problems* 3:1.

Friedrichs, Robert W. *A Sociology of Sociology.* New York: Free Press, 1971.

Goldman, Paul, and Van Houten, Donald. "Mangerial Strategies and the Worker: A Marxist Analysis of Bureaucracy." *The Sociological Quarterly* 18 (Winter 1977):108–125.

Gouldner, Alvin. *The Coming Crisis in Western Sociology.* New York: Basic Books, 1970.

Horton, John. "The Dehumanization of Alienation and Anomie." *British Journal of Sociology* 15:4 (December 1964).

———. "Order and Conflict Theories of Social Problems." *American Journal of Sociology* 71:6 (March 1966).

Hydebrand, Wolf. "Organizational Contradictions in Public Bureaucracies: Toward a Marxian Theory of Organizations." *The Sociological Quarterly* 18 (Winter 1977): 83–107.

Kuhn, Thomas. *The Structure of Scientific Revolutions.* Chicago: U. of Chicago Press, 1962.

Lange, Oscar. *Political Economy.* Vol. 1, Ch. 7. New York: Macmillan, 1963.

Lazarsfeld, Paul, et al. *The Uses of Sociology.* New York: Basic Books, 1967.

Lichtman, Richard. "Symbolic Interactionism and Social Reality." *The Berkeley Journal of Sociology* XV, 1970.

Marcuse, Herbert. *One Dimensional Man.* Boston: Beacon, 1964.

Marx, Karl, and Engels, Frederick. *The German Ideology*, Part One. New York: International, 1970 (1845).

Mills, C. Wright. "The Contribution of Sociology to Studies of Industrial Relations." *The Berkeley Journal of Sociology* XV, 1970.

————. "The Professional Ideology of Social Pathologists," in *Power, Political People.* New York: Oxford U. Press, 1963.

————. *The Sociological Imagination.* New York: Oxford U. Press, 1959.

Moore, Barrington. *The Social Origins of Dictatorship and Democracy.* Boston: Beacon, 1967.

Myrdal, Gunnar. *The Political Element in the Development of Economic Theory.* New York: Humanities, 1971.

Nisbet, Robert. *The Sociological Tradition*, Part 1. New York: Basic Books, 1966.

Ritzer, George. *Sociology: A Multiple Paradigm Science.* Boston: Allyn, 1975.

Robinson, Joan. *Economic Philosophy.* New York: Doubleday, 1964.

Schwendinger, Herman and Julia. *Sociologists of the Chair.* New York: Basic Books, 1974.

Szymanski, Albert. "Marxism and Science." *The Insurgent Sociologist* 3:3 (Spring 1973).

————. "The Practice of Marxist Social Science." *The Insurgent Sociologist* 7:1 (Fall 1976).

————. "Three Alternative Sociologies." *Humboldt Journal of Social Relations* 2:2 (Spring-Summer 1975).

————. "Towards a Radical Sociology." *Sociological Inquiry* 40:2 (Winter 1970).

Sternberg, David J. *Radical Sociology.* New York: Exposition University, 1977.

Therborn, Goran. "A Critique of the Frankfurt School." *New Left Review* 63 (Sept.-Oct. 1970).

————. "Jurgan Habermas: A New Eclectic." *New Left Review* 67 (May-June 1971).

Veblen, Thorstein. *The Higher Learning in America.* New York: Hill & Wang, 1951 (1918).

Chapter 2

Foundations of Radical Sociology

In this chapter we will outline the most important features of the Marxist sociological paradigm. All thinking in the social sciences is based on philosophical assumptions about the nature of the world, and more particularly about how thought is related to the physical world. The perspective that Marxism takes on these issues is known as "dialectical materialism." It incorporates elements from other related philosophies, and therefore many of its elements will not be unfamiliar to the student. Nevertheless, there may well be some elements that are new. In any event, some understanding of Marxist philosophical assumptions will make it easier for the reader to understand what we are attempting to do in the remaining chapters of this book. For these assumptions shape both the questions that are asked and the ways in which they are answered.

This chapter will also define basic empirical concepts used in sociology. First, we will explain what is meant by a "society" and show how this concept is used in radical as well as other sociologies. Second, we will examine the key characteristics of class societies.

DIALECTICAL MATERIALISM

Radical sociology is postulated on a *dialectical* conception of knowledge. This means that knowledge develops as part of an interaction between the thinker and the environment. Thought cannot develop in a vacuum without any link to the real world.

Social conflict reflected in sunglasses.

Photo by Neil Benson

But neither can the social world be known independently of the thinking human beings who make it up. Thinking, including the thinking of sociologists, is viewed as an integral part of the social process.

Dialectical materialism incorporates elements from classical philosophers such as Plato and Hegel. These philosophers developed the concept of the dialectic as a way of thinking in which knowledge advances as a consequence of a dialogue between two thinkers. One thinker advances a thesis, the second responds with an antithesis, and out of the interaction a new idea, the synthesis, emerges. But Marxism does not stop at this point. Rather, it goes on to say that these thinkers are not isolated individuals, but members of social classes. And the struggle between these thinkers is not so much intellectual as social. The dialectic of ideas is a reflection of the dialectic of class. Thus, first the capitalist advances the ideas and interests of capitalism (reflecting the reality of capitalist relationships). The workers growing out of this social system advance contrary ideas and politics through the labor movement. Out of this conflict, both the ideas for and the reality of a new socialist society emerge.

Dialectical materialism also accepts the basic tenets of scientific logic. It incorporates the basic idea of science as a method whereby theoretical generalizations are tested by empirical research. This means that once a notion about the world is formulated, whether on the basis of experience or reason, it is put to a test. The results of the test are then used to modify the original theoretical notion, and the modified theory is again tested. The results of the test of the more sophisticated notion are once again used to modify the theory to bring it into closer agreement with reality, and so on. Through this process, social theory can get closer and closer to reality, though without ever reaching perfect knowledge.

The process of testing theories cannot be the same in social science as in physical science. This is so because the social scientist is part of the social system that he or she is studying. Testing theories about society may involve simply making passive observations, offering predictions about what will happen in the future, and then waiting to see if these predictions come true. If the mythical "ivory tower" ever really existed, where academicians could write and lecture without anyone paying the slightest attention to what they said, then perhaps social science could be limited to this sort of passive scientism. Radicals, however, are committed to helping to change societies. The only ultimately effective way to test theories of how to change society is to put them into practice. Thus, radical sociologists believe that applied practice is an essential method for scientific research in the social sciences. Theories about political change must be tested through politics; theories of how to organize economic production must be tested through experimentation at the workplace; theories of socialist education must be put into practice in schools. In this way, the theory becomes part of the world in a way that astronomical theory never influences the motions of the planets. Thus, dialectical materialism works toward an ultimate unity of theory and practice.

Theory and Reality

Sociological theory must be both advanced by reason and disciplined by practice, whether the practice is scientific experimentation, political activity, or productive labor. Although theory is primary, practice is necessary. Practice is necessary in order to develop an understanding of the social world. Unlike radical sociology, most liberal and conservative sociology is based on the division of theory from research. During the 1950s and much of the 1960s sociology was divided into the two camps of the Grand Theorists and the Abstracted Empiricists—the proponents of a theory separate from research and of research techniques independent of theory. These two camps could maintain their respective positions only by rejecting the dialectical conception of the relation between theory and practice. While the Grand Theorists engaged in concept association and dissociation (illustrated by common-sense examples), the Abstracted Empiricists developed pretentious methodological techniques (Mills refers to it as the "methodological inhibition"). The empiricist camp came to use research methods, especially survey methods, in a ritualistic manner that revealed little concern with the differential applicability of techniques to research problems. Radical sociology, on the other hand, is concerned neither with abstract speculation about the world nor with research methods developed for their own sake. Radical sociology maintains that the separation of theory from research is nonsense. Ideas without verification are as worthless as verification techniques without ideas.

In some cases, sociological theory can be advanced by using data that have already been gathered for some other purpose. This might include analysis of census data or of historical reports gathered in the library. In other cases, the sociologist may physically observe what is going on in a group but attempt to avoid influencing anyone's behavior. Alternatively, the sociologist may use interviews or questionnaires to gather information. This inevitably influences the responses, since the questions are determined by the researcher and people will answer differently depending on what and how they are asked. All of these methods are fairly similar to those used in the physical and biological sciences, and these sciences also have the problem that their observation processes may affect the processes they are studying.

Some sociological theories can best be advanced through experimentation. It is possible to test some ideas in a classroom, or with a small group of students gathered together as subjects in an experiment. Many of the most important ideas in radical sociology, however, can be tested only through political practice. The best way to formulate a sociology of revolution is to form a revolutionary movement and put one's ideas into practice. This involves a process of experimentation that is logically identical to that used in a research laboratory. For example, the road to power followed by a social movement such as the Communist Party of China consisted of following a series of policies based on Marxist-Leninist theory but constantly modified in the light of the successes and failures of practice. The theory of the Chinese Communists became better and better as the Party's successes and failures were assimilated and as a better theory developed on which to base further practice. In the process the original ideas of Marx and Lenin were modified considerably. Theoretical development can also come through work experience. A group of workers may think up a more efficient way of producing a good, which they then put into practice. Their success and failure in introducing more efficient techniques is assimilated into their theory and a more correct practice of production is developed.

There is nothing mystical or unusual about this process. The logic of social science is more systematic and thorough than the logical processes used by nonscientists in their practical lives, but it is not qualitatively different. This is not to say that social science theories, including those of radical sociology, cannot be complex or difficult to understand. That happens, however, because of the complicated and often contradictory nature of social reality itself.

Contradictions

Probably the most important aspect of dialectical thinking, and also perhaps the most difficult to really grasp, is the idea of contradiction. The notion of contradiction captures the essential tragedy of social relationships in class society. People's intentions and aspirations are systematically frustrated by the very consequences of their actions. Since social relationships have a logic of their own, and social relationships are

Ted Goertzel

A contradiction. New housing is built in the suburbs while existing housing deteriorates in the cities.

nothing other than the interrelated actions of people, what people hope to have come out of their actions is negated by the social processes of class society. Things turn into their opposites because people try to make them stay the same. This notion of tragedy is essentially the same as that of classical Greek or Elizabethan dramatic tragedy. For example, in Sophocles' play, *Oedipus Rex*, the oracle prophesies that Oedipus will someday sleep with his mother and kill his father. Horrified by this prediction, Oedipus from that day onward structures his life to rationally minimize the possibility of realizing the oracle's prophecy. Nevertheless, the very course of action that was the most rational to follow to avoid sleeping with his mother and killing his father was exactly the course of action that most surely brought about that result. Such is the stuff of all classical tragedy, and such is the stuff of social relationships in class society.

An example of a contemporary contradiction facing the United States is the fact that the cost of maintaining world military superiority makes for a very slow rate of economic growth, which in the long run undermines the economic basis for exerting worldwide political hegemony. To be the world's number one power is thus inherently contradictory. The very course calculated to maximize worldwide power—heavy military spending—diverts productive resources away from uses that would result in increased productivity and growth and leads to the relative economic decline of the leading country relative to others. Eventually, some other country, once its more rapid rate of economic growth has taken it beyond that of the previously hegemonic power, will convert its economic basis into worldwide political hegemony. In turn, this new power will be faced with the same contradiction. Throughout the rest of this book we will have occasions to point to other contradictions in social relationships.

Scientific Laws

The dialectical method is similar to heuristic principles used in other sciences. All the "hard" sciences tend to see the world in a dialectical way. The concept of system, for example, is universal in astronomy, physics, chemistry, and biology. Likewise the concept of systematic change or evolution. These fields also categorize their subject matter in terms of opposing forces that are at the root of change—positive and negative charges, north and south magnetic poles, matter and antimatter, centrifugal and centripetal forces, and acids and bases. The unity of theory and practice or experiment is also a goal of most sciences. A dialectical methodology is an attempt to apply the scientific approach developed in other fields to the social sciences.

One goal of socialist sociology is thus to create a body of scientific laws similar to those that exist in other sciences. Scientific laws, of course, are not statements that something will always occur. They are rather statements about forces or tendencies that always operate under specified conditions. Thus, the law of gravity states that all things tend to fall toward the center of the earth. This statement, of course, does not preclude the possibility that balloons, airplanes, or rockets can counteract this tendency with other forces. Likewise, with social laws, the statement that A tends to do such-and-such is not a claim that A always does such-and-such, but only that there is a force operating to compel A to do such-and-such. Only if there are no effective countertendencies will A in fact actually do such-and-such. The actual outcome is the product of all forces or laws that are operating.

The basic logic of science is determinist. It assumes that behavior is determined by objective factors; if this were not so, behavior would be random and it would be impossible to form laws about it. Many people are prepared to believe this about physical particles but are reluctant to believe that their own behavior is determined by anything other than their own personal preferences or wishes. Of course, it is not possible to completely predict anyone's behavior since this is a result of a myriad of forces that have acted on that person throughout his or her lifetime. If an individual really wishes to control his or her own life, however, the only way to effectively do so is to study the forces that have shaped his or her personality and the forces in the social and physical environment that limit his or her alternatives. Similarly, if the people in a society wish to change their society, they must first understand the constraints imposed by their society. Radical sociologists are committed to acting on the world in order to change it, but in order to do this effectively they must focus on the ways in which social systems are determined by objective factors that are beyond any individual's conscious control.

The philosophical question of whether human behavior is totally determined by objective factors, or whether there is in the last analysis some degree of individual free will, is not crucial to radical sociology. What is important is to understand that radical sociology, like all science, seeks to explain behavior as it is determined by objective factors and that it assumes social structure is the source of human oppression. This means that the goal of radical sociology is the understanding of the forces behind human behavior. It is thus not so important what individuals or groups *think* are their motivations, but what they *really* are. Only in this way is it possible to uncover the laws that govern social relations, and to act effectively to change those relationships.

Social laws differ fundamentally from laws in abstract sciences such as physics in that they are specific to certain kinds of social systems. Just as many biological principles are valid only for certain species or types of organisms, social laws frequently apply only to specific types of societies. For instance, some laws apply only to capitalist societies, and even within that category some apply only to competitive capitalism while others apply only to monopoly capitalism. There are very few social laws that apply across the board to all societies. Such general social laws are limited to statements such as (1) people's ideas always tend to fit their social position and experience, (2) people always tend to act in accordance with their interests, and (3) all societies have to satisfy certain basic biological needs of their members. With the exception of principles such as these, in order to understand the operation of a society or its component institutions it is more or less sufficient to understand the social laws that govern the particular social organization. Each type of social organization operates according to its own set of laws and they are the principle determinates of what goes on within them.

The full range of phenomena can be analyzed into increasingly specific levels, called "levels of specificity":

1. Laws that apply to all matter.
2. Laws that apply to all life.
3. Laws that apply to all animals.
4. Laws that apply to all mammal interactions.
5. Laws that apply to all primate social relations.
6. Laws that apply to all human societies.
7. Laws that apply to all class societies.
8. Laws that apply to all capitalist societies.
9. Laws that apply to all monopoly capitalist societies.
10. Laws that apply only to certain levels of organization within capitalist societies, such as mode of production, state, ideology.
11. Laws that apply only to a concrete institution or process, such as ecology, the family, crime, imperialism, racism, social movements.

As the level of analysis gets more specific, more and more useful laws appear until the level of capitalist society is reached. Analysis on this level explains the most. As the system becomes still more specific, our analysis tends to explain less and less. Certain characteristics of monopoly capitalist societies can be explained in terms of the laws that apply to all matter. For example, because they are constructed out of matter, cities occur on the surface of the earth. Other characteristics of society are explainable in terms of the laws that apply to all forms of life, to all animals, or to all mammals—societies need to provide food, warmth, and shelter to its members. Some other aspects of society are products of the fact that society's members are primates or members of the species homo sapiens. Such facts as the year-round sexuality of women, the flexible hand, and the ability to speak have a tremendous social impact. Other aspects of monopoly capitalist society are either characteristics of all societies (such as the few we mentioned above), characteristic of all *class* societies (such as the functioning of the state), characteristic of all capitalist societies (such as the functioning of the military), or are specific products of monopoly capitalism itself. In later chapters we will discuss in detail the laws that originate at each of these levels.

Functional Analysis

It is society that must be the principal unit of social analysis. It is the characteristics of a societal type that fundamentally determine its component system of social relations, the modes of individual social behavior, and social change. It is the logic of a particular type of societal organization that is responsible for virtually all significant aspects of social relations within a society.

Another way of saying that all important social elements and processes are determined by the basic social structure of a society is by stating that these social behaviors have a *function* for the social structure or for the people in it. The function of a behavior is the contribution it makes to the survival of a larger system. Some behaviors are *functional* on a biological level. Food production, clothing production, child-care institutions are all necessary to meet people's biological needs. Other behaviors have a function at a higher level of specificity. All societies, for example, need some process for decision-making and for communication within the group. Decision-making institutions thus play a function on the level of all societies. The same social institution can play a function on more than one level at a time, however. Political institutions in class societies play a decision-making function necessary for all societies, but they also play a function that is specific to class societies. This is the function of maintaining the privileges of the upper class against the rest of the society. All class societies impose such universal imperatives as those for a state apparatus enabling a minority to control the majority. Capitalist societies impose additional functional requirements such as the need for a high level of unemployment to keep wages down and for a standing military force to protect economic interests. Monopoly capitalist society imposes further demands, such as the need for state regulation of the economy and universal education. Thus, a single institution, such as the American government, performs functions on a number of different levels of specificity. Some of these functions would not be needed in a socialist society, while others would be.

Functionalism is a method of analysis that explains social phenomena in terms of the functions they play. Conservative sociologists often use functionalist analysis as an argument against change. They say that since existing social practices perform a function for "society" they are necessary and should not be changed. Radicals do not accept this. The fact that an existing social practice may perform some function in maintaining an existing capitalist society is no argument for not changing it. Instead, it can be an argument for changing not only that practice but also the society as a whole!

While radical sociologists do not accept this sort of conservative functionalism that opposes change in the interest of preserving an abstract entity called society, radicals can make use of functionalist analysis. Marxist functionalism differs from conservative functionalism in that it recognizes that social practices are functional for historically specific kinds of social systems, which are eventually going to break down and be transformed into new social forms. Marxist functionalism is dialectical in that it recognizes that a given social practice need not be functional for more than one system level at a time. A social component or process that may come into existence because it is functional to the needs of the system at one level may at the same time undermine the system at another level. Also, a component or process generated by the operation of a social system may be both functional and dysfunctional, if it both contributes to and undermines the working of the social system. In fact, it is the development of such conflicts or contradictions that is the fundamental source of change within societies.

It is the normal functioning of a societal system that generates the forces that lead to its transformation. Societies, as we have seen, have contradictions; their normal operation generates forces that undermine their operation. Change comes about because of the existence and growth of these contradictions. For example, the normal operation of competitive capitalist society results in growing economic crises, large-scale property, and economic stagnation. These contradictions of the system result in the transformation of competitive capitalism into monopoly capitalism in order to attempt to resolve the contradictions. But monopoly capitalism too has contradictions, which become the motive force behind change in this type of social organization. Inequality, racism, sexism, war, and the continuation of the subordination of men and women to the social laws of capitalism (alienation) persist, resulting in movements of opposition to the continuation of this social form.

The growth of bureaucracies is another contradictory feature of capitalist societies. Bureaucratic forms are needed to enable the capitalists to maintain control of the large corporations that grow up as part of the monopolization process inherent in capitalist economies. But these forms lead to alienation and work dissatisfaction, which cause discontent with the system, forcing workers to unite in collective struggle to change their working conditions.

The notion of social contradiction as the motive force of social change is alien to almost all of liberal and conservative sociology. These sociologists look for change in either factors external to the system or simply consider it to be an accident. At best a few of these sociologists analyze the stresses and strains inherent in social systems that cause them to change *quantitatively,* that is, without fundamental transformations of their basic social relationships. Socialist sociology understands that all class societies are constantly in the process of *qualitative* change. Because of the internal contradictions of the normal and routine operation of their social structures they are turning into new forms totally different from what they temporarily are.

Explanation in terms of social structure or the nature of social relations is what is meant by "sociological materialism." The materialism of radical sociology assumes that the real relationships among people are responsible for the fundamental character of social organization and social process. Materialist explanation of real social relations is counterposed to the idealist mode of analyzing the world. Idealism looks to the ideas, spirit, will, values, or norms held by individuals or groups as the ultimate explanatory category. Idealism frequently rejects the scientific method of determining the nature of the world in favor either of a subjectivistic approach, which argues that one person's ideas about the world are as good as another's, or to a voluntarism, which maintains that people can change the world if they simply want to do so (that is, change their ideas about it).

Contrary to the claims of sociological idealism, it is the social relationships in which people participate that determine all the major aspects of society, individual behavior, and social change. The system of social relations is in turn determined by the distinctive mode of production of a society, that is, by the mutually conditioning system of the techniques of production on the one hand and the social relationships between the producers and those that control production on the other.

Although the techniques of production and the social relations of production mutually condition one another, it is the logic of the social relations of production that govern the actual technologies employed and the rate at which technology advances. The structure of relationships among people is determined by the mode in which people relate to nature to satisfy their material needs. People are driven by their biological needs to interact with nature and with other people in order to win from nature that which they need. Thus social relations are at base economic relations. Regardless of people's will or consciousness, it is ultimately the way people get a living that determines all aspects of their social life. Political, legal, moral, religious, philosophical, and all other kinds of ideas, as well as all basic types of familial, military, social, and political behavior, are fundamentally determined by social activities that are structured by societies' distinctive mode of production.

THE NATURE OF SOCIETY

Societies are created by people because only in association with other people can people meet their basic needs. A society consists of a system of social relationships between people that can basically satisfy or contain the biological drives of its members. But once a society exists, it takes on a life of its own. In addition to providing for the needs of its members, a society must provide for its survival as a social organization.

This much can be said for all societies. As simple societies grow and become wealthier and more complex, however, they develop a third characteristic. They develop systems of inequality or of social stratification. Some people become wealthier and more powerful than others. This seems to be necessary for societies to progress, to become larger and stronger, yet it is a source of conflict and contradiction as well. Social processes that are necessary to maintain the privileges of elites often conflict with the more elementary requirements of meeting basic biological and emotional drives and surviving as social organizations.

A society can be defined as a group that is more or less self-sufficient. Some primitive societies consist of as few as 50 or 100 people, yet they qualify as societies because they are essentially self-sufficient and provide for all their members' needs. Most of what goes on in these simple societies can be explained in terms of two variables: the biological needs of its members and the physical environment in which they live. Meeting the basic needs of hunger, warmth, and dryness takes up most of people's energy in simple societies because their technologies are primitive. They cannot harness the energy of animals or fuels to do this work but must do it themselves. Their remaining energies are spent on bearing and raising children, and on informal sociability among themselves.

Contemporary societies tend to have hundreds of thousands or millions of members. With the increasing importance of the government in modern societies, the boundaries of societies generally coincide with the boundaries of the nation-state. Yet even societies as large as the United States must meet the same basic human needs as are met by a primitive society of less than 100 people. In fact, it may not meet them so well since in addition to meeting basic human needs, and needs of social coordination, it must also sustain a system of social inequality that is often contradictory to those needs.

A good part of the institutions of all societies are devoted to meeting biological needs such as hunger, warmth, and dryness. The social institutions that meet these needs are referred to as the *economy*. Because these needs are so basic, the way they are met tends to shape the rest of the society. The need for sex is met primarily through the institution of the *family*. The family also meets other basic human needs, such as the drives for affection, approval, dignity, self-esteem, belongingness, and community. These two institutions meet most of our basic human needs, although these needs may also be met through other institutions. The drives for dignity, self-esteem, community, and belonging also contribute to the widespread prevalence of clubs, associations, ceremonies, patriotism, and racism, for example, while the drive for meaningful creative activity results in the universal presence of hobbies, participant sports, crafts, and games, which provide satisfaction that may not be present in economic life.

Other institutions meet other basic human needs. The drive for meaningful activity together with the propensity to attach meaning to things is one factor that results in the universal presence of world views such as those of religion, mythology, philosophy, or science. The need of human children for extensive care and socialization makes necessary some sort of family or educational institutions.

Functional Requisites of Societies

Much of what goes on in societies, however, must be attributed to the functional requirements of the social system itself. In order for society to continuously function to satisfy biological drives, it must continue to exist as a coherent system. To do this, it must fulfill a set of societal requisites. These can be called "integrative imperatives," since they are necessary for social integration or coherency. Four of these can be listed:

1. The societal need to replace society's members who age and die.
2. The societal need to preserve the health of its members against human diseases and the integrity of the society against threats from both animals and other societies.
3. The societal need to coordinate the society so that it can function properly.
4. The societal need to manage frustrated biological energies so that they do not disrupt society.

In summary, these four societal requirements can be referred to as the member replacement, safety, coordination, and safety-valve functions.

Every society, if it is to survive, must replace its members that die with new people. Therefore, it must provide for childbirth, and/or other means of recruiting new members, as well as for the socialization and education of new members so that they will be able to perform their roles. Much of the family pattern, children's games, and educational institutions are determined by this societal need. Every society must in practice have institutions for preserving the integrity of the group. It must defend itself from dangerous animals, epidemic diseases, other societies, and internal disruption or else it cannot continue to exist. This requirement accounts for many of the institutions of the military, public health, magic, and the police or their equivalents. Safety-valve institutions will be discussed in Chapter 6.

The members of a society must coordinate their efforts if they are going to realize the advantages of working together to satisfy their individual drives. The effectiveness of a group in achieving its ends is a function of its internal coordination. There is a wide range of mechanisms of social coordination: rational agreement, convergence of interest, habit, enjoyment in working together, and the power of leaders are some of the most important. The universal presence of language can be accounted for in terms of its contribution to this function. Leaving language aside, the most important mechanism of coordination, especially in complex societies, is power. By power is meant simply the ability to realize one's will. Giving power to an individual or small group is one mechanism of coordination. Society can coordinate itself through such means as the police, blood vengeance, the courts, economic incentives, the inculcation of common values by education, religion, and mass media, as well as by informal mechanisms of social approval and disapproval. Correspondingly, much of the structure and operation of these institutions is determined by the requisites of social coordination.

Primitive societies can be more or less completely explained in terms of how they meet biological drives and maintain social integration within the limitations of a specific physical environment. Class societies, where great differences in power, wealth, and privilege exist, cannot. In these societies, technological resources exist that make it easy to meet basic biological needs. As a consequence, the population grows rapidly, and the need for coordination becomes more difficult to meet. Technology also makes it possible to live in a wide variety of physical environments, modifying the environment to fit the needs of people (who naturally would require a warm environment). Thus, the more developed a society becomes, the greater the extent to which its organization is shaped by social requisites.

In analyzing class societies, we must always consider the extent to which social institutions contribute to the maintenance of the class structure. Most specifically, we must consider how they meet the requisites of the specific type of class system present in the society. This makes social analysis quite complicated, since a given institution generally fulfills functions on three different levels. For example, in class societies the family fulfills basic biological needs for sex and emotional support. It also fulfills basic societal needs for socialization by teaching the young skills needed by everyone in a society. Even more specifically, however, it socializes people to fit into a capitalist class society by teaching them to accept the particular position they have been born into in the class system. It also provides a safety valve for the frustrations its members suffer as members of class society. Likewise, most other institutions in class societies have this contradictory character. They exist to fulfill functions necessary for the survival of the society and of the people in it. And they also exist to meet the needs of the people on top of the society to maintain their privileges at the expense of those on the bottom. It is this contradictory nature of social institutions in capitalist society that creates conflict and leads eventually to the transformation of these societies into new and more advanced forms of social organization.

THE NATURE OF CLASS SOCIETY

Class societies are characterized by the division of the population into large groups of families that share a common economic and social position defined by the relationship of its adult members to the means of production. Social classes are ranked hierarchically or *stratified* into various levels essentially corresponding to their position in the production process. Members of classes share many things in common: their wealth, their income level, their occupational status, their educational level, and the general prestige or status they have in the community. People tend to live in neighborhoods, and to marry people from the same class. Of course, there are exceptions. Some people are mobile from one class to another. If this is merely a matter of an individual changing positions, it is of little importance. However, when changes in society force many people to be mobile, this may be of great significance.

There are many different theories of class in sociology. Conservative sociologists tend to see classes as hereditary groups that pass on traditions necessary for the maintenance of social order. They see the upper class as a valuable repository of aristocratic virtues. Liberal sociologists, on the other hand, tend to stress social mobility. They argue that social stratification is useful when it motivates people to work hard in order to win a higher position in society. (This is known as the "functional" theory of stratification.) The difficulty with this argument, however, is that there is little evidence that people's position in a class society is determined by how hard they work or how much they contribute to society. In fact, the probable relationship may be just the opposite: people on a lower level of society often work harder and contribute more than those on top.

While liberals see stratification as being functional in the sense that it is useful for society as a whole, radical sociologists believe that it is functional only for those on top. Radicals believe that class relationships arise out of exploitation, and that the only interest they serve is to make the rich richer and the poor poorer. Radicals favor a society without class divisions; ultimately they work towards a society without inequality. They believe that in a classless society people will work because they want to, and for the good of society, not so that they can make more money than someone else.

Radical sociology has a different theory of stratification than liberal or conservative sociology. The liberals and conservatives tend to place the greatest emphasis on the values held by people in different classes, and on the way in which they live. They thus emphasize the consumption patterns of members of social classes. Radicals, on the other hand, stress the *productive* side of class relationships. Following the social theories of Karl Marx, they argue that it is the social relationships growing out of economic production that create different classes. Someone must produce wealth before it can be consumed. A person's relationship to the production of wealth determines how much wealth he or she will have to consume, and hence the life style he or she will be able to afford.

Class and Economic Value

In most class societies there are two major classes. The dominant class is the one that owns or controls the means of production. In an agricultural society, this class owns the land. In an industrial capitalist society, it owns the factories. The other class, the class that is dominated or oppressed, is the class that does not own the means of production. This class is forced to work for the class that owns the means of production, in exchange for wages or for some other payment (such as a percentage of the crop in a sharecropping situation) that represents less than the *value* of what they produce.

A central tenet of Marxist theory is that it is *labor* that produces value. Of course, some things such as the air we breathe have great value in the sense that we must *use* them to survive. This *use value* is often inherent in the bounty of nature, as with plants that grow wild. However, *exchange value*, the commercial value of something in a market society, depends on how much work people must do to produce it. Thus, it is the people who do the work who produce value. Simply owning the land or a factory does not add any value for people. A capitalist who simply sits home and collects dividends, or a landlord who simply collects rents from the farmers who do the work, does not contribute anything to production. (Of course, an owner who actively manages his or her enterprise is performing a useful function. The proportion of his or her income that is attributable to actually working in the production process is not unearned income. With marginal classes, it is often difficult to distinguish between earned and unearned income.)

Class and Power

Class relationships are essentially relationships of *power*. As we have seen, by power sociologists refer to the ability to realize one's will even in the face of resistance from others. In class societies, the dominant class exercises power over the subordinate class by compelling members of that class to work for their benefit. There are four major types of power that can be identified in class societies; economic power, physical power, ideological power, and social power. By "economic power" is meant the ability to determine the behavior of others by manipulating the satisfaction or frustration of their material drives and wants through controlling the goods and services available to them, thus essentially bribing them to follow a certain course of action. By "physical power" is meant direct physical compulsion—the threat or actual use of physical force to compel someone to do a certain thing. By "ideological power" is meant the manipulation of people's beliefs and values to get them to follow a certain course. Ideological power can be exercised by creating wants or values in people through such means as advertising, early socialization, or education. It can also be exercised by controlling the channels of information either to make people believe that a certain thing or course of action will in fact satisfy their wants or values or to obtain access to better information than others in order to make better decisions than those lacking good information. By "social power" is meant the ability to have one's will prevail by using such means as control over prestige, group interaction, or social acceptance to get another to do one's bidding. Social power can be very compelling and is normally only resistable when an individual belongs to another group that places conflicting demands on him or her.

Power does not have to be actually exercised to be effective. The mere threat of the exercise of power is often sufficient to secure compliance. The mere threat of being fired, of being shot, or of being cut off from valued friends is usually enough to get an individual to realize the will of others. However, in order to maintain credibility, power must occasionally be actually exercised. Of course, the too frequent exercise of power may be counterproductive. It might alienate people to the extent that they may rebel against the demands of those with power.

The dominant class in society has an objective interest in maintaining a social structure that reinforces and increases its power, prestige, and income, while the subordinate class has an objective interest in decreasing or eliminating the differentials in these categories. The dominant class members can utilize the existing organizational structure of society to maintain and increase their privilege. Generally speaking, they are quite conscious of their objective interests. They have a high degree of "class consciousness" in the sense of being consciously aware of their interest and how to maintain it. The army, churches, state, and the corporations are all available for their service. The masses of the working people, on the other hand, must set up alternative structures in order to implement their interests in changing the structure of society. Labor unions and working-class-oriented political parties are probably the two most important forms of such organizations. Since working people must exist in a society dominated by institutions that reinforce the ideology of the upper class, it is more difficult for them to develop class consciousness. Often they are torn by conflicting loyalties, with their objective experiences leading them to feel solidarity with other workers, but the propaganda they hear from the schools, churches, and media reinforcing allegiance to the existing system. For class consciousness to develop among the working class, generally there must be a concerted effort made by organizers from leftist parties or labor movements.

Because of the propensity of human beings to seek world views or attribute meaning to things, and because of their tendency to believe that that which corresponds to one's behavior and satisfies one's drives and is in one's interests is right and good, all classes *tend* to develop a consciousness that justifies the pursuit of their interests. In order for the subordinate class to develop fully as a social class it must control its own institutions and propagate a counterculture of resistance. It must gain control of its own media and educational institutions, or develop enough political power to be able to gain control of a part of the established institutions in the society. The radical sociology movement is an outgrowth of an attempt made by progressive social movements in the 1960s to use the existing educational institutions as well as alternative media of communication to help build working-class consciousness.

Changes in Class Systems

The productive system in a society is constantly changing, partly as a result of technological developments and partly as a result of changes in social relationships manifested in social conflict. Radical sociologists see changes in the productive system as the basic source of social evolution, both in the past and in the future. They focus on the relations of production when studying the way in which society evolved from primitive hunting and gathering techniques to modern industrial societies. They also believe that continuing changes in the productive system will cause a continued evolution of society towards socialism. Political and social struggle is also necessary, however, to assure that society evolves in a humane direction. Modern technology makes socialism possible, but it may also facilitate fascism. Before we can intelligently participate in political struggles, we must have an understanding of the role of changes in the productive system in causing and channeling social changes.

The earliest forms of the division of labor were determined by people's biological nature. The main division was between women and men, with each sex playing a different role in the productive process. Women were pregnant or nursing during most of their fertile years and consequently had to stay close to the camp and focus their energies on gathering plants to eat and on household chores. Men were free to hunt. There was also some division of labor between younger and older people, with men who were too old to hunt staying in camp and working on crafts, medical arts, or other things that were within their biological limitations.

The first changes in the relations of production resulted from ecological or environmental factors. As the population grew in fertile river valleys, it became more efficient to settle in one place and plant crops rather than roam around gathering natural products. It became necessary to import some commodities from distant places, since not everything can be obtained in one place. Thus, a need for merchants and traders developed. When water was scarce or erratic, a need for flood control and irrigation developed. The earliest development of governmental institutions can probably be traced to this need to control the water supply, as well as the desire to protect valuable land and to secure internal harmony between various specialists. Gradually, greater specialization developed between food production and crafts, or between manual and intellectual labor.

Those societies that adopted these changed relations of production became larger and more powerful. They were able to spread to outlying areas, compelling more primitive peoples to adapt to their system. In so doing, they developed an elite, an upper class, which controlled the armed forces and which existed by extracting taxes or tribute from the productive classes in society. This elite class, of course, had an interest in the division of labor even if it was not functional for society as a whole. Thus, they tended to encourage further specialization in order to make the system better able to support them and their ambitions. With the development of a major division of labor social classes developed, with families passing on their position in the system to their children. Technology tended to be developed according to the interests of the dominant classes, and this class system assumed a logic of its own that became the principle determinant of social organization. Thus, as societies become more developed, their evolution tends to result from *social* rather than *ecological* factors. This process of social evolution will be discussed in detail in the next chapter.

For now, let us look in some detail at capitalist society as a form of class society. Capitalist society is, of course, the most familiar to the readers of this book, who, we can assume, live in capitalist societies. However, the class relations of capitalist societies are often less obvious and visible than those in feudal or slave societies. Relationships between lords and serfs, or between masters and slaves, are personified in specific individuals who know each other and interact on an interpersonal level. The

Capturing people to serve as slaves in the New World is portrayed in this work by Mexican muralist Diego Rivera.

relationships in capitalist societies are often more complex and hidden—for example, workers at a major corporation may never meet the owners of that corporation; people who work for government are only indirectly tied to the profit-making system. Thus the class nature of a society such as that in the United States is not immediately apparent to people living in that society.

Class Systems in American History

In any real society, also, the class system tends to be more complex than that of a theoretical society that is purely of one type or another. This is true because class relationships that were predominant under one type of society survive as minority classes once a new type of society emerges. For example, when the United States was founded there were three basic class systems. One was a system of self-employed farmers, artisans, and shopkeepers. Members of this class worked for themselves and sold their products on the free market. To the extent that they suffered from class exploitation, it was from bankers who lent them money at exorbitant rates, or from government officials who taxed them excessively, or from big merchants or middlemen who paid them too little for their produce and charged them too much for the goods they had to buy. There is still considerable nostalgia in the United States for this small-town or rural society of independent producers, although self-employed individuals today are a small proportion of the population. Marxists refer to this group of self-employed workers as the independent *petit bourgeoisie* (a French term that acquired special political-economic connotations in French history).

A second class system that existed historically in the United States was the slave system. This system was polarized between masters and slaves. It was concentrated in the South prior to the Civil War. The relationship between the master and slave under this system determined the whole nature of the Southern social and economic system, its ideology, its politics, its military organization, its family forms, etc. Slavery meant that only certain crops could be grown under certain conditions, it meant that the South was inherently expansionist, it meant that there were real constraints on industrialization, and it meant that the slaveholders would develop a sense of "aristocracy" and paternalism. The slave system was formally abolished after the Civil War, but remnants of it were reestablished under the Jim Crow system in the South, with sharecropping and other arrangements being used by the landowning white population to extract cheap labor from the black population. As we shall see in Chapter 11, racial patterns that grew out of this system still have a major impact in the United States.

A third class system that has existed in the United States since colonial days is the capitalist system. The two main classes in this system are the owning capitalist class and the nonowning working class. This class system was imported from England and grew rapidly in the United States and in other settler societies (Canada, Australia, etc.), where there was no old aristocratic class to oppose it. Capitalist relations of production tend to grow out of *petit bourgeois* relations of production because of the functioning of the competitive system. As some small producers become more efficient, or develop new techniques of production, they grow in size and hire more workers. The larger they get, the more efficient they become because of certain *economies of scale* (processes whereby it is cheaper on a per item basis to produce 1,000 items of something than to produce 10 or 100). Gradually, the larger producers force the smaller producers out of business. The entrepreneur who started the business, and in the early days did much of the work himself, becomes a capitalist who hires others to do the work. The capitalist system of productive relations has grown to the point where it is by far the predominant system in the United States. The *petit bourgeois* system of production survives primarily in marginal sectors of the economy, particularly in service industries where personal relationships between seller and customer are important.

Class Divisions in Advanced Capitalism

As capitalist industries grow, they tend to create new divisions in the class system. Large, complex organizations require a large group of professional managers to run things. These managers tend to be better paid than other workers, and because of the

As recently as two generations ago independent farming families were a major group in American society.

Industrial production is the core of the contemporary capitalist economy.

nature of their work have a good deal of control over what happens. Thus, they tend to grow into a separate class, a class that is in the middle between the workers and the owners. As society becomes more technically complex, it requires a better-educated population. It requires advanced medical and social service systems. These employees in education and the social services tend to be paid by the state, as do military officers and other civil service employees. They typically must obtain advanced educational credentials in order to obtain their positions. They, too, have a greater degree of control over their working conditions than do the masses of workers, and they control the labor of workers such as secretaries, assistants, janitors, etc. They thus are part of the middle class.

There are other divisions that tend to arise within the major classes in a capitalist society. There may be a division between bankers and merchants who merely circulate money and commodities and industrial capitalists who control industries that actually produce things. There is a division between manual workers who work with their hands and white-collar workers who do not. (It is important to remember that both manual and nonmanual workers use their heads.) These divisions are very complex, and tend to change as economic conditions change. Today, for example, we see that white-collar workers and professionals are tending to lose their middle-class status and find that their educational credentials no longer give them a privileged position different from that of less-educated manual workers.

The significance of these divisions within the class system in the United States is a highly controversial subject within radical sociology. Some writers adhere to a "new working class theory" and assert that college-educated professionals will be the most central exploited group in the capitalist society of the future. Others argue that these professionals are part of the *petit bourgeoisie* because of their middle-class life styles and their economic interest in preserving the privileges they have sustained under the present system. This issue will be discussed in some detail in Chapter 5, where we will also discuss the theory of social class more systematically.

The class system in the United States is constantly changing because of contradictions built into the capitalist economy. As corporations grow, they tend to form monopolies (or oligopolies, where a small number of producers together dominate a market). Inflation tends to increase. Government spending has to be increased to attempt to avoid a depression and to support the people who are thrown out of work by the tendency of capitalist industries to cut their labor force in order to make greater profits. This government spending creates a large class of state employees, many of whom aspire to middle-class careers for their children. The educational system is expanded as a means of giving people an opportunity for social mobility, but the number of jobs for educated people is stable or shrinks.

The capitalist system has been the most volatile system of relations of production in human history. In their never-ending search for higher profits, capitalists have brought about tremendous technological advances. A whole new class of industrial workers was created by capitalism. Societies became predominantly urban, and dependent on fossil fuels for energy. In order to motivate people to work within this system, promises of a better future were held out to entire populations. Rational thought was encouraged at the expense of tradition and mysticism. Thus, capitalism was an essential stage in human history; a stage that built the foundations for a better society in the future. Capitalism also created the contradictions that will make that better society possible. The germs of a new society are always present within the old. Understanding this potential for change in our society is only possible when we understand how the society is shaped by the relations of production that created it and that make further changes inevitable.

Summary

Radical sociology is based on a dialectical theory of knowledge. This means that knowledge is shaped by social reality, while at the same time our understanding of social reality is shaped by ideas. Sociological ideas must be tested both through scientific research and through applied practice, if they are to be objectively valid. While it is possible to formulate sociological laws that are valid on a wide range of levels of analysis, radical sociologists have found that it is most effective to formulate laws that apply to a specific type of society, such as capitalist society. On this level it is possible to specify the functions each element of society makes towards sustaining the system. At the same time, it is possible to study how each element of society contributes to social conflict and to the eventual breakdown of one type of society and its transformation into a new type.

Societies are inherently contradictory. This means that their normal operations generate forces that undermine their functioning and lead to social transformation. Societies are created to meet the basic needs of the people who belong to them. But once societies are created, they have a life of their own, and develop characteristics that are oppressive to many or most of the people who belong to them. The division of societies into social classes is oppressive to the majority of people who find themselves on the bottom, yet it survives because it is in the interest of those who exercise power. Dominant social classes often play a progressive role in developing new technologies and relationships of production, yet by so doing they create conditions that make them obsolete.

In its history, the United States has had three major class systems: the slave system, the system of self-employed producers, and the capitalist system. The first of these has been abolished, the second has sharply declined, while the third has become dominant and undergone a transition from competitive to monopoly capitalism.

Review Questions

---

1. In what ways can sociological ideas be tested through practice?
2. Explain the concept of contradiction. What contradictions can you think of that are inherent in the social structure of the United States?
3. What are some differences between the social sciences and the physical sciences?
4. Which level of analysis tends to be the most effective for sociology? Why?
5. Make a list of occupations, including high-paying and prestigious ones such as with the conservative use of functionalist analysis?
6. Is Marxist sociology materialist or idealist?
7. What are the basic integrative imperatives that must be met for a society to survive? How do these differ from meeting the needs of individuals in the society?
8. Is it possible for a social institution to fulfill functions on different levels of social organization? How?
9. How do liberal and radical sociologists differ in their analysis of the functions of social stratification?
10. What is the difference between use value and exchange value? How is each determined?

11. What are the different ways in which power can be exercised?
12. What was the chief form of the division of labor in primitive societies?
13. What three class systems have existed in the United States since its founding?
14. Which groups make up the middle class in advanced capitalist societies?

Suggestions for Further Study

1. Choose a specific institutional feature of American society, such as the educational system, the police force, the corporate economy, the churches, the family patterns, etc. Make a list of as many functions you can think of that this institution plays for the maintenance of American capitalist society. Be sure to list not only the obvious functions admitted by those in control of the institution, but also more subtle and less obvious functions. Now make up a second list of all the "dysfunctions." That is, of all the ways the same institution tends to interfere with the orderly functioning of society, creating conflict and pressures for change. Compare your list with those of other members of the class.

2. The dominant relations of production in American society have changed markedly during the last one hundred years. This means that these changes can often be observed in the generational history of specific families. With the help of your parents and grandparents, trace your family tree back for as many generations as possible. For each adult member of the family, indicate his or her relationship to the means of production, whether employer, worker in a capitalist firm, self-employed farmer or craftsperson, slave, slave owner, housewife, etc. How do the changes in your family reflect more general changes in the structure of society?

3. Make a list of all the social factors that have shaped your life and made you the kind of person you are. Consider the neighborhood you lived in, the type of friends you have had, the schooling you have had, the economic circumstances you have experienced, the mass media you have been exposed to, your religious experiences, etc. Discuss how your personality, attitudes, and opinions have been shaped by these social experiences.

4. Find a book that portrays life under social conditions markedly different from those with which you are personally familiar. For example, a novel portraying life on a slave-owning plantation in the South or on a medieval manor in Europe. Write an essay showing how people's lives differed because of the social conditions there.

5. Make a list of occupations, including high-paying and prestigious ones such as physician and lawyer, and less prestigious and poorly paid ones such as factory worker or secretary. Make a list of the functions that members of these occupa-

tions fulfill for society. What would happen if all members of this occupation were to withhold their services for a week, a month, or a year? Are the rewards received by people in each occupation commensurate with the contribution they make? If we paid less money to the higher-paid occupations, would they attract less qualified and motivated people? Are there occupations that are completely unnecessary? If so, why do they survive?

Selected Readings

DIALECTICAL AND HISTORICAL MATERIALISM

Bukharin, Nikolai. *Historical Materialism: A System of Sociology.* New York: Russell & Russell, 1965 (1925).

Cornforth, Maurice. *Materialism and the Dialectic Method.* New York: International, 1971 (1968).

———. *The Theory of Knowledge.* New York: International, 1971 (1963).

Engels, Fredrick. *Anti-Dühring.* New York: International, 1939 (1885).

———. *The Dialectics of Nature.* New York: International, 1940 (1927).

Lenin, V. I. *Materialism and Empirico-Criticism.* New York: International, 1970 (1908).

Mao, Tse-tung. *On Contradiction,* in *Selected Readings from the Works of Mao Tse-tung.* Peking: Foreign Languages, 1971.

———. *On Practice,* in *Selected Readings from the Works of Mao Tse-tung.* Peking: Foreign Languages, 1971.

Marcuse, Herbert. *Reason and Revolution.* Boston: Beacon, 1969 (1941).

Progress Publishers. *Fundamentals of Marxist-Leninist Philosophy.* Moscow: Progress, 1974.

Stalin, Joseph. *Dialectical and Historical Materialism.* New York: International, 1940.

Szymanski, Albert. "Dialectical Functionalism." *Sociological Inquiry* 42:2 (Spring 1972).

THE NATURE OF SOCIETY

Cornforth, Maurice. *Historical and Dialectical Materialism.* New York: International, 1971.

Durkheim, Émile. *Elementary Forms of Religious Life.* New York: Collier Books, 1961 (1915).

———. *Suicide.* Glencoe, Ill.: Free Press, 1951.

Engels, Frederick. *The Origins of Private Property, the Family and the State.* New York: International, 1972 (1884).

Freud, Sigmund. *Civilization and Its Discontents.* New York: Norton, 1962 (1930).

Genovese, Eugene. *The Political Economy of Slavery.* New York: Vintage, 1963.

Harris, Marvin. *Cows, Pigs, Wars and Witches*. New York: Vintage, 1974.

Malinowski, Bronislaw. *A Scientific Theory of Culture*. New York: Oxford U. Press, 1960.

Marcuse, Herbert. *Eros and Civilization*. Boston: Beacon, 1953.

Marx, Karl. *Capital*, Vol. I and Vol. III. New York: International, 1967.

Marx, Karl, and Engels, Frederick. *The Communist Manifesto*. Baltimore: Pelican, 1968 (1848).

Pareto, Vilfredo. *Mind and Society*. New York: Dover, 1963.

Reich, Wilhelm. *The Mass Psychology of Fascism*. New York: Farrar, Straus & Giroux, 1970 (1945).

White, Leslie. *The Evolution of Culture*. New York: McGraw-Hill, 1959.

———. *The Science of Culture*. New York: Grove, 1949.

Chapter 3

Social Development

The most interesting and important, and also the most difficult, problem in social science is the study of social change. It is much simpler to describe the situation as it is right now, or as it was at any particular point in time, than to understand how things got to be the way they are and where they are going in the future. If we are committed to changing societies, however, we must face the challenge of analyzing the process of social change. Only in this way can we have a basis for understanding what is going on in our society and world today, and what needs to be done to help things evolve in a progressive direction.

While the Marxist sociological paradigm stresses the fact that conflict and change are integral to the nature of class societies, this does not mean that changes are observable in all parts of these societies at all times. Even the most casual student of history can see that societies tend to have periods of apparent stability, followed by relatively brief intervals when rapid and dramatic changes take place. Of course, there are small changes going on all the time, but these may be of little apparent importance. Some countries may have coups d'etat and even violent uprisings quite frequently, but the society remains essentially the same after each change of government as it was before. Really dramatic revolutions, which change the social structure of a country and shape an era of world history, are much rarer. The French revolution of 1789 and the Russian revolution of 1917 are perhaps the two most significant examples. But what was it about these events that made them so important? Can we expect similar earth-shattering events in the near future?

Theory of Social Change

Answering these questions requires a theory of social change. It also requires a good deal of study of the ways in which change has taken place in the past, in order to check the validity of the theory. Marxism offers such a theory, and Marxist scholars have done quite a bit of research into historical changes in an effort to refine and test the theory. Although the specifics of the theory as applied to each historical situation are quite complex, its basic elements can be summarized briefly.

The Marxist theory of social change is a theory of *stages of development*. It is somewhat analogous to quantum theory in physics, in that it asserts that major changes in the structure of society are discontinuous. That is to say, there are relatively long periods of stability, followed by a fairly rapid transition from one type of society to another. The reason for this is the tension between the *structure* and the *superstructure* in society. The structure is the economic base on which society is built. Out of this base, there grows up a social superstructure: political institutions, religious beliefs, cultural patterns, etc. Included in the structure is an upper class that has a vested interest in the existing system. This class tends to resist change, since its members prefer to retain the privileges they have developed under the existing system. However, as they improve the efficiency of their exploitative system, the contradictions within it also increase. Eventually, these contradictions become so intense that the society breaks down and new groups assume control.

The rate of change varies from one type of society to another. In some societies, the contradictions in the economy are relatively weak, while the ruling class is very strong. These societies may go centuries without a major change in their social system. In other societies, the contradictions are great and the ruling class weak. Even in these societies, however, one cannot expect to see major changes going on all the time. Social change is much more rapid than geological change or than biological evolution. Compared to the lifetime of an individual, however, it is fairly slow. Some generations experience a major change in their lifetimes, others do not. As yet, the study of social change is not developed enough for us to make valid predictions of when major changes are going to take place. However, there has been a general tendency within capitalist society for the rate of change to become more rapid. Modern capitalism is much more prone to change than were previous types of society. Thus, those of us who are alive today are certain to see major technological and social changes during our lifetimes. There are almost certain to be revolutionary changes in the social systems of a number of countries, as well. Thus, understanding the process of social change is more important for us today than it was for people throughout most of human history.

Our past has exhibited a number of basic types of societies. In this chapter, we will discuss the following basic types: primitive, oriental despotic, slave or ancient, feudal, capitalist, and state socialist societies. Within each of these types there are subtypes as well, and we will discuss the most important of these. Primitive societies, for example, include hunting and gathering societies and horticultural societies. Capitalist societies can be divided into competitive capitalist societies and monopoly capitalist societies.

Each of these basic types of societies is defined according to the way in which its people are organized for economic production. It is this set of relations to production that determines the social structure characteristic of the type and that generates the pressure that eventually causes it to evolve into a more advanced type. The details of this process will be discussed for each type of society.

PRIMITIVE SOCIETIES

Primitive societies have a very low level of technological development. They mobilize only a small amount of energy per producer, have little or no significant division of labor, and little or no stratification. In their economic roles adults of the same sex are more or less interchangeable, and conditions of substantive egalitarianism and democracy generally prevail.

Very primitive societies are determined in their fundamentals by their ecology, that is, their relation to their physical environment. A primitive social organization develops a technology that allows it to secure a niche in its environment where the basic material drives of the society's members are satisfied. All the social institutions of a primitive society are normally synchronized to facilitate the full exploitation of this niche to the extent necessary to satisfy the group's material needs. The family forms, political organization, military organization, religious practices, etc., are all geared to maximal utilization of the physical environment. The only sources of systematic change in such simple societies are either changes in the environment or increases in population. Either of these factors may disturb the equilibrium that a primitive society has established with its physical environment and force the introduction of new, more efficient technologies that can better satisfy the material needs of its members. By decreasing the food supply and disturbing the ecological balance, these factors may force the society and its institutions to change. However, simple societies are normally very stable. They persist for thousands of years virtually unchanged unless forced to change by the operation of one or another of these factors.

One of the most vivid examples of the influence of a change in the physical environment was the rapid and revolutionary impact of the spread of the horse on the societies of Great Plains Indians. The integration of the horse into their culture radically transformed virtually all aspects of their life in a few generations.

Technological Change

The most simple primitive societies relied on hunting and gathering wild plants for food. Given their limited technologies, they were very dependent on their environments. There are basically only two social forces operating on very simple societies, the biological drives and propensities of their members (a constant) and the differences in their physical environments (a variable). This latter factor is the only variable systematically acting on these societies. Thus, the distinctive Eskimo culture can be fundamentally explained in terms of its maximal adaptation to its environment, as can the culture of the Plains Indians, the Arabian nomads, the Northwest Coast fishing cultures, the forest peoples of South America and Africa. People living in social groups with very backward technologies must maximally utilize their limited energies in extracting from their environment the material essentials of life in order to satisfy the material drives of their members.

As technology slowly developed under the pressure of growing population, it resulted in increased competition for scarce material resources (both within a tribe and among tribes). As a result the very primitive hunters and gatherers moved into *horticulture* (the cultivation rather than the mere gathering of food), and became increasingly able to control their environment. Technology gradually becomes a protection against environmental forces. It is the means by which people bring their environments under social control.

Gerhard Lenski has analyzed the correlates of technological development in primitive society (see Table 3-1). The data he used, based on hundreds of studies done by anthropologists who visited and observed primitive societies, shows that as technology improves in primitive societies there are tremendous changes in the social structure. It becomes profitable to own slaves once the technology has developed to the point that they can produce a surplus for their masters. Social classes emerge, together with political hierarchies and warfare designed to steal the surplus of other societies. The dominant class asserts its rights to ownership of land. All of this is possible because of increased productivity due to the new technology.

As technology develops people lose their dependence on the vagaries of nature.

TABLE 3-1. Correlates of Technological Development in Primitive Society

Society by Technology	PERCENTAGE OF SOCIETIES WITH EACH CHARACTERISTIC				
	Slavery	Powerful Chief	Significant Stratification	Frequent Warfare	Private Property in Land
Hunting and gathering	10	0	2	8	11
Simple horticultural	14	38	17	44	71
Advanced horticultural	83	63	54	82	60

(Source: Adapted from Gerhard Lenski and Jean Lenski, *Human Societies.* New York: McGraw-Hill, 1974.)

But this liberation from dependence on nature is at the expense of greater dependence on social institutions. In order to effectively produce and utilize an increasingly complex technology, a whole new set of social institutions and values are instituted that significantly undermine the authentic democracy and egalitarianism of more primitive society. As societies increase in technological efficiency (as the energy mobilized per person day grows) many changes in the social superstructure occur. For example, monetary payments come to be associated with marriage, sexuality becomes increasingly restricted, cruelty increases, the size and density of societies and settlements grow, settlements become more permanent, a division of labor develops, significant stratification appears, private property becomes more important, and the female becomes increasingly subordinate to the male.

Hunting and Gathering Societies

Hunting and gathering societies are the most democratic, egalitarian, and fraternal societies the world has ever known. Generally, the members of these societies are rather happy, provided only that their environment treats them well. Their social drives are generally well satisfied compared to advanced industrial societies. The main drawback in these societies is the frequently tedious labor involved in the satisfaction of material drives, the possibility of irregularity in food supply, the lack of adequate health facilities and possibly the lack of an adequate diet, and the consequent prevalence of sickness and a short life span. In these societies decision making takes place in assemblies of the whole tribe or at least of all its adult male members. There is very little real private property in the means of production, i.e., land; crime is handled by a system of blood vengeance (retaliation by the kin of a victim) rather than by any official apparatus; most are not strictly monogamous; sexuality is generally relatively free; a divorce tends to be a very simple matter; and political leaders have very little authority. In general, the repression of the social drives is at a minimum. Child-rearing practices tend to be very liberal and nonauthoritarian. As a consequence of all this there is generally a strong sense of community and dignity; most people engage in meaningful activities and participate in strong social relations based on mutual support.

Horticultural Society

Hunting and gathering societies developed horticulture (cultivation of the land with a hoe) for the first time only about 10,000 years ago. The discovery of seeds and plant cultivation had a momentous impact on social life. For the first time people could produce their own food rather than simply take what nature provided. This step differentiated people from all the other animals (except some species of ants and bees). The development of hoe technology meant that much more food could be produced in a work day. This allowed for the creation of an economic surplus, that is, of production significantly beyond that necessary to satisfy the material drives of the producers. The consequence of this was that a division of labor and the beginnings of a division between those who produced and those who controlled production was able to develop for the first time in human history. The fact that one person could now regularly produce enough to feed additional people thus opened up the possibility of the division of society into the rulers and the ruled. The process of social division was not fully realized, however, until the agricultural revolution and the introduction of the plow.

Early horticultural society's institutional structure still looked much like that of hunting and gathering society. The difference between them was more quantitative than qualitative. Decision making was still decentralized and political leadership was still based on persuasion, although a significant tendency was present for more power to be concentrated in the leaders. Although the differences in wealth and power were not great, they were significant. Concentration of decision making and stratification increased significantly with the discovery of metallurgy, however. Advanced horticultural society, which utilizes the metal hoe and metal weapons, is much more stratified than the less advanced horticultural society. There are now great disparities in wealth, prestige, and power, which have developed because of the large surplus produced by the metal hoe and consolidated through the increasing monopoly on the production of metal weapons and tools. Private property in the means of production now becomes significant and the position of women declines in relation to that of men. But there are still obstacles to a full development of class society in the relative backwardness of a hoe technology that is unable to produce enough surplus for full-scale stratification.

Breakdown of Primitive Society

The possibility of stratification and the development of classes occurs because of the development of a sufficient technology to allow for a significant surplus to develop. The realization of this possibility is a product both of functional necessities and self-interest. The first differentiation between those that engage in physical labor and those that engage in supervisory or other nonproductive type activities was most probably a result of the allocation of these positions on the basis of real or imagined increases in efficiency that would result from some people specializing in warfare, some in communication with the gods, or some in economic coordination. These early differentiations, with their consequent differential distributions of wealth, privilege, and power, were relatively small and directly related to what the members of a society thought was necessary to more effectively deal with their environments. The initial functional differentiation was enough, however, to allow people's innate biological propensity to act in their own interests to operate. As the authority of the more powerful and privileged strata became institutionalized, those that had authority acted so as to both consolidate and increase their power and privilege. As a result social classes were formed and the stratification system rigidified into a completely differentiated system, with those that produced on the bottom having virtually no power, privilege, or wealth and the few that supervised and came to actually "own" the economy on the top having a virtual monopoly of power, wealth, and privilege.

As the economic surplus grew, the producing masses went on living at a subsistence level, turning over an ever-increasing proportion of their income to the privileged. This privileged group, in turn, developed into a ruling class that lived in ever-increasing luxury.

One of the most basic processes that undermines the kin-based, fraternal organization of primitive society is the growth of trade. Commerce destroys the solidarity of primitive groups. Hunting and gathering peoples engage in very little trade. These peoples, as small as their societies are, tend to be self-sufficient in the means to satisfy their material drives. But as the technology develops, self-sufficiency is harder and harder to maintain, (1) because groups are now stationary, and cannot acquire all the things they could when they were nomadic, and (2) because the increasingly complex technology means that more and more diverse materials are required. Trade then becomes increasingly important as technology develops. A tribe comes to specialize in the supply or production of one or another item depending on its geographical location near a source of a certain metal, salt, a certain kind of food, etc. This specialization results in the creation of certain specialists within a tribe, both the people that collect or produce the trade goods and the people that specialize in the commercial process itself. As trade becomes more and more important for a tribe, these groups, particularly those that monopolize trade, begin to use their position to increase and consolidate their privileges and wealth. External trade thus generates internal differentiation, and consequently internal trade, among those who have become differentiated on the basis of external trade. Internal trade greatly accelerates the process of the destruction of the old communal ties and the generation of a rich and a poor that cuts across the old kinship ties.

There are a number of other processes operating to produce the first significant stratification. War leaders develop in order to coordinate military activities (both defense and raiding). Military success requires the coordination possible only through leadership. Military leaders become more important as the economic surplus grows as a result of the advance in technology. With a significant economic surplus there is now more to be won or lost in military combat; hence warfare is both more important and more frequent and military leadership more important. Military leaders who initially acquire their position for these purely functional reasons, just as do the traders, soon begin to take advantage of their superior position to consolidate and increase their power, privilege, and wealth.

Political leaders (or peace chiefs) arise in a similar manner. As population and population density increases within a society, the need for the coordination of economic activities grows. Hence the political leaders whose primary responsibility is to coordinate economic projects becomes increasingly important. Again, once these leaders are granted a functionally necessary amount of power and privilege they tend to use their position to consolidate and augment their advantage.

Specialists in religion likewise become more important with the development of horticulture and the consequent dependence on the weather to provide for crops. Primitive religions generally stress contact with supernatural forces that supposedly control the environment. As class societies develop, however, religion comes to stress issues of morality as it becomes necessary to teach people to accept their lot in an unequal society. These societies generally develop religions that have a supreme being who gives people moral rules to follow. As religion becomes more important, the religious leaders use their position to advance and consolidate their privileges.

Growth of Elites

There are thus four processes by which elites tend to be created in formerly classless societies:

1. The growth of trade and the trading classes.
2. The development of warfare and military elites.
3. The need for political coordination in larger and more complex societies.
4. The growing strength of formal religion.

It would appear that one or another of these four modes of the creation of an elite is more or less important in the emergence of classes in a given society, although all probably operate to some extent in many. The formation of a ruling class with a virtual monopoly of power, wealth, and privilege is the result of the full realization of any of these four principles. The different composition of various ruling classes in earlier societies is a function of the relative importance of one or another of these. In some societies the core of a ruling class was the merchants, in others the controllers of the state apparatus, in others the war leaders, and in still others religious leaders. But quite naturally, whatever may have been the predominant mode of an elite consolidating its power, once it becomes a ruling class it uses its power base to gain or attempt to gain a monopoly of power in all areas. Thus, an elite that may have come to secure a strong position because of its monopoly on trade uses its wealth to capture a monopoly on the control of the political apparatus, the military structure, and the religion, as well as to secure ownership of the land and the entire productive apparatus of the society. Likewise, elites whose power is initially based on the control of the political apparatus, the military structure, or religious ideology consolidate their position through gaining control over all other aspects of society. Thus, a mature ruling class, although it may maintain vestiges of its origins, especially in its traditions, tends to be multifaceted in its contemporary power base.

In those primitive societies where commerce broke down the kin-based primitive structure, the laws or principles of the exchange economy came to operate independently of the will of people, and the people came to be subordinate to the operation of markets. Thus, while the development of technology brings increasing control over the physical environment, it brings at the same time decreasing control over one's social relationships. The inherent laws of exchange come to dominate individuals and society. The network of social relations established in the process of getting a living come to gain control over people.

Increasingly, individual wealth and trade, wherever it occurs, has brought about more and more commodity production, which in turn has created greater and greater disparities of property and wealth. In order to safeguard the newly developed concentrations of private property and the newly acquired wealth, the old, kin-based fraternal system of primitive society had to be abolished and replaced by a state apparatus. This state apparatus was based on enforced jurisdiction over a certain geographic area rather than over a set of related people. It was unique in that it consisted of a group of full-time specialists in administration. The state apparatus made the rules for society and enforced these rules through its police, military, and penal apparatus. Blood vengeance was replaced by a full-time police force and the old militia system was replaced by a military organization made up for the first time of full-time soldiers. The state secured a monopoly on the use of physical force in the society.

The state apparatus also probably comes into existence for other kinds of economic reasons, either to regulate social production, especially to regulate water, or to regulate the production of slaves. But in all cases, the state was under the control of the most privileged groups in society to use as the instrument of their interests against the masses of the people.

The crystallization of class society occurred with the introduction of the plow. Through greatly facilitating weed control and the maintenance of soil fertility, the plow significantly increased the available economic surplus and hence the opportunities for those with more power and privilege to increase and consolidate their position. The greatly expanded political empires and increased commerce (a consequence of the increased economic surplus) necessitated the development of a written language with which to facilitate communication and record keeping. Cities developed as political and commercial centers because of the greatly expanded economic surplus produced by the peasants. The state reached its full development with the consolidation of absolute power, first by the ruling class, then by a single individual. The development of writing played an important role in the consolidation of absolute power and the hardening of society into two basic classes. Two distinct subcultures, one literate and one illiterate came about. Philosophy, literature, and art developed in the ruling class, while superstitions, mythology, and practical knowledge were the heritage of the masses.

All the various great world religions originated among the relatively oppressed groups in such empires, and all initially expressed the masses' aspirations for the satisfaction of their frustrated psychological drives and for universal brotherhood. However, all were soon co-opted by the ruling classes and were turned into tools of domination of the masses by the ruling classes. Churches of all faiths became instruments of social control and oppression, preaching subordination to the secular powers, contentment with one's lot, and future compensation for earthly misery in an afterlife where "the last shall be first."

We can classify four basic types of class society, that is, societies characterized by monumental differences between the class that produces and is governed and the class that controls production and the state apparatus: Oriental despotism, slave society, feudal society, and capitalism. Each of these basic social types is categorized by a distinctive mode of production or property relations. The institutional structure of each is synchronized to its fundamental mode of production.

ORIENTAL DESPOTIC SOCIETY

An Oriental despotic society consists of a powerful centralized state apparatus with a large body of officials that carries out the orders of a king or emperor whose authority is usually close to absolute. The state runs virtually everything in these societies—there is a state church, the economy is either directly owned by the monarchy or closely supervised by the state, and the military is kept closely under state control. Oriental societies have arisen directly out of primitive societies in fertile river valleys where it is imperative to build a state apparatus in order to control flooding and construct and regulate irrigation works, tasks impossible without central coordination beyond the capabilities of a primitive political apparatus. Once political leadership is generated in order to coordinate this effort, it takes advantage of its position by turning itself into a ruling class. Oriental despotic society can also result from the decay of a slave society or feudal society, and perhaps even from the overthrow of a capitalist society. In each of these cases there is a different basis for the power of the group that turns itself into the ruling class, but the shape of the resultant society is more or less the same.

This social form is highly stable so long as its basis in water control continues. At the base of Oriental society is the more or less sufficient village of preclass society. The Oriental despotic state is more or less superimposed on an economic basis identical with that of advanced primitive society except that the local villages are dependent on the state for water control. The villages provide a large share of their produce (the economic surplus) to the state apparatus, getting little or nothing other than water control in return. Their standard of living is probably worse than it was in primitive society, but having given up their older kin-based egalitarian system with its popular militia, they can do nothing about it. Even when these empires are conquered or when rebellions of despair on the part of the underlying population throw up new leaders, mere change in personnel is the only lasting result. A new king or emperor takes over the state apparatus and all remains as before. Although these types of societies tend to oscillate somewhat between strong central power and decentralization, the only thing that breaks into this oscillation is the impact of trade imposed from the outside. Oriental despotisms, oscillating back and forth between very strong and weak central states, lasted thousands of years until external stimuli in the form of trade, forced on them by Europe, resulted in their collapse.

Oriental despotic societies oscillate from extreme centralization to relative decentralization because of the inherent interest of the ruling class in constantly increasing its share of production by extracting more and more from the underlying population. In this process the state becomes more and more autocratic until finally resistance breaks out in the form of widespread banditry, rebellion of outlying officials, or spontaneous uprisings on the part of the masses. Meanwhile, the ruling class itself, as it gets used to ever-increasing luxury, loses its military traditions and increasingly neglects its social functions, which were the original basis of its authority. Subofficials come to be given or take more and more responsibility. The economy as well as the military situation deteriorates, both because of the degeneration of leadership and because the increasing pressure on the underlying population destroys their motivation to make good soldiers or enthusiastic workers. Eventually, the subofficials rebel, or the people spontaneously revolt or commit acts of massive resistance. As a result of this reaction the personnel of the old ruling class are either totally displaced or undergo a massive infusion of new blood, stratification is somewhat mitigated, and the state apparatus is somewhat decentralized with the now popular outlying officials obtaining considerable authority. But soon the tendency towards increasing stratification and increasing central power asserts itself, since it is in the interests of the most powerful groups in society to pursue such a course. Eventually, the centralized state again begins to disintegrate and the cycle starts over. This cycle would appear to be endemic to Oriental societies. Each cycle is basically the same as the last without any significant long-term change.

SLAVE SOCIETY

Slave society developed directly out of primitive society with the growth of trade, military conquest, and the consequent enslavement of other peoples. It was also recreated by European industrial capitalists in the Carribean region to meet the needs of their new economic system. The central relations of production are those between the producing *slaves* and the *free citizens* that own them on the one hand and among the free agricultural and craft producers on the other.

Unlike Oriental despotic society, slave society is fundamentally unstable and tends to break down into a different type of social organization. As the population of the citizen ruling class grows, or as the productivity of the land is exhausted by inefficient slave labor, wars of conquest are required in order to provide all the citizens or slaveholders with sufficient land. These wars of conquest, as in the Ancient World, result in a greatly expanded number of slaves, who as a matter of course come under differential ownership because of the operation of markets. Slave labor becomes cheaper than the free agricultural labor of citizens, and hence drives the small independent producers out of the market and off the land. Large estates (plantations) utilizing slave labor come to displace the system of small landholding. Thus, the basis of ancient slave society was inherently self-contradictory. The resolution of this contradiction was the transformation of ancient slave society into a form of Oriental despotic society (as in Rome). That is, the normal functioning of this type of society results in its transformation. The very attempt to reproduce it leads to the establishment of a small ruling class, a large class of proletarians, and a large class of slaves.

The type of society that results from this process can be categorized as an advanced Oriental despotism. It is not necessarily based on water control, although it is weakened to the extent that it does not have such a functional base. Without any functional justification in the eyes of its people, such as the control of flooding and irrigation provides in the classical type, it becomes pure despotism. Such societies can survive in spite of their lack of a functional basis because of their superiority to the earlier form in communications, transportation, and military technique, which they can utilize to maintain control over the underlying population.

As Oriental despotic societies crystallize out of ancient slave society, such as the Roman Republic, commodity production and trade regress, villages become more self-sufficient, and the central state becomes an increasing burden on the villages. The formally free proletarians merge with the old slaves as part of a single class of producers legally tied to their villages but having more rights than the old slaves. The late Roman Empire was such a social organization. It collapsed in the West through a combination of its internal weaknesses and external invasions. But the empire did survive in the East, where its functional basis in water control meant that its internal structure was stronger than that of the West. The same types of invasions did not lead to its collapse. The barbarian invaders of the West tried again and again to set themselves up as a new ruling class as their cousins had successfully done in China, India, and other places, but because of the inherent weakness of the social fabric in the West, they failed. The intense exploitation of the underlying populations, the elimination of a class from which to recruit loyal soldiers, and the collapse of commodity production, together with the lack of a functional basis, meant that the empire could not stand. In the Eastern areas of much more erratic rainfall, the state apparatus, although it was equally predatory, did have a functional basis and hence was able to survive for a thousand years after the fall of Rome. The Oriental society in the West deteriorated into feudal society.

FEUDALISM

Feudalism is most likely to arise and be stable in those areas where there is sparse population and no need for water control. While in Oriental despotic society the power basis of the ruling class is obtained through its control of the central state apparatus, in feudal society political power is based on the military power of the feudal lords. The predominant relationship among individuals in the ruling class are military relations of personal loyalty, rather than relations of officials to their absolute ruler. Feudalism is characterized by unfree producers—serfs, who, although tied to the land and subject in many respects to the lord of the land, have more autonomy than slaves. While slaves predominate in societies with markets for slaves and the commodities they produce, serfs predominate in feudal society, where markets of any kind are insignificant. Political power is highly decentralized in feudal society with only weak ties between one local center and another. There are minimal obligations between the local lords, who are political rulers as well as owners of the land. The interrelations among the lords are predominantely of a military nature. The feudal economy is more or less self-sufficient, with each manor or local center providing for almost all of its needs. Virtually no trade exists except perhaps for trade in salt and a few metals and luxury items unattainable on the local level. There is also little division of labor. The basic crafts necessary to sustain an agricultural society based on a very primitive plow technology and a few varieties of service personnel are all there is. Most production is for local use, not for exchange.

Feudalism is typically established through the military conquest of internally weakened despotic societies. The advanced primitives who conquered the Roman Empire, once they despaired of establishing themselves as a new ruling class, had to resort to the already existing military ties among themselves to provide the political structure of the new society. The conquered land was parceled out by the military chiefs among their principal lieutenants in exchange for a promise to provide military service in time of need. Eventually, the free peasants, descendants of the barbarian conquerors, and the descendants of the protoserfs of the despotic empire merged into a more or less homogeneous unfree peasantry under the common exploitation of the loosely linked class of lords. The weak ties among the lords made for perpetual warfare among them directed to gain or protect one or another advantage. This constant warfare forced all free peasant descendants of the barbarians to seek the protection of some lord by becoming his serfs. The medieval serfs, unlike the slaves of more commercial systems, generally worked part of the time for their lords and part of the time for themselves.

Breakdown of Feudal Society

Feudalism would probably not be considered a very impressive or important type of society if we did not know that capitalist societies first emerged out of feudal societies. Feudal societies were in many ways more backward than Oriental despotic societies. They lacked much of the magnificent art and culture of the great empires of the Orient and the Middle East. Medieval Europe, under the feudal system, was a relative backwater compared to China, India, or the Arabic world during the same historical period.

It is often the case, however, that evolutionary advances can best take place in a society that is not the most advanced in the world system. Such a society can take advantage of the privilege of backwardness. It can import ideas and technological advances from abroad, yet it lacks the fully developed and centralized political and military dominant groups of the more advanced countries. Thus, capitalism first developed in feudal Europe, rather than in the Oriental despotisms of India, China, or Arabia. In these Eastern societies, the central state was too powerful to permit a rival source of power to grow strong enough to compete with them.

As European explorers and traders came into contact with the more wealthy and advanced societies of the East, they brought back products that sorely tempted the relatively unsophisticated feudal nobility of Europe. As with much of the breakdown of primitive societies, the transition from feudalism to capitalism was stimulated by commerce. Once capitalism was established in Europe, it spread through commerce and conquest throughout the globe, conquering even the proud societies of China and India. The original development of capitalism in Europe, however, was a unique historical event. An event that irrevocably changed the entire world. It was an event that was not forced on the Europeans from the outside but that developed out of tensions and contradictions inherent in European feudalism. This transition was of such importance in shaping the world in which we live today that it is worth reviewing in detail.

One of the variables that caused feudalism to break down was an increase in population. Increased population density created an impetus for technological innovations, a growing division of labor, and the migration of people off the land and into towns. The competition among the more or less autonomous lords for military conquests and prestige also produced a demand for more and better goods, encouraging the growth of towns and trade. The surplus population was pressured off the land and allowed to stay in the growing towns, where they gradually come to form an urban proletariat. A class of rich merchants and a set of guilds developed early in the towns under the pressure of the economic demand of the rural lords. This new class grew rich through employing the people pushed off the land. The growth of trade and the resultant increasing division of labor dissolved the feudal relationships among the lords and between the lords and serfs. Serfs were freed in some areas to become wage workers on the land (although in other areas serfdom was greatly intensified and the serfs were turned into virtual slaves in order to increase the now marketable surplus gotten out of them). In the lords' struggle for dominance over one another it became more and more important to cultivate the favor of the towns and their chief merchants and guild masters. The struggle grew more and more intense as the means again became available for the creation of Oriental despotic empires.

In pre-industrial economies commerce provided a major impetus for social change.

Ross Koppel

Emergence of Wage Labor and Capital

In the relatively overpopulated rural regions and in the towns free laborers everywhere replaced unfree laborers as the basic producers. This transformation of serfs into free workers was a product of the greater profitability of wage labor in areas of overpopulation and the pressures of an increasingly sophisticated technology. Serfdom (as well as slavery) mitigated against the use of technological improvements since people who are forced to work, and who gain nothing from it, have no incentive to be careful with tools. Free laborers, who can be fired or promoted, unlike unfree laborers, have a great incentive to master technology and consequently are much more careful. Likewise, the employment of wage workers under conditions where there is a surplus of people willing to work for wages forces wages down to a minimum and results in greater profits than does the utilization of unfree labor. Unfree serfs (and slaves) must be fed and sheltered regardless of whether or not there is work for them, or regardless of whether or not they are too old or too sick to work. Slaves also require a large initial capital investment for their purchase. Wage workers, on the other hand, are paid by the hour, only when their labor is desired. The initial cost of wage workers in zero, and the cost of upkeep is less than for serfs or slaves. A free labor force can thus be extremely flexible and correspond perfectly with the owner's need. Unfree labor generally requires closer supervision to be efficient than does free labor. Again, this is because of the lack of incentive of unfree laborers. Wage workers, particularly when paid on a piecework basis, can be counted on to regulate themselves to a considerable extent.

Within a market economy unfree labor is preferred to free labor only when laborers are scarce. As a more inefficient and expensive mode of production, it is resorted to only when enough free laborers cannot be found to work at a low enough wage. Thus, in Eastern Europe the impact of the revival of commerce with Western Europe resulted in an intensification of serfdom because of sparse population. In Western Europe, where there was a population surplus, the same intensification of trade resulted in the freeing of the serfs.

The prolonged and intense competition among the feudal lords for hegemony and the attainment of a number one position in a recreated semi-Oriental despotism meant that the bourgeoisie of the towns were courted by all sides. The struggling lords needed goods, especially military goods, in order to fight their wars. It was the bourgeoisie that could both supply the goods and loan the money to buy them. At the same time the bourgeoisie tended to favor the forces that looked most like they were winning because the profitability of commerce and the prosperity of the towns depended on increased centralization to enhance trade and to eliminate the feudal restrictions on commerce and trade (such as local customs duties, different monetary systems, different measurement units). The town bourgeoisie was happy to support the most likely aristocratic candidate for hegemony and later the centralizing monarchy against the feudal nobilities. They wanted an end to the perpetual wars that disrupted trade as well as an end to the great barriers to growing trade thrown up by decentralized political units. The prolonged period of feudal strife and the struggle within each emerging nation between its king and its nobility, and among the various nations for superiority, within Europe gave the bourgeoisie an enormous impetus, increasing their power and wealth. This impetus proved to be the crucial determinant of the breakthrough of capitalism against the very strong tendencies leading toward the crystallization of a new, more advanced form of Oriental Despotism that almost succeeded everywhere in Europe in the seventeenth and eighteenth centuries.

Preconditions for Capitalism

There are a number of necessary conditions for the development of capitalism out of feudal society: (1) the generation of free laborers, (2) the generation of moneyed wealth, (3) a sufficient level of skills and technology, (4) markets, (5) and the protection, rather than the hindrance, of the state. These conditions must be generated by precapitalist society *before* capitalism can develop by its own dynamic. Once capitalism is established, it no longer needs a precapitalist system to provide it with these inputs; it rather produces and reproduces these conditions itself through a kind of feedback mechanism. Once the accumulation of capital gets going, it proceeds on its own.

By "capitalism" is meant the system of social relations where the principal relations of production are between free laborers and the owners of the means of production. In this system labor power is a commodity with a price like any other. The producers themselves are not the property of other individuals; nor do they own their own means of production—they are thus free in this two fold sense. Lacking ownership of the tools necessary to gain a living, they are forced to sell their time to the capitalists so that they may eat.

Capitalism did not necessarily *have to* develop out of feudalism, although it might possibly be the case that capitalism can develop *only* out of feudalism. Feudal societies had existed previously without capitalism resulting from their breakdown. Strong tendencies toward capitalism as the dominant mode of production existed in advanced horticultural and in ancient slave society, but always without realizing themselves. Always, Oriental despotism was the result. We must examine why the tendencies toward increased commercialism present in advanced horticultural society, slave society, and feudal society only once reached their culmination in the creation of a capitalist system of social relations. We must examine why the universal tendency for a ruling group to crystallize society into an Oriental despotism, thereby securing their monopoly of power, privilege, and wealth, was frustrated in Europe.

The universal tendency for Oriental despotism to develop in a situation of growing commercialism almost reached its natural culmination in the sixteenth to eighteenth centuries in Europe. During this period very strong absolutist monarchies did develop. In these absolutist monarchies the ruler was virtually all powerful and the state became a strong central coordinating institution in society and the dominant force in the economy. Although most actual production took place in units owned by either the landlords, the guilds, or private individuals, the state's hand was heavy everywhere through economic regulation and state monopolies.

As powerful as the absolutist monarchies were, however, the monarchs never succeeded in fully subordinating the merchant class, which remained a major power and which eventually gave birth to the capitalist mode of production. The merchants were simply too important to the kings to be brought under total royal control. The protracted and intense competition among the relatively small nation-states of Europe, together with the struggles between the nobility and the centralizing monarchs within each state, meant that the bourgeoisie was wooed by all. The bourgeoisie's technology and control of trade was a very valuable asset to all the competing forces. Thus, the bourgeoisie increased in their power and wealth until finally they were in a position to force a dissolution of the quasi-Oriental Despotisms and establish republics. Either formal republics, like those of France and Switzerland, or constitutional monarchies, like those in England and Holland. The bourgeoisie eventually achieved power in all Western European countries because of its powerful economic position.

There were two other very important and more or less unique forces at work in early modern Europe that led to the capitalist breakthrough: the high level of technology reached and the rapid expansion of markets due to the colonial expansion of Europe. It would seem to be the case that the higher the level of technology of a decentralized, nonmarket economy the more likely that its dissolution will result in capitalism.

A relatively high level of technology means that unfree laborers are inefficient producers (because of their lack of motivation in handling complex machinery). A relatively high level of technology also encourages the employment of large and varying numbers of workers in one enterprise and consequently favors flexibility in the labor force. These factors together favor free labor relations over unfree. The early technological advances in Europe were themselves at first stimulated by the competition among the various countries and between the nobles and the centralizing monarch in each country, who desired more efficient weapons of war and higher standards of luxury. But, once capitalism was institutionalized, its own internal logic of competition became the dynamic producing ever more technological advance.

The third force, together with prolonged political competition and the relatively advanced state of European technology, that produced the capitalist breakthrough was the vast new market opportunities opened up by the colonial expansion of Europe. It was the technological superiority of Europe, specifically its development of the gun and the sail, that allowed it to subordinate the world. Colonial expansion produced a great influx of gold and silver and a consequent inflation, which improved the position of capital against the landlords and workers and served as a lubricant of trade. In late feudal times rents and wages were set largely by tradition; therefore in the event of inflation the real cost of both declined and the share going to profits greatly increased. Capital accumulation was thus greatly facilitated. Meanwhile, the importation of large amounts of gold and silver served to make the exchange of commodities much easier than under the older system of barter.

The exploitation of raw materials in the colonial areas directly produced large fortunes. Likewise, the slave trade that supplied the labor force for the New World plantations resulted in great concentrations of wealth. Fortunes made in these colonial enterprises, and in colonial trade and plunder in general, found their way eventually into the pool of funds available for capitalist accumulation. The colonial areas, of course, also supplied cheap raw materials to the growing industries within Europe, and at the same time provided them with vast overseas markets for their produce. Both of these processes were of crucial importance in the early days of the formation of capitalist enterprises. Finally, the coastal ports that became the centers of the colonial trade were generally free of the guild restrictions on free enterprise that stymied the development of capitalist firms in the older cities. The early capitalist enterprises then grew up in new towns free of guild restraints, under the direct stimulation of the markets and supplies of colonial areas, and financed by the fortunes made in colonial enterprises.

Because of the great accumulated wealth and power of the bourgeoisie, it could not be crushed by the despots as had previous bourgeoisies. The European bourgeoi-

Peasants in southern Mexico.

Ted Goertzel

sie was larger, richer, and more powerful than any the world had known before, and it was far too essential for the prosperity of the kingdoms to even attempt to destory. Royal attempts to limit the prerogatives of the commercial class in both England (early seventeenth century) and France (mid and late eighteenth century) failed, and eventually the bourgeoisie everywhere in Western Europe transformed its great economic power into direct political power. As a result the quasi-Oriental despotic societies that had grown out of feudalism were destroyed or fatally undermined in the English Civil War of the seventeenth century, in the French Revolution of the eighteenth century, and in the various processes of revolution and reform in most of the rest of Europe during the eighteenth and nineteenth centuries. The earlier absolute monarchies were almost everywhere replaced by republican forms that pretty much served as executive committees for the reconciliation and administration of bourgeois interests.

How did feudal society generate the free laborers necessary for the formation of capitalist enterprises? As trade expanded, many peasants were pushed off the land and into the cities, thereby creating a class of proletarians who needed to find work, even at the lowest wages, if they were to eat. As a market developed for agricultural products, especially for wool, peasants were driven from the land as the lords converted to the most profitable use of their estates—sheep grazing. Lands that had traditionally been held in common for grazing, watering, wood gathering , etc., were increasingly expropriated by the now profit-oriented lords, who by depriving the peasantry of their use, forced even the peasants with rights to their own property off the land and into the cities. Once trade became a major force it greatly accelerated the process, initiated by overpopulation, of forcing peasants into the urban proletariat. It was primarily the textile industry that benefited from, as well as caused, this forced proletarianization.

The state played an important facilitating role in this process. The state, after some struggle, came to support the lords in their expropriation of the common lands. In England, the country in which industrial capitalism first developed, the state also facilitated the accumulation of capital through its expropriation and sale of Church lands and much of the royal domain to commercial land interests.

DEVELOPMENT OF CAPITALISM

The process of capital accumulation is destructive of non-capitalist relationships. Once established, capitalism destroys all obstacles to its continued growth. Capitalism, moreover, is not a static system. By its very nature it must constantly expand. Its factories create more demand for raw materials, the supply of which in turn displaces more peasants, turning them into a cheap labor force as well as consumers of the products of the textile goods industires. The more capitalist enterprises the greater are the inherent forces leading to the establishment of still more capitalist enterprises, until eventually the whole economy is brought into the capitalist system of social relations, and feudal, slave, and other relations are reduced to, at best, archaic vestiges within the broader framework of the capitalist system.

It is the pursuit of profit that drives this process. Each producer must take advantage of the growing possibilities to sell more or else go under in the competitive struggle with other producers. Sell more and more, make more and more, accumulate more and more—such is the inherent tendency of capitalism. Capitalism, once it is set in motion, continues to expand because of the insatiable drive to increase profits. Unlike other systems of production, capitalist production is oriented not to consumption needs but to the maximization of profit.

The first capitalists were the merchants and artisans who began hiring day labor outside of the restrictive guild system under the protection of the king. Early industrial capitalist enterprises developed for the most part outside of the established towns, either in rural areas near sources of water power and away from the guild restrictions or in and around the new seaports stimulated by the colonial trade and also free of the guild restrictions on production, labor relations, and marketing. There was a discontinuity between the development of commercialism centered in the old cities and the development of industrial capitalism in the new industrial towns. The interests of commercialism led to a close alliance with the absolutist monarchies to the mutual advantage of both. The result of the alliance between the commercial bourgeoisie and the monarchs was the establishment of monopolies and the stabilization of the system of guild production. Industrial capitalists had to break through this system. They accomplished this only with the support of the central state, which needed the goods they were producing. In England the state only slowly came to support industrialization. But after England had shown that industrial capitalism was the basis of economic and military supremacy most other European countries quickly followed suit by actively supporting and at times even creating a class of industrial capitalists.

At first the early industrial capitalists used the same technology as the guild system. But gradually the logic of capitalism, which is geared to increasing profits, forced the development of constantly improving technology. In the early years the putting out system, in which the capitalists would supply the raw materials to families who worked in their home, as well as small-scale production under a single roof directly supervised by capitalists, prevailed. But gradually larger and larger enterprises developed and all production became concentrated under direct capitalist control. Beginning in the eighteenth century in England industrial capitalism took off. The logic of the system dictated that each individual capitalist had to constantly introduce new technology in order to increase or even just maintain his level of profits. Meanwhile workers could demand more pay as the supply of the unemployed was depleted. This at first meant that workers had to be paid more by the capitalists so that they could secure enough laborers to work. Then as wages rose labor-saving technology was introduced to replace workers, thus increasing the number of unemployed. The rising number of the unemployed then bid down wages by offering themselves to the capitalists as a lower wage than those who kept their jobs. In addition, under completely competitive conditions, the best way to increase one's profits, vis-à-vis other capitalists, is to introduce an innovation that allows one to sell cheaper than the next guy. Once one capitalist introduces such an innovation, all are required to do so under pain of going out of business, since competition forces down the prevailing prices below the old cost of production. These two very powerful forces operate under competitive capitalism to insure that a technological revolution occurs just as soon as capitalism becomes institutionalized as the prevailing mode of production. The extraordinary technological revolution that began around 1750 has so radically changed the means of production and the standard of living of the producing classes that the average producers of just two hundred years ago had much more in common with a peasant of three thousand years ago than they do with an average producer of today. Never has the world seen anything like the capitalist-induced technological revolution of the last two hundred years.

Capitalist relations did not become the predominant relations of production in most of Western Europe until the late nineteenth century. Before that time, in spite of the rise of commercialism, most production took place in guilds, in households, or was done by peasants. A potpourri of productive relations prevailed for the hundreds of years from the decline of simple feudalism with its classical lord-serf relationship to the widespread predominance of industrial capitalism.

Simple feudal society consisted of a manor-based economy without significant commerce. Only in this simple form of feudalism was the serf-lord relationship the

A medieval castle.

more or less exclusive form of productive relationship. In advanced feudalism, with its free towns based on trade, the serf-lord relationship, although it still prevailed in modified form on much of the land, was displaced in the towns by the guild system of master-journeyman-apprentice relations combined with day labor. Advanced feudalism gradually developed into a transitional form of social organization that has variously been referred to as "commercial capitalism," "mercantilism," or "commercialism." Such was the predominant form of economic relationships under the quasi-Oriental despotic restoration of the sixteenth through the eighteenth centuries. The big merchants together with the lords of the land, who themselves were now producing for markets, were the major economic force (although both were politically subordinate to the monarchs). This economic type, which may best be called "mercantilism," was based on the full gamut of productive relations, no one of which was hegemonic. Agricultural wage labor, free peasantry, serfdom, and chattel slavery in the colonies were all major relations of production on the land, while guild relations, wage labor in preindustrial capitalist manufacturing, domestic production, and wage or serf labor in state monopoly manufacturers were the predominant relations of production in the towns. Only gradually did the wage-labor relationship come to displace all the others. This did not take place in most of Western Europe until after 1850, although it occurred earlier in England and in many towns of Western Europe.

CAPITALISTS' STRUGGLE WITH OTHER CLASSES

It was competitive capitalism that emerged out of the potpourri of the economic relations of mercantilist society: a competitive capitalism that gained hegemony because of its overwhelmingly superior power to promote technological advance and hence the production of ever cheaper commodities. Industrializing capitalism swept all before it as it dissolved the less efficient serfdom, slavery, guild, independent peasant, and artisan production. Rapidly growing industrial capitalism quickly brought the industrial capitalists to dominance over both the older merchant rich and the agricultural lords, both of whose economic positions were based on commercialism rather than on capitalist relations of production. The hegemony of the capitalists did not occur, however, without a long struggle between them and the other two groups. In the United States the Civil War was fought for political supremacy between the industrial capitalists of the Northeast and the less efficient slaveholding commercial plantation lords of the South. In England there was a protracted struggle throughout the nineteenth century for control over the state between the industrial capitalists on the one hand and the commercial and landed interests on the other. This struggle was replicated on the Continent. The various segments of the wealthy classes in the countries that were later to industrialize were thrown together by their common fear of revolution as the working class grew to maturity. But eventually everywhere, even in countries such as Germany, where the landed interests held the greatest share in political power until World War I, the industrial capitalists acquired the greatest control over the state. Often, however, this was accomplished only after merging through marriage (both sexual and financial) with the wealthy commercial and landed families.

Emerging industrial capitalism had great difficulty securing adequate labor power to run its factories. Peasants forced off the land by growing commercialism resisted the degrading and tedious labor of the factories that demanded 12, 14, 16 hours a day 6 or 7 days a week under the most miserable conditions for a wage that barely allowed one to keep one's family alive. Therefore, the state had to resort to a wide range of Draconian measures geared to forcing people into the mills. Begging, petty theft, and vagrancy were made crimes punishable by death or deportation to the labor-starved colonies. Welfare of any kind was given only under circumstances that forced the recipients into conditions even more degrading and humiliating than work in the mills (the poorhouse system, for example). A working class had to be created. The displaced peasants had to be broken to accept industrial discipline and, moreover, to internalize the motivation to work. At first the pay of workers was purposely kept low so that they would have to work 70 to 90 hours a week just to live. Peasants came to the mills with the sensible idea of working only as long as necessary to eat. Therefore, if by working only through Wednesday they could earn that amount, they preferred to quit until the next Monday. Capitalists found it was necessary to destroy this work attitude by decreasing pay and forcing people to work until the working class as a whole adopted the work ethic—an inner compulsion to work based on a fear of the poorhouse and on attitudes inculcated by religions such as Puritanism and Methodism that transformed religious belief into work motivation. Sexual restrictions were also increased until the late nineteenth century. England, at the peak of its industrial power, experienced a repressive sexual atmosphere in Victorianism. All the psychological drives were systematically frustrated by the tedium of industrial labor, which took up virtually the whole of a worker's nonsleeping hours. The psychological drives blocked from satisfaction were tied up in the worker's character structure, with the aid of religion and the fear of the poorhouse, to produce a character structure with a compulsion to work. Capitalism pretty much succeeded in generating a personality type in its working class that internalized submissive attitudes and the desire to work for a wage and to get ahead rather than to merely work long enough to live. The economic coercion by the capitalist of his employees together with the internalization of the capitalist value system resulted in a new type of producer—the modern industrial worker.

DEVELOPMENT OF MONOPOLY CAPITALISM

The inherent logic of competitive capitalism meant that the least efficient producers were constantly being forced out of business by the more efficient, the size of enterprises increasing in the process. The size of businesses increased, both because the more efficient were buying up the least efficient and because as technology developed, a larger and larger minimum investment was necessary. The result of this process was the undermining of the competitive basis of early capitalist productive relations and their succession in the latter part of the nineteenth century by monopoly relations. As the capitalists in each sector of the economy were shaken down to a handful of firms, agreement was everywhere reached among the last remaining giants to respect one another's interests and to set monopoly prices to the mutual benefit of all.

A system that might best be called "simple monopoly capitalism" was the result. From the 1890s until around the 1930s in the United States and Britain this system was dominant. Monopoly prevailed in the economy, while the state played only a slightly more active role than it did during the competitive phase of capitalism. Its role was focused on preserving property rights, enforcing contracts, crushing unions, and preserving law and order, that is, keeping the working class compliant and lubricating the relations among capitalists.

Although the state began assuming some important regulatory functions during this period, for the most part the state let the natural laws of monopoly capitalism work themselves out. The consequence of the natural working out of the laws of monopoly capitalist society was the worst depression the world has ever known—that of the 1930s. The result of this experience was the full institutionalization of state monopoly capitalism in England and the United States. This social type, which can also be referred to as "corporate capitalism," has the same economic basis as simple monopoly capitalism but differs in two important ways from it. First, the state plays the central role in regulating the economy in the interests of the capitalist class as a whole. It determines interest rates, exchange rates, the rate of unemployment, attempts to set the rate of growth, regulates prices and wages, and when necessary, takes over and operates sectors that are no longer profitable but are essential for the operation of the whole capitalist economy. Second, trade unions are not only recognized but they are encouraged as mechanisms to increase the control over labor and defuse working-class disruption of society. In a system of collective bargaining the organizations of workers become supervisors of the conditions of the negotiated contracts. These contracts charge the unions with preventing spontaneous strikes, slowdowns, rule violations, etc. At the same time collective bargaining diverts working-class discontent from the issue of power and control over the productive process to negotiations about wages and fringe benefits with which the system can deal relatively easily. Since the state has legalized unions and provided them with certain privileges, it can and does (as with the Taft-Hartley Act) threaten to take them away whenever the unions are threatening to become radical or too militant. The privileges granted unions, in addition to serving as a club to keep them in line, act as an incentive for union bureaucrats to develop. These bureaucrats, because of the system of closed shops and management support, do not need the authentic support of their rank and file. Union bureaucrats generally happily collaborate with managers and the state against the interests of the working class.

These two innovations of mature monopoly capitalism mean that the economy runs much smoother than it did earlier. Working-class discontent is contained, while poverty and unemployment are kept from exploding the system. State monopoly capitalism is the current mode of production in all the developed capitalist societies.

DEVELOPMENT OF SOCIALISM

The world today is in the midst of a transition to a new type of society—socialist society. This transition is in many ways similar to the transition from feudalism to capitalism. It is a worldwide phenomenon, it promises to completely revolutionize the ways in which people live, and it is a process that is very difficult or impossible to stop once it has begun. Just as capitalist society had its roots in the contradictions of feudal society, socialism has its roots in the contradictions of capitalist society. Socialist visions have existed throughout human history, in the sense that people have dreamed of idyllic societies in which everyone is equal and all basic human needs are fulfilled. The very earliest human societies had a form of primitive communism. But these societies suffered from the oppression of nature; they lacked the technology or economic organization to completely meet their members' biological needs. Industrial socialism, based on the abundance made possible by modern technology, is possible only after the necessary advances that have been made by capitalism.

Socialist movements emerged in the 1830s in England and France among industrial workers who united in struggle against the extremely oppressive conditions forced on them by early capitalism. These early socialists used a variety of tactics. Some united in petition campaigns, demanding reforms from the government. A few found financing to set up utopian communities where they could experiment with communal forms of living. As the movement grew, however, two tactics emerged as primary. One was the formation of labor unions to lead struggles against particular employers and of cooperatives to attempt to establish a better life now. The other was to form socialist political parties to struggle either for influence within the existing state or to overthrow that state and replace it with a system responsive to the needs of workers. By the time of the Europewide crises of 1848, brought about by economic contradictions in the capitalist economy, socialist movements were contenders on the political scene. Karl Marx and Friedrich Engels wrote *The Communist Manifesto* as part of this movement in 1848.

These early socialist movements were in many ways premature. The industrial working class on which they were based was still a small minority of the population, and capitalism had not yet fully developed to the point where a transition to socialism was possible. The socialists were crushed in 1848, and again in the Paris uprising of 1871. Often the repression was harsh; for example, after the crushing of the Paris Commune in 1871, 17,000 people were executed. But despite this, the socialist movement always reorganized and grew stronger because it was based on social conditions that became steadily more central to capitalist society.

During the last half of the nineteenth century, the socialist movement developed into an international movement. The First Workingmen's International was formed in 1864 and was heavily influenced by Marx and Marxism, although there were anarchist and other political tendencies within it as well. The First International collapsed in 1876 because of internal conflicts and repression, but a second International was formed in 1889 and still exists today, representing a moderate wing of the social democratic movement.

As capitalism spread throughout the world, socialism inevitably followed. And, just as capitalism first emerged in a relatively backward agrarian society, socialism often found fertile ground in countries that were just entering capitalism. These countries suffered from imperialist exploitation by the more advanced capitalist countries, so their economic problems were more severe and they lacked the resources to make concessions to buy off labor or socialist movements. They also suffered from the consequences of wars created by imperialist rivalries between the great powers.

The first successful socialist revolution took place in Russia in 1917 as a direct consequence of the massive destruction suffered by that country and its armed forces in World War I. Russia was very much a backward country at the time; a large majority of its population being peasants. The political party that took power, the Russian Communist Party, had not had time to organize a substantial political base among the peasantry. Its primary bases of social support came from the industrial workers, who were less than 10 percent of the population, soldiers (most of whom were from peasant backgrounds), and some middle-class intellectuals who were radicals out of ideological conviction. It was able to win power because it was a highly disciplined political organization in a country that was falling apart, because it had a leader, V. I. Lenin, who was highly flexible and insightful, and because it offered the peasants, soldiers, and working people what they wanted: "peace, land, and bread."

The Russian revolutionaries fervently hoped that socialist revolutions would occur in other countries, after their example. There were attempts in other places, most importantly in Germany, but they failed. This left the Soviets isolated, surrounded by hostile capitalist countries, and in charge of a country that had not yet gone through the industrialization process which would provide the basis for a smooth transition to a fully socialist system. Most of the population was backward and poorly educated.

Development of State Socialism

Faced with these conditions, the Soviet Communists decided to industrialize their country as quickly as possible. While they in part relied on private ownership of the means of production for a period of time during the 1920s, as quickly as possible they created a new form of society. This type of society is perhaps best labeled "state socialism." It is socialist in the sense that productive wealth is publicly rather than privately owned and controlled. There is no capitalist class which owns the factories, no one who is exempt from the necessity of working for a living, and there is far more equality and participation than in capitalist countries. Many of the persistent problems of capitalism are eliminated, such as the need for unemployment or for periodic depressions. What cannot be eliminated, however, is the need for many hours of arduous work in order to build an industrial base. Socialist movements that take power in an underdeveloped country cannot change the laws of physics or economics. They cannot instantly create an abundant society, let alone create the type of military machine that the Soviets soon needed to defeat Hitler. These societies need a mechanism for accumulating wealth and for investing it in enterprises that will build the society in the long run but not immediately provide abundant consumption goods for the working population.

In the Soviet Union a powerful state apparatus was created to fulfill this function. The state made basic economic decisions for society, rather than allowing them to be made by supply and demand as in a market economy. It used popular mobilization, discipline, and strong economic incentives to maximize production. It also dealt harshly with its political enemies. This system was successful in obtaining a very rapid rate of industrial growth at a social cost that was considerable, though probably less than that suffered by the English working class during England's period of rapid industrialization. It was a cost borne by all levels of society, including leading members of the Communist Party.

The sociological laws that apply to state socialist societies have not yet been studied to anywhere near the extent that they have been for capitalist societies. Indeed, there is a vigorous controversy on this issue among Marxist writers and groups. Some argue that state socialism is a temporary phase on the road to communism (a stateless, classless society based on the principle of "from each according to his ability, to each according to his need"). They think that it is a period referred to by Marx as the "dictatorship of the proletariat," during which the proletariat exercises firm rule over social classes that are remnants of the old capitalist society. Once these remnants die off or are reeducated, the need for this dictatorship should gradually decline and the state wither away. This is the official Soviet interpretation of their own system.

Other Marxist authors are much more pessimistic. These include the Chinese, who generally argue that Soviet state socialism has evolved back towards a kind of capitalism, a form of state capitalism in which a new ruling class has emerged based on control of the state apparatus. This ruling class allegedly uses the state to expropriate the wealth produced by the workers, and then spends it for its own enjoyment.

The best evidence we have about Soviet society suggests that, although there is a power elite there, and significant inequalities of income exist, distinct social classes that are able to pass on their social positions to their children have not crystallized. There is considerable economic and social equality, compared to capitalist societies. Very considerable participatory democracy exists in Soviet society on the local level, although the higher reaches of decision-making remain more closed. Power to a great extent is exercised by dedicated Communists with close personal and family links to the working class. However, a powerful state apparatus is a dangerous thing, which can be misused to the benefit of those who control it. Socialism will not be secure until political power is firmly democratized, with the working population fully participating in every level of decision-making, from the factory and neighborhood to national policy and foreign affairs.

Americans are better informed about the problems of Soviet society than they are about the many advantages the socialist productive system has brought to the people there. While the Soviet Union is not as wealthy a country as the United States, the economy has grown steadily and so have the living standards of the people. The economic gap between the United States and the Soviet Union has been steadily closing: in 1955 the Gross National Product per capita of the Soviet Union was 36 percent that of the United States. By 1968 it had risen to 47 percent. Wages and consumption more than doubled during this same period.

There is no unemployment in the Soviet Union. Instead there is a shortage of labor and workers are actively sought out by enterprises. Seventy percent of women between 16 and 59 years of age are employed. By the late 1960s, about half of all preschool children were in child-care centers run by the state or by employers. The state covers about 80 percent of the cost of running these centers, and fees are charged according to income, with low-income workers often paying nothing. There is maternity leave with full pay for 14 weeks. Retirement is at age 60 for men and 55 for women, with pensions of at least half the wage level. However, because of the labor shortage, older people are encouraged to continue working even while receiving their pension benefits.

While there is significant inequality in pay, the range is considerably less than it is in the United States. Industrial workers are relatively well paid, bringing in higher incomes than farmers, clerical, trade and service, and education and culture workers. The average pay of managers is about one and a half that of skilled workers, although managers (as do workers) also receive special bonuses when their enterprise's economic goals are fulfilled and fringe benefits such as use of company cars and vacation homes. Income inequality is lessened, however, by the fact that many essential products such as milk and bread are sold at subsidized prices. Medical care and other social services are provided free, while housing is provided at very low cost, averaging about 7 percent of income levels. These benefits are available to all, and consequently tend to be of proportionately more value to lower-income people, lessening the effective degree of inequality in consumption.

The highest-paid people in the Soviet Union are prominent artists, writers, leading university administrators and professors, and scientists. By 1973, industrial workers were earning an average of 146 rubles a month, state government workers were earning an average of 185 rubles, educational and cultural workers averaged 121 rubles, and state farm workers averaged 116 rubles (a ruble is worth slightly more than a U.S. dollar). The very highest incomes were about 10 times those of industrial workers. In the United States, by contrast, there were about one thousand individuals in 1973 who had incomes of at least one million dollars, while the annual average wage in manufacturing was $8,632.

These higher-paying positions cannot be passed on from generation to generation through inheritance, since the managers in Soviet society do not own the factories they run. Access to scientific and managerial positions is largely through the educational system, and education is free in Soviet society right through the university level, with living allowances provided as well for university students. Admission to universities is competitive, based on grades and achievement exam scores, although it is true that children raised in the homes of intellectuals tend to do better in school and are more likely to be admitted to universities. The Soviets have at times attempted to compensate for this by requiring a period of work after high school as well as by favoring students with work experience. However, they are concerned about any policy that tends to favor students with less academic ability and poorer preparation. This is a major issue in Soviet society, just as it is in the United States today.

There are many problems in Soviet society, such as inadequate housing, alcoholism, long lines in stores, shortages of consumer goods, etc., which are quite familiar to American readers. Often these problems are exaggerated by the American media, which does not explain the true differences in the systems of the two countries. For example, in America there is always plenty of food in the supermarkets, while in the USSR one must often wait in line and sometimes there are shortages.

However, in the USSR everyone has enough income to buy food, while in the United States, despite apparent abundance, there are people suffering from hunger and malnutrition. The food is in the stores because many people who need it cannot afford it. Other differences, such as the smaller number of private cars and the greater use of public transportation, may make more sense to us as we discover the tremendous costs of our own system.

Despite the remaining problems, Soviet society provides for the needs of its people much more adequately than did the capitalist regime that came before it. The same can be said for the Chinese and Cuban socialist systems. State socialism has proven to be an effective method of achieving rapid industrial development in an agrarian country while providing for the people's basic needs to be met. Thus, it is not surprising that all the other countries that have adopted socialism since World War II have adopted state socialist forms. These countries have also relied heavily on charismatic leaders, people such as Mao Tse-tung and Fidel Castro, who are capable of inspiring the people through the force of their personalities. The socialists in these Third World countries have generally had a broader base among their populations than did the Russian Communists. The Chinese, in particular, have been highly sensitive to the danger of a bureaucratic elite trying to move towards state capitalism. The Great Proletarian Cultural Revolution led by Mao Tse-tung himself was an attempt to counter this tendency by criticizing leaders who had lost their revolutionary dedication and by giving the people a greater voice in decision-making. The political controversies raging in China today generally center around the question of how much emphasis should be given to egalitarianism and socialist ideals and how much economic inequality has to be used as an incentive to assure rapid economic growth.

Socialist Movements in Advanced Capitalist Societies

As yet, no advanced capitalist country (with the possible exception of Czechoslovakia) has made an indigenous transition to socialism. As these countries move towards state monopoly capitalism, they have so far proven capable of avoiding the really serious and prolonged crises that would make socialist revolution possible. In part, they have been able to do this because of their dominant position in the world economy, in part because their advanced economies makes it possible to support a substantial nonproductive middle class and to give in to many of the demands of the workers. While no one can be sure what will happen in these countries in the future, until now conditions have facilitated the growth of social democratic movements that work to reform the capitalist system. These movements have grown to major proportions, coming to control the government for long periods in many Western European countries. They have succeeded in implementing many reforms in collaboration with liberal capitalists, such as unemployment insurance, socialized medicine, free public education, etc., which have greatly improved the lives of the people in these countries. In many cases, however, the leaders of these parties seem to have become so satisfied with the reforms they have obtained, and with the personal rewards of leadership, that they have abandoned real commitment to socialism as a goal.

Radicals are divided on the question of whether this reformist approach is a valid way of working towards socialism or whether it tends only to patch up the defects of capitalism and thus to defuse movements that might lead to more meaningful change. The leading Marxist movements of Western Europe, including the powerful Communist Parties of France, Italy, and Spain, have adopted a strategy of seeking power through democratic elections. They have repudiated the concept "dictatorship of the proletariat" and have at times formed alliances with democratic socialist parties. This course has been tried by other Marxist parties in the past, most recently by those of Chile, and has resulted in the right-wing forces abandoning the rules of democracy and imposing fascist dictatorship. Whether this will happen in Europe, or whether a reformist transition to socialism will be possible, remains to be seen.

The United States remains perhaps the most backward of advanced capitalist countries in terms of its political development. While there was a fairly powerful socialist movement in the United States in the late nineteenth and early twentieth centuries, it was destroyed through a combination of repression of radical leadership and concessions to many of the practical demands of the labor movement, such as the eight-hour day, social security, and unemployment insurance. There are many reasons why socialism has been retarded in its development in the United States, including the long, open frontier tradition, the exploitation of racial and ethnic differences by the ruling class, and the great wealth of the country based both on its natural resources and on its dominant role in the world economic system after World War II. In the light of past experience in social evolution, it is not surprising that new forms of society should develop more quickly among societies that are less advanced under the old form. Thus, socialism may advance more quickly in the less-developed capitalist countries.

There is every reason to believe, however, that socialism will at some point emerge as a powerful mass movement in the United States as well. The costs of maintaining world dominance have put a great strain on American society. The same economic contradictions of capitalism exist in the United States as everywhere else, and should eventually produce a similar political result. Socialism is in a way the logical culmination of the ideals that inspired many of the revolutionaries of 1776 to create the United States. The belief in human rights which inspired the American Bill of Rights cannot be realized without guaranteeing everyone full rights to economic as well as political decision-making. The pragmatic and utilitarian belief in the "greatest good for the greatest number," which underlies much of our English tradition, cannot be realized except under a system that guarantees the greatest good for the working class, which in fact constitutes by far the greatest number of people in our society.

Summary

The most difficult and important problem in social science is to understand how societies change and evolve over long periods of time. Marxist theory postulates that societies pass through distinct stages of development. During each stage we can observe a more or less stable type of society. As each type of society matures, the contradictions inherent within it develop until it breaks down and is transformed into a new and more advanced type of society.

Societies in human history can be classified into five types. *Primitive* societies are small and egalitarian. They rely on hunting and gathering to obtain sustenance from the bounty of the land. As they develop horticulture they create the wealth that undermines their egalitarianism and makes possible the development of *Oriental despotic* societies, where a powerful military state apparatus extracts tribute from agricultural villages. *Slave* societies also develop when agricultural labor becomes more productive, but they are an inherently unstable form of societal organization. *Feudal* societies develop where population and resources are too sparsely scattered to support a strong Oriental despotism, or during periods when the central authority of an Oriental despotic society is weakened through internal decadence or warfare. Feudalism is most important because it provided the necessary conditions for the emergence of *capitalist* society in Europe in the Middle Ages. Capitalist society, once established in Europe, used its superior economic and military technology to conquer the world. At present, the world is in the midst of the breakdown of capitalism due to its internal contradictions. *State socialist* societies have emerged following workers' and peasants' revolutions in a number of countries.

Review Questions

1. The Marxist theory of social change postulates that social change originates in which institutional area of society?
2. What was the first major technological advance made by primitive peoples?
3. What are some of the social traits that became more frequent once societies developed horticulture?
4. What is the role of commerce and trade in social change?
5. When did the state originate as a social institution?
6. What is the basic form of economic production in Oriental despotic societies?
7. Why do Oriental despotic societies tend to be cyclical in their political organization?
8. What characteristics of feudal society facilitated the emergence of capitalism?

9. How do the relations of production in capitalist society differ from those in feudal society?

10. In what ways were feudal peasants forced to become capitalist workers in the early days of capitalism?

12. What is the role of profit in the capitalist system? How does this differ from other economic systems?

13. Why is competitive capitalism inherently self-destructive?

14. When was state monopoly capitalism fully institutionalized in the United States and England?

15. When did socialist movements first emerge, and in what sense were they premature?

16. In what ways have socialist relationships of production changed the living conditions of people in the Soviet Union?

17. What strategy have the socialist movements of Western Europe adopted in an attempt to win power?

Suggestions for Further Study

1. Go to the library or a bookstore and find an anthropological monograph describing a primitive society. Describe the ways in which the people of that society obtain(ed) food, clothing, and shelter. Then briefly describe the other key aspects of their society: the kinship and family system, the division of labor between the sexes, the religious and spiritual beliefs. In what ways do these social practices serve to help maintain the productive system of their society? How can the differences between that society and our own be explained as being necessary because of the different productive systems? If your instructor can arrange to show a film covering life in a primitive society, the same exercises can be done with the film.

2. Max Weber offered an interpretation of the development of capitalism that differed from the one presented in this book. Look up a summary of his viewpoint in another textbook or reference work or read it in the original. How does the difference between his interpretation and the one given in this book reflect the fact that he was working within a different paradigm? To what extent are there empirical, factual differences that could be resolved by research?

3. Choose one social institution that is of particular interest to you, such as education, health care, child rearing, or marriage patterns. Find out how this is or was organized in a particular society belonging to a type other than capitalism. To what extent can you explain the differences that you find as being made neces-

sary by the different productive systems in the society you chose? If possible, form teams of students with each team looking at the same institution in a different type of society.

4. Make a list of ten technological inventions you have used during the last week that did not exist two hundred years ago. When were these inventions made? How are they produced and controlled in our society? Would it have been possible to produce or use these inventions in American society as it existed at the time of the Revolution?

5. Imagine how you would live if you knew you would receive the same income no matter what kind of work you did. In what ways is your present life style conditioned by the need to obtain an income within the limitations of our capitalist society? Can you really imagine living without those constraints? Or within the constraints provided by some of the other types of societies portrayed in this chapter?

Selected Readings

PRIMITIVE SOCIETY

Childe, V. Gordon. *Social Evolution*. New York: Meridian, 1963 (1951).
———. *What Happened in History*. Baltimore: Penguin, 1954.
Engels, Frederick. *The Origin of the Family, Private Property and the State*. New York: International Publishers, 1972 (1884).
Farb, Peter. *Man's Rise to Civilization*. New York: Dutton, 1968.
Harris, Marvin. *Culture, Man and Nature*. New York: Crowell, 1971.
Krader, Lawrence. *Formation of the State*. Englewood Cliffs, N.J.: Prentice-Hall, 1968.
Lenski, Gerhard. *Power and Privilege*. New York: McGraw-Hill, 1966.
Morgan, Lewis Henry. *Ancient Society*. Cambridge, Mass.: Harvard U. Press, 1964.
White, Leslie. *The Evolution of Culture*. New York: McGraw-Hill, 1959.

PRECAPITALIST CLASS SOCIETIES

Anderson, Perry. *Lineages of the Absolutist State*. London: New Left Books, 1974.
———. *Passages from Antiquity to Feudalism*. London: New Left Books, 1974.
Bloch, Marc. *Feudal Society*. Chicago: U. of Chicago Press, 1961.
Elkins, Stanley. *Slavery*. New York: Universal Library, 1963.
Genovese, Eugene. *In Red and Black*. New York: Vintage, 1968.
———. *The Political Economy of Slavery*. New York: Vintage, 1967.
———. *Roll Jordan Roll*. New York: Vintage, 1974.
———. *The World the Slaveholders Made*. New York: Vintage, 1969.

Hindness, Barry, and Hirst, Paul. *Pre-Capitalist Modes of Production*. London: Routledge & Kegan Paul, 1975.

Hobsbawm, Eric. *Introduction to Karl Marx: Pre-Capitalist Economic Formations*. New York: International, 1965.

Lenski, Gerhard. *Power and Privilege*. New York: McGraw-Hill, 1966.

Marx, Karl. *Pre-Capitalist Economic Formations*. New York: International, 1968.

Pirenne, Henri. *Economic and Social History of Medieval Europe*. New York: Harcourt, Brace & World, 1937.

Polanyi, Karl. *Primitive, Archaic and Modern Economics*. Boston: Beacon, 1971.

Polanyi, Karl; Arensberg, Conrad; and Pearson, Harry W. (eds.). *Trade and Market in the Early Empires*. Glencoe, Ill.: Free Press, 1957.

Rostovzeff, Mikhail. *Social and Economic History of the Roman Empire*. Oxford, G.B.: Clarendon, 1957.

Sorokin, Pitrim. *Social and Cultural Dynamics*. New York: Bedminster, 1937.

Weber, Max. *General Economic History*. New York: Collier, 1911 (1923).

Wittfogel, Karl. *Oriental Despotism*. New Haven: Yale U. Press, 1957.

DEVELOPMENT OF CAPITALISM

Aston, Trevor (ed.). *The Crisis in Europe 1560–1660*. New York: Anchor Books, 1967.

Beard, Charles. *An Economic Interpretation of the U.S. Constitution*. New York: Macmillan, 1962 (1913).

Cheyney, Edward. *The Dawn of a New Era 1250–1453*. New York: Harper & Row, 1936.

Dobb, Maurice. *Studies in the Development of Capitalism*. New York: International, 1963.

Hacker, Louis. *The Triumph of American Capitalism*. New York: McGraw-Hill, 1965 (1940).

Hilton, Rodney (ed.). *The Transition from Feudalism to Capitalism*. London: New Left Review, 1976.

Hobsbawm, Eric. *The Age of Revolution*. New York: New American Library, 1962.
———. *Labouring Men*. New York: Basic Books, 1965.

Kuczynski, Jürgen. *The Rise of the Working Class*. New York: McGraw-Hill, 1967.

Lefebvre, George. *The Coming of the French Revolution*. Princeton, N.J.: Princeton U. Press, 1947.

Lenin, V. I. *The Development of Capitalism in Russia*. Moscow: Foreign Languages Press, 1956.

Moore, Barrington. *Social Origins of Dictatorship and Democracy*. Boston: Beacon, 1966.

Polanyi, Karl. *The Great Transformation*. Boston: Beacon, 1957 (1944).

Thompson, E. P. *The Making of the English Working Class*. New York: Pantheon, 1966.

Wallerstein, Immanuel. *The Modern World-System: Capitalist Agriculture and the*

Origin of the European World-Economy in the 16th Century. New York: Academic, 1974.

————. "The Rise and Future Demise of the World Capitalist System." *Comparative Studies* 16:4 (Sept. 1974).

Williams, Eric. *Capitalism and Slavery.* New York: Capricorn, 1966 (1944).

Yinger, Milton. *Religion in the Struggle for Power.* New York: Russell & Russell, 1961 (1946).

CAPITALIST SOCIETIES

Aronowitz, Stanley. *False Promises.* New York: McGraw-Hill, 1973.

Brady, Robert. *Business as a System of Power.* New York: Columbia U. Press, 1941.

Chirot, Daniel. *Social Change in the Twentieth Century.* New York: Harcourt, Brace & Jovanovich, 1977.

Domhoff, G. William. *The Higher Circles.* New York: Random House, 1971.

Faulkner, Harold. *The Decline of Laissez-Faire: 1897–1917.* New York: Harper & Row, 1968.

Hayes, Carlton. *A Generation of Materialism.* New York: Harper & Row, 1963 (1941).

Hobsbawm, Eric. *The Age of Capital: 1848–75.* New York: Scribner, 1975.

Kolko, Gabriel. *Main Currents in Modern American History.* New York: Harper & Row, 1976.

————. *The Triumph of Conservatism.* Chicago: Quadrangle, 1967.

Lenin, V. I. *Imperialism: The Highest Stage of Capitalism,* in *Selected Works,* 3 vols. New York: International, 1967 (1917).

Marx, Karl. *Capital,* Vol. I, Vol. III. New York: International, 1967 (1867, 1894).

Mills, C. Wright. *White Collar.* New York: Oxford U. Press, 1956.

Perlo, Victor. *The Empire of High Finance.* New York: International, 1957.

Sweezy, Paul, and Baran, Paul. *Monopoly Capital.* New York: Monthly Review, 1967.

Vagts, Alfred. *A History of Militarism.* New York: Free Press, 1967 (1959).

Weinstein, James. *The Corporate Ideal in the Liberal State.* Boston: Beacon, 1969.

Wiebe, Robert H. *Businessmen and Reform.* Cambridge, Mass.: Harvard U. Press, 1962.

SOCIALIST SOCIETIES

Bettleheim, Charles. *Cultural Revolution and Industrial Organization in China.* New York: Monthly Review Press, 1974.

Bornstein, Morris, and Fusfeld, David (eds.). *The Soviet Economy.* Homewood, Ill.: Irwin, 1974.

Goldwasser, Janet, and Dowty, Stuart. *Huan-Ying: Workers' China.* New York: Monthly Review Press, 1975.

Gregory, Paul, and Stuart, Robert. *Soviet Economic Structure and Performance*. New York: Harper & Row, 1974.

Hopkins, Mark. *Mass Media in the Soviet Union*. New York: Pegasus, 1970.

Kanol, K. S. *China: The Other Communism*. New York: Hill & Wang, 1967.

Lane, David. *The End of Inequality*. Baltimore: Penguin, 1971.

Milton, David; Milton, Nancy; and Schurmann, Franz. *The China Reader: People's China*, Vol. IV. New York: Vintage, 1974.

Myrdal, Jan. *Report from a Chinese Village*. New York: New American Library, 1965.

Nettl, J. P. *The Soviet Achievement*. New York: Harcourt, Brace & World, 1967.

Osborn, Robert. *Soviet Social Policies*. Homewood, Ill.: Dorsey, 1970.

Parkin, Frank. *Class Inequality and Political Order*. New York: Praeger, 1971.

Schramm, S. T. (ed.). *Authority, Participation and Cultural Changes in China*. Cambridge, G.B.: Cambridge U. Press, 1973.

Schurmann, Franz, and Schnell, Orville. *The China Reader*, Vol. III; *Communist China*, Vol. IV. New York: Vintage, 1967.

Sidel, Ruth. *Families of Fengsheng: Urban Life in China*. Baltimore: Penguin, 1974.

Skilling, H. Gordon, and Griffiths, Franklin (eds.). *Interest Groups in Soviet Politics*. Princeton, N.J.: Princeton U. Press, 1971.

Sweezy, Paul, and Bettleheim, Charles (eds.). *On the Transition to Socialism*. New York: Monthly Review Press, 1971.

Wheelwright, Edward, and McFarlane, Bruce. *The Chinese Road to Socialism*. New York: Monthly Review Press, 1970.

Wilczynski, Josef. *The Economics of Socialism*. Chicago: Aldine, 1970.

Yanowitch, Murray, and Fischer, Wesley. *Stratification and Mobility in the USSR*. New York: International Arts & Sciences Press, 1973.

Chapter 4

The Corporate Economy

When most people are asked what problem in life most concerns them, they respond that it is the economic welfare of themselves and their family. People spend much of their energies on earning a living, or preparing to earn a living, or trying to find some other way to survive. Despite the centrality of economic factors to our lives, however, most people are bored by economic issues. While our own work lives may be exciting (but more likely are not), there is little human drama in the working out of impersonal economic forces.

This aversion to economics is especially understandable in capitalist society, because the laws of the market are often presented as eternal and unchangeable. Inflation, unemployment, poverty, and the other problems generated by capitalism are treated as if they were incurable diseases best left to specialists who have been trained to deal with such unpleasantness. In fact, however, economic systems are much more changeable than biological ones. We are more capable of curing ourselves of capitalism than we are of cancer or diabetes. Knowledge of this fact may not make economics easier or more exciting, but it does make it more important.

Economic systems can be changed in two ways. One way is to change the technology, the physical means by which economic production is carried out. Throughout history we have seen a change from hunting and gathering, to gardening, to more developed agriculture, and finally to industrial production. Technical change tends to be continuous and incremental, through a series of small advances, although occasionally a major invention such as the plow or the steam engine will revolutionize productive processes.

An important industrial site—the Ford Motor Company's River Rouge plant.

The other way to change the economy is organizationally. We can change the social relations between people as they engage in economic activity. Of course, technology and social organization are related. Hunting and gathering requires a small band of hunters, while automobile production in large quantities requires a factory with hundreds of employees. But the organization of production is not completely determined by technology; there are alternative ways of organizing both the production and the distribution of goods within the same basic technical system.

A key factor in the organization of an economy is the way in which decisions are made—decisions about what is to be produced, who is to do what kind of work, and how and by whom the products are to be used. One way of making these decisions is communally, through collective decision making in a group. This method prevailed in primitive societies, and can be used by groups within larger societies as well. Another way to make economic decisions is by tradition. This was done in feudal societies, where tradition required that the serfs turn over a certain amount of their produce to the lord each year, regardless of its value on the market. Of course, such exploitative traditions had to be backed up by power, specifically by at least the threat of physical force. Oriental despotic societies tended to rely heavily on political power to make economic decisions, although they reinforced their power through the weight of tradition as well.

MARKET ECONOMIES

Capitalist societies rely on the *market* to make most economic decisions. Those of us who have grown up in capitalist societies tend to take the market, the interplay of supply and demand, as if it were a law of nature. But there is nothing in nature which guarantees that production will decrease if the price goes down and increase if it goes up. Under a market system, no one is responsible for producing food or homes or automobiles. People are motivated to produce something only if they can make a profit by doing so. And people are entitled to consume something only if they have enough money to buy it. The fact that someone's father was a shoemaker or farmer does not mean that he is expected to continue in the same profession, as it did in societies governed by tradition. Rather, the successful individual in a market economy is expected to go wherever the rewards are greater.

The market system is, of course, familiar to most readers of this book because they have grown up under it. What is important is to recognize that this system is not inevitable, not the only way of organizing an economy. It is a system that has both advantages and disadvantages, and that works better under certain conditions than under other conditions. Market systems work best when there are a large number of producers and a large number of consumers of any commodity. Under these conditions, no small group of producers or consumers can interfere with the market, purposely restricting production or consumption in order to distort the workings of the law of supply and demand. Thus, relatively speaking, the market system worked fairly well in frontier America, where there were thousands of small farmers and craftsmen who could produce the basic commodities needed by most people.

There are problems with the market economy. The free interplay of supply and demand inevitably leads both to great inequality and to business cycles, or alternations of prosperity and depression, and the depressions cause considerable suffering. They also tend to get worse and worse over time. If market forces are truly allowed to function freely, there will always be those on the bottom who fail to compete successfully and starve to death. The early capitalists believed that this was necessary, in fact, that it was sometimes God's way of purging the human race of incompetents and misfits. They carried this so far as to allow over a million people to starve in Ireland when they relied on a crop that was susceptible to the potato blight. Today, however, all but the most doctrinaire capitalists recognize the need to interfere in the market economy to provide at least a wretched minimum of subsistence for those on the bottom.

Growth of Monopolies

The most central defect in the market as a means of making economic decisions is that it is self-destructive. There is an inherent contradiction in the market system; the more efficiently it works, the more it undermines the conditions that enable it to work effectively. As the market system rewards the best producers, these producers receive more resources. The additional resources enable them to improve their advantage over other producers to the point that they drive these producers out of business. There is thus a general law that free competition leads to monopolization. Of

Ted Goertzel

Small businesses survive on the fringes of the economy.

course, there are exceptions to this law, as in businesses where large size is a disadvantage because of the personal nature of the services rendered. But in most industries, the law holds. From over a hundred automobile producers in the 1910s, America is down to four today. A similar concentration goes on in almost every industry, although it is often concealed from the consumer by a proliferation of brand names used by the same company. Independent grocers are driven out of business by supermarkets, family restaurants by franchised fast food outlets, small shops by shopping centers. Small business survives only by filling odd niches in the economy, or by picking up the less profitable fringes of the business.

This process has been going on for a long time; an intense period of monopoly growth took place during the 1890s, for example. Monopolies dominate the major sectors of the economies of the United States and the other advanced capitalist countries. While market mechanisms continue to play an important role in these economies, it is a myth to refer to them as free economies in the sense of being governed by markets free of monopoly control. The economy of the United States today is characterized by a system of *monopoly* capitalism, that is, by a system which is dominated by large privately owned corporations.[1]

Under monopoly conditions depressions tend to become more severe, for rea-

1. Strictly speaking, the U.S. economy is dominated by *oligopolies*. These are small groups of firms that dominate a particular industry. Since oligopolies function in the same way as monopolies, however, the distinction is not important.

sons which will be discussed later. In the 1930s the capitalist economies of the developed world entered a crisis which was unprecedented in its depth and scope. As a consequence, the state began taking a much more important role in regulating and controlling the economy in support of the monopoly corporations. All sorts of government regulatory institutions were created or reinvigorated. Deficit spending was used by the state to attempt to bring the economy out of the depression. The spending was never quite enough until World War II, but since then massive military spending, together with other state spending, has been used to shore up the economy. The state has continued to play a central role, as the "invisible hand" predicted by the early theorists of capitalism clearly did not do the job. Consequently, the system presently predominant in the United States can best be called "state monopoly capitalism."

ORGANIZATION OF THE MONOPOLY CAPITALIST ECONOMY

The United States economy is dominated by giant monopolistic corporations. The inherent logic of these corporations, and of their relationships with one another and with their workers, determines the basic characteristics of the entire society—its values and beliefs, its political forms, its educational system, its military policies, etc. Each decade, the control of the economy by these corporations becomes stronger. In 1976, the two hundred largest manufacturing corporations controlled 58 percent of the assets in this sector.

These corporations are controlled by the *capitalist class* of American society. The capitalist upper class is a small, cohesive group, consisting of approximately one half of one percent of the American population. This class relies on inherited wealth to sustain its economic and social position. It plays an active role in making decisions in its corporate role, through control of stock and positions on boards of directors, and by control of managerial positions. A study of the 15 largest banks, the 15 largest insurance companies and the 20 largest industrial firms in the mid 1960s showed that 53 percent of their 884 directors were members of the social upper class. Most of the other 47 percent were professional businessmen who had been socialized into the corporate world through a long process of promotions and advancement through the ranks of the corporate world.

How Monopolies Are Controlled

There are different mechanisms by which major corporations are controlled. One mechanism is stock ownership. Most stock in large corporations is owned by small shareholders, either directly or through mechanisms such as pension and mutual funds. Thus, wealthy individuals who own at least 5 percent to 10 percent of the stock of a corporation can generally exercise effective control over its management. Some corporations are clearly controlled in this fashion, many by the families that originally

A center of financial activity—the New York headquarters of Chase Manhattan Bank.

owned them, such as Ford, Alcoa, Gulf Oil, Sun Oil Co., Du Pont, Weyerhauser.

In another mechanism of control, effective power resides with the managers. Some argue that managers of large corporations can become independent of any set of stockholders because of the great diversity of stock ownership and the resultant apathy of stockholders. According to this theory members of management reappoint themselves to their positions by means of their control over the proxies of a significant number of stockholders. The *managerialists*, who advance this theory, assert that each giant corporation is more or less autonomous in its operations. Each management is motivated to maximize the profit of its own corporation rather than that of any wider familial fortune or interest group. To the extent that corporations become wealthy enough to be financially independent, they may be independent of banks or wealthy families.

A third mechanism of control is through banks and other financial institutions. When corporations are unable to generate enough capital internally for their operation and expansion they must turn increasingly to the banks. The banks provide financing, but only in return for control over corporate policies. The banks not only give loans tied to the observance of certain conditions but they also put bank directors on the boards of the corporations to which they loan money. Some Marxists who have studied the U.S. economy argue that financial institutions are the heart of the system of corporate capitalism and that the financial institutions attempt to maximize the profits of the set of corporations that they have an interest in, rather than merely maximizing the profit of each corporation taken separately.

Proponents of this position cite evidence to show that the assets controlled by financial companies have been rising as a percentage of national wealth (it was 30 percent in 1929 and 47 percent in 1965) and that the proportion of the funding of non-financial institutions by financial institutions has likewise been growing since the end of World War II (it was 30 percent in 1964, and 43 percent in 1968). They also point out that the share of the largest financial institutions in the assets of all financial institutions has been growing. The ten largest banks, for example, in 1970 had over 25 percent of all the deposits. During the 1950s, eight New York banks accounted for one half of all loans to all corporations with over 100 million dollars in assets. Most of the very largest corporations are financial, not industrial.

The particular mechanism of control does not make a critical difference to the system, however, since all three mechanisms serve to reinforce the interests of the upper class. There may be cases where the interests of a particular family or financial interest group will distort the system in their limited interest. For example, at one time the DuPont family held approximately 10 percent of the stock of the U.S. Rubber Company and 25 percent of the stock of General Motors. This was a controlling interest in both cases, because the rest of the stock was diversified among small shareholders. At this time, the DuPont representatives made U.S. Rubber sell tires at cost to General Motors. This meant that U.S. Rubber lost money, while G.M. gained extraordinarily high profits. Since the DuPonts owned a larger share of G.M. than of U.S. Rubber, they gained from this arrangement.

Professional managers, on the other hand, are probably more likely to defend the growth of their own particular corporation. Their success, however, is determined by the rate of profit that the corporation attains and the amount of capital under its control. Although most managers hold a very small proportion of their corporation's stock, they hold enough that the success of the corporate stock is important to their own income and financial security. Moreover, their identities are tied up with their corporations. Their personal status and prestige are products of that of their corporation and of their position within the corporation. Consequently, managers have the same incentives to maximize the profits of their corporation as individuals or families that own controlling shares.

Prices, Profits and Planning

The corporations are governed by profit maximization, regardless of how they are controlled. The rate of growth of a corporation, its size, its credit rating, the price of its securities, etc., are all functions of its profits. Everything about corporations is regulated by the guiding principle of profit maximization.

Because of the tremendous size and stake of the corporations, they must plan. They must rationally allocate their resources and have a good idea of what to expect in the future in terms of the supply of raw materials, labor supply, and market trends. Thus, they typically must have long- and short-term projections in all these areas. But since corporations in themselves are unable to effectively control their environment, they rely heavily on the state, whose foreign and economic policies they largely control, to regulate and guide the society and economy in their common interest. The state helps out a corporation when it is in financial difficulty (e.g., Lockheed), develops new technologies when they are too expensive for any one corporation to develop (e.g., atomic energy and space exploration), and engages in all kinds of regulatory activities and long- and short-term quasi-planning of the economy.

Shortly after the formation of the modern corporations, an implicit, if not explicit, agreement was reached among them to avoid cut-throat price competition designed to bankrupt one or another of them. Instead, since this time, almost all the corporations have been run according to a strong social norm that dictates a prohibition on price competition and the systematic avoidance of risk-taking.

But even with quasi-planning of the whole economy, fundamental competition between the corporations still exists in areas other than prices. Corporations still relate to one another and to their workers and consumers through markets, although these markets are highly monopolized and regulated by the state in the collective interest of the corporations. The giant corporations, because of their monopoly position, are price makers, that is, they are in a position to, and do, set the prices at which people will buy their products. This privilege is denied people in competitive markets where the price people pay is a function purely of demand for a product and the cost of producing it. In competitive markets the suppliers are completely subject to the vagaries of market forces. But since there are so few suppliers in a monopolized market, the suppliers can easily collude to set the prices at an artificially high level. Consumers are then in a position to buy at this monopoly price or go without.

Prices do change in monopoly capitalist society, although generally only in one direction—up! Since price cutting is a violation of the norm against competition, prices can normally only increase. The means by which this is accomplished in societies like the U.S., which have laws against explicit price setting by monopolies, is through the institution of price leadership. A traditional firm, usually the largest and most powerful in its field, is the first to raise its prices. If the other companies want the price level to rise they soon follow suit. If most do not follow suit, the price leader will then rescind its announced price increase (temporarily). This process accomplishes in an only slightly more cumbersome manner the same result as overt price setting. The consequence of the ban on price cutting as a threat to the rule of live and let live is that there has been a constant inflation since the institutionalization of monopoly corporations around 1900. An examination of the buying power of the dollar from 1790 to 1900 would show that its value fluctuated but remained stable on the average so that it bought more or less the same in 1790 as it did in 1900. However, since 1900 inflation has progressed at a more or less steady rate. The only significant deflation since 1900 has been that of the Great Depression.

Corporations compete with one another for expanded markets through advertising and marketing and by increasing their profit margins by reducing their costs. Their competitive energies are channeled into these two courses rather than going into price competition. Products are designed with great care for their salability. Tremendous sums are spent on packaging, advertising, and market research. The slightest advantage or the most trivial gimmick in the absence of a price differential may be enough to secure a greatly expanded share of the market unless one's competitors quickly follow suit. A classical example of this is the advertising of airlines. Because the airlines regulate their own rates through control of the government regulatory agencies, there is no competition in ticket prices. Therefore, they compete for a volatile customer market by offering more up-to-date in-flight films, steak and lobster, prettier stewardesses, etc.

CONTRADICTIONS OF MONOPOLY CAPITALISM

Rising Rate of Profit

The effort to reduce costs as a major way of increasing profits has the consequence of giving a major impetus to technological development. As a result, labor productivity and the advance of technology increases as rapidly under monopoly conditions as under competitive conditions. This tendency for costs to be reduced, combined with the norm of no price competition, means that profits tend to rise in the corporate world as the gap between price and cost grows. Thus, there is a tendency for profits to rise both absolutely and relatively as the system develops. The tendency of profits under monopoly conditions is the opposite from that under competitive capitalism, where because of price competition and the forced reinvestment of virtually all profits, profits tend to decline rather than rise.[2]

A recent Harvard study documented the tendency for profits to rise under monopoly capitalism. This study covered 57 corporations which were involved in 620 separate businesses. They found that the greater the share of the market for a given product that a company monopolized, the higher its rate of profit. The findings are summarized in Table 4-1.

---

2. Technically it is the gap between actual price and the cost of production that tends to rise. This difference is not the actual profit that appears on a company's books, but is rather what Paul Baran and Paul Sweezy in their book *Monopoly Capital* call the economic surplus, the difference that is, between the price of output and the socially necessary costs of producing it. There are a number of claims on profits—rents, interest, advertising and selling expenses, insurance, taxes to support the government, etc., which must be deducted from the surplus before the book profits of a corporation are obtained.

TABLE 4-1. Monopolization and Profit Rates

Market Share	Return on Investment
under 7%	9.6%
7–14%	12.0%
14–22%	13.5%
22–36%	17.9%
over 36%	30.2%

(Source: Joe Cappo, *Chicago Daily News,* May 17, 1977)

Underconsumption

The fact that profits tend to rise in monopoly capitalist society means that it becomes more and more difficult for those profits to be spent. Because profits not spent will not in fact be produced, the tendency for economic stagnation grows. Unless everything that is produced is bought, much of the profit anticipated will not be realized. Everything produced will not be bought unless people have enough buying power to buy everything produced. Rising prices together with decreasing wages relative to total output means that it is more and more difficult for working people to buy the total output of their labor. It is also increasingly unlikely that the output will be bought out of profits. Instead, the wealthy and the corporations will try to save an ever-increasing percentage of the GNP. But attempts to save that do not correspond to someone else's deficit spending logically cannot occur. Therefore, the tendency to save out of profits results in underconsumption.[3]

There are basically four possibilities open for the growing surplus of monopoly capitalist society being utilized: (1) increased consumption on the part of those who receive the rising profits, (2) increased investment on the part of corporations in new productive plants, (3) waste by the corporations in the process of attempting to sell

---

3. A simplified example of underconsumption follows. Let us assume the following: Corporate output is 100; the profit margin (p) is set at 30 percent of output; investments out of profit (i) is $\frac{1}{3}$ of profits; profit class consumption (c) is $\frac{1}{3}$ of profits; attempted savings out of profit (s) is set at $\frac{1}{3}$ of profits; wages (w) is 70; at time period 1: $100 = 70w + 30p (10i + 10c + 10s)$. But, total effective demand $70w + 10i + 10c = 90$, or 10 less than the value of the output 100. Therefore, in the next period, output will be limited to 90, which the corporations think on the basis of their experience, they can sell.

Thus, at time period 2: $90 = 63w + 27p (9i + 9c + 9s)$. But still 90 is greater than $63w + 9i + 9c = 81$. Therefore, production must be limited still further in time period 3.

This tendency of the economy to contract will go on until all attempts to save out of surplus have been frustrated. That is, until all surplus finds have outlets in consumption or investment.

This actually can happen without a very great contraction because (1) profits decrease faster than value of output, and (2) the propensity to save decreases faster than profits. But to the extent that profit margins are maintained or increased and the rate of investment and consumption out of profits is decreased the contraction is greater. Hence the tenacity of depression under conditions of simple monopoly capitalism.

their goods (advertising and marketing), and (4) government spending to buy up the products of the corporations that they cannot sell to the public because of their working classes' lack of purchasing power. Each of these will be examined in turn.

Increased Consumption by the Wealthy. The main obstacle to increased spending on the part of those who receive the profits is what has been called Engel's law—the higher a person's income the higher the proportion of income that is saved, that is, the more income someone has, the less important to him or her is further spending compared with building up savings. The rich attempt to save more than the middle and working classes. Also important is the fact that corporations do not distribute all profits to their stockholders, but rather accumulate reserves and maintain liquidity. Hence distributed profits do not keep pace with real profits. Thus little relief is found in this quarter.

New Investment Outlets.   There are two basic kinds of new investments in capitalist enterprises, *inside* and *outside*. Inside investment is a firm's normal investment in expanded plant and equipment. This does not include significant technological change or totally new markets but rather is investment based on normal technological improvements and normal market growth. If inside investment were to absorb the growing surplus, investment would have to grow more rapidly than the Gross National Product (since the surplus that would be channeled into inside investment grows more rapidly than GNP). If inside investment were to absorb the surplus, the ratio of the value of investment goods to the value of the output of consumption goods would have to constantly rise. That is, new investment would have to be disproportionately in capital goods used to produce more capital goods, not in the production of consumption goods themselves, since the buying power of the masses of people is contracting relative to the GNP. This would mean, for example, that steel mills would be built to produce steel to build more steel mills, whose output would be used to build still more steel mills, etc. All this would be based on a relatively constant demand for steel for purposes other than building more steel mills. Such a process, as should be apparent, makes no sense and would not be engaged in for long by any sensible capitalist who could see that any such pattern of investment would be built on sand. If there was ever overinvestment in the productive goods sector (relative to what is necessary for the production of consumption goods) an economic crisis would result. When it was realized that disproportionate surplus capacity existed, the bubble would burst. If these inside investment outlets were the only ones available, the system would have long since bogged down in permanent depression.

The second type of private investment opportunity available in capitalist society is outside investment. This type of investment is induced by factors not integral to the normal operation of the productive process. We can list four: growth in population, new methods and new products, foreign investment, and epoch-making innovations. Population growth can slowly absorb part of the growing surplus as new con-

Ted Goertzel

The introduction of the automobile was an epoch-making event for the U.S. economy.

sumers are born and come of age, but on the one hand this process is too slow to be able to absorb very much of the surplus and on the other, by providing more and more laborers to the corporations, it helps aggravate the problem of surplus.

Foreign investment is a real possibility for absorbing the growing pool of profits. Capital that cannot be profitably invested at home can be invested overseas. However, although empirically this would appear to be a real possibility for surplus absorption, because of the monopolization of the world markets, overseas investment results in the value of repatriated profits being greater than the value of new overseas investments. Thus, the operation of overseas investment processes aggravates rather than alleviates the problem. New methods and products help absorb some of the surplus. But under monopoly capitalist conditions innovations are introduced with careful consideration given to profit maximization so as not to make past investments worthless. There are no larger competitive forces compelling old capital to be scrapped when it becomes outdated. Thus, new methods and new products do not absorb an extraordinary amount of investment funds, so the problem is not resolved here. There are, however, a very few "epoch-making innovations" that do shake up the entire pattern of the economy and create vast investment outlets in addition to the surplus they directly absorb. We can list three of these: the steam engine, the railroad, and the automobile. Each had tremendous repercussions on the economy and opened up great new horizons for investment. Of the steam engine little more need be said. From 1850 to 1907, 40 to 50 percent of all new investment was in railways. From 1915 to 1929 automobile production became the center of new investment (either in car production itself, or in oil, steel, rubber, concrete, and other products stimulated by the demand of automobile production and its necessary accoutrements). Following World War II a second great wave of automobile expansion occurred which gave a further great impetus to investment. In the last 100 years first the rapid expansion of the railroads and then the growth of the automobile culture have gone a long way towards absorbing the economic surplus and preventing the natural tendency of monopoly capitalist society to result in stagnation from exerting itself.

Corporate Waste. A third possibility for absorbing the growing pool of surplus lies in nonproductive corporate spending designed to increase the spending of consumers without giving them more money. The sales effort creates all kinds of jobs for public relations people, salesmen, advertising people, newsprint producers, research and development people, etc., whose jobs are geared to increasing sales. Thus, the sales effort directly absorbs a high and growing share of the total surplus (which thus never actually appears on the books as profits). This type of work, designed to excite interest in the products of corporations thereby insuring that people buy what is produced, is essential for the operation of the corporations. It helps absorb the surplus not only through the wages of the people involved but also through insuring that consumers spend all that they earn (so as not to add to the surplus through bank savings and petty investments) and *more* (through buying on credit). The deficit spending induced by advertising means that large numbers of consumers are regularly spending more than they are earning (getting deeper and deeper in debt), thus allowing the profit-earning classes to save (spend less than they receive).

Advertising and packaging efforts appeal to people's psychological anxieties and drives rather than their material needs. They promise social acceptability (no bad breath or body odor), play on the drive for self-esteem and dignity (own a new luxury car), and pander to sexual frustrations (be beautiful and popular). Advertising is not only geared to stimulate demand for the product of one particular company but also is designed as propaganda for goods in general. It is geared to combatting the natural tendency for satiation to temper a person's desire to work and consume ever more. It must constantly stimulate us to insure that we have a limitless horizon of material aspirations, so that it can succeed in its relentless war against savings and for the system that delivers the goods. Lastly, the sales effort serves as propaganda for the monopoly capitalist system itself. Since material goods are everywhere flaunted as the goal of life by the media, the system that however slowly and inequitably does deliver material goods to the people is legitimized in spite of its fundamental frustration of the human needs for dignity and community.

The share of advertising in the GNP has increased enormously during the history of monopoly capitalism. In 1867, the costs of advertising totaled only $40 million dollars a year; in 1890, $360 million; in 1929, $3,400 million; and in 1976, $18,450 million. Most research and product development engaged in by the corporations is directed to planning obsolescence—that is, in making products so that they will not last, or so that people will not want to own them for very long. It has been estimated that the annual cost of automobile model changes comes to 2½ percent of the Gross National Product. The income of all nonproductive workers, those who are directly involved in the sales effort together with those involved in other institutions that facilitate the operation of monopoly capitalist society but make little or no contribution to the socially necessary costs of production (salespeople, people involved in finance, insurance, real estate, advertising, planning obsolescence, lawyers, etc.), amounts to approximately a third of the GNP.

Government Spending.   All the mechanisms discussed so far are unable to sustain the absorption of the growing surplus generated by monopoly capitalism even though the sales effort makes a valiant attempt and epoch-making inventions can succeed in staving off the tendency for stagnation for a while. Increasingly, as the surplus has grown and the other mechanisms have shown themselves to be inadequate, the government has stepped in to insure that the remaining surplus was taken care of. Since the institutionalization of state monopoly capitalism during the Franklin Roosevelt administration, the state has considered it its obligation to insure sufficient demand in the economy. This has occurred without hurting the profit opportunities of the corporations because the state buys up the goods the corporations would otherwise be unable to sell, thus allowing the attempt to save on the part of the corporations to be realized. The state can accomplish this through a combination of deficit spending (which is the most efficient) and through simple massive spending covered by tax collections. Deficit spending on the part of the government is a very effective mechanism. To absorb the surplus, the government in effect prints money that it uses to buy the products of the corporations. The attempt of the rich to sell without buying (i.e., saving) is therefore balanced by the government's buying without selling (i.e., deficit spending). Deficit spending is more potent as an absorber of surplus than expenses covered by taxes. But such expenditures are also very important in creating demand. The government taxes people—mostly not the rich—to pay for its expenses. But since it is committed to spending the money before it collects the taxes, it adds to the GNP by the amount of its expenditure, even though it later recovers this in taxes. Deficit spending is better because the money the government uses to buy products does not return to the government in taxes but is instead spent by the corporations on the products of other corporations, who in turn spend much of it on the products of still other corporations. Thus, a *multiplier* effect results as the money originally spent does more than double duty in stimulating the economy for a while. Stimulation through deficit spending will result in reduced unemployment rather than in inflation as long as there is significant unemployment in most sectors of the work force and underprotection in most sectors of industry. Government taxation does not significantly infringe on the savings of the rich because of their great political power (although this would certainly be a logical way to eliminate the surplus problem). Instead, taxation is effective mainly on the working classes, whose incomes are thus channeled into subsidies granted by the government out of tax funds to the corporations so that they will be able to sell all the goods they produce and hence realize great profits.

Government spending has become the major mechanism in the economy for creating income through turning idle capacity into production. Corporate interests since the Great Depression have favored the ever-expanding role of government spending in the economy as the only practical way of avoiding stagnation and insuring the continuance of profits. Trends in overall government spending are shown in Table 4–2.

TABLE 4-2. United States Government Spending as a Percentage of GNP

Year	Spending (all levels)
1903	7.4
1929	9.8
1939	19.2
1949	23.1
1961	28.8
1968	32.8
1975	36.7

(Source: U.S. Bureau of the Census, *Historical Statistics and Statistical Abstract of the United States, 1977.*)

The government, which now spends approximately one-third of the gross national product, is restricted in the types of activities it can spend its money on by the powerful forces that control the state. Civilian spending of most kinds is limited by the opposition of vested interests to any endeavors that would interfere with their profitability. There exists an alliance of vested interests that support one another and vetoes government spending in virtually all civilian areas. For example, electric power companies oppose government spending on public power projects that could provide power at cheaper rates than the private power companies, because such public companies would then take this sphere of exploitation away from private companies. The American Medical Association opposes aid to medical schools and scholarships to medical students because this would result in so many doctors that the price of medicine would fall to within reasonable bounds. Urban real-estate interests oppose low-cost public housing because this would not only take away from them a very profitable sphere of investment but because massive public housing would undermine the rent structure of the country, affecting both private and public housing, thus depriving developers, real estate investors, mortgage companies, and banks of vast sums of money. The railways, airlines, and communications companies oppose government takeovers in these spheres unless, like in railway passenger service, the private operations are running at a loss. What they prefer is that government take over profitless industries so that they can recoup a profit in their sale that they otherwise would have no possibility of realizing. There is basic opposition to improving the quality of education because of its function for the system. The educational system in capitalist society is geared to providing the corporations with the properly trained labor force it requires. Quality education is needed for the minority who are being trained for the professional occupations such as engineers, scientists, and teachers, as well as for managers and those that support the corporations in government and university positions. But most of the jobs offered by the corporations require an inferior education that is designed to train people for lowly economic positions without giving them unrealizable aspirations that can only result in trouble for the corporations. Therefore, corporate interests combine to oppose all government aid to education beyond what is necessary to provide for the labor needs of the corporations. There was, for example, a big increase in government support to education in the 1950s to aid in the cold war and to staff the profitable military-industrial complex. In the early seventies, however, aid to higher education was cut back as the universities began to produce more engineers, teachers, and scientists than the profit-oriented corporate economy could absorb.

There are a few areas where government spending is not blocked by private interests. One of the most important of these is spending on highways, which consumes a large share of government revenue on all levels. A conglomerate of automobile manufacturers plus the rubber, concrete, steel, and petroleum industries, together with highway construction firms, have forced large government outlays in the construction of the roads without which the automobile complex would be impossible. Space is another area where the large corporations force sizable government expenditures because such spending is highly profitable while not hurting vested interests. During the post-World War II period the most important area of government spending was on the military.

Military Spending

Military spending is ideal for the corporations. Since there are no private armies, spending in this area competes with no one while requiring a wide range of very expensive products that benefit almost all industrial sectors. Moreover, unlike any other area of spending (except space spending to a lesser degree) patriotism (based in the authoritarian character and energized by the frustration of people's psychological needs) can be mobilized by the state to drum up support for gigantic levels of military spending while at the same time intimidating all opposition. Lastly, military spending is perfect as a mechanism of surplus absorption, because far from being pure waste (like space) it is very useful for the corporations in advancing their imperial aims throughout the world. We will discuss these aspects of surplus absorption further in Chapter 10.

War spending has increased until recently both as a percentage of GNP and as a percentage of government spending. In 1929 war spending represented only .7 percent of the GNP, but by 1960 it had grown to 10.7 percent. It was military spending that made the difference between economic prosperity and economic stagnation in the postwar years. The percentage of the labor force employed in war industries and the military plus the unemployed has been more or less constant since the middle of the Great Depression at around 17 percent. In 1939, 1.4 percent were employed in war-related activities and 17 percent were unemployed, while during most of the 1960s approximately 10 percent were employed in war-related activities and 6 percent were unemployed.

LIFE UNDER MONOPOLY CAPITALISM

There are a number of ways in which the economic forces of monopoly capitalism affect the everyday lives of the people who live within monopoly capitalist societies. The variables that most effect the lives of ordinary people in these societies are wages, prices, and unemployment. These variables seem to move erratically, almost to have a life of their own. We read in the paper that the inflation rate has topped 10 percent or that the unemployment rate has stabilized at 7 percent as we read that the temperature is 88 degrees and the humidity 95 percent. We may get the impression that as little can be done about the first set of figures as about the second. And in a sense this is true. Unemployment and inflation are as much a feature of the economic system in which we live as heat and humidity are part of our meterological systems. Thus, it is not possible to eliminate these problems, *unless* we are willing to abandon the system altogether. Even within the confines of the system, however, wages, prices, and unemployment rates can be and are manipulated. One of the ways in which state monopoly capitalism differs from competitive capitalism is that these economic variables are regulated *within limits* by the state and by organized economic interests.

Minimal Wages Under Competitive Capitalism

Under competitive conditions the capitalists were forced to resist every demand for wage increases because if they did not they could not compete with other capitalists.

Labor unions were prohibited or suppressed, and the state did not intervene in the economy except to insure a compliant, low-wage labor force. Consequently, wages tended to approximate the *minimum* needed to survive and raise a family in the society in question. If workers were not paid enough to feed, clothe, and shelter themselves and their families, the system would die out. But there was always a large number of unemployed people who were forced by the threat of starvation to seek work that would enable them to survive. Thus, wages tended to remain stable at a bare minimum level.

The only thing under competitive capitalism that broke this pattern was the business cycle. During boom periods, when capital accumulation expanded under the pressures of forced investment, more and more workers are employed until labor shortages develop. During these periods, the pool of unemployed workers goes down, and capitalists are forced to pay their workers higher wages in order to keep them on the job. As a consequence of this increase in wages,. however, profits go down. Low profitability forces the capitalists to introduce machinery to displace the workers. This labor-saving technology results in workers being laid off, and in wages being forced down.

Thus, under competitive capitalism, the rate of unemployment and the rate of technological change are inversely related. The greater the unemployment, the less the need for new technology to maintain profits, and vice versa. Under monopoly capitalism, the same basic logic operates to interrelate the level of wages, the rate of technological change, and the rate of unemployment. However, under monopoly capitalism new variables are entered into the equation. These new factors make it possible for wages to grow steadily for long periods of time. They also make it possible to lessen the fluctuation in the unemployment rate, to keep it from going too high *or too low*. Through introducing these new variables, monopoly capitalism is able to control to a considerable extent the crises built into competitive capitalism.

Increasing Wages Under Monopoly Capitalism

The new factors that are responsible for the increase in real wages under monopoly capitalism are (1) the interference of the state, (2) the development of labor unions, and (3) the ability of monopoly corporations to pass wage increases on to consumers through higher prices.

Under monopoly conditions the corporations need *not* resist every wage increase out of fear that their profits will be reduced if not altogether eliminated because of competition. Once capitalists gain control over the prices they charge for their goods, they are able to collectively raise their prices to compensate (or often overcompensate, using an increase in wages as an excuse to increase profits) for increased wages. Not only does control over price allow the corporations to raise their prices to compensate for increased wages but it also allows them to raise wages in order to insure worker loyalty to their enterprises, reduce employee turnover, keep unions out, obtain better workers, and minimize trouble from workers.

The state also has come to play a major role in advanced monopoly capitalism in increasing real wages. Partially because of its desire to minimize social disruption and prevent radical change, and partially in order to maintain a healthy, technically competent and well-motivated work force, the state enforces minimum-wage laws, restrictions on the employment of women and children, provides welfare, which acts to put a floor on wages, and enforces collective bargaining. This state interference insures that real wages stay above the subsistence level.

Lastly, the organization of strong trade unions has forced the corporations to grant wage increases. Their success in this has been possible, however, only because of (1) the new ability of the corporations to pass increases on to consumers and, (2) the support of the state.

Causes of Inflation and High Taxes

While these three changes in the system have helped to control the basic problems of low wages and unemployment, they have created new problems. The biggest of these are inflation and high taxes. Prices rise steadily under monopoly capitalism for two reasons. First, because corporations keep raising their prices in order to increase their profits and to make it possible to pay higher wages to their organized workers. Organized workers then win greater dollar paychecks through union contracts, only to see them taken away by higher prices. Second, because the state has to print more money to cover the costs of its deficit spending. Every time the state does this, it is in fact taking a hidden tax from the pockets of workers who do not have capital investment opportunities that enable them to avoid inflation.

Inflation and taxes thus become key contradictions in monopoly capitalist society. Everyone is for cutting inflation and taxes, but always at someone else's expense. Imposing strict price controls, the logical solution, does not work because capitalists would refuse to produce goods if they were not able to sell them at profitable price. Holding down wages, generally done through phony "wage-price controls," which in fact control only wages, or increasing the unemployment rate, works only as long as the labor union leadership can be persuaded to accept it at the expense of their members. Cutting taxes works only if one is willing to cut state services, lay off government workers, or force the welfare population into even greater misery. Thus, despite the universal dedication of capitalist politicians to cut taxes and inflation, little is done. This is not so much a result of dishonesty on the part of the politicians as of their commitment to work within a system that objectively makes it impossible to resolve the problem.

Under monopoly capitalism, the wages that a particular group receives are largely determined by their political and organizational strength. Some workers, such as airline pilots, truckdrivers, or city sanitation workers, occupy critical positions in the economy. If they organize effectively, they may be able to force their employers to pay them high wages. Professions such as medicine, which are effectively organized to keep down the number of people able to get training in their field, can extract high prices for their services. Other professions or occupations that are less central to the economy, or that are less effectively organized, do much more poorly. The remuneration an individual or members of a group receives for their work has little or nothing to do with the value of their contribution to society. Similarly, the prices we pay for the commodities we buy has less and less to do with the value of them to the consumer or with the amount of labor that went into producing them. They depend largely on how effectively the producers organize to restrict supplies.

Monopoly capitalism has found temporary solutions to the problems that Karl Marx expected would bring an early end to capitalism. It has not been necessary for the workers to get poorer and poorer each year. There are limits, however, to the processes that are used to shore up the system. Government spending cannot increase forever; nor can inflation be allowed to increase indefinitely without catastrophic effects on the economy. Once inflation gets out of hand, it can rise over 100 percent a year, as it has in some Latin American countries in the last few years or in Germany in the post-World War I period. The laws of monopoly capitalism are not yet sufficiently understood, by either Marxist or non-Marxist economists, for us to know exactly what the limits are or when they will be reached. However, a consensus seems to be emerging among liberal and conservative economists that it will be necessary to slow down the increases in wages and find some way to get people to accept the fact that their incomes will no longer continue to rise. Both liberals and conservatives agree on the need to cut government spending and restrain wage demands. Thus, there is some reason to believe that the limit to the expansive capacities of monopoly capitalism may have been approached by the 1970s.

At the present moment, the "energy crisis" is being used as an excuse to cut back on people's real incomes. While it is of course true that our economies have been built on nonrenewable fossil fuels, and these will eventually run out, the current "energy crisis" has been created by the capitalist energy companies that created the current wasteful energy system in the first place. These firms have profited enormously, while the ordinary citizen is forced to suffer. Most Americans are suspicious of the claims of the oil companies, but they do not yet see a viable alternative to simply accepting the dictates of these firms, and of the government agencies they control, and simply cut back their use of energy while paying inflated prices. Only when they recognize that the crisis is of economic rather than geological origin will they be able to consider a true solution to the problem.

RECENT TRENDS IN THE AMERICAN ECONOMY

In the last decade, the United States seems to have entered into a phase similar to that entered by England after World War II. This is a period of stagnation or decline, which is caused by a nation being too long in a leading role in maintaining the world capitalist system. As the strongest country in the period after World War II, the United States was able to afford to make concessions to its working class and to increase state expenditures to maintain the middle class. It was able to make super-profits by investing in foreign countries that were under its indirect control. In doing so, however, it ran up huge bills for military and social expenditures. The Vietnam war, in particular, cost much more than any possible benefit, yet it was considered necessary to maintain the credibility and prestige of American imperial forces.

During the Vietnam period, social tensions got out of hand. Blacks were rioting in the ghettos, and students were rioting on campus. The army was falling apart as soldiers deserted in large numbers, refused to follow orders, or even started shooting at their own officers rather than at the supposed "enemy" in Vietnam. Meanwhile, countries such as Germany and Japan, which had been freed from imperial expenses by losing World War II, were able to rebuild their industrial plants and outcompete the United States. Their economies grew at the expense of the older industrial plants of England and the United States. The United States began to experience balance of payments problems and was often able to pay its bills only through its highly productive agricultural sector.

Forced Cuts in Military Spending

In response to these trends, ruling class leaders instituted changes in the economy. They instituted a rapid change in the main focus of government spending away from the military and towards social expenditures, principally in the form of indirect subsidies to the corporations for research and development, training, and retirement benefits for workers. Under the pressure of international competition from Western Europe and Japan, U.S. corporations have had to reduce their costs to remain competitive. In order to meet the prices of its international competitions, whose wage bills have been considerably less than those of the American corporations, they have had to turn to the U.S. government to subsidize as much as possible of their costs. In order to pay for these subsidies, military spending has had to be reduced. In 1960, direct military spending (excluding veterans' benefits and interest on old war debts) was 8.9 percent of the Gross National Product. In 1970 it was still 8.1 percent, but by 1975 it had decreased to 5.7 percent.

Recently, military and social expenditures in the United States have come to play more or less the same economic role as they have for some time played in the other advanced capitalist countries. The eighteen leading capitalist countries of the world spent an average of only 3.8 percent of their GNP on military expenditures during the late 1960s. During the same period these countries averaged 25 percent of their GNP's on nonmilitary expenditures. Only Israel and Great Britain among the other leading capitalist countries spend as much as 4 percent of their GNP on the military. On the other hand, only Japan and Australia, of these countries, spent less on social expenditures than did the United States.

Government attempts to stimulate the economy with military spending included the proposed B-1 bomber.

It has been the force of international competition that has moved the United States to change the relative role of military and social expenditures in its economy. The heavy reliance on military spending has undermined the technological advance of the U.S. economy. The best U.S. resources, scientists, technicians, and laboratories had concentrated on producing better weapons rather than on increasing industrial productivity. In terms of its effect on the rest of the economy, military spending can be compared to digging giant holes in the ground and then filling them back in again. That is, while it provides jobs for workers and sales for corporations, it is almost pure waste in terms of adding anything productive to the rest of the economy (or in increasing the living standards of Americans). Bombs, unlike machine tools, have no effect on increasing productivity in other sectors of the economy. The other advanced capitalist countries have been able to put almost all of their energies into increasing productivity, and hence, to greatly expanding the sale of their products at the expense of the United States. As a consequence of the allocation of resources and skills during the twenty-year period of 1950 to 1969 the average growth in real GNP per capita was 2.0 percent in the United States, while it was 3.8 percent in other advanced capitalist countries. The sharp differential in growth rates was manifested in the rapid deterioration of the U.S. balance of trade position as the U.S. lost more and more of both its overseas and domestic markets. Foreigners came to produce quality industrial goods cheaper than the U.S. was able to do.

Heavy military spending in capitalist economies is thus inherently self-contradic-tory. It was adopted during World War II as a mechanism to solve the economic crisis of advanced capitalism in the United States, but eventually led to a further eco-nomic crisis resolvable only by the decrease in military spending and the transforma-tion of the military industrial complex into a "social-industrial complex." Another aspect of this contradiction is manifested in the changing international role of the United States. In order to secure and maintain its number one position in the world in the period from 1943 to the 1970s the United States had to spend enormous sums on its military establishment. But, as we have seen, the costs of maintaining the dom-inant position in the world is gradually to lose the economic base for being able to maintain it. This is the irony of world hegemony. The position of world leaders is inherently contradictory. No nation can indefinitely maintain leadership. Not even the United States of America.

Contradictions of Contemporary Capitalism

Because of the tendency for prices to rise and costs to decline in monopoly capitalist society a serious contradiction arises. Monopoly capitalism has a strong tendency to economic stagnation of the kind that occurred in the 1930s because of its inherent in-ability to find adequate outlets for the economic surplus it generates. Although such factors as the railway and automobile booms and the sales effort have played a vital role, the most important factor in preventing the realization of the tendency for stag-nation to set in in the period from 1940 to the mid-1960s was government military spending. It was only the military spending associated with World War II and the Cold War that brought the United States out of the Great Depression and only this military spending that prevented its return. In order for the high levels of military spending to be acceptable to the majority of American people anticommunist hysteria and patriotic sentiments had to be inculcated in the masses of the American people. Only very recently has government social expenditure come to replace military ex-penditures as the prime means of preserving economic prosperity. Government spending has continued to grow as a percentage of the GNP as the only way to avoid economic stagnation, but the composition of this spending has changed as the needs of the corporations for increasing productivity and reducing their wage bill are com-ing to triumph over the nonproductive need for military hardware.

By making these changes, members of the ruling class hope to patch up the sys-tem once again. Increasingly, they are attempting to build economic alliances with the Western European countries and with Japan in order to get these countries to help to share the costs of the military and to coordinate their economic policies. They are attempting to put the blame for the current economic crisis on the oil-producing nations, or on the environmentalists, or on any other scapegoat they can find. In their efforts to save the system, they may make some real concessions to the working class, such as instituting a system of socialized medicine or improving welfare state measures to the level currently provided in Scandinavia and Northwestern Europe. As long as the basic industries in the economy are organized around the profit system, however, there are limits to what can be done. Somehow the profits must be paid out of the wealth created by the workers. Only by converting to a socialist economic system will it be possible to design a system that is truly oriented towards meeting human needs.

Summary

The capitalist economy in the United States relies on the market to make basic decisions. This system provided for fairly rapid economic growth, at the expense of very low wages paid to workers, during the early stages of capitalist development. As the market system develops, its own inherent contradictions tend to undermine it. Small producers are forced out of business, as production becomes dominated by a small number of monopolistic corporations. Economic crisis sets in as the concentration of wealth in the hands of capitalist corporations creates an insufficiency of demand for the products of those corporations.

The economic contradictions inherent in monopoly capitalism have made it necessary for the state to assume major responsibility for regulating and stimulating the economy. The upper-class-controlled banks and corporations retain effective control of state economic policy, and use it to stimulate demand through government spending while minimally ameliorating the worst human consequences of the system through welfare programs. The state also supports a large number of middle-class individuals who provide a political buffer between the upper and working classes.

While these state policies have prevented a repetition of the major economic crisis of the 1930s, they have created new problems, such as inflation and high taxes, both of which are borne primarily by working people. The United States has recently gone through a period of cutting the share of its income going to the military, as it became too much of a burden to police the entire world capitalist system. As the United States loses its favored position in the world economic system, the contradictions inherent in monopoly capitalism can be expected to continue to develop.

Review Questions

1. What are the different ways in which economic decisions can be made?
2. What are some of the defects of the market as a method of making economic decisions?

3. What are the three different ways in which the corporate economy is controlled?

4. What mechanisms are used to fix prices in the American economy?

5. Under monopoly capitalism, do profits tend to rise, fall, or remain constant over long periods of time?

6. Do monopoly capitalist firms make greater or lesser profits than competitive capitalist firms?

7. What are the ways in which the surplus wealth produced by monopoly capitalism can be consumed?

8. Why is it difficult for consumers in a monopoly capitalist economy to consume as much as the economy is capable of producing?

9. Why has advertising grown as a percentage of the Gross National Product in the United States?

10. How much of the American Gross National Product is spent by government today?

11. Why are military spending and spending on highways both highly desirable from the point of view of monopoly corporations?

12. How do wage rates and labor negotiations tend to differ under monopoly capitalism from the way they were under competitive capitalism?

13. Why do budget deficits and inflation continue, despite continual pledges from politicians to end them?

14. How has the role of military spending in the American economy changed in the last decade?

Suggestions for Further Study

1. Choose one of the large corporations included in *Fortune* magazine's list of the top 500 corporations. Investigate this corporation, using standard reference works such as Standard and Poors' and Moody's guides to corporations, copies of the annual report of the corporation, or reports in business magazines. Identify the major stockholders and directors, and see if you can find out their wealth and income. Determine how much profit the company made, and if possible find out average wages paid to its workers and prices charged consumers. Determine its linkages to other corporations, and its investments abroad in either developed or Third World nations. Make a list of the brand names used by the corporation in marketing its products.

2. Investigate a major bank in your area by obtaining a copy of its annual report and any other information you can get. Determine who the major stockholders are,

and what other significant business interests they have. Find out where its moneys are invested and to whose benefit.

3. Find a newspaper or mail-order catalog that is at least twenty years old. Note the prices advertised for various products and compare them with prices being advertised today.

4. Make a list of twenty products you or your family own. Try to estimate how much this product is worth to you by using the following criteria: how much would someone have to pay you to obtain your agreement not to use this product for one year? How does the value of the product to you correspond to its market value? How does it correspond to what you would estimate to be the actual cost of producing the article?

5. Purchase a mass circulation magazine, and clip out advertisements for consumer products. What implicit promises are made in the advertising which are not actually offered by the product? How many advertisements can you find that suggest that the owner of a specific product is likely to be surrounded by beautiful women or handsome men? How do advertisements in men's and women's magazines differ? How about magazines aimed at businessmen? Television advertising aimed at children?

Selected Readings

Baran, Paul. *The Political Economy of Growth.* New York: Monthly Review, 1957.

Baran, Paul, and Sweezy, Paul. *Monopoly Capital.* New York: Monthly Review, 1966.

Dobb, Maurice. *Political Economy and Capitalism.* New York: International, 1945.

Eaton, John. *Political Economy.* New York: International, 1963.

Edwards, Richard, et al. *The Capitalist System.* Englewood Cliffs, N.J.: Prentice-Hall, 1972.

Finch, Robert, and Oppenheimer, Mary. "Who Rules the Corporations?" *Socialist Revolution* 1:4,5,6 (July–December 1970).

Gold, David; Y. H. Lo, Clarence; and Wright, Erik Olin. "Recent Developments in Marxist Theories of the Capitalist State." *Monthly Review* 27:5,6 (October–November 1975).

Gordon, David M. (ed.). *Problems in Political Economy: An Urban Perspective.* Lexington, Mass.: Heath, 1971.

Green, Mark J. *The Monopoly Makers.* New York: Grossman, 1973.

Horowitz, David (ed.). *Marx and Modern Economics.* New York: Monthly Review, 1968.

Kidron, Michael. *Western Capitalism Since the War.* Baltimore: Pelican, 1970.

Lenin, V. I. *Imperialism: The Highest Stage of Capitalism,* in *Selected Works, 3 vols.* New York: International, 1967 (1917).

Leontiev, A. *Political Economy.* San Francisco: Proletarian, n.d.

Luxemburg, Rosa. *The Accumulation of Capital.* New York: Monthly Review, 1944 (1913).

Mandel, Ernest. *Late Capitalism.* New York: Humanities, 1975.

———. *Marxist Economic Theory.* New York: Monthly Review, 1969.

Marx, Karl. *Capital: A Critical Analysis of Capitalist Production.* Moscow: Foreign Languages, n.d. (1867).

———. *Capital: The Process of Capitalist Production as a Whole,* Vol. III. Moscow: Foreign Languages, 1962 (1894).

Mattick, Paul. *Marx and Keynes: The Limits of the Mixed Economy.* Boston: Sargent, 1969.

Menshikov, S. *Millionaires and Managers.* Moscow: Progress, 1969.

Mermelstein, David (ed.). *The Economic Crisis Reader.* New York: Vintage, 1975.

O'Connor, James. *The Corporation and the State.* New York: Harper & Row, 1974.

———. *The Fiscal Crisis of the State.* New York: St. Martin's, 1973.

———. "Question: Who Rules the Corporation, Answer: The Ruling Class." *Socialist Revolution* 7 (Jan.–Feb. 1971).

Perlo, Victor. *The Unstable Economy.* New York: International, 1973.

Robinson, Joan. *Essays in Economic Growth.* New York: St. Martin's, 1962.

———. *An Introduction to the Theory of Employment.* New York: St. Martin's, 1960.

Sweezy, Paul, and Magdoff, Harry. *The Dynamics of U.S. Capitalism.* New York: Monthly Review, 1972.

Sweezy, Paul. *Modern Capitalism and Other Essays.* New York: Monthly Review, 1972.

———. *The Present as History.* New York: Monthly Review, 1953.

———. *The Theory of Capitalist Development.* New York: Monthly Review, 1968.

Sweezy, Paul, and Magdoff, Harry. *The Dynamics of U.S. Capitalism.* New York: Monthly Review, 1972.

Szymanski, Albert. "Military Spending and Economic Stagnation." *American Journal of Sociology* 79:1 (July 1973).

Veblen, Thorstein. *The Theory of Business Enterprise.* New York: Scribner, 1902.

Wright, Erik. "Alternative Perspectives in the Marxist Theory of Accumulation and Crisis." *Insurgent Sociologist* 6:1 (Fall 1975).

Zeitlin, Maurice (ed.). *American Society, Inc.* Chicago: McNally, 1977.

Chapter 5

Class
in American
Society

Because of the central role of classes in modern societies, all sociological paradigms must somehow deal with class differences. The division of societies into classes is a complex phenomenon, and each paradigm usually emphasizes those aspects of it which best fit into its overall perspective on society. Conservatives tend to see class inequality as good. They feel that classes reflect natural differences in human abilities and values, and that for society to function well it is necessary for everyone to remain in their proper place in society. They tend to identify upper-class values as good and lower-class values as deviant or dysfunctional for society.

Liberal sociologists most frequently take classes for granted. They prefer to focus on other things, usually on more limited phenomena such as suicide rates, mental illness, family problems, political attitudes, population trends, work attitudes, or whatever. In studying these phenomena, they find that they can explain many of the differences they observe by comparing people from different social classes. They are less likely to raise the question of where classes come from, or how the class system itself can be explained. When they do address this question, they often fall back on the conservative argument that classes are necessary to motivate people to perform well for society.

Radical sociologists have a much more fundamental interest in class. As socialists, their goal is to help end the division of society into classes. As Marxist scholars, they use the concept of class to draw the links between the economic structure of society and the social, political, and ideological superstructure. Class is a central concept in the radical sociological paradigm, not merely a variable that can be used in research studies when it is convenient.

ECONOMIC CLASS AND SOCIAL CLASS

In this book, we will present a systematic conceptualization of class which is based on Marx, as well as on the work of other authors within the radical tradition who have written on the question. We will begin by drawing a distinction between *economic class* and *social class*. Economic class and social class are closely related. In fact, a central tenet of Marxism is that economic class determines social class. But it is useful to distinguish the two for analytic purposes.

By "economic class" we refer to a set of individuals who have the same relationship to the means of production. We have seen that the economic classes that exist in a society depend on the productive system within which the classes exist. The dominant class is composed of those individuals who own or control the means of production. The subordinate class is composed of those individuals who do the actual production but who do not own or control the means of production. In capitalist societies, the two basic economic classes are the capitalists and the workers. The capitalists own the factories, while the workers own nothing but their own labor power which they must sell to the capitalists. In feudal or peasant societies, the two classes are the landlords and the peasants or serfs, with one class owning or controlling the land and the other being forced to work for them in order to live.

In these basic cases, it is relatively simple to define economic classes. There are, however, many instances when more subtle distinctions must be made. For example, there are some individuals who own a small plot of land or a small workshop. These individuals need not sell their labor power to anyone else, but neither can they afford to hire anyone else to work for them. These individuals constitute a middle class, intermediate between the owning class (people who can live without working, through rent, dividends, interest, or other unearned income) and the working class. There are other individuals, such as managers in large corporations, who have tremendous control over productive wealth, but *own* relatively little of it. Ownership is the only complete form of control, since only when someone owns something can he or she give it to his or her children, or sell it for money, or dispose of it completely at will. But the control that is exercised by a manager in a large corporation, or by a bureaucrat in a state capitalist system, is also important and is part of their relationship to the means of production. *Control of the means of production is the key variable that determines economic class.* Control means the power to assign the means of production to a chosen use, to put them into operation, and to dispose of their products.

By "social class" we mean a large set of freely intermarrying families who share a common lifestyle and a common status or prestige ranking in the society based on a

Differences among social classes are reflected in the lifestyles characteristic of different neighborhoods.

similar economic class position. Members of a social class tend to have a great many things in common. They tend to have the same general level of education, to live in the same sort of neighborhood, to have about the same income level, to have jobs with similar status and economic rewards, to use the same speech patterns, to wear similar styles of clothing, and in many ways to have similar values, attitudes, and perspectives on life. It is important to note that social classes are composed of families. Thus, children are raised in an environment that is largely determined by their social class, and learn the attitudes and behavior patterns appropriate for that class. Women who are housewives belong to the social class of their husbands, although their economic position is that of housewife (a position left over from preindustrial societies where the basic division of labor was by sex).

Economic class and social class are very closely linked. Liberal sociologists tend to overlook this fact, and to focus on social class while paying less attention to economic classes. Max Weber, the most prominent liberal sociologist who wrote on this question, drew a distinction between "class" (similar to our concept of economic class) and "status" (similar to our concept of social class). He stressed the fact that these were not always identical, focusing, for example, on groups that had had high status in the past, but whose class position was being undermined by social change. Weber also argued that political power, or organized "party" affiliations, were conceptually separate from class or status. While it is possible to keep these three variables distinct *conceptually*, the most important fact *empirically* is that they are closely interrelated.

In fact, social class and economic class are so closely related that it is common both in colloquial and sociological English to use the term "class" to refer to both of them. The term "class," used in this unmodified sense, refers to a social class whose family heads belong to the same economic class. The central variable that can best be used as an index of class position is *occupation of the head of the household.* In contemporary American society, the occupation of the head of the household determines both his or her relationship to the means of production *and* the income and status level of his or her family.

CLASS AND OCCUPATION

Some occupations involve only a minimal degree of control over working conditions. These working-class occupations tend not to involve skills that take a long time to learn, or to require extensive formal education. Workers in these occupations are fairly easily replaceable, in the sense that a new worker with no special training can learn the job in a short time. Holders of these jobs, regardless of whether they work in factories, offices, or service establishments, are part of the *working class.* The only way they can raise their incomes above the bare subsistence level is to organize collectively, since as individuals they can easily be replaced.

Other occupations involve control of the means of production. The most precise example is that of an individual who owns a large enterprise, controls the daily operations of the enterprise personally, directs the labor of the employees, and enjoys the

Occupation is a major index of economic class. Within one company there are both professionals and workers.

ability to spend the profits earned by the enterprise. Such an individual is part of the *capitalist class*, although his or her social position within the class depends on the size of the business. Other occupations, such as managers and directors of large corporations, are essentially involved with control of production even though they do not involve formal ownership. Such occupations tend to command very high salaries and prerogatives, such that the individuals who hold them can integrate themselves and their families into the capitalist class.

There are still other occupations which are in the middle between those that have little or no control of the means of production and those that have great control. These include small businessmen who control only a small amount of productive wealth. They also include individuals who have advanced educational credentials or technical skills which enable them to exercise considerable autonomy in their work. Such individuals are not so easily replaceable. Often, the nature of their work is such that they cannot be closely supervised and in fact they often supervise the work of others. These individuals must work for a living, but they are often able to demand pay or benefits that enable them to sustain a higher standard of living than that of the working class. Thus, they constitute a "middle class" intermediate between the capitalists and the working class. These middle-class individuals often play a key role in political and social conflicts, since they can ally themselves either with the workers or with the capitalists, depending on the circumstances of the particular situation.

Changes in the Occupational Structure

We can get an overall picture of the relative numbers of people in each economic class by looking at occupational statistics gathered by the federal government. Table 5-1 shows the percentage of the economically active people who fell into each of several occupational categories in various years. It shows that certain categories have increased, while others have decreased. Farm workers have declined to a very small segment of the labor force. Managers, officials, and proprietors have also declined significantly. Manual workers have remained constant as a percentage of the working population, while service workers, clerical and sales workers, and professionals have increased. These changes reflect technological and organizational changes in the society, such as the decline of small business, the mechanization of agriculture, and the growth of the service sector of the economy. Such changes have a tremendous effect on people's lives, since people must move from one position to another, or children must go into different occupational categories than their parents, in order to make these changes possible.

There is not always an obvious link between occupational categories and social classes. In general, we can say that middle- and lower-level managers, officials, and proprietors are primarily middle class. Professionals are mostly middle class, although recent economic trends have emphasized their vulnerability to the same economic conditions that affect working-class people. Because of increased unemployment, professionals are losing much of their control over their working conditions. Thus, the

TABLE 5-1.   Major Occupational Groups in the Civilian Labor Force, 1900–1977

Year	OCCUPATIONAL GROUPS AS % OF LABOR FORCE					
	Professional and Technical	Managers, Officials and Proprietors	Clerical and Sales	Craftsmen and Foremen	Manual and Service	Farm
1977 (April)	15.3	10.5	24.5	13.1	33.7	3.0
1970	14.6	8.3	25.0	13.8	35.2	3.1
1960	11.4	8.5	22.3	14.3	37.1	6.3
1950	8.6	8.7	19.3	14.2	37.4	11.8
1940	7.5	7.3	16.3	12.0	39.5	17.4
1930	6.8	7.4	15.2	12.8	36.6	21.2
1920	5.4	6.6	12.9	13.0	35.1	27.0
1910	4.7	6.6	10.0	11.6	36.2	30.9
1900	4.3	5.8	7.5	10.6	34.3	37.5

(Source: U.S. Bureau of the Census, *Historical Statistics* and *Statistical Abstract of the United States, 1977*. Figures for 1977 are not strictly comparable with prior years because of reclassification of census occupational categories.)

lines between economic classes are somewhat fluid, responding to economic trends. It is also true that not all economic differences result in the formation of distinct social classes.

In some societies, landlords and capitalists form two distinct social classes, with distinct lifestyles, political beliefs, and patterns of social interaction. Given the fluidity of wealth in the United States, however, the same families may invest either in land or in industrial capital. Thus, large landlords are part of the social upper class, while smaller ones are part of the social middle class. Similarly, in some societies, those individuals who own industrial capital may form a distinct group separate from those who own financial capital. Major political and social conflicts may emerge between these two groups. In the United States, however, the same families tend to be involved in both the financial and the industrial spheres. The Rockefellers, for example, traditionally owned major interests in both the Standard Oil Companies and the Chase Manhattan Bank. Thus, it does not seem to be critical whether banks or industrial corporations control the economy. Both are under the control of the same social upper class.

CLASS DIVISIONS AND CLASS CONSCIOUSNESS

Classes vary in the extent to which they are organized as social groups. The upper class in most societies tends to be the best organized, with exclusive clubs, schools, and social affairs. They tend to have a high degree of *class consciousness*, that is to say, of understanding of their place in society and of their interests as a class in relation to other classes. They also have considerable capacity to act politically to express their class interests. Other classes, such as the working class in our society, have a much lower level of class consciousness. Although working-class people are certainly aware of differences in wealth and power, they do not often have a clear understanding of the economic basis of their own class or of how they are exploited by the capitalist class. Nor are they effectively organized in a political party that expresses their class interests. In other societies, such as those of Western Europe, the working class is much more class conscious and expresses its political interests through labor, socialist, or Communist parties that are explicitly organized along class lines. Development of class consciousness is not an automatic process, but one which usually requires considerable educational effort by groups of political organizers.

The lines between social classes may be relatively sharp in some societies. In others, they may be blurred. There are various factors that account for this. Probably the most important factor is the nature of the economy. In a simple traditional economy, there tends to be relatively few occupations and the gap between the peasantry, who make up the vast majority, and the small aristocracy is great. The middle-class groups are small. A complex industrial capitalist economy has much more occupational diversity, and a larger middle class. Class divisions are somewhat blurred in a large city with a diverse economic base, while they are sharper in a community dominated by a single industry such as mining or steel or auto production.

Another factor that influences the class system is *social mobility*. This refers to the extent to which individuals can move from one class to another. Generally speaking, mobility is high during periods of rapid economic change. Thus, while the United States was making the transition from an agrarian to an industrial economy, rates of mobility were high. When the economy becomes more stable, the rates tend to decline. Americans have been accustomed to relatively high rates of mobility, due to rapid economic development and expansion and to the immigration of foreign ethnic groups into the lower levels of society. As the mobility rate lessens, we can expect the lines between social classes to become sharper.

The class system is dynamic. It changes in response to changes in the economy. Some classes become more important, others become less so. For example, in 1940 self-employed persons (mostly middle class) constituted 22 percent of the economically active population in the United States. By 1976 this declined to 8 percent. This change is due to the growth of large corporations, which force small enterprises out of business. Those self-employed persons who remain are mostly marginal farmers or shopkeepers who are barely able to survive against the competition of the more efficient and better-connected giant corporations. In some cases, supposedly self-employed people are really under the control of large corporations. This includes franchise holders who "own" a gas station or fast-food restraurant. Their costs, prices, and way of doing business are effectively controlled by the larger corporation, which profits handsomely from their labor. Socially, most self-employed persons are integrated into the working or middle classes. They are often heavily in debt to banks, and work long hours for the relatively meager incomes they are able to extract from their businesses.

On the other hand, a few people recorded in the statistics as "employees" are actually highly paid managers of large corporations who are *de facto* capitalists because of the control they exercise over the means of production. Overall, we can conclude that at least 75 percent of the United States population is working class. This working class produces most of what is consumed in society. Because they do not own the means of production, they must sell their labor time to those that do—to the capitalists—or they must find a job working for some agency of the government that is effectively in the control of the capitalist class. The nature of the capitalist economic system requires that the vast majority of these workers be paid less than the value of what they produce. Unless this were the case, the capitalist system would not function since there would be no profit. No owner would hire a worker unless he or she anticipated that the worker's pay would be less than the value of the added output produced by the new worker.

Capitalism creates divisions within the working class. For example, a group of unemployed or underemployed individuals, living on welfare or other minimal sources of income, exists. This makes the workers who do have jobs feel that they have some vested interest in the system, because they are better off than the very poor. A strata of highly skilled and well-paid individuals whose income and working conditions are better than those of the mainstream of the working class also exists. These individuals often feel that they have a vested interest in the system. The existence of such people is important also because it gives some possibility of mobility to working-class people. While it is virtually impossible for ordinary working-class people to become capitalists, it is possible for some of them to rise into the middle class or at least the skilled trades. Thus, the existence and growth of a middle class and skilled trades is useful for the capitalist system as a whole.

Social class divisions are more subtle and complex than economic class divisions. Important changes are also taking place in these social class divisions. These details can best be understood by analyzing the conditions of each social class separately.

THE WORKING CLASS

The working class of modern capitalist society is composed of very diverse segments. Its main components are industrial workers (workers who run machines, nonfarm laborers, and craftsmen and foremen), service workers (those that work in restaurants, laundries, hotels, and the like), farm workers (those who labor for someone else on the land), and clerical and sales workers (those who do the menial, everyday, routine work in offices, supermarkets, and retail stores). Some consider many or most employed professional and technical wokers, such as most teachers, engineers, scientists, airline pilots, social workers, technicians, and the like to be part of the working class. If that is so, these workers constitute a distinct stratum within the working class since their degree of control over the means of production, and of their own and others' labor power, is significantly greater than that of other members of the working class. We will discuss this group more fully when we discuss the middle class, but recognize that in many ways they share something in common with the working class as well. They must sell their labor power in order to survive.

Men as Heads of Households

Table 5-1 provided data on the overall occupational distribution in the United States, including both men and women. For many purposes, however, it is more significant to look only at the occupation of the head of the household. We have noted that the occupation of the head of the household tends to determine the social class position of the entire family. Since in our contemporary society men are most frequently the heads of families, it is instructive to look at the distribution of men in various occupations. This is presented in Table 5-2 (comparable data for women are in Chapter 12).

Many of the trends are the same when we look at trends in men's occupations as when we look at the total workforce. Farm labor decreased from over 40 percent of the male workforce in 1900 to less than 8 percent in 1976. The professional and managerial classes have increased. The main difference is the smaller increase in the clerical and sales group and the greater increase in the craftsmen and foremen category. Some writers have interpreted census occupational statistics as showing an increase in the "middle class" over the "working class." They do so by considering all white-

TABLE 5-2.   Male Occupational Structure in the United States, 1900–1977

	OCCUPATIONAL GROUPS AS % OF MALE LABOR FORCE					
Year	Professional and Technical	Managers, Officials and Proprietors	Clerical and Sales	Craftsmen and Foremen	Manual and Service	Farm
1977	14.8	13.6	12.6	20.9	33.9	4.3
1960	10.9	13.6	13.0	19.0	34.0	9.6
1930	4.8	8.8	11.6	16.2	33.8	24.8
1900	3.4	6.8	7.4	12.6	28.2	41.7

(Source: U.S. Bureau of the Census, *Historical Statistics* and *Statistical Abstract of the United States, 1977.* Figures for 1977 are not strictly comparable with prior years because of reclassification of census occupational categories.)

collar workers, including those in clerical and sales work, as "middle class." By including women who work as secretaries and sales clerks in the "middle class," they greatly exaggerate the size of this group. Actually, women who work in these jobs do not have sufficient control over their own labor, or over the labor of others, or over their own working conditions, to be considered anything but working class. Many of them are married to men with blue-collar jobs. When we look at the male occupational distribution, as an index of the overall position of American families, we see that the manual working class strictly defined (craftsmen and manual workers) remains a majority of the work force. Of course, this strict definition is much too restrictive. While there is no clear, formal line between working-class and middle-class jobs, it is clear that most farm workers and clerical and sales workers should be considered in the working class. So should many workers whose jobs are classified in the professional and technical category. Looking separately at male occupations, it is clear that approximately three quarters of the families in America are working class, with close to one quarter middle-class (and less than 1 percent upper-class).

Most of the women in the labor force, including most clerical and sales workers, come from manual working-class (industrial plus service) families (as defined by the occupation of the husband or father). These women in earlier years tended to be housewives. As these manual working-class women leave the home for the salesroom and office and leave behind them the isolation and parochialism associated with housework to mix with more people like themselves, as well as go into direct and sustained contact with representatives of the capitalist class, their manual working-class attitudes and values are reinforced. The on-the-job experiences of manual working-class women thus comes to reinforce the experience of manual working-class men. The members of the family now have much more in common than they did when only the husband left the home and the wife stayed home with the children. Thus, in no sense can the rapid growth in the sales and clerical occupations, due to the corporation's changing labor force needs, be considered to be strengthening a clerical and sales *class* at the expense of the manual working class. Manual working-class women are employed mostly in stores that cater primarily to manual working-class people or in lower-level jobs in offices that approximate the conditions of industrial labor. In both types of occupations the control over one's work and the subjugation to the authority of one's boss is at best only equal to that of a manual worker. Most male clerical and sales workers, it should be noted, have higher paying, higher status, and often supervisory jobs.

Occupational Differences in the Working Class

Industrial work tends to generate solidarity among workers as well as produce in them an understanding of the production process that includes a realization of the superfluousness of capitalists. Large numbers of these workers are put together into common conditions of labor, labor in which there is little emotional involvement, and are generally treated like adjuncts to the machines they tend. It is clear to such workers that they are different from their bosses both in power and knowledge of the production process. Their common oppression and work experience, facilitated by structured opportunities to talk among themselves, results in the development of a common consciousness of class and an increasing willingness to struggle together to increase their control over their lives.

Male clerical and sales workers often labor under very different conditions. Although the conditions of their labor are coming increasingly to resemble those of manual workers, they tend to maintain strong ties to the capitalist class and relative privileges, especially in status (these people are "employees" not "workers" and they receive a "salary" not a "wage"). They tend to imitate upper-class values, dress, morals, and lifestyles. Such workers tend to be more isolated from one another on the job, either socially, by the presence of managerial personnel or physically, by the structure of their work. Unlike production workers they tend not to have an understanding of the productive process since they are physically isolated from it. Thus they do not tend to feel that capitalists are superfluous as much as do industrial workers.

Service and farm work tends to be very much like industrial labor in terms of the lack of control over the production process, the subjugation to authority, and the lack of identification with the boss and his values. In fact, there is a high rate of transfer from all of these three occupational categories to the others. It is much easier to move from farm work to working in a restaurant, to tending a machine in a factory, than it is to move from either of these to the salesroom or office. Thus, we are justified in grouping these three very similar types of occupations as manual working class since all three work predominately with their hands.

Causes of False Consciousness Among Workers

In order to perpetuate the class system, it has been necessary to instill in the American working class a false consciousness of its interests and of the nature of the social forces acting on it. The members of this class have been conditioned to think that they are unable to run their own lives, that they need people to supervise them, and that those who hire them deserve all kinds of power and privilege, while they themselves are lucky to get a living wage. It had been necessary to inculcate the work ethic into the members of this class so that they would internalize the motivation to work for economic incentives beyond subsistence. Wherever a working class has been created the basic desire of people was to work only as long and as hard as was necessary to get the customary minimum of material satisfaction. Workers had to be broken to industrial discipline. Starvation, religion, the penal system, and the poorhouse were used to inculcate the work ethic.

Among the factors that account for the acceptance by the U.S. working class of upper-class values are the brainwashing effect of the mass media, especially of television and education; the co-option of the trade unions into the political and economic apparatus of societal control; the periodic terror directed against radicals in the working class, and the consequent elimination of radical leadership and the radical tradition of this class; the great prosperity of the last generation, together with the overwhelming propaganda in the media for the importance of material goods as a source of happiness; and the gratitude to the New Deal and to "America" for providing the working class with what they never had during the Great Depression or in the "old country."

Submissiveness and feelings of inadequacy are inculcated into manual workers in order to "keep them in their place" and performing the jobs the system needs done without significant opposition. Manual workers are taught in school, brainwashed in the military service and by the media, and constantly told on the job that they must respect experts, that the capitalists own and control industry because of their superior knowledge, hard work, or abilities, that technicians and scientists have qualitatively different abilities that must be deferred to, that they themselves are in their lowly positions because they are lazy, didn't have the proper schooling, aren't bright or ambitious enough, etc. Without these feelings of inadequacy, so carefully built up in working people by the institutions controlled by the upper class, the system could not function, since working people would refuse to put up with the subhuman way they are treated. Even professional workers are subjected to this brainwashing. Although initiative and autonomy are encourageed in them, these traits are delimited to very narrow areas by the ideology of professionalism so carefully developed in professional workers. It is defined as inappropriate for professional workers to question the goals of the projects they work on, or to decide for themselves what they will participate in. Professional workers come to feel just as inadequate in areas outside of their "expertise" as anyone else—physics teachers, for example, who can't fix cars or biologists who can't cure an infection.

It might be expected that as a new generation of workers grows up—without a memory of the hard times of the old country or the Great Depression, and hence who feel no particular debt to the system; who have never known serious material deprivation, and hence who are not so impressed by the affluence the system is supposed to bring; who have had much more education, and hence in however distorted fashion, more exposure to abstract and historical ideas than their parents; who tend to read or listen to underground media, who do not take the union bureaucrats seriously (they do not remember the founding of the CIO in the 1930s); and who have little instinctual fear of "radicals" because they never experienced the McCarthyite hysteria—they will become increasingly class conscious. This class is very likely to develop into a full-fledged class-conscious social class clearly distinct from the upper and middle classes.

The Lumpenproletariat

Below the working class is a group that is the most victimized and oppressed element in society. This group, which can be called the *lumpenproletariat* in classical Marxist terms, consists of people who are not regularly employed and who do not own any form of wealth that produces income. There are many reasons why an individual may fall into this class: physical or mental disability, lack of ability to support minor children, rejection of societal values, racial or ethnic discrimination, or a propensity towards illegal activities. In this group must be included beggars, street prostitutes and pimps, welfare recipients, professional illegal gamblers, professional thieves, muggers, drug dealers, con artists, hustlers of all kinds, and "hippies" who choose to join the lumpenproletariat by voluntarily rejecting productive labor and attempting to live off the system.

The lumpenproletariat is not exploited by the capitalist class in the way that workers are, because they are not regularly employed. They do play a function for the system, however, to the extent that they are a reserve labor force that can be sometimes called upon to do seasonal work or to work as strikebreakers or thugs. They also serve as a scapegoat, to the extent that workers can be persuaded that it is this group that is causing taxes to rise. Under most conditions, because of its lack of a systematic relation to the means of production and the highly diverse nature, the lumpenproletariat does not develop much class consciousness or engage in unified class behavior. An exception may be when members of a racial or ethnic group are forced into this class by discrimination; in this case they may develop militant antidiscriminatory or nationalist movements, but even here their political participation is likely to be erratic and undisciplined.

THE MIDDLE CLASSES

Marxist economic theory shows that there are basic tendencies within capitalist economies which encourage capitalist societies to polarize into two classes. As the size of monopoly corporations grows and grows, wealth and power tend to become more concentrated. Independent businessmen are forced out of business, family farmers are pushed off the land, independent professionals are forced to work for large bureaucracies which undermine their autonomy, skilled artisans find that their products are no longer marketable. People with college degrees find that they cannot find jobs that are "appropriate" for their educational level. The middle class is in a precarious position, always in danger of losing the privileges and prerogatives it has been able to obtain in the past. Yet, the middle class remains very important in American culture and politics. What is the explanation for the existence of a middle class? What can we expect about its future?

Liberal and conservative sociologists tend to emphasize the values held by middle-class people, their personal or business skills, and their educational credentials. Certainly, these factors are important, more so for middle-class people than for members of other social classes. Because they lack great quantities of wealth, the basic way middle-class people can sustain their position is through their skills or credentials. And the best way they can pass their position on to their children is to see that they obtain similar abilities through schooling or other means of socialization. But the personal traits of middle .class people cannot explain their economic base in our society. This has been discovered by many middle-class people in recent years who have worked hard to obtain advanced degrees, have improved their interpersonal skills, cut their hair short and pressed their suits, and nonetheless ended up working as taxidrivers. While personal skills are important to the success of any individual middle-class person, the success of the middle class as a class depends on economic conditions.

The American middle class, whether employed or self-employed, is a single social class. Members of the middle class live in middle-class neighborhoods, send their children to middle-class schools, have middle-class speech habits, enjoy middle-class recreational patterns and reading habits, etc. They think of themselves as middle class, and are so considered by others. Economically, however, middle-class people have a variety of relationships to the means of production. In fact it can be said that there are middle classes rather than a single middle class (in terms of economic class).

Economic Bases of the Middle Class

Some middle-class people are self-employed. They own the tools necessary for their own labor, but do not own enough wealth to enable them to live off of the labor of others. This group is part of a competitive economy. Their success depends on how hard and how effectively they work. Often, they tend towards individualist ideas since their experience leads them to believe that success or failure is a matter of individual merit. These self-employed people are often placed in a precarious position by competition from large corporations which have resources that are vastly superior to theirs. Every year more small businesses fail than are started. As a consequence of this insecurity, some small-business people become quite conservative, hoping to turn back the course of history to a period when small business was more prosperous. They often find it difficult to blame their condition on big business, since they identify with businessmen as a group, so they may turn their hostilities towards some other group, such as liberal intellectuals or members of some racial or ethnic minority. Because of the decline of small business, the traditional self-employed middle class is of relatively little importance in the United States today. The possibility of self-employment does, however, play a safety-valve role, giving many workers a goal they believe may eventually enable them to escape from dull and oppressive jobs.

While small-business people are declining, however, other sectors of the middle classes are increasing. One of these is the group of middle and lower managers. Managers are people whose responsibility is to organize and direct the work of others. As corporations grow, there is a need for more managers to staff the enlarged chain of command. The top managers have considerable power and very large incomes and tend to become integrated with the owning class. Beneath them, however, is a large group of second- and third-level managers. These individuals are in an intermediate position; they have greater control over their conditions than do the workers, but considerably less than the top management. Success in their work, however, generally requires that they identify with the interests of top management. They are part of a hierarchy, and have the possibility of rising within that hierarchy if they are successful in helping the corporation to meet its profit goals. Managers tend to identify closely with the goals and ideologies of the ruling class, even though in many cases they have little real autonomy or ability to share in the fruits of the capitalist enterprise.

Another sector of the middle classes that is increasing in size is the professional and technical class. Most members of this economic class share with workers the necessity of selling their labor in order to obtain an income. But they have important skills, which enable them to demand higher pay and better working conditions than those of manual, clerical, or sales workers. The nature of their work, also, typically requires that they be given a certain degree of autonomy, and that they have real control over the work of others (secretaries, assistants, etc.). There is as yet no way in which the work of a college teacher or physician can be standardized, routinized, and controlled to the extent that the work of a typist or assembly-line worker can be. Most of these professional and technical workers perform labor that is socially necessary—indeed, they are often motivated to a considerable extent by a desire to be of service to humanity. In this sense their work differs from that of many managers, advertising workers, and sales people, whose work is largely created by the profit motive in capitalist society but could be dispensed with in a socialist society.

Thus, the middle classes contain diverse economic groups. For this reason, it is difficult to make a simple statement about the social, economic, or political role of the middle class. We said earlier that there is a fundamental tendency for the independent middle class to decline as capitalist societies polarize into two classes. This is true, but there are also countertendencies at work that make for an increase in the size of the employed middle class. One is the growth of the *nonproductive* sectors of the private economy. As monopoly capitalism develops, it becomes necessary for more and more money to be spent on sectors of the economy that do not directly produce commodities the capitalists can sell for profit. This includes many sectors of the commercial economy, such as banking and credit, retail and wholesale trade, real estate brokerage, advertising, etc. These enterprises *circulate commodities and money,* and thus keep the system working, although they do not actually produce anything. The growth of this sector, necessary to keep the economy stimulated and avoid depression, tends to increase the size of the middle class since many of the occupations in this sector require middle-class educational skills.

Another area that tends to grow under monopoly capitalism is the state-financed service sector of the economy. This includes a whole collection of organizations that are involved in *maintaining and reproducing the social system itself,* rather than in producing goods—for example, schools, hospitals, social welfare agencies, mental health institutions, and other government service agencies. These tend to grow as the state assumes the responsibility of trying to deal with needs which people have that are not otherwise met by capitalist society. Many middle-class people work in these agencies. Often, they are liberal or even leftist people, with considerable intellectual training, who are seeking some sort of career that will enable them to help other people.

Economic Pressures on the Middle Class

There is, however, a limit to the growth of both the *circulation* and the *reproduction* sectors of the economy. Both of these must be financed by wealth created by the productive sector, the sector that actually produces useful goods. The circulation sector is financed by collecting interest, mark-ups, commissions, etc., all of which create a drag on the economy if they are increased. The reproduction sector is financed primarily by taxes and secondarily by fees paid by individuals who require services. There are limits to both of these sources of revenue, and indications are that these limits may be being reached.

Thus, while there are short-term tendencies that encourage the number of middle-class jobs to grow, these have their limits. Our educational system, however, continues to expand to the point where it can supply many more people trained for middle-class roles than there are middle-class jobs. Thus, we can expect to see the salary advantages enjoyed by middle-class professionals decline in the future. (The exceptions may be those occupations such as doctors and lawyers that effectively restrict the number of people getting professional education in their field.) As the costs of maintaining government service agencies become too great, we can also expect the government to introduce cost-cutting measures that will decrease the number of positions or make the work simpler so that it can be done by workers with less education. The welfare system, for example, may be reformed so that recipients get checks in the mail without requiring the services of a social worker to inquire into their eligibility.

As much as is possible, the capitalist system will do away with the need for highly educated middle-class labor. It is more profitable to hire an unskilled or semi-skilled worker, or even a paraprofessional if necessary, than to pay for a highly educated middle-class professional. We can expect to see technology evolved in ways that will make this possible. Computer technology has already eliminated or routinized the jobs of many white-collar workers. Drugs are used to control mental patients, eliminating the need for costly therapists. Of course, this process is not always successful. The attempt to make education more efficient by replacing teachers with teaching machines was rejected by students as well as by teachers. Even in our supposedly media-dominated culture, no one seems to want to go to college by television. A computer program has been written to carry on therapeutic interviews, but no one seems satisfied with a computer terminal as a therapist. Some middle-class professions will necessarily survive, since not all human needs can be met by modern capitalist technology. However, the number of middle-class jobs will be far short of the number of people (including most of the readers of this book) who are seeking educational credentials in the hopes of obtaining one.

Technical and professional employees are forced to sell their labor power to the corporations or to the state, which, although they generally allow some autonomy in the details of job performance, direct the goals as well as the outlines of the work of this group. That is, the group is not free to select its own work goals or to determine the general ways in which their work is performed. These are dictated by the profit maximization principle of the corporations. The greater job autonomy and privileges of this group are offset by their greater aspirations and understanding of the operation of the system. As much as it is able to understand that it has the power in its hands to run the economy, this group feels its oppression in its subordination to the will of others who are motivated by profit rather than by usefulness.

The Middle Classes and Politics

Politically, the middle classes play a highly diverse, heterogeneous role. Middle-class intellectuals have often played a key role in revolutionary movements. Such key leaders as Karl Marx, V. I. Lenin, Mao Tse-tung, and Fidel Castro came from middle-class backgrounds. Because of their intellectual training, middle-class people tend to be more interested in politics and to have more clearly defined political ideas than working-class people. They are especially active in movements such as the antiwar movement, the environmental movement, and the women's movement, which seek to correct specific social injustices. Most frequently, it is professional people who are active in these liberal movements. Right-wing movements also rely on middle-class people for much of their leadership and support. Small-business people, and highly paid professionals such as lawyers and doctors, are more likely to be drawn in this direction. The diversity of politics among the middle class reflects the diversity of economic positions within the middle class.

It is not at all clear how the American middle class will respond to the financial squeeze that is being thrust upon them at the present time. One possibility is that they will turn to right-wing or neofascist movements that will promise to help protect

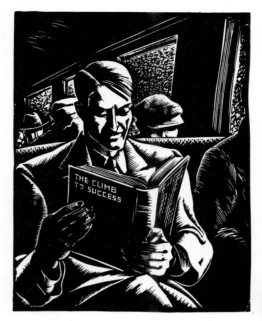 

Linocuts by artist Giacomo Patri depict his struggle as a young man to pursue a middle-class

their privileges against the claims of the working class. Another is that they will recognize that they are truly workers, despite their professional degrees, and throw their lot in with the working class. This is the only course that will enable them to preserve the most positive and humanistic elements of middle-class careers.

THE CAPITALIST CLASS

Included in the capitalist class defined economically are those individuals whose primary source of income comes from *owning* or *controlling* the means of production. This includes people who do not have to work for a living but who can live throughout their lives on income from stocks, bonds, rents, interest payments, or other sources of income that do not require work. Also included are top-level managers and state officials whose job it is to supervise the labor of others, who have the power to hire and fire workers, and who do not perform menial labor themselves. These individuals are usually able, in a capitalist society, to use their control of the means of production to pay themselves very high salaries and benefits. They function as members of the capitalist economic class.

Not included in the capitalist class are small-business people who employ only a

career. During the Depression, Patri turned to the labor movement to work for social change.

few workers at most, and who thus rely primarily on their own effort for their living. Nor would we include elderly people who live off the interest and principal of their savings during their retirement years. It is not the legal technicalities of ownership that determine economic class membership but the real relationship that an individual has to the means of production during his or her lifetime.

While in terms of economic theory any individual who lives off ownership rather than by working is part of the capitalist class, the American capitalist *social* class or upper class is more restrictive. It does not include small capitalists who employ only relatively few workers; nor does it include upwardly mobile top managers or even most self-made millionaires. Smaller capitalists are socially part of the middle class, although many "self-made men" and top managers are in the process of becoming socially integrated into the capitalist class. The social class of capitalists includes those who own large amounts of wealth and some of the top managers of major corporations. As a social class, it naturally includes the members of their families as well. This social upper class is the most class conscious of all classes. It has the most defined traditions, the highest degree of interclass interaction, and the most distinct boundaries of any social class in society. Simply being extremely wealthy or employing or controlling large numbers of workers is not enough to be fully accepted into this social class. Because of its position at the pinnacle of American society it has developed exclusivist traditions that dictate that time as well as money are necessary criteria for general acceptance by other members of this class. One must have had the proper breeding and the proper school, club, and familial ties as well as sufficient wealth. The sure sign of full upper-class membership is being included in the *Social Register*, a list of names and affiliations of those wealthy individuals considered socially acceptable by the upper class. As a rule at least one's parents and more likely one's grandparents need to have been very well off to make it into this listing. In the early 1970s there were about 110,000 men and women in the *Social Register*. This number then is the most minimal definition of the size of the upper class. Since it is very difficult for minorities, Jews, and even Catholics, as well as the eccentric rich to get listed, and because self-made millionaires cannot get listed, the real size of the upper class is considerably larger than this figure. Those listed in the *Social Register* do, however, represent the heart of the upper class in America.

This national upper class was formed at the same time as the corporations in the period between the end of the Civil War and the first decade of the twentieth century. It is made up exclusively of rich businessmen, their families, and their descendants. It is closely knit by a wide range of economic and social institutions. The economic institutions that bind it together include stockholding (it owns about half of all corporate stock outright), shared positions on boards of directors of business corporations as well as nonprofit corporations such as universities, financial houses, and corporate law firms. The last two institutions are central in smoothing the operation of upper-class-controlled corporations. The social institutions that tie this class together include a high rate of intermarriage (which after about five generations has led to a high degree of interrelation), private schools, elite colleges (including the right fraternities and clubs), exclusive city clubs, summer resorts, debutante balls, distinctive upper-class sporting activities such as fox hunting, yachting, and polo, and distinctive cultural activities such as charity balls. The upper class is national, not local in its orientation. A high degree of geographical mobility, including a great deal of seasonal migration, its pattern of boarding school attendance, multiple club memberships, and summer and winter vacationing, together with its constant traveling for business activities and involvement in the government, pretty much dissolves regional loyalties in favor of a national consciousness in this class.

Upper-class children go to special prep schools such as Groton, St. Paul's, St. Mark's, Exeter, and Andover. Further, they go to special universities. Sixty-seven percent of all Social Register listees with college degrees as of the mid 1960s have gone to only three colleges—Harvard, Princeton, and Yale. A study of 476 top executives who went to college showed that 86 percent received their undergraduate degrees from one of these three institutions. The prep schools and the elite colleges reproduce the upper class as a social class, at the same time assimilating into it children of the new rich. These educational institutions also serve to co-opt a few of the very brightest members of other classes into the upper class. This allowance for social mobility is essential for long-run social stability. Attendance at upper-class schools guarantees that the upper-class child will mingle with upper-class children, learn upper-class values, manners, and speech patterns, receive invitations to debutante parties and social gatherings and consequently marry other members of the upper class.

Exclusive clubs for the male members of the upper class are central institutions for upper-class integration and coordination. Among the best known are the Pacific Union in San Francisco, the Links and the Knickerbocker in New York, and the Somerset in Boston. Also important, but not as exclusive, are the Harvard, Princeton, and Yale clubs, especially in New York City. Admittance into one of the top clubs is the surest sign that a wealthy family has become socially acceptable. Membership is the essential proof that one is a gentleman. The clubs provide an informal atmosphere in which new members of this social class can be initiated into the mores that govern gentlemanly behavior. They provide a place where the groundwork for major business deals can be laid, and where economic and political differences within this class can be smoothed over in a friendly manner. The clubs also serve as an important tie to the national upper class for upper-class members from smaller towns.

It is impossible for people with "new money," no matter how wealthy they may be, to be fully accepted into the upper class. Only the second generation of wealth can hope to achieve such status and then only by a long and arduous route of wrangling dinner invitations, hiring the right social secretary, sending one's children to the right schools, making the right marriages, and getting into the right clubs.

Although the upper class is united by its common traditions and social institutions, it nevertheless has certain basic internal conflicts that are mostly structured along economic lines. This is still the case even though these antagonisms have been somewhat lessened by the prevalence of increasingly diversified stock portfolios, which come more and more to replace family owned businesses. Such classical antagonisms as heavy industry versus retailing and light manufacturing, industrialists versus bankers, business liberals versus the Old Guard, and Protestants versus the ethnic rich, continue to be important. The first two involve basic differences over economic policies, such as the price of steel, the balance of payments, or the interest rate, while the third involves the two major ideological groups within the upper class: corporate liberalism (one of whose major journals is *Fortune* magazine) and the Old Guard conservatives (represented by such organizations as the National Association of Manufacturers and the right wing of the Republican Party). The corporate liberals have been ascendant since before World War II. This group implements its interests through such key organizations as the Council on Foreign Relations, the Business Council, and the liberal wing of the Republican Party (see Chapter 8). Another important division within the upper class more broadly conceived is that between the traditional Anglo-Saxon Protestant upper-class rich who have traditionally controlled the Republican Party and the ethnic (predominantly Jewish and Irish) rich, traditionally excluded from the *Social Register* but who have traditionally controlled the Democratic Party outside of the South.

INCOME AND WEALTH DIFFERENCES IN THE UNITED STATES

The most immediate consequence of the division of society into classes is a highly unequal distribution of income and wealth. Some people have great concentrations of money, others less than they need. Despite efforts at reform, since 1900 there has been no significant shift in the income distribution in the United States. Since that time, one third of the income in the country has gone to the top 10 percent of income earners, while the share of the lowest 20 percent of the income earners declined from 8 percent to 4 percent by 1960.

In 1922, the top 1 percent of the adult population controlled 32 percent of all personal wealth in the country. In 1957 the figure was 26 percent, while in 1969 it was 25 percent. In 1957, one percent of all adults held 25 percent of all cash, and 32 percent of all government bonds. Looking at specific families, we find that in 1937 the Du Pont family was worth $574 million; in 1964 their wealth had reached $7,629 million. The Mellon family, worth $341 million in 1937, had reached $4,768 million by 1964. For the Rockefellers, the figures were $397 million in 1937 and $4,742 million in 1964. In 1971, the wealthiest 1 percent of the people owned 51 percent of the value of all corporate stocks. This compared with 52 percent in 1959 and 62 percent in 1922. This overwhelming concentration of ownership in the corporations is the basis of both the wealth and the power of the American capitalist class.

The family fortunes are often concentrated in key banks and corporations, allowing the billionaires to control even more money than their own personal wealth. In the case of the Rockefellers, their traditional control of Chase Manhattan Bank, the Standard Oil companies, and other corporations has enabled them to control assets of over fifteen times their personal wealth. This makes them the most economically powerful family in the United States, although they are third in personal family fortune.

The major corporations are tremendous power resources. They are increasing as a percentage of the total U.S. economy. The top 100 corporations controlled 39 percent of the total corporate manufacturing assets in 1947. By 1968 this had risen to 49 percent. The assets of the larger corporations exceed the Gross National Products of most countries, making these countries vulnerable to economic subversion by the corporations. Recently, for example, the President of A.T. & T. offered to help finance secret CIA subversion of Chile under the Allende government. He could well afford to do this. In 1974, A.T. & T. had total assets of $74 billion, while the Gross National Product of Chile was only $8.8 billion. A comparison of the assets of other corporations with the GNPs of various countries is given in Table 5-3.

Inequities in the Tax System

Taxation has had no appreciable effect on the income distribution since 1900. The rich have been able to use various loopholes in the tax laws written for them to avoid paying such a large part of their income to the government that their relative position

TABLE 5-3. Comparison of the Size of U.S. Corporations with the GNP of Various Countries,* 1974

BIGGEST 35 U.S. CORPORATIONS RANKED BY ASSETS (in billions of dollars)		SELECTED COUNTRIES OF THE WORLD RANKED BY GNP (in billions of dollars)	
AT & T	$74.0	United States	$1440.0
Bank of America	60.4	Soviet Union	797.0
Citicorp	57.8	Japan	448.0
Chase Manhattan	42.5	W. Germany	385.0
Prudential Life	35.8	France	292.0
Metropolitan Life	32.7	China	223.0
Exxon	31.3	United Kingdom	192.0
J. P. Morgan	26.0	Canada	136.0
Manufacturers-		India	79.0
Hanover Trust	25.7	Poland	76.2
Chemical Bank	22.2	Spain	70.0
General Motors	20.5	Netherlands	67.1
Banker's Trust	20.4	E. Germany	59.9
Continental Illinois	19.8	Mexico	56.9
First Chicago Corp.	19.1	Switzerland	44.8
Western Bancorporation	18.7	Argentina	36.7
Equitable Life	17.6	Iran	30.9
Texaco	17.2	Denmark	30.7
Security Pacific	15.5	Indonesia	18.0
Ford	14.2	Greece	17.2
Mobil	14.1	Nigeria	16.6
IBM	14.0	S. Korea	14.8
Aetna Casualty	13.9	Philippines	12.1
New York Life	13.0	Peru	10.6
Wells Fargo	12.7	Thailand	10.5
Marine Midland Bank	12.7	Pakistan	9.4
Gulf	12.5	Chile	8.8
General Telephone and Electric	12.0	Ireland	7.3
John Hancock	11.8	Cuba	6.1
Standard, Calif.	11.6	S. Vietnam	3.4
Sears	11.3	Ghana	3.4
Charter New York Corp.	11.3	Syria	3.0
ITT	10.7	Guatemala	3.0
Crocker National	10.3	Burma	2.8
Mellon National Corp.	9.9	Dominican Republic	2.8
Travelers	9.8	Haiti	.8

(Source: *Fortune*, May 1975 and July 1975.)

(Source: U.S. Arms Control and Disarmament Agency, *World Military Expenditures and Arms Transfers 1965–1974*, 1975.)

*A comparison of corporate assets with GNP is not *strictly* justifiable since GNP and assets are different concepts. Another comparison might have been made between government budgets and corporate profits. Assets and profits are the only two measures of a corporation's size that apply across the board to all types of corporations. Although not strictly valid, the comparison used here does give a general idea of the power of the corporations compared to that of various countries. The types of corporations listed among the top 35 should be noted. Twenty-two of the 35 are financial (including insurance) corporations; five of the remaining 13 are oil companies.

to other groups in society would be effected. One of the ways the rich have avoided the effect of the progressive income tax has been through taking an increasing proportion of their income in kind, for example, expense accounts. One study showed that 37 percent of all Cadillacs registered in Manhattan were registered in the name of corporations, while 80 percent of all meals in expensive restaurants and 35 percent of all Broadway tickets were charged to corporations. The rich who receive most of their income in forms other than salaries are also in a good position to underreport their income on their tax returns. While only 3 percent of wage and salary income goes unreported, 27 percent of entrepreneurial profits, 14 percent of dividends, and 58 percent of interest is unreported. Also, as the tax rate went up, corporations distributed a decreasing proportion of their profit to their stockholders holding an increased amount as undistributed income.

Even when these three factors are ignored and only the actual rate of taxation on reported income is examined it can be seen that the tax burden on the very rich is rather light. The rich have developed numerous ways to avoid paying taxes. Table 5-4 contrasts the percentage of an average family's income that is actually paid in federal taxes with the percentage that the law seems to call for.

TABLE 5-4. Percentage of Family Income Taxed by Federal Government

Family Income	Legal Rate	Actual Rate (after using all loopholes)
$ 10,000–$ 11,000	12.4	7.6
20,000– 25,000	20.8	12.1
75,000– 100,000	46.0	26.8
200,000– 500,000	58.0	29.6
500,000–$1 million	60.5	30.4
over $1 million	63.1	32.1

(Source: Phillip Stern, *The Rape of the Taxpayer.* New York: Vintage, 1972.)

Few rich individuals pay more than 35 percent of their reported income to the government. In addition to not declaring their income and taking income in kind, they use the loopholes of capital gains, deferred compensation, tax-exempt interest, depletion allowances, trust funds, gifts, and creating foundations to avoid paying taxes. The capital gains loophole allows much of the profits the rich make on their investments to be taxes at one half the regular rate. Certain types of securities are tax exempt: many raw material investments allow greatly disproportionate deductions every year (22½ percent of gross income deductible from taxes owed in every year). Taxes are also avoided by setting up tax-exempt foundations to do the bidding of those that set them up, trust funds for one's children, and gifts to relatives. Not only has the progressive federal income tax not affected the income distribution of the country but the system of inheritance taxes has had no significant effect on the inheritance of wealth.

Some individuals and corporations have mastered the techniques of legal tax avoidance to the extent of paying no taxes at all. In 1969 there were 761 individuals who reported an income of over $100,000 but who paid not a cent in taxes. (There were 56 who reported an income of over $1,000,000 who paid nothing.) According to a Congressional study, in 1976 United States Steel paid no taxes on its income of $518 million, Mobil Oil paid 4.5% of its revenues in taxes, and Exxon paid 8%.

Although the tax structure of the federal government is theoretically progressive, it has had little or no effect on the redistribution of income. Since Franklin Roosevelt's administration even the theoretically progressive income tax system has been steadily undermined, with tax increases being across the board (such as the surtax), while tax decreases favor the higher brackets. Although the federal income tax is still somewhat progressive, its effect is counterbalanced by the regressive nature of state and local taxation, the various loopholes for the rich in the federal tax structure, and the ability of corporations to raise their prices in order to pass on tax increases (just as they do wage increases) to the consumers (the working class). Leon Keyserling, the head of Harry Truman's Council of Economic Advisers estimated that in the 1950s those in the $0–$5,000 class paid 38 percent of their income directly and indirectly in taxes, those in the $5,000–$10,000 bracket paid 22 percent, and those making over $10,000 paid 32 percent. In 1958 those in the $0–$4,000 class paid approximately $6 billion dollars in federal taxes while at the same time receiving approximately $4.5 billion in all types of welfare benefits. The net effect of taxes and welfare on the poor is to take away from them money that they would otherwise have used to satisfy their essential needs.

According to the U.S. Department of Labor's official definition only about one half of the people of the country earn enough to live reasonably comfortably. One third of Americans do not meet the Department's standard for even the minimum basic necessities. When we compare the poverty in which large number of Americans live with the astronomical incomes and fortunes of the upper class, we see the tremendous economic inequality in the United States. Neither the progressive income tax, welfare legislation, nor the minimum wage has had any significant effect on this great inequality.

Welfare and the Poor

The presence of the poor in capitalist society is no more an accident than is the fortunes of the rich. The poor perform an essential function for capitalism. On the one hand, the economic system needs a large pool of unemployed to put pressure on those that have jobs in order to keep wages down. It is only the presence of large numbers of underemployed or unemployed people seeking work and desperate enough to work for low pay that keeps those that have jobs from demanding higher wages. There is a strong correlation between the rate of unemployment and the rate of change in the rate of wages. Without the unemployed poor, the system's profitability would tend to dry up. The poor also perform an essential function for the system in providing cheap unskilled labor for the most degrading, boring, and menial jobs—garbage collection, dishwashing, janitorial and domestic work, heavy physical labor, seasonal agricultural labor, etc. Unless there was a group of poor workers, there would be no one to perform the essential services that this group provides at such low pay. Lastly, the poor are necessary to reinforce the goals of the better-paid working class. Their continuing presence is a constant threat to the working class. Failure to comply with the capitalist system's demands will result in a similar fate for oneself and one's family.

The welfare system from its inception in sixteenth-century England to the present has been organized to implement the functions described above as well as to serve as a general mechanism of social control over the potentially disruptive poor. Relief began as a response to the mass disturbances of urbanized displaced peasants in the sixteenth century. Historically, whenever the poor have engaged in civil disorders, welfare has been expanded in order to restore order. Welfare as a social control operates to co-opt the potentially disruptive poor. The worst abuses of the system are alleviated by "relief," which is granted as a "privilege" upon evidence of good behavior, political loyalty, and the surrender of one's privacy and much of one's dignity to those that supervise the welfare programs. In the absence of welfare, control over the poor decreases during times of great unemployment (with the withering away of the economic sanctions associated with jobs). Welfare or "unemployment insurance" then tends to expand in these periods as an alternative system of social control. When large numbers of people are suddenly barred from their traditional occupations, the entire structure of social control is weakened and in danger of collapse. As political and economic stability is restored, welfare programs are contracted if not outright abolished, expelling those who are needed in the labor market. Welfare is, in principle, in conflict with the operation of capitalist markets and is only instituted in order to make the whole system work without major disruption. Massive welfare violates the work ethic and prevents the free operation of markets. As long as it is in existence there is a real danger of large numbers of people electing not to work, or not to apply themselves fully to work (since the option of going on relief is not as threatening as starvation). In the absence of significant threats to social order, the natural course for capitalist society to follow is to minimize welfare, thereby reinforcing the work ethic and increasing the pressure on the employed.

Thus, welfare functions to regulate the labor force, to enforce work norms, and to provide an adequate motivation for people to work. To demean and punish those who do not work and who are the recipients of welfare is to exalt by contrast even the meanest labor at the lowest wages. The aged, disabled, insane, and others who are not of use as workers are left on the relief rolls and their treatment is so degrading and punitive as to instill in the working class a fear of the fate that awaits them should they relax.

The workhouse was instituted in English society in the middle of its industrial revolution as a means of motivating the poor. In order to force displaced peasants into the factories, all those who were unable or unwilling to take factory jobs, had to enter into the workhouse where conditions were even worse than in the factories (if they did not want to starve). Conditions in the workhouses were intended to insure that no one with any conceivable alternative would seek public aid. The workhouse system was designed to spur men to offer themselves to any employer at any time on any terms. This is still the guiding principle of all welfare systems in capitalist societies. Welfare is normally given only under the condition that the poor behave in certain ways and on the condition that they be willing to work even at the most degrading jobs for the lowest wages. State policy toward the poor thus must be understood as an appendage to the corporate labor control policies.

Poverty is *not* a matter of the lack of education or of motivation. If everyone had a Ph.D. and was motivated to work 16 hours a day, the system's functional need for unemployed people and a pool of low-paid unskilled labor would still operate to produce poor people. But such a situation would be very unstable, since such a highly educated poor would be unlikely to blame themselves for their poverty and unemployment and consequently would be very likely to be socially disruptive. The system must then be careful on the one hand not to "overeducate" its workforce and on the other to get the poor to adopt a "culture of poverty" that legitimizes their failure in their eyes as their own rather than society's fault.

Summary

Class stratification is a basic feature of capitalist and other class societies, and class analysis provides an understanding of the link between the economic structure of these societies and their social and political superstructures. An individual's *economic class* is determined by his or her relationship to the means of production. The economic class of the head of the household is the fundamental variable determining the *social class* to which his or her family belongs. Therefore, these two dimensions of class are closely related empirically. The occupation of the head of the household thus provides the simplest index of *class position*, i.e., of membership in a social class the family heads of which belong to the same economic class.

The working class is the largest class in American society, constituting about three quarters of the population. It includes industrial, service, farm, clerical and sales workers and their families. These workers do not own or control their own means of production and have fundamental control over neither their own nor the labor of others.

The capitalist class constitutes less than 1 percent of the American population. Members of this class owe their tremendous power to ownership and control of corporate wealth. This class is cohesive, thanks to an extensive network of private clubs and schools and neighborhoods where they interact closely with their social equals. Despite their small numbers, they play a decisive role in American society.

The middle class, defined as including professional and technical employees and managers and proprietors, constitutes about a quarter of the American population. Some middle-class people are self-employed in small businesses, others have managerial positions where they help to control the labor of other people. Many, such as teachers or social workers, work for government agencies in professional positions where they help to reproduce the social system. As a social class the middle class is fairly cohesive, but the diverse economic interests of the members of this class lead to contradictions on the political and ideological level that make the middle class quite controversial in radical sociology.

Review Questions

1. What is the difference in definition between economic class and social class?
2. Which one variable is the best index of economic and social class position for American families?
3. Approximately what percentage of American families fall into the working, middle, and upper classes?
4. Which occupational group has greatly declined as a proportion of the U.S. workforce during the last century?
5. Since 1900, the proportion of manual and service workers in the U.S. labor force has increased, decreased, or remained stable?
6. Which class in American society is the best organized and has the highest degree of class consciousness?
7. Women who work as clerical and sales workers belong to which social class?
8. What types of attitudes are taught to workers to make them accept their position in a capitalist class system?
9. How do people in the *lumpenproletariat* obtain a livelihood?
10. What three different relationships to the means of production are commonly found in the middle class?
11. What aspects of the monopoly capitalist economy have kept the middle class from shrinking as a proportion of the workforce?
12. What are some of the traits that classify an individual as being in the upper class?

13. Since 1900, the distribution of income in the United States has become less equal, become more equal, or retained about the same degree of inequality?

14. What percentage of their income do wealthy individuals actually pay in federal taxes?

15. What proportion of the American people do not meet the Labor Department's standards of the income necessary to purchase minimum basic necessities?

Suggestions for Further Study

1. Describe the different social classes that were represented in your high school. Did both middle- and working-class families send their children to the same school? Were there any upper-class students? If so, did each class take different courses? Did friendship cliques and dating patterns generally remain within classes, or did they cross class lines frequently? Can you draw social distinctions within the working or middle class, i.e., between upper-middle-class and lower-middle-class children? How do the class distinctions correspond to different neighborhoods in the community from which the high school drew students? You may wish to compare your analysis with that of A. B. Hollingshead in the book *Elmtown's Youth*.

2. Examine the ways in which your own life has been conditioned by the social class into which you were born. How did this affect the neighborhood in which you lived, the schools you attended, the friends you had, the relationships within your family? How did the expectations that significant others had for you reflect your class position?

3. Read a selection of the wedding announcements in *The New York Times*. Keep a record of the occupations and other information published about the social positions of the parents of the young couples being married, about the schools they attended, the clubs or organizations they belong to, and their own occupations or plans. Which types of people, out of the many millions in the New York metropolitan area, are deemed important enough to have their marriages mentioned. Contrast this with metropolitan newspapers that circulate in your area, or with local community newspapers.

4. Get together with a group of students from your class to do a small survey of people from different social classes in your community. Assign each student to interview a few people from different neighborhoods. Variables that you might include on your survey are political party preferences, voting behavior, educational plans for their children, attitudes towards labor unions, satisfaction with their job, feelings about women's roles in society, and the like.

Selected Readings

Anderson, Charles. *The Political Economy of Social Class.* New York: Prentice-Hall, 1974.

Andreski, Stanislaw. *Military Organization and Society.* Berkeley: U. of California Press, 1968 (1954).

Aronowitz, Stanley. *False Promises.* New York: McGraw-Hill, 1973.

Baltzel, E. Digby. *Philadelphia Gentlemen: The Making of a National Upper Class.* New York: Free Press, 1958.

———. *The Protestant Establishment.* New York: Random House, 1964.

Bendix, Reinhard, and Lipset, Seymour Martin. *Class, Status and Power,* 1st ed. Glencoe, Ill.: Free Press, 1958.

———. *Social Mobility in Industrial Society.* Berkeley: U. of California Press, 1959.

Blauner, Robert. *Alienation and Freedom: The Factory Worker in His Industry.* Chicago: U. of Chicago Press, 1964.

Boyer, Richard, and Morais, Herbert. *Labor's Untold Story.* New York: United Electrical Workers, 1965.

Braverman, Harry. *Labor and Monopoly Capital.* New York: Monthly Review, 1974.

Chinoy, Ely. *Automobile Workers and the American Dream.* Boston: Beacon, 1965.

Corey, Lewis. *The Crisis of the Middle Class.* New York: J. J. Little, 1935.

Domhoff, G. William. *Bohemia Grove and Other Retreats.* New York: Harper & Row, 1974.

———. *The Higher Circles.* New York: Random House, 1971.

Domhoff, G. William, and Ballard, Hoyt (ed.). *C. Wright Mills and the Power Elite.* Boston: Beacon, 1968.

Edwards, Richard; Reich, Michael; and Gordon, David. *Labor Market Segmentation.* Lexington, Mass.: Heath, 1975.

Ehrenreich, Barbara and John. "The Professional/Managerial Class." *Radical America* 11:2 and 3 (March–April and May–June 1977).

Fitch, Robert, and Oppenheimer, May. "Who Rules the Corporations." *Socialist Revolution* 1:4,5,6 (July–Dec. 1970).

Gitlin, Todd, and Hollander, Nancy. *Uptown: Poor Whites in Chicago.* New York: Harper & Row, 1970.

Goldthrope, John; Lockwood, David; Bechhofer, Frank; and Platt, Jennifer. *The Affluent Worker,* 3 vols. Cambridge, G. B.: Cambridge U. Press, 1969.

Gordon, David. *Theories of Poverty and Underemployment.* Lexington, Mass.: Heath, 1977.

Gorz, Andre (ed.). *The Division of Labour.* New York: Humanities, 1976.

———. *Strategy for Labor.* Boston: Beacon, 1967.

Hamilton, Richard. *Class and Politics in the U.S.* New York: Wiley, 1972.

Heller, Celia S. (ed.). *Structured Social Inequality.* New York: Macmillan, 1969.

Hill, Judah. *Class Analysis: The United States in the 1970's.* Emeryville, Calif.: Class Analysis, 1975.

Hollingshead, August, and Redlich, Fredrick. *Social Class and Mental Illness.* New York: Wiley, 1958.

Johnson, Stephen. "How the West Was Won." *Insurgent Sociologist* 6:2 (Winter 1976).

Kerr, Clark, and Siegel, Abram. "The Interindustry Propensity to Strike," in Clark Kerr, *Labor and Management in Industrial Society.* Garden City, N.Y.: Doubleday, 1964.

Kolko, Gabriel. *Wealth and Power in America.* New York: Random House, 1962.

Lipset, Seymour Martin; Trow, Martin; and Coleman, James. *Union Democracy.* Garden City, N.Y.: Doubleday, 1962 (1956).

Lockwood, David. *The Blackcoated Worker.* London: Allen and Unwin, 1958.

Loren, Charles. *Classes in the United States.* Davis, Calif.: Cardinal, 1977.

Lundberg, Ferdinand. *The Rich and the Super-rich.* New York: Stuart, 1968.

McWilliams, Carey. *Factories in the Field.* Santa Barbara, Calif.: Peregine, 1971 (1935).

Mallet, Serge. *Essays on the New Working Class.* St. Louis: Telos, 1975.

Mandell, Betty Reid (ed.). *Welfare in America: Controlling the "Dangerous Classes."* Englewood Cliffs, N.J.: Prentice-Hall, 1975.

Matles, James, and Higgens, James. *Them and U.S.* Boston: Beacon, 1975.

Menshikov, S. *Millionaries and Managers.* Moscow: Progress, 1969.

Miller, Herman. *Rich Man, Poor Man.* New York: Crowell, 1964.

Mills, C. Wright. *The New Men of Power.* New York: Harcourt, Brace & World, 1948.

————. *The Power Elite.* New York: Oxford U. Press, 1956.

————. *White Collar.* New York: Oxford U. Press, 1956.

Morland, John. *The Millways of Kent.* Chapel Hill: U. of North Carolina Press, 1958.

Parkin, Frank. *Class Inequality and Political Order.* New York: Praeger, 1971.

Perlo, Victor. *The Empire of High Finance.* New York: International, 1957.

Piven, Frances Fox, and Cloward, Richard. *Regulating the Poor.* New York: Vintage, 1971.

Poulantzas, Nicos. *Classes in Contemporary Capitalism.* London: New Left Books, 1975.

Roach, Jack, and Roach, Janet (ed.). *Poverty.* Baltimore: Penguin, 1972.

Sale, Kirkpatrick. *Power Shift.* New York: Random House, 1975.

Sennett, Richard, and Cobb, Jonathan. *The Hidden Injuries of Class.* New York: Vintage, 1973.

Serrin, William. *The Company and the Union.* New York: Knopf, 1973.

Shostak, Arthur. *Blue-Collar Life.* New York: Random House, 1969.

Stinchcombe, Arthur. "Agricultural Enterprise and Rural Class Raltion." *American Journal of Sociology* 57:2 (Sept. 1961).

Szymanski, Albert. "Race, Sex and the U.S Working Class." *Social Problems* 21:4 (June 1974).

———. "The Petty Bourgeoisie in the Advanced Capitalist Countries." *Synthesis* 1:4 (Jan. 1977).

———. "Trends in the American Class Structure." *Socialist Revolution* 2:4 (June 1974).

Tumin, Melvin (ed.). *Readings on Social Stratification.* Englewood Cliffs, N.J.: Prentice-Hall, 1970.

Wolf, Eric. *Peasants*, Chs. 1, 23. Englewood Cliffs, N.J.: Prentice-Hall, 1966.

Wright, Erik Olin. "Class Boundaries in Advanced Capitalist Societies." *New Left Review* 98 (July–Aug. 1976).

Chapter 6

The Individual in Class Society

Radical sociology begins with a recognition that human societies are made up of people. People who must eat and drink and have shelter, and who seek meaningful social and sexual relationships with other people. A basic value assumption of radical and other humanistic sociologies is that social arrangements must be judged according to how well they meet people's needs. In class societies many people suffer unnecessarily from hunger, inadequate housing and medical care, and other deprivations of their basic biological needs. Radical sociologists are committed to helping to bring about social arrangements that will not impose unnecessary suffering of this sort on anyone.

Beyond physical deprivation, people in class societies often suffer from frustration of their emotional needs. They find their work lives dull and uncreative, their intimate relationships unfulfilling, their social, religious, or political affiliations lacking in meaning. Often these problems are dealt with on an individual level, through psychological counseling or therapy, by joining a meditation or spiritual group, or by taking drugs. But when such problems affect large numbers of people, sociologists look to something in the organization of society itself for the cause. Conservatives generally argue that it is the responsibility of individuals to conform to social arrangements, to fit into the status quo no matter how difficult the adjustment may be. Radicals insist that societies were made by people, and should serve the needs of people. When they fail to do so, they should be changed.

Given this humanistic emphasis in radical sociology, it is important to begin with an analysis of human nature. People's biological nature has an important impact on human societies, making them different from societies that have evolved among other species. Human nature sets limits on societies, but also gives them great potentialities for growth and change. We will begin with a discussion of the aspects of human biology that are relevant to social structure. We will then discuss the effects that social arrangements have on people, especially in terms of their propensity to accept existing social arrangements or to challenge them.

BIOLOGY AND SOCIETY

The fact that the members of human societies are advanced primates means that the nature of social relations between them is quite different from what it might have been had societies evolved among cats, fishes, or birds. Human beings are not the only species to live in societies. Fairly complex societies exist among insect species such as termites, bees, and ants. These societies resemble contemporary human societies in significant ways, especially in their use of the division of labor and in their hierarchical organization. They differ largely in their changelessness; since the behavior of insects is largely determined by instincts, they do not learn new patterns of behavior that would permit change in their social organization.

   Simple societies also exist in other animal species. Among these are the societies of other higher primates such as gorillas and chimpanzees. Gorilla and chimpanzee societies differ only slightly from the very primitive human societies of a mere 10,000 years ago. Both are characterized by a division of labor between the sexes and an economy based on hunting and gathering. Although the biological differences between *homo sapiens* and other primates are relatively minor, they were sufficient to allow humanity to develop complex societies out of the very primitive social structures shared by the higher primates. Thus, evolution crossed a critical threshold with the development of human beings. Once this threshold was passed, the rate of social change accelerated a thousandfold. Change no longer occurred primarily because of genetic mutations and adaptations forced by changing environments. It occurred through new behavior patterns which were invented by people and passed on from generation to generation through language.

Human Biological Capabilities

People's biological nature made this possible. Biology gave people many capacities not shared with other animals, and deprived them of some capacities that other animals do have. People lack true instincts such as those that determine the behavior patterns of many other species. We do have biological differences between the sexes, a highly developed capacity for rational thinking, an exceptional facility for learning, great flexibility in behavior, a virtually unique ability to use language, a flexible hand,

and keen daytime color vision. While we share each of these capacities with some other species, no other species has all of them. All of these capacities have had consequences for our social organization.

As with other primates, there are sexual differences in the human species. Males and females are not equal in physical strength, on the average, or in the capacity for bearing and feeding babies. Since men are physically stronger than women and not constrained by pregnancy, childbirth, and breast feeding, it has been functional for technologically primitive societies to assign the roles of hunter and warrior to males. With the development of advanced technology, made possible by people's intellectual and linguistic capabilities, such sexual differentiation is no longer functional for societies.

The fact that human beings lack true instincts means that we have no specific and definite inherited or unlearned responses that follow or accompany a specific and definite sensory stimulus or organic condition. Since we do not have instincts, we must learn how to do everything that is necessary for our survival. Even the sex act among higher primates must be learned. Children are essentially blank slates on which society, largely through their parents, writes. This gives human societies tremendous flexibility.

The ability to speak and the flexible hand have been essential for the development of societies. The ability to speak, which we share only with certain birds (who do not have the mental capacity to use it fully) and perhaps with dolphins and porpoises, allows us to communicate our experience and knowledge easily to others and to build up a body of knowledge that grows from generation to generation. The dexterous hand, which we share with the other higher primates, allows us to make and use tools and in general to manipulate and shape our environment. This characteristic is essential. Recent evidence has suggested that the dolphins and porpoises are equal if not superior to people in their mental capabilities. They lack, however, the capacity to physically control their environment in the way that people can.

The year-round sexual receptability of human females is a characteristic shared with other primates. It encourages people to form long-term ties between males and females, rather than mating during a certain period of the year and then retreating into single sex groups. Closer relationships between fathers and children than in many other species is a result.

The fact that people normally stand erect, with their hands free for work, is certainly a useful capability, as is our keen binocular color vision, which is a great aid in hunting and hence in survival.

Physical and Biological Drives

Human biological nature gives us more than capabilities. It also gives us motivation. People are born with drives that must be fulfilled for the organism to survive. Drives are powerful parts of our biology. Failure to satisfy them leads to frustration and ultimately to death, mental illness, extreme unhappiness, drug addiction, or some other retreat from reality. There are two major types of drives: physical drives and psychological drives. Two physical drives are of key significance for human social organization: the drives for food and for warmth. These together compel people to produce, or at least gather, food and to obtain shelter and clothing. Social production, which is at the center of social life in all societies, is oriented around these two drives. Other physical drives are just as important biologically, but do not require so much social effort to satisfy. These include the drives of thirst, for sleep, for air, and for urination and defecation.

The psychological drives are somewhat more difficult to divide into categories, but they are just as important. Frustration of these drives leads to mental illness, depression, and eventually to death. Psychological drives include the drive for affection or approval from others, the drive to be treated with dignity or respect in order to maintain one's integrity and self-esteem, the drive to engage in creative or meaningful activity, the drive to participate in social interaction with other people and to experience solidarity or belongingness with other people, and the drive for sexual release. Sex is perhaps unique in the extent to which it involves both physical and emotional aspects. All of these psychological drives are different aspects of what Sigmund Freud called "libidinal energy."

All people feel the need to receive affection or approval from others. "No man is an island," even though he may have developed a personality or character structure that pushes other people away. The drive for affection or approval is common to all people and finds its realization through familial relationships, friendship, and work relations. More than this, people are driven to seek relationships that provide them with self-respect. People need dignity. They react against being treated as subhumans or as fools. This, more than any of the other drives is the root energy behind rebellion, revolution, and Messianic religion. Blacks and women joined radical movements in recent years not so much because they were hungry or unloved but because they were denied dignified treatment as the equals of white men.

This drive for dignity can find expression in two fundamentally different ways. On the one hand, feelings of self-respect can be obtained at the expense of others, i.e., one can come to evaluate oneself as better or worse than others. For example, great pride can be taken in being white, being a man, being an American, or in being an "A" student. But the drive for dignity or self-respect does not have to be channeled into invidious comparisons. A full sense of dignity or self-respect can be obtained by simply mastering a certain craft, art, or sport, regardless of whether or not someone else succeeds or fails. What form the satisfaction of the biological drives for dignity takes is a matter of the values and options that the individual's society affords.

People seem also to have a drive compelling them to do well at one or another kind of activity and to be free of boring routine. This drive for creativity or meaningful activity is given institutionalized release in all societies through either work or play activities. Crafts, sports, and hobbies are all universal and are, in part, results of this drive. People also seem to be driven to seek communal relationships with others, that is, to participate in intensive social groups. They feel a need for solidarity and belongingness with other humans. This is the case even when this drive is overwhelmed by forces in our character structure compelling us toward egoism and individualism. In all societies and classes, the tendency to participate in groups for nonproductive reasons can be noted.

Lastly, common to all more advanced animals is the drive for sexual release. This drive, however, is usually tied up in the structure of our character with other drives, such as the drive for approval and affection or the drive for self-esteem, as well as with other factors. All societies develop ways of institutionalized release for the frustration produced by this drive. Marriage forms are in part determined by this universal drive.

There is a hierarchy of drives. That is to say, some drives are more potent than others and demand satisfaction before the others. Generally speaking, the physical drives take precedence over the psychological drives. Even among the physical drives, some take precedence over others. The drive for air clearly comes first, perhaps followed by defecation-urination, warmth-dryness, thirst, hunger, and sleep. It is more difficult to order the psychological drives, although probably the drives for affection, approval, and dignity are the strongest.

Human Propensities

In addition to the drives, people's biological nature provides them with weaker tendencies or propensities, which pressure them to act in certain ways but do not cause great frustration if they are not realized. Often the propensities influence the way in which people go about satisfying their drives. Some human propensities include the tendency to attribute meaning to things or to seek a world view; the tendency towards inertia in beliefs, values, and behavior patterns; the tendency to believe that what corresponds to one's drives and interests is true and right; the tendency to protect one's self; and the tendency to sympathize with other members of the species. Somewhat weaker tendencies include the propensity to be consistent in one's beliefs, values, and behavior; the propensity to act according to one's beliefs; and the tendency to seek out new experiences.

People in all societies try to give meaning to their world, to understand how and why things got to be the way they are, and what is going to happen in the future. This propensity is the major force behind human mythologies, religions, and sciences.

Once people come to believe a certain thing, they normally persist in this belief unless new social forces operate to change their beliefs. Thus, people are generally conservative in persisting in their orientations. This principle may be labeled "inertia." Somewhat counter to this tendency is a weaker force making people uncomfortable with the routine and pressuring them toward seeking release from boredom in new experiences.

There is a rather strong tendency among human beings to bring their beliefs and values into line with their interests and actual behavior. Because of the innate need to attribute meaning to things, members of the species *homo sapiens* normally feel it necessary to justify their behevior by developing rationales for it. When an individual or group changes its interests or its behavior, it normally also changes its beliefs and values to correspond. For example, a woman who is brought up a good Catholic when faced with her sexual desires may modify her religion to develop a personal version of Christianity that allows for sexual experiences. When she later marries and regularly practices birth control, even if she remains a Catholic, she is likely to develop a belief that in spite of what the Pope says, birth control is all right. Likewise, men who are involved in the censorship of pornography may justify their watching and reading of such material by an ideology that claims they are protecting the community, while in actuality they enjoy the stimulation it provides.

There is a much weaker tendency for members of *homo sapiens* to act according to their beliefs. This is probably so weak as to be without effect unless reinforced by a socially learned character structure that serves to actually motivate people. Both of these tendencies are specific cases of a broader tendency leading people toward consistency. People feel a general need to be consistent in their beliefs and in their behavior. As is obvious to the most superficial observer, the manifestation of this tendency in social relations is quite minor except in the respect indicated above—people do try to rationalize their interests and behavior. If no other force is operating, there is a tendency for people to be logical or internally consistent in their beliefs and values, but if for any reason there are forces operating to bring people to hold contradictory beliefs and values, or to engage in contradictory actions, then these later forces prevail without much resistance.

Members of *homo sapiens* have, as do all animals, a tendency to protect themselves from harm. Thus, certain aspects of warfare, shelter, and communication are explainable in terms of biologically given propensities. Members of *homo sapiens* also have an innate tendency to sympathize with the suffering of their fellows. They share this trait with the other higher primates and perhaps the higher insects. Although this trait is often overwhelmed by superior forces in our learned character structure, it appears that there is a relatively strong force leading us to help, or desire to help, fellow human beings who are suffering. However, under the pull of contradictory forces, in capitalist society this tendency is frequently overwhelmed (although often not without resulting guilt).

Our listing of innate capacities and propensities is not meant to be all encompassing. There are undoubtedly other aspects of human nature that make a difference for our social organization. We have rather here tried to list the characteristics that seem to have the greatest bearing on social relations.

All the drives, propensities, and capacities we have discussed are universal to all members of *homo sapiens*, although they may vary somewhat in any given population. There is no evidence that different ethnic groups, classes, or societies have any systematic differences in these biological characteristics. Nor is there any evidence that people's biological nature has changed, at least since the development of horticulture. While there are individual variations within societies, there is no evidence that these variations have had any effect on the social organization of societies. Social differences cannot be explained by biological capacities, drives, or propensities, since these factors do not vary systematically among social groups.

Biology, Culture, and Repression

What does vary is the culture, or learned behavior patterns, in different societies or groups. Our actual feelings or wants are determined both by our drives and by the culture in which we live. We want things that our society has taught us are desirable. Many of these wants correspond to biological drives, but others do not. All societies, however, must give at least minimal satisfaction to the drives of most of their members. Therefore, many if not most drives are channeled by societies into culturally approved wants that are generally conscious desires. Each society or subgroup encourages a limited range of the possible solutions to the biological desires of human beings, frequently limiting satisfaction to very narrow channels and imposing great restrictions on the timing, type, and distribution of satisfactions. For example, some societies or subgroups put high value on eating snakes, worms, insects, pork, beef, or human flesh as a way of satisfying the drive for hunger. Others absolutely prohibit eating such material as a socially acceptable means of satisfying the hunger drive. Likewise, the sex drive is channeled in widely varying manners. In some groups, young people of the same sex are the most prized sexual objects, while in other groups it is people of the opposite sex. There are all kinds of social variations on the preferred forms and objects of sexual intercourse. Genital intercourse with someone of the opposite sex is probably the preferred form in most societies only because of its societal survival value. Since only such forms of sexual release will result in children to carry on a society, it is natural that there has been a strong selective factor operating in social evolution in favor of this cultural trait.

Wants can be classified as either "true" or "false" depending on whether or not a want corresponds to a drive. Those wants that do not correspond to drives can be classified as "false," while those that are more or less identical with a drive can be classified as "true." For example, a desire for a drink of salt water could be classified as false, while a desire for fresh water would be true. The energy behind human motivation appears to be the tension created by the frustration of drives, not the presence of wants. Members of *homo sapiens* are driven by the frustration of their drives regardless of their conscious desires. Thus, the satisfaction of wants cannot result in

Ted Goertzel

Some industries grow in response to frustrated physical, psychological, and social needs.

authentic satisfaction unless an underlying drive is also satisfied. Likewise, the frustration of a conscious want may be irrelevant to motivation if an underlying drive is satisfied. For example, we might want a steak dinner very badly, but after eating our fill of rice lose all appetite for steak, since our underlying hunger was satisfied. Or our desire for four new cars instead of our present three could be totally satisfied without in the least relieving the underlying tension that is the source of the energy for our conscious want—which in fact lies in the frustration of a social drive, perhaps for affection or dignity.

There are in most societies inherent contradictions in satisfying various drives. That is, the process of satisfying one drive frequently means that other drives have to go unsatisfied. Specifically, some limits must be put on the satisfaction of the psychological drives (libidinal energy) in more technologically backward societies in order to successfully satisfy the physical drives. In other words, under those conditions where long hours of tedious labor are necessary in order to satisfy the drives of hunger, warmth, dryness, and thirst, the drives for affection, approval, dignity, community, creative activity, and sex may have to be repressed. In order to get the necessary labor done, people in a technologically backward society may have to be motivated to engage in tedious labor. Their pursuit of libidinal satisfactions must then be constrained not only during work but nonwork time as well, since in order to secure motivation the contrast between the pleasures of leisure and the tedium of labor must be removed. Thus, sexuality, dignity, community, and affection might have to be limited for the sake of production.

It is an object of some contention just how much repression of the libidinal energies or psychological drives is necessary under conditions of primitive technology. Sigmund Freud and Herbert Marcuse argue that it is quite a bit, while Wilhelm Reich argues that it is very little. In any event, we can define that part of libidinal repression that is necessary for production given the level of technology as "necessary repression" and all other repression of the libidinal energies as "surplus repression." Even a superficial examination of primitive tribes shows that in almost all cases the amount of libidinal repression is much less than that experienced in class and especially in capitalist societies. Therefore, we know that both the total amount of repression and the socially necessary repression under capitalist society is much greater than the socially necessary minimum for even the most technologically backward societies. This additional repression is needed in order to maintain the unequal social structure that does not permit everyone to realize their drives.

The more technologically advanced a society, the less the socially necessary level of repression (if we assume population density to be constant). However, as society developed from its primitive to its monopoly capitalist form total repression of the libidinal energies increased. The rapid increase of surplus repression became necessary in order to remove the growing possibility of authentic physical and psychological drive satisfaction from people's consciousness. In order to preserve the prevailing system of domination and privilege, the vested interests in society must encourage ever greater repression of the libidinal energies. The less necessary repression becomes, the more repression there must be. If the libidinal drives were released, their satisfaction in affectionate, dignified, communal, and creative relations and activities would immediately disrupt the highly stratified class society with its institutionalized individualism, tedium, hierarchy, and competitiveness.

Since frustration of drives is an inevitable consequence of class society, it is necessary that such societies have institutionalized ways of dealing with the tensions that result. In order to cope with the frustration of the physical drives for food, clothing, and shelter, class society has police, religion, mysticism, and drugs to contain or redirect popular concerns. These mechanisms are readily understood and need not be dwelled upon. If a society that is technologically capable of feeding, clothing, and sheltering its people nevertheless denies to a significant proportion of its people these satisfactions in order to sustain the privileges of a dominant group, then people's consciousness of their frustrations must be removed through drugs, religion, or mysticism. This is the significance of slogans such as "There'll be pie in the sky when you die," "The real reality is the spiritual not the material," or "It is more difficult for a rich man to pass into heaven than it is for a camel to pass through the eye of a needle." If the elite groups fail to suppress frustration of the physical drives from people's consciousness, then societies turn to outright terror in the use of police and the military to prevent the poor from satisfying their drives, now fully conscious as wants.

The handling of psychological drives is more complex, although again societies have patterned ways of dealing with the frustrations they produce. There are a number of ways of dealing with frustration:

1. The collective institutionalized mechanisms of dealing with frustration.
    a. Those involving displacement of means.
    b. Those involving displacement of objects.
    c. Those involving displacement of both means and objects.
2. Individualized but patterned ways of dealing with frustration.
3. - Noninstitutionalized, but patterned, collective responses to frustration.

The first two basic types listed above are the safety-valve mechanisms of a society, that is, the ways it copes with frustration in order to render it socially harmless. The third is the result of the failure of safety-valve functions and results in the breakdown of society. Societies have, then, two essential courses to cope with frustration, and they usually use both. They institutionalize such things as witchcraft, mass nonparticipant sports, Messianic religion, racism, anti-Semitism, extreme nationalism, and war enthusiasm as ways of channeling the collective energy of the frustrated masses into pursuits that not only are not harmful to the existing form of social organization but also frequently strengthen it. Societies also pattern various individualized responses to frustration. Frustrated individuals who cannot find substitute satisfactions in one or another form of collective safety-valve institutions are drawn into such things as neuroses, psychoses, suicide, Messianic religion, and consciousness-contracting drugs.[1] All these phenomena are highly patterned and vary characteristically by classes, races, societies, and over time as a consequence of the amount of unrelieved libidinal frustration in each group.

Three forms of the collective safety-value institutions can be distinguished. Witchcraft, voodoo, and hostility expressed in wit are examples of the displacement of means. That is, hostile energy is directed against a frustrating object but in ways that do not normally actually result in any harm coming to it. Mass sports, anti-Semitism, racism, and war hysteria are examples of the displacement of the object. Hostility is directly expressed, but against something other than the actual source of frustration. Here hostility and aggression is projected into a relatively harmless object away from the more powerful real source of frustration.

1. Emile Durkheim's study of suicide demonstrated that a whole class of suicides—anomic suicide—is caused by the frustration of the drive for community (and perhaps affection-approval as well). He showed that the greater the frustration of this drive in a social group, the higher its suicide rate: that more Protestants kill themselves than Catholics; more Jews than Christians; fewer minorities than majorities; more men than women; fewer married than single; fewer people in larger families than in small families; more professionals than proletarians; more rich than poor; and more of the population in general in times of war and revolution than in normal times.

If both modes of safety-valve processes fail, then noninstitutionalized collective responses ensue. Rebellion and perhaps, eventually, revolution occur. Hostile and aggressive energy is directed against the cause of frustration in ways that attempt to eliminate frustration. Rebellion and revolution cannot be understood without understanding the source of energy motivating their participants and the reasons for the breakdown of the redirective safety-valve institutions.

SOCIALIZATION AND CHARACTER STRUCTURE

Since all people are born with essentially the same genetically determined nature, the vast differences in personality or character types between the sexes, among classes, races, nations, and people living at different times are all a consequence of social environments. Biology sets limits and provides capabilities; societies determine what will be done with the capabilities. Thus, human biological nature provides the ability to learn languages, but whether a child grows up speaking English or Chinese depends on the language used in the family and community where he or she is born. In more general terms, what people are, what they think and want, and their characteristic ways of behaving are all functions of the accident of who their parents are. Each society attempts to shape its children's character in ways that make them fit into existing social arrangements. For example, hardness and strength have been encouraged in boys and suppressed in girls in favor of weakness and softness. This supports social arrangements where men are expected to be assertive in dealing with the world, while women are supposed to be emotional and supportive of others. Similarly, working-class children have been taught to be compliant and submissive to authority, while upper-middle-class and upper-class children have been taught initiative and independent thinking.

Theories of Socialization

Social psychologists have made extensive studies of socialization, that is, of the ways in which people learn socially acceptable behavior patterns. There are many different paradigms within this field, each of which corresponds to a different aspect of the process. *Behaviorists* such as B. F. Skinner stress the role of rewards in teaching correct behavior. A child is rewarded with praise or social acceptance if he or she behaves properly. This paradigm tends to describe socialization processes in authoritarian settings where one person or group holds all the power and another group can be manipulated more or less at will. This approach applies best to rats or other animals kept in cages for experimental purposes, but it can also be used in institutions such as reform schools, mental hospitals, or prisons. It is much more difficult to use behaviorist theory to explain socialization that takes place in situations where both partners to the process are rewarding (and punishing) each other. In this case behaviorism becomes a theory of *exchange* and there must be an analysis of the resources available for exchange and the motivations of each participant.

Behaviorist theories often tend to appeal to conservatives who identify with authority and hope to find ways that it can be used more effectively to control people's behavior. Liberals and radicals are more likely to stress *cognitive* paradigms, that is, they use theories which pay attention to the conscious mental processes that people use in learning socially acceptable behavior. People are able to learn correct behavior by watching other people and modeling themselves on correct behavior. Thus, boys learn to be men by watching their fathers and girls learn to be women by watching their mothers. *Modeling theory* stresses the use of role models in socialization. This sort of theory can be used by liberals or radicals who wish to change traditional behavior patterns. For example, school textbooks can be changed to portray blacks and women in positions of authority and responsibility in the hope that black children and girls will model their future behavior on these role models.

Other theories, using a cognitive approach, stress the role of language in socialization. *Symbolic interactionist* theorists stress the fact that language is a key tool for human interaction and study how people use words and concepts to understand their social world. Sociologists such as Charles Cooley and George Herbert Mead have written extensively on the ways by which people develop conceptions of themselves by internalizing images that other people have of them. People first react to input from specific people who are significant to them; later on they develop a more generalized image of themselves and of behavior that is appropriate in society. These theories can also provide some guidance in changing societies. For example, some feminists place emphasis in changing words that convey a sexist image of society. Thus "chairman" becomes "chairperson," or the pronouns "he" or "his" are no longer used to refer to both men and women in abstract sentences. There is as yet, however, no evidence about how effective these changes are in actually changing social behavior.

Neither the behaviorist nor the cognitive approaches to socialization place emphasis on people's biological nature. For this reason, we believe that they are inadequate for radical sociologists. Radical sociology requires addressing the question of how social arrangements meet or frustrate human needs. Socialization is a two-dimensional process. It is not merely the pouring into us of the prevailing values, beliefs, and behavior patterns of our society and subgroups. These social norms must necessarily relate to our innate biological drives. Socialization involves structuring the ways in which people seek and obtain gratification and the mechanisms by which we protect ourselves from disappointment. Our emotional energies become attached to appropriate beliefs and values. Thus, socialization is a process of interaction between social pressures and human nature. A basic goal of radical sociology is to find social forms that satisfy rather than frustrate human needs. Systematic frustration of human needs is undesirable both on humanistic grounds and because it tends to develop personality traits in people that are inconsistent with a good society.

Radical sociologists are often critical of the specific theories advanced by Sigmund Freud. Freud's views on the socialization of women in modern societies have been controversial, especially within feminist circles. While radical sociology need not accept every specific conclusion that Freud reached, the Freudian social-psychological paradigm does provide a more adequate conceptual basis for considering the relationship between the individual and society. Freud distinguished between the *id* (basic biological drives), the *superego* (the representation of social norms in the personality), and the *ego* (the rational, calculating elements in the personality). Freud also stressed the importance of the unconscious mind, dealing with mental processes which have been repressed or which are so deeply rooted in the personality that we are not aware of them. The Freudian *psychodynamic* paradigm is more adequate than the behaviorist or cognitive paradigms in analyzing the interrelationship between social forces and biological drives.

Freud argued that personality characteristics are largely formed during childhood. As we grow up we develop behavior patterns that determine the ways in which we satisfy not only our physical drives but also our nonphysical or emotional needs. *Social character* is the form in which our emotional or libidinal energy is shaped by the adaptation of the nonmaterial drives to the particular mode of existence of a given society. It in turn determines the thinking, feeling, and action of individuals. It anchors the prevailing ideology of our society and subgroups deeply within our own personalities.

Character Structure in Capitalist Society

Character structure typically is formed in the young child between the time of birth and the age of four or five. It is formed initially as a kind of protection or armoring against the dangers threatening the child from the outer world. The child must develop ways of dealing with the anxiety and frustration caused by his or her inability to control the environment. The human infant is unable to obtain food or drink or warmth and physical comfort except by relating to the adults in his or her life. Freud placed great emphasis on the ways in which basic biological needs are met—for example, the child may be fed whenever it cries, or on a rigid schedule, or arbitrarily. Toilet training may be gradual, when the child is biologically mature enough to handle it, or it may be imposed too early with strict punishment from the parents. There are also important variations in the handling of emotional needs. Fondling and emotional closeness may be readily available from both parents, or there may be conflict with the parent of the same sex for the affection of the parent of the opposite sex.

During the first four or five years, the child learns to function in the home environment where he or she was born. Of course, these environments vary in different social classes, in different countries, at different times, and among different racial and ethnic groups. The expectations often vary, also, depending on whether the child is a

Differences among social classes are reflected in various social activities.

By Ross Koppel

boy or a girl, or has siblings, older or younger or both. The character structure that the child develops depends on the interaction between basic biological and emotional needs and this social environment. As the child goes out of the home into the neighborhood and school, and on to work as an adult, a similar process continues, although the changes that take place are not nearly as marked as those during the crucial first years of childhood where the child is utterly dependent on the parents. (Children raised in institutions, of course, have special problems.)

In societies characterized by inequality between social classes, people must be socialized to accept social conditions that are not in their own best interest. We must all be taught to compete for "success," even when that success does not actually bring satisfaction of our basic needs. We must be taught to accept authority, even when that authority compels us to repress our own needs in order to satisfy those of the system created by the upper classes. Continually adapting to such conditions creates character traits destructive to the human personality in that they work in a direction opposite from our primary social drives. People thus frequently become incapable of sexual enjoyment, of giving or receiving affection, they desire to be isolated from people, find it impossible to be creative, etc. These socially imposed character traits become the central forces motivating people's behavior. They channel the energies of the biological and emotional drives into patterns that provide only inadequate substitutes and partial tension release. Such substitute gratifications cannot be fully satisfying even though they may avoid the consequences of full frustration. As a result, people in class societies are unhappy much of the time. They cling desperately to patterns that provide limited satisfactions, or which at a minimum provide some relief from feelings of guilt and anxiety. They develop character traits that minimize the pain caused by the impossibility of fully satisfying their basic needs within the confines of a repressive society.

Character structure is thus the bridge between the individual and class society. Character structure provides the anchoring of the individuals to their social position by channeling people's biological energies in the direction necessary for the smooth functioning of society. Libidinal energies are attached to the collective values of God, Mother, and Country, as well as to the functions necessary for the individual to perform. Each individual tends to be attached to his or her social position and to accept the legitimacy of existing social arrangements. Every social order needs to produce in the masses of its members that character structure which it needs to thrive.

Individuals, through the mechanism of character formation, come to want to do what they have to do. People's libidinal energies are molded so that they become willing to perform their social functions. People are thereby made into "good" workers, "good" citizens, "good" soldiers, "good" housekeepers, etc. Character formation anchors in people the drive to work and to follow orders. The libidinal drives are suppressed and turned around in the formation of character to get people to accept their own degradation. The more unequal a society and the greater the gap between what is technologically possible and what the existing reality provides, the more important character formation becomes. The more dangerous the possibility of a breakthrough in libidinal gratification, the more necessary the surplus repression fixed by character structure to remove the alternative possibilities from people's consciousness and to secure the attachment of libidinal energies to authoritarian ends.

Authoritarianism

Perhaps the most important aspect of character structure in class societies is its channeling of energies into *authoritarian* character traits. Authoritarian personality traits develop when people are forced to deal with rigid and arbitrary authority. Under these conditions, people become afraid to express or even to acknowledge their own inner urges and needs. They often tend to project their own inner needs—needs that may have been repressed into the unconscious mind—onto other people. They are afraid that unless people are rigidly controlled they will become unruly and uncontrollable.

People with authoritarian personality structures tend to place great reliance on people or groups with power and authority. They believe in hierarchy and obtain vicarious satisfaction by identifying with those in power. They often seek security by rigidly conforming to traditional norms and behavior patterns. They are afraid to examine their own feelings and emotions because of what they may find there.

Of course, authoritarian tendencies are found in the character structures of all people whose experiences have been especially frustrating. Children raised in a home where the parents are strict disciplinarians or even abuse their children are more likely to develop authoritarian personalities than children raised in more liberal or permissive homes. Students in an old-fashioned school that requires everyone to conform simultaneously to detailed instructions from the teacher are more likely to develop authoritarian patterns than those who enjoy a more permissive educational environment.

Authoritarian character traits have broad implications because of the tendency of people to form consistent world views that enable them to feel they understand the world around them. Although an authoritarian character may originate in childhood experiences, it tends to persist throughout life and to influence how one deals with all types of authority—the authority of one's boss, religious leaders, God, political leaders, the state, professors, husbands, etc. People generalize the attitude they have adopted toward their parents to all forms of authority; they project their father and mother into the heavens, the state, and the economy. Thus, the basis for submissiveness and compliance to the will of the powerful is psychological. It originates within the family, is reinforced in the school, and carries over into all aspects of class society.

Authoritarian tendencies in a population tend to make people susceptible to fascist political movements. These movements are characterized by a strong leader with a dominant personality, have an irrational and authoritarian ideology, and generally choose some minority group as an outlet for their followers' frustrations. Thus, Germans who were raised in homes with a domineering father, and who consequently suffered uncertainty in their lives caused by economic crises, may have turned to Hitler as a strong father figure who could bring order to their lives. They readily believed that the Jews or Communists were the cause of all their problems, because their character structure conditioned them to project their own needs onto other people. They feared that the Jews were doing the things that they themselves would do if only they dared.

Personal racism and sexism have their roots in authoritarian character structures. Thanks to authoritarianism, white people in America may be persuaded that it is the black family on welfare, rather than the powerful corporate executive, that is causing their economic woes. Men may be persuaded that women must be kept in an inferior and strictly regulated social position, lest their deeply buried "evil" tendencies be released. Authoritarian longings for order and discipline may sometimes be so severe among middle-class people who are suffering from career problems, for example, that they will pay hundreds of dollars to spend two weekends sitting on hard chairs in an auditorium listening to an EST leader call them demeaning names, while denying them even the right to go to the bathroom, get a drink of water, or eat, except during infrequently scheduled breaks. Nothing could be a greater indictment of capitalist institutions than the fact that two weekends of this may in fact make the individual a more willing, enthusiastic, and successful cog in the machine.

Fortunately, authoritarian socialization is not always effective in suppressing people's natural drives. Healthy parents often succeed, despite the pressures they themselves suffer, in providing a supportive and liberating atmosphere for their children. Healthy people have a strong tendency to take the strictures of authority with a grain of salt, and to seek ways to meet their needs as best they can. Liberal and radical people working within the school system, or in the helping professions, may find ways to help people understand their own feelings and needs and how these relate to the larger society. Often, however, those people who are most oppressed by the system may not have the resources to escape the repression built into the system. Consequently, movements for change often emerge first from among people who have had enough advantages to create a tolerable environment for themselves and their families within the present system.

Summary

Human beings as a biological species have definite needs that must be fulfilled, and capabilities that enable them to meet these needs. Physical needs or drives that are particularly significant for human societies are the drives for food and warmth, which provide the basis for economic behavior. The psychological drives for affection, approval, and self-respect are crucial in providing a key motivation for resisting oppressive social conditions. Culture prescribes approved ways of meeting people's needs. It also creates false wants or desires that serve to motivate people to conform to social norms even when doing so does not fulfill their fundamental drives.

Societies exist because human beings in isolation cannot satisfy their emotional drives; nor can they effectively meet their physical drives. All societies repress the drives of their individual members to some extent. In primitive societies this is done because resources are scarce, or because it is necessary for everyone to do tedious labor in order for the group to survive. In advanced, class-stratified, societies the amount of repression is much greater than that which is necessary for the survival of the group. This surplus repression is needed in order to ensure a surplus for the ruling class. Safety-valve mechanisms are created in these societies in order to absorb the frustration created by surplus repression.

Children born into a society must be socialized into accepting the rules of that society. This can be done with rewards and punishments, through modeling, or through direct teaching. In a repressive class society, this socialization process often creates authoritarian personality or character structures in people as they become afraid of their inner feelings which are repressed by those in authority.

Review Questions

1. What species other than human beings can be observed to live in societies?

2. Which biological traits of human beings make our form of societal organization possible?

3. What physical and psychological drives must be met for the human organism to survive?

4. Which human propensities account for the development of ideologies and religions?

5. Why is surplus repression necessary?

6. What is the role of safety-value mechanisms in a society?

7. What are the advantages of behaviorist theories of socialization for those in power in a social institution?

8. What are the advantages of the Freudian paradigm in studying socialization?

9. At what age do the basic elements of the human character structure tend to be formed?

10. What are the traits of the authoritarian character structure?

Suggestions for Further Study

1. Make a list of the activities that fill your typical day. Which drives are met through these activities? Which drives must be frustrated in order to complete your activities? In what ways have you been taught that it is not "good" to satisfy your own drives? Do you believe that these teachings are justifiable?

2. Visit an introductory lecture for EST, Lifespring, or some other popular "self-improvement" course being sold in your area. What sorts of frustrations does the course promise to help solve? What solution is offered? How difficult is it to resist the sales pressures put on you? (If you are weak in resisting sales pressures, you may want to skip this suggestion.)

3. Find an opportunity to observe a small child under five years of age, either at home or in a school or play setting. See if you can observe the ways in which the child's behavior and thinking are shaped by the environment. How much of the learning is through direct verbal instruction, how much is through observation and modeling, and how much through rewards and punishments from the environment or from other people? If you can observe more than one environment, see if you can detect differences.

4. Purchase a popular magazine sold at a supermarket checkout counter. See how

people's frustrated drives are dealt with, both in the editorial matter and in the advertising. How many cures for defects such as obesity and baldness are offered? How many opportunities to get rich quick? How do the stories provide an opportunity to escape from the boredom of everyday existence and satisfy one's needs in a fantasy world?

Selected Readings

Adorno, T. W., et al. *The Authoritarian Personality.* New York: Harper & Row, 1950.

Chakotin, Sergei. *The Rape of the Masses.* New York: Avon, 1940.

Durkheim, Émile. *Suicide.* Glencoe, Ill.: Free Press, 1951.

Freud, Sigmund. *Civilization and Its Discontents.* New York: Norton, 1962 (1929).

———. *The Future of an Illusion.* New York: Doubleday, 1953 (1927).

———. *The Group Psychology and the Analyses of Ego.* New York: Bantam, 1966 (1921).

Fromm, Erich. *The Crises in Psychoanalysis.* Greenwich, Conn.: Fawcett, 1971.

———. *The Dogma of Christ and Other Essays.* New York: Holt, 1963.

———. *Escape from Freedom.* New York: Avon, 1971 (1941).

———. *The Sane Society.* New York: Holt, 1953.

Goertzel, Mildred; Goertzel, Victor; and Goertzel, Ted. *Three Hundred Eminent Personalities.* San Francisco: Jossey-Bass, 1977.

Henry, Jules. *Culture Against Man.* New York: Random House, 1965.

Marcuse, Herbert. *Eros and Civilization.* Boston: Beacon, 1952.

Marx, Karl. *Economic and Philosophical Manuscripts.* New York: International, 1964 (1844).

Maslow, Abraham. *Towards a Psychology of Being.* Princeton: Van Nostrand, 1962.

Mitchell, Juliet. *Psychoanalysis and Feminism.* New York: Pantheon, 1974.

Pareto, Vilfredo. *The Mind and Society.* New York: Harcourt, 1935 (1916).

Pavlov, Ivan P. *Lectures on Conditioned Reflexes.* New York: International, 1941.

Reich, Wilhelm. *Character Analaysis.* New York: Farrar, Straus & Giroux, 1972.

———. *The Mass Psychology of Fascism.* New York: Farrar, Straus & Giroux, 1970 (1945).

———. *Sexpol.* New York: Random, 1972.

Skinner, B. F. *The Behavior of Organisms.* New York: D. Appleton-Century, 1938.

Wells, Harry. *Pavlov and Freud.* New York: International, 1956.

Chapter 7

Culture and
Class Consciousness

The concept "culture" has played an important role in social science. As it is used in social science, "culture" refers to socially shared and transmitted knowledge. Culture includes beliefs about how the world is and about how it ought to be. As we have seen, culture is transmitted from one generation to another through the socialization process. For a person to be a member of a society, he or she must know basic things about the culture of that society. An American, for example, must know that when meeting someone you shake his or her hand, that a fork is used for eating food, that red means stop and green means go, that men wear pants but women can wear either pants or dresses. All of these things are quite obvious to anyone socialized in American culture and need little comment.

It is not surprising that anthropologists tend to place great emphasis on the concept of culture. In studying diverse primitive societies they are constantly working with cultural beliefs that are different from those in our own society. A good part of their work consists of cataloguing these beliefs and the practices which correspond to them, and trying to show how the beliefs fit into the structure of the particular society. But why should culture be of concern to sociologists who are working in a society the basic cultural patterns of which are well known to their readers?

Conservative sociologists often place emphasis on culture because they believe that values and ideas are the central factors that hold societies together. Thus, they argue that American society is capitalist because American culture stresses competitive values, or that America is a democratic society because Americans believe in democracy. Conservatives tend to stress beliefs that are *national* in character. They appeal to patriotic or nationalist sentiments in order to avoid dividing societies along class lines. Thus, we are taught to feel strong emotions when we hear the national anthem or recite the pledge of allegiance. Such feelings of loyalty to our own national and ethnic group can be used to encourage us to follow the leadership of the dominant groups within the society.

Radical sociologists place less emphasis on culture, since they do not believe that culture is the central factor which shapes the nature of society. They recognize that some cultural practices are simply arbitrary rules which make it possible for us to live together. For example, it makes no difference whether we all drive on the right side of the street or on the left side of the street, but it is important that we all agree on one or the other. These cultural norms are not problematic, however. They do not merit the extensive discussion often given them in introductory sociology books which imply that most social norms are of this nature.

There are times, however, when the study of cultural beliefs is important to radical social scientists. One is when these beliefs conflict with human nature or distort objective reality. When the culture requires that we suppress our needs for sociability or repress our sexual drives, radical sociologists question whether the norms are useful or necessary. When we are told that Pepsi-Cola will make us "young, fair, and debonair," we wonder what it is in our society that generates such obvious lies. The radical anthropologist Jules Henry studied "pecuniary pseudo-truths." These are beliefs which are not true, and which everyone knows are not really true, but which are part of our consciousness nonetheless because of the influence of advertising on our thinking. For instance, no one really believes that "Pango Peach" color by Revlon comes from "east of the sun and west of the moon where each tomorrow dawns," or that it is "so succulent on your lips and sizzling on your fingertips (and on your toes, goodness knows)," that it will be your "adventure in paradise." But American women do buy lipstick in the belief that it will somehow make them more attractive or make their lives more exciting.

Culture and Social Class

Radicals are interested in cultural ideas that reflect the interests of specific social classes. In most cases, the middle and upper classes are in control of those institutions in society that define our culture. Through the churches, the media, and the educational institutions they propagate a set of beliefs that are generally consistent with their own view of the world. Through these institutions the upper and middle classes encourage the belief that American society is just and democratic, and that everyone receives a fair reward for the work he or she performs. These cultural beliefs are useful for defending the privileges of those who are on the top in our society. If the working class can be taught to accept these ideas, they will be less likely to rebel against the system that represses them.

There are sets of ideas that correspond to the distinctive structured life experiences and interests of every class in capitalist society. People in a given class may or may not actually hold such ideas, however, since the actual consciousness of a class is a product of its experiences and interests *and* of its exposure to the media, education, religion, and the state. The upper class in capitalist society uses its control of these institutions of cultural production to propagate to the working classes ideas that correspond to the experiences and interests of the upper classes. As a result, false consciousness, or an invalid understanding of the real structure and operation of society, is systematically spread throughout all classes. Thus, the higher in the class system a class is, the more likely it is to have a true consciousness, since the more compatible its experiences and interests are with the ideas it gets from the cultural institutions. Working-class people are very likely to have a high degree of true consciousness about practical questions associated with their daily life, since these questions relate closely to their everyday experiences. But on more abstract religious, philosophical, moral, or political questions that are far removed from their daily experiences they tend to accept the ideas put forth in the media and thus acquire a false consciousness (as with their attitudes on China, Vietnam, Communism, and the like). While only consistent forces operate on the consciousness of the upper class, conflicting forces operate on that of the working classes. As a result, only under certain special conditions (which will be examined in Chapter 14) do working-class people clear their heads and gain a true consciousness of the forces operating on them.

Ideas do not create themselves. They are created in a specific social context and for a specific purpose. Once they are created and accepted by large numbers of people, however, they come to have a power of their own. Once ideas become rooted in the character structure of individuals, they become powerful social forces. Ideas arise from the experiences and interests of one or another class (material forces) and change only when the underlying forces that produce and reproduce them change. But as long as they are held they can have considerable influence on human behavior. The more intensely we believe in an idea, the more influence that idea has.

Culture and Personality

Human beings act towards things in good part because of the meaning those things have for them. Almost all human action is influenced by what we think things are and how we think things will respond to our actions. Our response to the flag of our country or party, to a cross or swastika, to a man with a bishop's or a judge's robe, to a sensuously dressed person, etc., are all a product of learned meanings we give these things. These meanings are not intrinsic. They are rather a product of society and our socialization into it. Another way of saying this is that such meanings are "symbolic." They bear no innate relation to the material objects that represent them. They are quite arbitrary. There is nothing about a certain combination of stars and

In recent years, patriotic values have often been a source of social conflict.

bars that invokes patriotic feelings. We have to be conditioned through years of schooling to have patriotic reactions when such a combination is presented.

The meanings we give to things arise in the process of our interaction with others—especially with powerful others such as parents and teachers. These meanings learned in such interactions are not arbitrary; nor are they completely uniformly constructed by all. The meanings passed on to us by our parents and by the schools are highly structured by society, but always there is a little slippage. Also, there are idiosyncrasies in our parents, teachers, and learning situations so that no two persons ever come out exactly the same. However, we are not really free to significantly change our mentors or to innovate very much in the meanings we receive. The mechanisms of social control over us are too powerful. These mechanisms range from beatings and scoldings, to pats on the back, love, approval, and acceptance.

There are two dimensions in understanding the social significance of cultural ideas: (1) their content, and (2) how deeply they are held. Although simply believing in the socially encouraged meanings of things has a considerable impact on our behavior, unless such meanings are anchored in our character structure or personalities, they may well become ineffective as motivating forces in situations where action on the basis of these meanings is not reinforced by other people. Ideas are often accepted by people who are not really touched by them. The real influence of any idea depends on the extent to which it appeals to the psychic needs in those who hold it. Ideas not rooted in the powerful needs of the personality will have little influence in a crisis situation or when the individual has conflicting forces acting on him or her.

Such unrooted ideas will have an influence only when what the ideas impel is the easiest course for the individual to follow. A classical example of this was the behavior of the German working class when the Nazis came to power in the 1930s. Although most of them voted for, and intellectually supported, the Communists and Socialists, they did not fight for their ideas. They instead pretty much went along with the Nazi appeals to their gut feelings of patriotism. Another example of the failure of unrooted ideas to influence behavior is in religion. There are great numbers of "Sunday Christians" who attend Church and profess faith in the doctrines of their faith but whose economic life is uninfluenced by these principles. In both cases the unrooted ideas came into conflict with much more powerful forces—patriotic feelings rooted in the German character structure and economic self-interest in the second example. In both cases the ideas give way. Such does not happen to all ideas, however. Revolutionaries and Christians have often been known to sacrifice their lives to advance their goal of realizing their ideas. But this occurs only when the ideas they hold are fully integrated with their deepest needs, i.e., when they become part of their character structure.

Not all behavior is guided by meanings. Often we do things without understanding why or deceiving ourselves as to our real motivation. The basic forces in our character structure are the primary forces impelling us to behave in our typical ways. Whether or not we are attracted to a strong leader, whether or not we feel strong attachments to our country or party, our attitude towards our parents, and our close relationships with people of the opposite sex, for example, are in their fundamentals determined by our character structure. Each of us, when questioned, will interpret our behavior towards each of these things in a relatively rational way, accounting for it with a recitation of a plausible meaning that these things *should* have for us, e.g., "I am patriotic because the U.S. is the best country in the world," "I don't kill because my religion says it is a sin," "I am unhappy because I'm not married," "I work hard because I want to pass something on to my children," etc. In fact such "meanings" as these, and a great many more, often have little or nothing to do with what is really motivating people. Our real motives are often unconscious. But since we have learned to appear to be rational and to accept society's definitions of acceptable motives we use a language of meanings that is epiphenomenal. Such meanings are often self-deceptions, as well as deceptions of others, and cover for what we really feel. Meanings in such a case play no role in our behavior except to alleviate guilt and get others to support us. This can be demonstrated by the frequency and suddenness with which people often change their behavior when their underlying feelings change, and, consequently, just as rapidly change their interpretations of their motives. It can also be demonstrated by observing the lack of effect that theoretical refutations of the rationales for doing something have on actual behavior. When one rationale is destroyed, typically another one is developed to rationalize the same behavior. Thus, our motives run much deeper than the mere intellectualized meanings we give things. Only those who cannot admit the power of nonrational forces in their own behavior could fail to recognize this fact.

Ideas indigenous to the dominant classes are often adopted by and become great motivating forces for working people. This occurs in good part because the frustrations of working-class life are channeled by the worker's character structure in ways that support the maintenance of the class structure. Workers come to adopt the ideas of the upper classes which are transmitted *directly* by the mass media, schools, and churches, or, *indirectly*, through the mediation of close relatives (especially parents) or friends. We often trust those personally close to us more than we do the impersonal media and, consequently, give much greater credence to what such people think. But the impact on our thinking of the institutions of reality definition (the media, schools, and churches) is no less because of this, since the ultimate source of ideas is still concentrated in these same institutions. Only if relatives and friends acquire their ideas from alternative media, schools, or organizations (such as radical political parties) will what we accept from them be any different from what we acquire from the dominant institutions directly.

Both the character of ideas and the intensity of one's belief in them (i.e., their motivating power) are a function of one's social position. This is true of all types of beliefs—religious, political, philosophical, ethical, aesthetic, and scientific. For example, in those countries whose political systems offer a real alternative between political parties, it is always the case that the higher up one is in the class system, the more likely he or she is to support the more conservative of available choices, while the lower down one is in the stratification system, the more frequent is support of the more radical alternative. For the last generation in France and Italy approximately 50 percent of the manual working class has voted for the Communist Party, while only about 5 percent of the middle and 1 percent of the upper middle classes have expressed the same preferences. A similar phenomenon is found in religious choices in the United States. Not only does religious belief vary as a function of class position, but the depth of religious commitment varies as well. The further down in the stratification system, the more people's drives are frustrated and thus the greater the amount of energy they have for religion. As a result Episcopal, Presbyterian, and Unitarian services are highly subdued and intellectualized, with very little emotional involvement in songs or ceremony. Among Catholics, Methodists, and non-fundamentalist Baptists, services involve somewhat more participation and somewhat less intellectualizing but nevertheless do not require very much emotional energy. Among the churches and sects of the poor, however, there is very little intellectualizing. Instead there is tremendous emotional involvement of the people in religious services, even in some cases to the point of physical orgasm.

RELIGION

Cultural ideas are often expressed through religious institutions. In primitive societies, religious ideas are largely concerned with nature. Religious rituals are used in an attempt to bring rain or sunshine, to ward off disease, or to provide plentiful game for the hunters. In these societies there is no clear distinction between religion and other areas of cultural belief. In class societies, however, religion frequently comes to be dominated by the ruling classes. Often, religion is integrated with the state and people are required to accept the tenets of a specific religion. Religion comes to be used as a mechanism of social control over working people. In these societies, religion provides a consolation for the suffering of people on earth and a projection of one's hopes into the future. Religious theology is a projection of the earthly social structure into the heavens.

The theological descriptions of the relationships among the gods and their relatives (such as the Virgin Mother and Her Son), angels, saints, and regular people closely reflect the relationships among people in the society in which the religion originates and is currently held. There is a particularly close correspondence between the postulated relationships between God and human beings and the real relationship between the earthly rulers and the earthly ruled. Polytheistic religions, for example, existed in societies without central authority. Religions with gentle and humane gods grew out of societies with nonauthoritarian families and political structures. Patriarchical family structures are correlated with wrathful and unmerciful concepts of God. Monotheistic religions did not generally develop until after the foundation of Oriental despotisms. The gods of Judaism, Christianity, and Islam are projections of the omnipotent and omniscient emperors of Rome, Egypt, and other despotic empires.

Religion is an intensely emotional experience. People can only relate to it when it allows for the expression of sentiments people *know* to be true. What people *know* to be true is a direct product of their biological needs and their structured frustrations as well as their life experiences in general. Both of these later forces are a product of the social, economic, and political organization of society. Religious morality is often used in practice both to hinder the development of class consciousness and to reinforce respect for existing authority. Concretely, most religions, particularly the religions of the working class and the poor—Baptistism, Methodism, the Messianic sects, and Catholicism—have condemned in their sermons and literature radical political involvement, preaching either political abstention or submission to governmental authority. The notion of hierarchy and place is integral to all the Christian churches. The belief in the omnipotence of God and the doctrines of submission and sin have traditionally been generalized to include a submissive attitude toward political authority. These doctrines reinforce feelings of inadequacy in the working classes and build into them a respect for power. Christianity, as well as the other "world religions," accordingly serve as a major support to all the authoritarian class institutions of capitalist society.

It is no accident that religious institutions are usually conservative. Most institutionalized religions are in fact controlled by members of the upper class, who sit on their boards, who supply or promote their Popes and Bishops, and who make generous financial contributions. Moreover, when the lower-class leadership of less socially

Religion can offer comfort for the oppressed and alienated in society.

acceptable churches are given privileged status, they often take advantage of their position (in a manner fully analogous to trade union leaders) to consolidate and extend their power. In this process they come to identify with upper-class ideology and institutional forms in opposition to their own people.

Oppressed people need consolation. Their religions are a reflection of their needs. In Marx's words:

> Religious suffering is at the same time an expression of real suffering and a protest against real suffering. Religion is the sign of the oppressed creature, the sentiment of a heartless world, and the soul of soulless conditions. It is the opium of the people.

Religion, like consciousness-contracting drugs, allows oppressed people to deal with their oppression by desensitizing themselves to it rather than trying to change their condition. The underlying motivation for oppressed people becoming heroin addicts is identical with that for becoming enthusiasts of some Messianic cult. It makes no more sense to intellectually criticize religion for being an illusion, than it does to pass laws against taking dope. Both are merely symptoms of deeply felt needs being denied by an oppressive society. Marx goes on:

> The abolition of religion as the illusory happiness of men is a demand for their real happiness. The call to abandon their illusions about their condition is a call

185

The wall sign in revolutionary Portugal reads: "Religion, the Opiate of the People."

Ted Goertzel

to abandon a condition which requires illusions. The criticism of religion is, therefore, the embryonic criticism of this vale of tears of which religion is the halo.

Because religion does provide consolation to people, it normally serves a very conservative function. By preaching acceptance of the existing order and obedience to existing authorities in favor of preparing for the much more important afterlife, it serves as a powerful legitimating force for the status quo. What matters the humiliations of seventy years compared with the riches of all Eternity? Render unto Caesar the things that are Caesar's—i.e., power and wealth, for you shall inherit the earth.

The specific mandates of religious authority not to steal or kill and not to engage in sexual activities support the existing structure of private property, handicap resistance, and reinforce the repression of the social drives (which serves as energy for authoritarian character structures).

The ruling class cannot, however, directly control what goes on in every church in the land. For this, they must rely on middle-class ministers, priests, and rabbis. Under certain conditions, these ministers may come to challenge certain aspects of the dominant culture. Thus, the black churches in the southern United States generally served to help black people survive the humiliation of living in a segregated, racist society. When the possibility of change in racial conditions emerged in the 1950s and 1960s, however, a few religious leaders such as Martin Luther King, Jr.

were able to use their positions to lead movements for social change. These movements were limited in their scope, but they did help to mobilize discontent during their early stages. Similarly, some religious leaders during the 1960s were active in the movement against the war in Vietnam.

Middle-class people often take cultural ideals quite seriously, even more so than upper-class people. This is because their careers are intimately tied up with ideas. Preachers who make their living teaching the ideals of Christianity may come to take those ideas so seriously that they try to apply them by working to advance the cause of the poor and oppressed. Educators who teach the principles of democracy to their students may try to act on those principles to attempt to bring about a true realization of the cultural ideals of equal justice for all. Thus, while religion plays a predominately conservative role in society, there are some religious leaders who play a progressive role in social movements.

MASS MEDIA

Control over the mass media—radio, popular magazines, the press, and especially television—is an extremely important mechanism by which to control people's consciousness. Control over the media means that the meanings given to social things is defined by the upper class. A more or less common consciousness is inculcated in the masses of working people through manipulation that precludes the emergence of effective opposition in the society. False needs are created which are superimposed on the individual. The influence of the mass media, supported by the network of personal contacts with the informal opinion leaders in all classes (who themselves receive their opinions from the media), sets the limits within which public opinion debates the controversial issues of the day. The mass media determine the framework within which decisions are made. Consequently, basic issues almost never get raised—issues such as who should own the factories, should the work week be twenty hours, should personal fortunes be abolished, etc.

Again, the media propagate the ideas and images they do because of how they are controlled. The media are for the most part big corporations, and like all corporations they are both interested in making profits and are directly controlled by the rich. Most of the influential magazines are owned by members of the upper class, e.g., *Time, Newsweek, The New Republic, The Nation, The New York Review of Books, The National Review*. The three major networks, NBC, CBS, and ABC, are run by members of the upper class. A large number of the more important newspapers as well as the news services are owned by members of the upper class, or are controlled by large newspaper chains, such as Hearst, Knight, and Scripps-Howard. The many upper-middle-class-owned newspapers and radio stations are largely dependent on the big media corporations for their news.

In addition to being controlled by the requirements of corporations and being run by upper-class people, the media have additional social control exercised on them through advertising. The threat of a withdrawal of advertising money in the event that a media institution should support antisystem ideas is a major force insuring against deviation from the system.

While the media are owned by upper-class individuals and corporations, they must rely on middle-class editors as well as reporters to do the actual day to day work of presenting the news. These reporters are often much more liberal or even radical in their ideas than their employers. When a split in the ruling class develops, they may be able to play a somewhat autonomous role. Thus, when Richard Nixon violated the rules of the game by sending his agents to violate not only the offices of the Socialist Workers Party and other radical groups but also those of the Democratic Party, liberal reporters were able to pursue the issue to the point of forcing the politicians to do something about it. Newspaper reporters are often quite cynical about the system, because their work gives them detailed knowledge of much corruption that is hidden from public view. Sometimes they are able to make a stir by exposing some particularly blatant abuse to the public. These exposés can be useful in selling newspapers, but as long as they deal only with specific scandals they do not undermine the system itself.

The American news media are primarily concerned with selling commodities since their revenue comes from advertising. They tend to stress sensational events which interest readers or listeners. They pay attention to social movements when such outrageous tactics as sit-ins, mass disruptive demonstrations, or hijackings are used because an audience can be attracted for the commercials. They give little space to interpretative reporting, which would help their readers to understand the less exciting but more important economic and social forces that shape their lives.

EDUCATIONAL INSTITUTIONS

The function of schooling in capitalist society is to produce the kind of people the system needs, to train people for the jobs the corporations require and to instill in them the proper attitudes and values necessary for the proper fulfillment of one's social role. People must not only be trained in the necessary skills, but they must also receive the correct ideas and be inculcated with a proper respect for authority.

Because the society needs a wide range of skills and because it has different requirements in the kinds of ideas and respect for authority people should have, educational institutions vary greatly in the kinds of education they provide. On the one hand, they must train an elite group of people capable of governing society. This particular group must have a broad and liberal education, be taught to identify with broad values and be encouraged in its autonomy and initiative, since it will have to make decisions. Of course, the existing privileged classes channel their own children into this kind of educational institution. Most "free schools" are run by and for the

Ted Goertzel

Circle time at a "progressive" school.

upper middle class. The vast majority of positions in the society, however, require more or less menial labor and the ability to follow orders. Thus, most children have to be processed by educational institutions geared to producing people who are functionally suited to these roles. The vast majority of the children of the working class receive this type of education. Feelings of inadequacy are cultivated in the children and they are systematically turned off to self-development. For the schools to operate otherwise would put them at loggerheads with the businessmen that control them. The job of the schools is to "produce" the kind of "products" that the corporations need. There is a relatively small "market" for well-educated and independent-minded "commodities." However, since the continuity and strength of any class system requires the continual infusion of the brightest, most creative, and best motivated members of other classes into the upper class's ranks, the school system must provide for the co-option of a relatively few working-class children who show extraordinary potential into the ranks of the privileged.

The consequence of the differential needs of the system is a great variation in the quality of school systems, ranging from excellent private schools for the upper and upper middle class to mere disciplinary institutions in the urban ghettos. Even within the same school there are tracks for different classes of people who are being prepared for different careers—college, vocational, business. People from higher-class backgrounds are almost automatically put into the college tracks, while minorities and the white poor are almost automatically put into the vocational and business tracks.

Public education was made universal (or virtually universal) in this country during the crucial years of the consolidation of monopoly capitalism, at the same time as the other key institutions of this social type—the mass army, the universal franchise, the welfare system, trade unions, patriotism, mass sports, etc.—were also being institutionalized. In the face of the massive migration of workers from Europe to feed the rapidly growing factory system, there developed an increasing fear (and reality) of massive social disorders emanating from this class. Compulsory public education was instituted at this time as part of the effort to integrate the working-class immigrant into American society. It was designed to instill in them ruling-class ideology and patriotism as well as proper work attitudes. Civics and American history have long been central to the curriculum of American junior and senior high schools. The examples in math problems as well as the selections in reading exercises focus on reinforcing capitalist ideology: "If Joe pays $100 for 20 pairs of shoes and $50 for his overhead, how much profit does he make if he sells all his shoes at $10 a pair?" Readings stress individualism and middle-class values and are often permeated with sexism and racism. Heroes, even when the action takes place in Third World countries, are normally white male individuals.

Reading, writing, and arithmetic, instead of the classical subjects of Latin, Greek, history, philosophy, and rhetoric, have come to be stressed in the public primary schools since these former skills are required by industrial capitalism in its laboring force. Meanwhile, the private schools to which the elite sent their children, for a long time continued to stress the classical education best suited to produce a ruling-class mentality. The public schools stress the principles of discipline, order, punctuality, and cleanliness because these are the qualities desired in a good worker. The inculcation of these values is as important as the three Rs. Learning to stand and march in lines, to be on time, not to miss days, to ask permission to go to the bathroom, not to talk unless spoken to, to show respect for the teacher, etc., are central processes in the education of the American working-class child who must later respond correctly in a factory situation. Unless conditioned in the schools to factory discipline, the work force would be very unruly once it was employed. The schools, too, are highly competitive institutions. This is epitomized in the system of differential grading. Students internalize the ideal of striving for better and better grades *as individuals* against their fellow students. They are encouraged never to be satisfied with their grades, but rather always to try to improve their positions. The competitive grade-seeking attitude is carried over into industry as the never-ending pursuit of money and the constant striving for more and more of it even at the expense of one's fellow workers.

Higher Education

Universities, like the grade schools, are synchronized to serve the needs of the system. Most institutions of higher education function to train the highly educated employees needed by the increasingly technologically sophisticated corporations, and to propagate a highly sophisticated ideological defense of corporate capitalism in its social science and humanities programs. The so-called "social sciences," as we saw in Chapter 1, are mostly geared to providing legitimation to the corporate system, although some practical techniques for social control are also taught in these disciplines. The presence of business schools to train middle-level corporate managers and of ROTC programs reflects an orientation that pervades the entire university.

Just as the grade-school system is highly differentiated to provide the different types of people the system needs, so is the university system. The different tracks within a university (professional schools, engineering, liberal arts, etc.) each recruit largely from a distinctive class. Of course, they also train people for distinctive functions. Colleges and universities themselves vary immensely in their functions and in the quality of the education they provide. There are basically three levels to the stratification of the university system. The highest level is the elite schools, the Ivy League, Stanford, Berkeley, the University of Chicago, and a handful of others, which are geared to training the new ruling class and the elite of the professions. As we have seen, most upper-class, often prep school, graduates go to these schools, but the very brightest and most promising students of other classes are also recruited and subsequently co-opted into the privileged strata after graduation. The middle-level higher educational institutions are composed of the state universities and colleges and the less prestigious private schools. These schools recruit the sons and daughters of the working and middle classes and train them for lesser professional positions. A great many of these graduates end up performing caretaker functions for the system as parole officers, welfare workers, social science teachers, and the like. The lowest level of educational institutions, the junior or community colleges, have grown the fastest in recent years. These institutions have two functions: (1) the training of skilled workers, such as mechanics, hairdressers, technicians, etc., and (2) the "cooling out" of those who aspire to professional jobs but who can't get into the regular colleges because of restrictions on enrollment geared to synchronizing college output to the needs of the corporations. Typically, the two years of junior college become grades 13 and 14 of high school, with the alienation of the high-school experience increasing to prod most community college students to give up their aspirations and accept skilled or semiskilled work careers.

The enrollment in each of these types of institutions is synchronized with the needs of the corporate system both through the trustees that govern them and the state and corporate institutions that finance them. The quality differential of each level is maintained by the same mechanism. For example, in California during the 1960s, 60 percent of all of the state system of higher education funds went to the universities, 30 percent to the state colleges, and only 10 percent to the junior colleges. This is in spite of the fact that their enrollments are more or less in inverse relation to their funding.

As is the case with the governance of virtually all important institutions of American society, the universities are controlled by the upper class. Members of the social upper class sit on the boards of trustees of the universities. They are further responsible for a great deal of their funding through family endowments, personal gifts, foundation grants, corporate donations and contracts. One third of all the trustees of the thirty most important universities in the United States in the 1960s were listed in the *Social Register*. The trustees of major universities and of state university systems are made up largely of top businessmen, corporate lawyers, and members of the power elite (i.e., individuals from institutions directly controlled by the upper class). About 50 percent of all college and university trustees also sit on the boards of trustees of private corporations. Businessmen, not educators, run higher education. Universities are very much like any other business except that their product is properly trained employees rather than profits.

Of course, the universities cannot be staffed by upper-class people. There aren't enough of them; nor do they have the time or interest. Middle-class professors and administrators do the day to day work of teaching courses, writing articles and books, and making administrative decisions within the policies set by the boards of trustees. This group of professional educators likes to think of itself as independent of social pressures and dedicated only to truth and academic freedom. Certain medieval traditions, such as life tenure for faculty members, are retained, giving credibility to the myth of the independence of the university.

To an extent, the middle class does succeed in maintaining its independence from the ruling upper class. Day to day decisions about course offerings, hirings and firings, content of courses, degree requirements, etc., are made by faculty and administrators. However, the ruling class has a variety of devices, such as control over research funding and departmental budgets, that can be used to encourage faculty members who wish to have successful careers to avoid stepping on the toes of powerful interests. University faculties themselves are highly stratified. Some older professors have "tenure" and are given the power to pass on the careers of the younger, "untenured" professors. Generally, this older group becomes somewhat conservative because its members enjoy a secure and privileged position in society.

These conservative senior professors generally control the graduate programs where college teachers are trained. In these programs, imagination and creativity are often discouraged in the interest of churning out "competent professionals" who are willing to work on problems considered safe by the system. Control over graduate fellowships, passing of examinations, and recommendations for jobs is used to encourage graduate students to learn to work within accepted paradigms. As the radical sociologist Thorstein Veblen remarked, graduate education most frequently cultivates a trained *incapacity* to understand society. It does this by enforcing the use of liberal and conservative paradigms that limit consideration to certain selected aspects of society.

These controls are not always successful. A certain percentage of faculty and students become attracted to radical ideas during the course of their reading and study, or because of their involvement in radical social movements. During periods of conservative dominance in the society, such as the McCarthyist period in the 1950s, these radicals are forced to conceal their views or to risk being fired or expelled. They are able to survive in the system only when there is some powerful social constituency that protects them. During the 1960s, college trustees and administrators were frightened of radical student protest on campus. Consequently, they were cautious about firing radical professors or expelling radical students. During this period, a good many radicals began academic careers. By today, there are a number of radical academicians who hold tenure in American universities. If they are able to retain sufficient support from students, or from other constituencies in the community, they may be able to assure that the universities remain open to radical as well as to liberal and conservative ideas.

In general, the upper class and corporate elite attempt to use the cultural institutions of society to propagate ideas that are in their own class interest. To do this, they must rely upon middle-class professionals who staff these institutions. If these professionals think of themselves as an elite group with special privileges and prerogatives, they are likely to share the conservative and liberal ideas of the ruling class. There are limits, however, to the ability of the system to buy off middle-class professionals. As the university system has grown, it has become too expensive to pay high salaries. As more and more people have sought graduate education in the hopes of following middle-class careers, there has developed a surplus of teachers at all levels in the system.

More and more, many middle-class professionals are coming to see that their condition is increasingly similar to that of workers. They must sell their labor power to an employer in order to sustain themselves, just like workers. The wage they receive, the working conditions they must accept, and their opportunities for advancement largely depend on economic forces beyond their individual control. Consequently, many middle-class professionals are increasingly turning to unionization in an effort to defend their economic interest. Such unions in some cases work to protect the privileges that professionals have received in the past. But it is unlikely that professional unionism will be able to protect these privileges without support from the broader working-class labor movement. If middle-class professionals wish to retain their professional integrity and independence, they must seek support from workers. They cannot expect the public to support payment of increased tax moneys to them unless the public is receiving fair benefits for the money they pay in taxes. True independence for educators and other professionals from the demands of capitalism will require an alliance with the working class.

In class societies, culture is not a neutral instrument of societal survival. Cultural ideas and beliefs are used as a mechanism of maintaining the hegemony of the ruling class over the society. Those who work in the intellectual and artistic fields in these societies cannot be oblivious to this. Attempting to ignore the political and ideological implications of their work will inevitably lead to accepting the ideas of the dominant class of the society, since these ideas permeate the thinking of all people socialized in the society. Intellectual work in class societies must necessarily be part of the class struggle.

Summary

Cultural beliefs in primitive societies are designed to help people to live together and confront their common environment. In class societies, however, cultural beliefs are shaped by institutions in the control of the upper and middle classes. People in the working class in capitalist societies are often brought to accept ideas that are really in the interest of the dominant class. In some cases these ideas are accepted on only a superficial level, in others they become a deeply ingrained part of people's character structures.

There are three major institutions of cultural production and indoctrination: the church, the school, and the mass media. Churches are class stratified, with people from different class backgrounds attending churches with varied beliefs and practices. Religious ethics often stress submission to secular authority, while providing comfort for the oppressed by promising relief in the spiritual world. The mass media are controlled by capitalist corporations, and function to shape opinion by choosing certain issues as important and by presenting only a limited range of alternative positions on issues. Education, also, is highly stratified. Middle- and upper-class children receive progressive, quality, early education, then go on to elite universities. Working-class children are exposed to educational systems that often teach them little more than the necessity for accepting authority. Ideas created in the elite graduate schools are diffused throughout the system.

Review Questions

1. Why do working-class people often have false consciousness?
2. Give some examples of how ideas can be used as rationalizations to justify behavior that is based on deeper psychological needs.
3. What is meant by the concept "culture"? Why do conservative and radical sociologists differ in their analysis of the role of culture in society?
4. In what ways do the characteristic religious beliefs and practices of the various social classes in American society systematically differ?
5. What was Marx's analysis of the role of religion in society?
6. In what ways do members of the upper class exercise control of the mass media in American society?
7. How does the primary-school education given to middle-class children in American society differ from that typically given to working-class children?
8. How does the structure of the educational system in American society reflect the needs of the capitalist economy?

9. How are American colleges and universities stratified in terms of the types of students they teach and the programs they offer?

10. In what ways does the structure of graduate education in the United States encourage conservatism?

Suggestions for Further Study

1. On three Sunday mornings, visit churches in different neighborhoods. Choose a storefront church in a poor neighborhood, a church in a working-class neighborhood and a church in a wealthy suburb. Observe the behavior and dress of the parishioners. What needs do they appear to be fulfilling through attending church services. Observe the way in which services are conducted, and note the dominant theme of the sermon, songs, and other messages presented. Do your observations accord with the generalizations presented in this chapter?

2. Do a systematic content analysis of a portion of the mass media serving your area. You can choose a radio or television station or a daily newspaper. Keep track of the news stories covered, in order of prominence (determined by their location in the paper and by the space given to them, or by the time given on electronic media). In what ways are certain issues emphasized and others minimized? In editorials or other places where opinions can easily be determined, what range of opinion is presented? What opinions are notable by their absence? What alternative issues and perspectives might be presented by a more radical media? As a group project, you can compare different papers and stations, perhaps including radical ones.

3. If you can obtain permission to do so, perhaps through your college's education department, visit classrooms in different parts of the city and observe the differences in conditions, class size, the type of lessons presented, and the behavior of students and teachers. If you can't observe this directly, get the information secondhand by interviewing students who have done student teaching in different schools. Do the differences correspond to the generalizations presented in this book?

Selected Readings

Bernays, Edward. *The Engineering of Consent*. Norman: U. of Oklahoma Press, 1955.

Bowles, Samuel, and Gintis, Herbert. *Education in Corporate America*. New York: Basic Books, 1976.

Chakotin, Sergei. *The Rape of the Masses.* New York: Alliance Press, 1940.

Cornforth, Maurice. *The Theory of Knowledge.* New York: International, 1971 (1963).

Domhoff, G. William. *Who Rules America?* Englewood Cliffs, N.J.: Prentice-Hall, 1967.

Freud, Sigmund. *The Future of an Illusion.* New York: Doubleday, 1953 (1927).

Fromm, Erich. *Escape from Freedom.* New York: Harcourt, Brace & World, 1940.

———. *Psychoanalysis and Religion.* New Haven: Yale U. Press, 1950.

Goode, Erich, and Faberman, Harvey. *Social Reality.* Englewood Cliffs, N.J.: Prentice-Hall, 1973.

Katz, Michael. *Class, Bureaucracy and Schools.* New York: Praeger, 1971.

———. *The Irony of Early School Reform.* Cambridge: Harvard U. Press, 1968.

Laternari, Vittorio. *The Religions of the Oppressed.* New York: New American Library, 1963.

Lipset, Seymour Martin. *Political Man.* New York: Doubleday, 1959.

Marcuse, Herbert. *One Dimensional Man.* Boston: Beacon, 1964.

Marx, Karl, and Engels, Frederick. *The German Ideology.* New York: International, 1970 (1845).

———. *On Religion.* Moscow: Foreign Languages, 1955.

Niebuhr, M. Richard. *The Social Sources of Denominationalism.* New York: Meridian, 1959 (1929).

Packard, Vance. *The Hidden Persuaders.* New York: McKay, 1957.

Pope, Liston. *Millhands and Preachers.* New Haven: Yale U. Press, 1971 (1942).

Pareto, Vilfredo. *The Mind and Society.* New York: Dover, 1935.

Reich, Wilhelm. *Character Analysis.* New York: Farrar, Straus & Giroux, 1949.

———. *Mass Psychology of Fascism.* New York: Farrar, Straus & Giroux, 1970 (1945).

Schiller, Herbert. *The Mind Managers.* Boston: Beacon, 1973.

Smith, David. *Who Rules the Universities?* New York: Monthly Review, 1974.

Spring, Joel. *Education and the Rise of the Corporate State.* Boston: Beacon, 1972.

Veblen, Thorstein. *The Higher Learning in America.* New York: Hill & Wang, 1957 (1918).

Weber, Max. *The Sociology of Religion.* Boston: Beacon, 1964.

Worsley, Peter. *The Trumpet Shall Sound.* New York: Schocken, 1968.

Yinger, J. Milton. *Religion in the Struggle for Power.* New York: Russell, 1961.

Chapter 8

The Capitalist State

Those of us who have grown up in contemporary societies tend to take the existence of the state for granted. While we are often suspicious of politicians, and resent intrusions of the state into our own lives, we accept the government as a necessary evil. If we study anthropology, however, we will learn that primitive societies have lived without a state, that is to say, without any organization having a monopoly on the legitimate use of force. Leadership was primarily a matter of moral suasion, while disputes were settled between kinship groups (sometimes violently). The state emerged when societies developed social classes. The classes that monopolized wealth needed an armed force of some kind to protect their possessions. They needed a mechanism for controlling the ways in which this force was used, and for making sure that everyone played their appointed role in the social order. The state, then, originated as an instrument of oppression, and was used quite openly by those in power to advance their own interests.

What does this history have to do with us today? Does our modern democratic state also serve the interests of the dominant class, or is it a neutral instrument reflecting the interest of society as a whole? Should our goal be to weaken the state or to strengthen it? Is it possible to conceive of a modern society without a state? What would it look like? Before we answer these questions, we must examine the role which the state plays in modern capitalist societies. We can then question whether changing the nature of the society would change the need for governmental institutions.

197

THEORIES OF THE STATE

The different paradigms in sociology naturally offer different interpretations of the role of the state. Conservative sociology asserts that the state plays a useful and necessary leadership role in society. Conservatives feel that elites are inevitable in human societies, both because inequality is inherent in human nature and because social organization requires coordination and leadership. Conservatives tend to be fearful of too much participation by the "masses" in decision making, since they feel that unsophisticated people may be misled by demagogues or dishonest politicians. They favor a strong state led by dedicated leaders who share their perspective on how societies should be run.

Liberal sociologists tend to minimize the importance of the state. While conservatives see the state as strong, and the rest of the society as fragmented and weak, liberals feel that society is well organized into pressure groups that keep the state in line. They see the state as a compromising mechanism that weighs the pressures on both sides of issues and then makes decisions that try to take both sides into account. This pluralist view of the state is consistent with the official ideology of democracy, which is incorporated in the formal constitutional structure of the American government.

The pluralist view of the state is idealized; it is an image of things more as they are supposed to be than as they really are. In fact, there is a tremendous imbalance in the power of some "pressure groups" as opposed to other "pressure groups." Many of the groups that the pluralists study are factions within the business class. The working class is represented by few groups, and generally has much less influence. The liberal perspective on the state tends to focus on mundane, day to day infighting within powerful groups and classes. It tends not to see the larger context in which this politicing takes place. This tendency not to see the forest for the trees is, as we discussed in the first chapter, a general characteristic of the liberal sociological paradigm.

In many ways, the radical theory of the state is closer to the conservative theory than to the liberal theory. Radicals agree with conservatives that power in capitalist societies is held by small elite groups that are able to remain relatively impervious to the pressures of nonelite groups. Radicals differ in that they think this is not a good thing. They also differ in that they think control by a small elite is not implicit in human nature, or an inevitable necessity for any human organization. Radicals believe that this control by a small elite is needed to sustain the dominance of society by the capitalist class.

The radical theory of the state provides more than just a moral critique of exploitative political institutions. It also provides a guideline for analyzing political change. It asserts that changes in the political system reflect changes in the economy and in the class system. The role of the state in society has changed throughout history, because of changes in the underlying class system. The state today plays a very different role from that played by the state in the early days of competitive capitalism.

As the economic structure of society changes, we can expect further changes in the role of the state. In a fully developed socialist society, without class inequalities, there would be no need for a state that would monopolize the legitimate use of force in order to dominate subordinate classes. Of course, there would be the need for some governmental institutions to do planning and overall coordinating, but their decisions would be made by and in the interest of the society as a whole and would be accepted by the vast majority of people, who would be directly involved in making decisions that affect their lives. Any disciplinary problems that remained could be handled democratically by local community groups.

In a sense, liberals, conservatives, and radicals share common visions of the ideal government. All want a government that will act in a disinterested way to benefit the society as a whole. Conservatives argue that this can best be accomplished by having the state run by an elite of wise, dedicated men. Liberals believe it can be done by allowing all interests in society to pressure the state, in the hopes that it will respond in some equitable fashion. Radicals argue that it is impossible to have true political democracy in a society without economic democracy. As long as there are rich and poor, the rich will be able to use their economic power to distort the political system away from serving the interests of the people as a whole. In the remainder of this chapter, we will examine this argument in detail, showing how the capitalist class has maintained control of the United States government and what it has done with this power.

DEVELOPMENT OF DEMOCRATIC INSTITUTIONS

All class societies have states that perform military, police, and judicial functions. Without such an institution it would be impossible to protect the property of the owning class. The state is a very powerful instrument. Indeed, in order to be effective it must be more powerful than any other group in society. In some societies, the state is so powerful that it exercises effective ownership or control over productive wealth. In Oriental despotism the state itself is the chief owner of the means of production.

Capitalism developed in societies where the state was relatively weak. As we have seen, in the feudal societies of Europe, local aristocrats retained many of the prerogatives of state power. This meant that the central governments were weaker than they were in most of the Oriental countries. The early capitalists were members of the middle class in these feudal societies. They tended to be hostile to the state, because the state was controlled by feudal lords who did not share their interests. Through a combination of violent revolution and political and economic pressures the capitalist classes of Europe managed to overthrow the feudal state.

Once the early capitalists overthrew the feudal state, they proceeded to establish a state that would fit the interests of their social class. They wanted a state that would

Successful social movements like the French Revolution have led to modern parliamentary de-mocracy; Le serment du jeu de paume *by L. David.*

not interfere in economic life, except to protect the rights of those who had property. Ideally, they felt that the state should be limited to preserving law and order, guaranteeing private property at home and abroad, collecting taxes, and mediating between privileged groups.

In their efforts to assure that the state would not reassert itself as a despotic force in society, the early capitalists invented political institutions that were designed to limit the power of the state. Their ideals were expressed in documents such as the American Declaration of Independence and the French Declaration of the Rights of Man and Citizen. They were crystallized in republican constitutional forms that attempted to restrict the powers of the state, and to protect the rights of the individual. They were especially interested in protecting the property rights of the individual, and in most cases voting was restricted to those who owned a certain amount of property.

The democracy that was instituted by these early capitalists was quite limited. It was generally restricted to white, male property owners, and it was heavily biased in favor of those classes with large amounts of wealth. Nevertheless, it constituted a historical advance in the struggle against arbitrary oppression by the state. Those countries that did not have capitalist revolutions, such as Germany and Japan, but where the state itself led the transition to capitalism for nationalistic reasons, eventually developed more authoritarian institutions.

Parliamentary democracy is a legacy of these early capitalist revolutions. Parliamentary forms were used in order to balance off the interests of diverse segments within the capitalist class. They were also used to provide some mechanism for protecting society against abuses of power by the executive branch of government. Whenever possible, capitalists prefer to use parliamentary or congressional institutions as a mechanism for defining and expressing their class interest.

But democratic institutions are also dangerous for capitalists. The same institutions that are used by capitalists to protect themselves from arbitrary abuse by the executive appeal to the working class as means to protect themselves from abuse by the capitalists. Once democracy is established, even for a limited group in society, other groups always demand to be included. In some cases, such as in France in 1848, the demands of the working class for equal protection from the state for their interests lead to revolution. In these cases, as we shall see, the capitalists abandon their fidelity to democracy and turn to a strongman of some sort to restore order.

Origins of the Monopoly Capitalist State

Throughout the period of competitive capitalism, most capitalists in the U.S. and Great Britain remained loyal to the ideal of a weak state governed by parliamentary institutions. Whenever these democratic institutions got out of hand, they turned to a military leader or other strongman to restore order. But as soon as possible, they returned to liberal democracy. When monopoly capitalism began to grow near the end of the nineteenth century, however, capitalists found that they required different services from the state. They needed a central authority that would maintain order in society in a stable and continuous way, preventing the cycles of order and disorder that followed the fluctuations of the competitive market economy. In the twentieth century they increasingly needed a state that would take control of the economy, regulating credit and monetary policy and spending money when necessary to prevent depressions.

Monopoly capitalists were freer than competitive capitalists to make concessions to workers. If a competitive capitalist was forced to raise wages or cut working hours, he would be unable to compete with other capitalists and would be forced out of business. Monopoly capitalists could simply pass on the increased wages to their consumers through higher prices. Since they held a monopoly, their customers would have no choice but to pay. Since they were so strong economically, the monopoly capitalists could afford to give the working population more rights. They expanded the franchise to include larger and larger segments of the population. They expanded welfare services, instituted universal education, and recognized trade unions. They permitted mass political parties, which channeled and disciplined the political energies of the working population. They developed the mass media, mass observer sports (baseball, football, soccer), and systematically inculcated patriotic values and racist sentiments into the working class. They also encouraged the revival of religion among this class. At the same time as they were extending rights to the working class and developing subtle methods of social control, they were systematically repressing radical groups.

All of these phenomena were closely related, and all were a result of the newly developed needs of monopoly capitalist society. In order to forestall massive disruptions and possible revolution, to create a working class that would instead work willingly and more or less identify with the ruling class, and very importantly that would make good soldiers to fight in the imperialist wars made necessary by the competition of the major capitalist countries for advantages in the Third World, it was necessary to give the working class a sense of participation in society—a feeling that it was *their* society and that the interests of the ruling class were *their* interests. Therefore, the proper loyalties had to be created and anti-ruling-class sentiments dissipated. Bismarck in Germany and Disraeli and Gladstone in England led the way in institutionalizing these policies. It was no accident that these two countries were the two most powerful military and economic powers on earth. The extension of the franchise, the expansion of welfare, and the recognition of trade unions were directed to increasing the sense of participation, while the encouragement of religion, racism, nationalism, the development of compulsory education, and the development of a popular mass media all were directed to controlling the minds of the masses who were now formally participating in politics as well as serving in the new mass armies. These institutions were all directed at securing the enthusiastic loyalty of the underlying population for the policies of the ruling class. At the same time, systematic policies of repression and later of co-option were used against socialists to eliminate any sense of a realistic alternative in the minds of the working classes to the rule of the capitalist class.

The role of the state in U.S. society was greatly expanded in the two decades after 1900 (the so-called Progressive Era) and again in the decade after 1933 (the New Deal and more importantly, World War II). It was during these two periods that the monopoly capitalist state reached its mature form. In both phases of its development the impetus for its expansion came from the giant corporations. After a decade or so of mergers and corporation formation, by around 1900 it was apparent that the movement to establish monopolies in order to stabilize economic conditions and realize super-profits was faltering. There was a contradiction in the corporate system. The super-profits made by the new monopolies were being reinvested and in the process were undermining the very monopolies that produced them. Thus the competition that the monopolies had been formed to eliminate was being restored. The new corporate giants needed economic stability, long-term predictability, and security from government interference. That is, they needed permanent elimination of the intense competition among themselves, control of the erratic fluctuations of the economy, the ability to plan future actions, and protection from political interference from state governments which were on occasion hostile to business interests.

Expansion of State Functions

The inability of the corporations and banks to secure the above goals for themselves led them to turn to the state for assistance. Only state regulation could solve these problems. A number of regulatory agencies were set up to control the sectors of the economy that the corporations wanted regulated. Each of these regulatory commissions was essentially controlled by the "regulated" industry itself. Thus, self-regulation of the corporations was instituted under the legal sanction of the state. Among the most important regulatory agencies set up around this time were the Interstate Commerce Commission, the Pure Food and Drug Administration, the Federal Trade Commission, and the Federal Reserve Banking System. The ICC set rates for the railways, thereby outlawing the price competition that had become so destructive of profits in many areas. The FTC outlawed business practices that undermined public confidence in the products of the large corporations. Banking reforms were designed to prevent panics and insure stable interest rates.

Not only did the expansion of state activities include the self-regulation of business and insure stability and predictability for the corporations but it also served as a safety valve against democratic and radical ferment (for example, demands for nationalization of the railways and banks that the Populists put forth in the 1890s) by allowing the corporations to claim that abuses had been ended by federal "control" over the corporations.

The programs begun during the Progressive Era were completed during the Franklin Roosevelt administration. The programs of the New Deal were initiated and pushed through by individuals and groups from the upper class. Roosevelt himself came from an old social upper-class family. Most of the programs of his administration were originally formulated and pushed by the National Civic Association and the American Association for Labor Legislation, two organizations controlled by far-sighted members of the American upper class. In the face of the worst depression the country had ever known, and the potential of massive disruption that its continuance could have had, a series of government programs were instituted that were designed to increase the stability of the system through a combination of the carrot and the stick. On the one hand, the government extended benefits to the working class and, on the other, it used the threat of retracting these benefits in the event that the recipients did not behave as the government wanted. The two most important pieces of legislation in the New Deal period were the Social Security Act and the National Labor Relations Act.

The Social Security Act of 1937 provided for minimum state aid to the unemployed, the aged, the disabled, and dependent children. The system was financed half by a tax on wages up to a maximum figure and half by a tax on corporations (which in fact pass on much of their share in the form of higher prices). Payouts were given in proportion to the amount paid in, not need. The act was passed in the face of massive popular agitation for large welfare payments to be financed out of the general revenues and thus served to reduce the push for much more substantial programs.

The second major piece of legislation that rounded out the corporate state was the National Labor Relations Act, which gave well-behaved labor unions the support of the federal government. The upper-class-run National Civic Association and the American Association for Labor Legislation had long desired to institutionalize collective bargaining. These organizations were convinced that officially recognized unions would be a bulwark against radicalism and the development of a third party based on labor. They felt, moreover, that these unions would serve as a mechanism of social control over the laboring classes, insuring their obedience to the terms of labor contracts designed to increase capitalist control over labor. The recognition of labor unions stabilized the work force, hindered unanticipated strikes, and set up the union apparatus as a second policeman to enforce labor discipline. The National Labor Relations Board was given power to recognize unions and provide procedures to guarantee the right to organize and to bargain collectively. However, the granting of these rights was conditional on government approval of union policies. After 1947 NLRB rights were removed from unions with Communist Party members as officials. It should be noted that the first two chairmen of the NLRB were members of the social upper class, Lloyd Garrison and Francis Biddle.

MECHANISMS OF RULING CLASS DOMINATION OF THE STATE

There are four key mechanisms that the capitalist class in the U.S. uses to control the state: (1) the special interest process, (2) the process of selecting officeholders, (3) the policy formation process, and (4) the maintenance of ideological hegemony.

Special Interest Process

Each group of corporations maintains its own business associations, which coordinate their interests and systematically influence the appropriate congressional committees and regulatory commissions. These business associations together with the individual corporations are the major force operating on Congress and the commissions. Through extensive lobbying, financing campaigns, granting of favors to friendly congressmen, offering jobs to members of regulatory commissions once their term is up, transporting officials around the world and socializing with and establishing close friendships with congressmen and regulatory commission members, business groups are normally able to exercise definitive influence over legislation in the Congress as well as effective control over the policies of the regulatory commissions.

Selection Process

Candidates for both elective and high appointive office are in large part selected by the upper class and the corporate institutions they control. Their control over the political parties by means of financing and the media allows them to handpick and promote likely candidates for top-level positions. Often the upper class itself provides the incumbents of top-level elective and especially appointive office. It requires tens of millions of dollars to get elected president and very large sums to get elected to the Senate or the governorship of large states. Despite public financing for presidential campaigns, most of the financing for the early stages of a campaign comes from the rich. This early financing determines which candidates are treated as "credible" by the media. Through their control over the financing of candidates, the rich can either get themselves elected (the Kennedys, Rockefellers, Roosevelts), or they can operate behind the scenes to choose candidates who are committed to their principles (Eisenhower, Johnson, Nixon, Reagan, Carter).

The rich finance all large rightist or moderate parties that have a real chance of coming to power so that they might secure access to and control over the national political leadership regardless of which particular party is in power. Although most of the old rich in the United States finance the Republican Party, most of the funding for the Democratic Party comes from new money and the ethnic rich (the Jews and Irish especially). Leading members of both parties are from the social upper class—Rockefeller, Goldwater, Percy, Taft in the Republican Party and Lindsay, Stevenson, Roosevelt, and the Kennedys in the Democratic Party. Other top figures in both parties have been developed by the corporate rich, who seek out ambitious politicians, especially lawyers, who have no particularly strong political interests or ideology, and support them in exchange for political favors. In the course of the relationship between the young and ambitious politicians and their benefactors, the politicians (who have no particular position on most things themselves) come to think like their financers. Consequently, it is not necessary to maintain close controls on these politicians, as they behave in ways for which they have been programmed and allow easy access to themselves for the capitalist class. Such men as Eisenhower, Nixon, and Johnson fall in this category. Eisenhower, although a very popular war leader, knew or cared little about politics. He was an excellent puppet for the corporate rich. Both Nixon and Johnson were picked out and promoted by the local corporate rich in their respective areas (Southern California and Texas). Many other top figures, such as Rusk and McNamara, were associated with top upper-class-controlled institutions (Wall Street law firms, financial houses, foundations, or leading corporations), and shifted directly from them into the very top levels of government. In the period from

1932 to 1964, 5 of the 8 Secretaries of State were listed in the Social Register (i.e., were at least second-generation rich), 8 of the 13 of the Secretaries of Defense were listed, as were 4 of the 7 Secretaries of the Treasury. In addition, such figures as Rusk and McNamara (not upper class themselves but closely tied to upper-class-controlled institutions) were in these top positions almost all the rest of the time.

Policy Formation Process

Most of the basic decisions made and policies followed by the state originate in upper-class-controlled policy-formation institutions such as certain key universities, think tanks, foundations, and above all the consensus-seeking policy planning groups. These institutions provide the state, especially the executive branch, with ideas, personnel, policy recommendations, and information on which to make decisions either directly or by way of "blue ribbon" commissions and "task forces." Certain universities such as MIT, Harvard, Yale, Princeton, Johns Hopkins, the University of Chicago, Berkeley, Stanford, and Cal Tech, especially in their centers for international studies and special research institutes, provide expert advisers and ideas to the key policy-planning committees. Both these universities' activities and the key policy-making groups themselves are financed by the upper-class-controlled corporations and foundations. Among the most influential policy-planning groups are the Council on Foreign Relations, which formulates basic policies and long-term programs for U.S. foreign policy, the Committee for Economic Development, the Business Council, and the Trilateral Commission. Each of these organizations is mostly comprised of members of the upper class and the elite of upper-class controlled institutions who are especially interested in the areas of the organization's specialty. Through their regular conferences, discussions, and publications they formulate basic policies. These policies are then transmitted to the state by means of providing the leading personnel to implement state policy (Henry Kissinger, for example), providing briefings and reports for government officials, and by direct consultation with state officials.

Ideological Hegemony

Through its domination of education, religion, the mass media, and the state itself, the upper class heavily influences the popular consciousness. Through both the ownership of the media, which are themselves giant corporations, and the flow of advertising income that sustain them, the upper class regulates the organs that heavily influence the popular consciousness of political issues. As we have seen, it is the media and the education system that for the most part determine what is and what is not of legitimate public concern. Public control of industry, disbanding the military, etc., are simply dismissed as not serious issues. The media have come to play an increasingly important role in securing upper-class dominance of the state as the old political machines in urban areas, which used to insure the vote for upper-class-controlled candidates in return for minor favors, have declined.

One of the most important aspects of the formation of consciousness is the inculcation of patriotism in the working class. To the extent that the working class puts "their" country ahead of their interest, the ruling class, which sets state policy, benefits. A patriotic working class that puts country ahead of class is ideal for the ruling class, which thereby secures loyal followers for whatever adventures it wants to pursue. Patriotism has been actively inculcated in the U.S. working class since the late nineteenth century. Universal education stressing citizenship and American history, the institutionalization of nationalist rites before all activities in which masses of working people participate (at the beginning of the school day, at the beginning and end of each TV day, the beginning of football and baseball games, etc.), parades on national holidays, the cult of the flag, and the nationalistic hysteria of the two world wars, all have deeply ingrained in the popular consciousness an identification with "America." Such inculcation has been the basis of the hegemony of the ruling class over the minds of working people. As long as the working class identifies the state with their country, they will of necessity identify with the ruling class that controls the state. Consequently, they will willingly implement the ruling class's policies even to the extent of volunteering to fight its imperial wars against people with whom they in fact share a common interest.

THE FUNCTION OF ELECTIONS

Elections with universal suffrage serve three important functions in capitalist society: (1) They are very powerful mechanisms for giving people the feeling that state policy is in their interest. Voting gives people the illusion that they are controlling the state. It is thus a powerful cement for the system. (2) An election is a thermometer of discontent. It is a notice to the ruling class when it must take certain actions to preserve its rule. In response to elections, the ruling class institutes policies of repression, co-option of radical leaders, or minor reforms to take the energy out of opposition movements. (3) Elections serve as a very useful mechanism for the resolution of differences within the ruling class. They are a definitive way of choosing the officeholders for a given period. Other mechanisms of selecting officials have the drawback of causing hostility in one or another segment of the ruling class that may get the worst of the deal. Elections allow the various segments of the upper class to compete among themselves for special consideration by the government through financing and otherwise supporting one or another party's candidate. When a sector of the upper class loses, it can always look forward to the next election and to the pressures that regular elections put on incumbents to attempt to mediate all differences with the ruling class. Any system of permanent selection of officeholders, through nonparliamentary forms, makes for alienation and potential disruption of the system by segments of the ruling class itself. Parliamentary institutions with universal suffrage are hence the ideal form of the bourgeois state.

Historically, there has been a strong correlation between parliamentary forms of government and highly commercial societies. Ancient Greece, medieval Hanseatic League cities, Venice, Holland, Switzerland, and England were all republics in their prime. This contrasts sharply with the Oriental despotic empires based on the direct exploitation of the underlying peasants, where power was concentrated in one man rather than a parliamentary body representative of the various interests in the upper class. This evidence, together with the development of parliamentary forms paralleling the development of capitalism almost everywhere in the world, strongly suggests that there is a functional relationship between parliamentary forms and commercial economics.

Parliamentary forms are best suited to achieving compromise among the powerful. Unlike agrarian despotisms, where almost all the rich are either landlords or bureaucrats, in commercial societies the upper class is highly diverse. There is no simple class will which is easily determined. In the presence of widely diverse interests within the elite, strongman rule would alienate large segments of the rich and powerful. Parliamentary forms minimize the alienation of the rich and provide the best institutional structures within which to work out compromises. Strongman rule further alienates the working classes, whose willing consent to upper-class rule is made all the more necessary by the undermining of their traditional loyalties through their involvement in a commercial economy to which nothing is sacred but the pursuit of money. Lastly, commercial economies depend on the ability to predict the behavior of political authorities. The rule of law, rather than the arbitrariness of a dictator, is necessary because of the fragile nature of economic relations involving a wide range of contracts, market expectations, wage and price fluctuations, etc. Business cannot be subject to arbitrary decrees and be profitable. The best guarantee of moderation and avoidance of arbitrariness is the parliamentary form, where the commercial class itself governs in a manner that necessitates compromise within itself in the development of policies agreeable to almost all. Over the long run, parliamentary democracies have proven to be the most powerful militarily, the most rapidly growing economically, and the most stable politically of all capitalist regimes. Whenever parliamentary forms and the universal franchise have been abolished in capitalist society, the long-term weakening of the society has always resulted in increasing pressures for a restoration of republican forms.

Political parties are an essential aspect of parliamentary rule by the upper class. Mass political organizations such as the Republican and Democratic parties in the United States and the Christian Democratic parties of Europe were developed to channel the political sentiments of people in ways harmless to the rule of the economic elite. In the United States, the urban party machines, by doing small favors for the working class, secured their loyalty and insured the unchallenged rule of the capitalist class. The religious parties of Europe accomplished the same purpose through their use of religious values. Nationalistic and conservative parties controlled directly by the ruling class also have been able to secure massive popular support by stressing nonclass issues, playing up patriotic and racist themes, and introducing pseudoleft programs (such as the expropriation of Jewish businessmen, attacks on intellectuals, opposition to foreign migration, restrictions on unpopular minorities such as blacks, and the like). Conservative parties use such issues as immigration, religion, anti-Catholicism, anti-Semitism, racism, and hostility against urban or rural areas to secure the votes of working people whose real interest lies with parties attempting to mobilize them on the basis of class interest.

The bourgeoisie supports republican institutions when they work, i.e., when they in fact function to develop and implement a class will against the rest of society. Only under a grave and continuing threat of working-class or peasant revolution have economic elites turned away from parliamentary forms and the universal franchise. If the traditional strongman regime fails, or if this is unworkable because of massive discontent, the ruling class turns to the support of fascist movements. Strongmen such as Francisco Franco, or Charles de Gaulle, with whom the masses can identify as a father figure, who respect most of the traditional bourgeois privileges, and who utilize a minimum of terror, are preferred. The bourgeoisie is always interested in law and order and due process in order to insure its own security, and naturally wants a minimum of disruption of society. Only when things are very bad will it too turn to fascist movements like those of Hitler and Mussolini. The support of fascism occurs when both the industrial working class and the middle classes of independent farmers, white-collar employees, independent artisans, and small businessmen become alienated from the system. In such circumstances the upper class normally establishes an alliance with the movements based on the middle classes. This alliance pursues a program of smashing radical and working-class organizations, giving economic benefits to the middle classes, and implementing strong racist and nationalist state policies to channel class hostilities into forms supportive of the ruling class. Support of fascist movements is potentially very dangerous for the ruling class, as the German upper class learned. Bringing a popular mass movement, like that of the German Nazis, to power means that the upper class may have to share real power with it. Eventually, it may even lose its guiding role (as was the case in Germany after five years of business dominance of the Nazis).

FUNCTIONS OF THE STATE IN MONOPOLY CAPITALIST SOCIETY

The two principal functions of the capitalist state are (1) to contribute to the formation of a unified class will out of the more or less divergent interests within the ruling class, taking into account the demands of the upper middle classes of local businessmen, rich farmers, and other local elites, as well as the danger of major disruptions of the system from the working classes; and (2) to implement the tempered common will of the ruling class against the rest of society. The second basic function consists of the following major subfunctions: (a) the protection of private property and the preservation of law and order, (b) the containment of discontent stemming from the working class, (c) the regulation of the economy as a whole in the interest of the corporations, (d) the provision for the self-regulation of the corporations within the limits of what is beneficial to the corporate order as a whole, (e) the protection of the foreign investments and the trade position of the corporations, (f) provision for the economic and social infrastructure of the corporations.

Forming the Will of the Ruling Class

Before the collective will of the ruling class can be implemented, it must be formed and tempered. This is the first function of the state apparatus—to contribute to molding the divergent interests and attitudes of the ruling class into a political policy more or less agreeable to all segments of that class. This process of forming a collective will completes what was begun outside of the formal political apparatus in such ruling-class organizations as the Council on Foreign Relations, the Business Council, the Committee for Economic Development, and other key institutions and foundations mentioned previously. The process is completed in the regulatory agencies, in the government advisory committees, and in the top policy-making bodies of the executive branch of the government, as well as sometimes in the committees of the Congress.

Much of the time, though, the function of the Congress, especially the House, is not to develop a common will for the ruling class but rather to temper ruling-class policies in the face of the demands of local elites. Regional upper-class people frequently control the key committees of Congress (especially those of the House) and have powerful voting power there. As a result programs that were initiated by and have the full support of the national upper class, such as foreign aid and welfare, frequently run into major difficulties in the Congress (again particularly in the House) from people who have no interest (unlike the national ruling class) in such programs. In order to maintain its rule, the upper class must deal with the local elites. Concessions must be made to them in order for the basics of the corporate liberal policy to be implemented. The local elites are usually satisfied if they can obtain a high level of agricultural support for the rich farmers, oil depletion allowances, military bases, dams, and the wide range of other giveaway and pork-barrel programs that the Congress parcels out. In exchange, the Congress is generally happy to let the executive branch run basic economic and foreign policy. Thus, the executive branch under the close supervision of national upper-class individuals and institutions, declares war, signs treaties, allocates foreign aid, controls prices and wages, regulates trade, controls interest rates, and does just about whatever else it desires. Normally, the executive is more sensitive to rumblings from below than is the local upper-class- and upper-middle-class-influenced Congress. As a result, it is usually the President with the support of the upper class and its institutions, such as the Rockefeller and Ford Foundations, who is in the vanguard of liberal reform policies designed to defuse popular discontent and prevent major civil disorders. Thus, it has been the Presidency in the last forty years that has initiated and pushed through Congress, against the wishes of most of its upper-middle-class and regional upperclass constituency, civil rights and labor legislation, welfare expansion, and other liberal programs.

Among the major antagonisms within the ruling class, which the state must compromise to produce a common class position, are the differences between (1) heavy industry and consumption goods manufacturers over such issues as monopoly pricing (the more competitive light consumption goods industries tend to favor antitrust actions against their suppliers, the monopolistic heavy industries); (2) industrialists and bankers over such issues as the interest rate (manufacturers as borrowers tend to favor easier credit and inflation, while the bankers as lenders tend to favor tighter money and less inflation); (3) war industries and consumption goods manufacturers over such issues as the continuation of wars and high levels of military spending (war-related industries favor ever-increasing military expenditures and the perpetuation of wars); (4) export and domestically oriented industries over such issues as the level of tariffs (export-oriented industries favor a low level of tariffs, while domestically oriented industries, which must face overseas competition, favor high tariffs); (5) international corporations with investments primarily in manufacturing facilities in Europe and Canada and international corporations with investments primarily in raw material extraction industries in the Third World over such issues such as the importance of opposing all socialist, communist, and nationalist regimes in the Third World and the importance of the balance of payments crisis; (6) international corporations with investments in the Third World and those with great interest in developing trade with Russia and China over such issues as the continuation of the Vietnam war and the recognition of the People's Republic of China.

In addition to these fundamental differences of interest within the ruling class there are two other major differences that must likewise be moderated and compromised: (1) the antagonism between the traditional Anglo-Saxon social upper class, the ethnic rich of Jews and Catholics (predominantely Irish), and the nouveau riche, especially those whose wealth is based on Texas oil and defense contracts; and (2) the antagonism between the business liberals who have been dominant since 1933 and the Old Guard conservatives who have been subordinate although occasionally very vocal since that date. Beginning with the Roosevelt regime in 1933, the business liberals and the institutions they control—the CFR, BC, CED, and the major foundations—have been hegemonic in the ruling class. However, older intransigent forces continue to be very influential through such organizations as the National Association of Manufacturers and the right wing of the Republican Party.

Social conflict with the existing govern-mental structure is reflected in this photo.

Photo by Neil Benson

Imposing the Will of the Ruling Class

Once the common will of the ruling class is developed it is implemented through the state apparatus. At the very core of state policy in all forms of capitalist society are its guarantees of private property. Its police, courts, and prisons punish all forms of violations against private property (stealing, robbery, theft, embezzlement, trespass, etc.) not authorized by the logic of the capitalist system (such as the foreclosure by banks of small businessmen). The state enforces contracts made among capitalists and between capitalists and the working class, as well as administering a complex system of business law to regulate the way businesses relate to each other. It enforces law and order in general, preventing crimes of violence from endangering the ruling class itself and from disrupting the productive lives of the working class.

Another central function of the state in all stages of capitalist society is the containment of working-class discontent. This has historically been accomplished through a combination of co-option and manipulation on the one hand and repression on the other. As we have seen, unions have been recognized and welfare granted as mechanisms of control. Systematic repression (the House Un-American Activities Committee, the FBI, conspiracy trials against prominent radicals, etc.) has been a traditional part of American history from the great trials of radical labor leaders beginning with the Haymarket riots of 1886 down to the show trials of the Black Panthers in recent years. Pressure against, if not outright censorship of, the media (such as in World War I when socialist literature was denied bulk mailing rates) has likewise been a consistent part of the policy of repression. On the other hand, handsome monetary incomes, appointment to government committees and agencies, invitations from the President, etc., are used to reward those working-class leaders loyal to the ruling class. Minor reforms are offered to the masses, in order to separate them from militant leadership. The combined policy of repression-co-option has proven to be very effective in destroying the Industrial Workers of the World, the Populist Party, the Socialist Party, the Communist Party, and recently the Black Panthers. Each of the potentially major threats that have developed against the corporate capitalist system since the late nineteenth century has been successfully turned back.

The state regulates the economy as a whole in the interest of the ruling class and the corporations. It has three major tasks in this area: (1) to insure an adequate level of total economic demand in the economy, (2) to insure an adequate and trained supply of labor at low enough wages to allow the corporations to make a "healthy" profit, and (3) to stabilize and regulate economic conditions to insure a high and sustained rate of profit. The very important state function of insuring an adequate level of demand for the products of the corporations through ever-increasing government spending on waste and wage subsidies has already been discussed. The government must also provide the corporations with a supply of properly skilled workers who are willing to work for relatively low wages. To accomplish this the state allows the unemployment rate to remain sufficiently high so that workers will be willing to work because they fear that others who are willing to work for less will take their places. It further regulates the working class through antistrike legislation and injunctions, wage guidelines, and restrictions on militant unions, secondary boycotts, picketing procedures, and the like. To provide the corporations with workers trained to do the jobs the corporations need, the state provides basic education as well as job retraining programs to all levels of the working class. Thus, the cost of training the corporations' workers has in large part been socialized.

To stabilize the economy and facilitate the making of profits, the state manages taxation, prints and controls money, regulates interest rates (and hence influences the rate of investment), controls trade through tariffs, and subsidizes industries directly and indirectly through outright grants (such as those to builders of merchant ships, aircraft corporations, corporate farms, and the giveaway of public timber, oil rights, and the like), loans and loan guarantees (for businesses near bankruptcy), and by developing technologies that are turned over to private corporations for exploitation once they become profitable (such as atomic energy, space satellites, and all the spin-offs of military research).

As already noted, the state sanctions the self-regulation of a number of the key sectors of the economy. The Interstate Commerce Commission regulates the railways, while comparable agencies regulate the airlines, the food industry, the banks, commerce, etc. Regulatory agencies not only serve as self-regulators of each corporate sector but they also serve to regulate each sector in the interests of the corporate system as a *whole*. Hence, the rate of profit in certain natural monopolies such as electric power and communications are kept lower than the power companies and A.T.&T. would like because all corporations must buy these services and they resist paying exorbitant prices. Likewise, much of the regulation of the banks and the stock market serves to stabilize the economy as a whole and to benefit almost all the industrial corporations that must utilize their services. Finally, the regulatory agencies serve to temper the more blatant abuses of the corporations in order to prevent or defuse massive working-class hostility to the operation of the corporations. It is better to make a high rate of profit over a long period of time than to attempt to get rich overnight with the consequence of shattering public faith in corporate capitalism.

The foreign policy of the capitalist state is governed almost exclusively by the needs of the giant corporations for protecting and advancing their overseas investments and trade positions. To this end, embassies and consulates are maintained in most of the world's major cities and a massive army, air force, and navy are stationed throughout the world. These apply great pressure on all countries to facilitate the profit making of the U.S. corporations. On a more general level the foreign policy of the United States is geared to containing Communism and preventing not only communist revolutions but also socialist and nationalist regimes from interfering with U.S. investments. (See Chapter 10 for a full discussion of these processes.)

Maintaining the Infrastructure

The state provides an economic and social infrastructure for the operation of the corporate economy. Not only does it insure a properly educated and skilled working class willing to work at low wages for the corporations but it also insures a minimum level of health and housing to the working class in order to keep it in reasonable condition to be effective employees. The state also either provides or guarantees the corporations a reliable supply of power (through publicly owned facilities if necessary), communications (through publicly owned facilities such as the post office), and transportation, i.e., it builds and maintains highways, canals, airports, rivers, and even takes over the railways and airlines when they cease to be profitable to the corporations.

A look at the federal budget will illustrate the functions and priorities of the state. If we *exclude* welfare transfer payments such as social security—which largely pay back out money that employees and employers have paid in—we find that in 1977, 54 percent of federal expenditures went for the military, veterans' benefits, and interest on the largely war-incurred national debt. Fourteen percent was spent on health, largely because of the increase in medicaid payments. Eight percent was spent on education, training, employment, and social services; 1 percent on agriculture; 6 percent on natural resources, environment, and energy; 6 percent on commerce and transportation; 3 percent on community and regional development; 3 percent on revenue sharing with states and municipalities; 3 percent on international affairs; 2 percent on science, space, and technology; 1 percent on general government administration; and 1 percent on law enforcement and justice.

These patterns of federal spending have been changing, reflecting changing international pressures on the U.S. economy, discussed in Chapter 5. Table 8-1 shows these trends in the percentage allocation of U.S. federal government spending in all major categories *including* income security (social security and welfare). The most remarkable trend has been the decline in spending on the military and the increase in spending on income security and health. Veterans' payments and interest payments are primarily payments for past military adventures, and they are difficult to cut since the obligation has already been incurred. While the military remains a central element in state expenditure, budgetary allocations change, reflecting the overall needs of the capitalist economy during each historical period.

THE MILITARY

The military is the very core of the state as an institution. The state is by definition the social institution that successfully claims a monopoly on force in a geographical

TABLE 8-1. Federal Budget Outlays, by Function, 1960–1977

	% OF TOTAL OUTLAY FOR SELECTED CATEGORIES		
Categories	1960	1970	1977 (est.)
National Defense	49.0%	40.3%	24.3%
Veterans' Benefits	6.0	4.4	4.5
Net Interest on National Debt	7.5	7.3	7.2
Income Security	19.8	21.9	33.6
Health	0.9	6.7	9.6
Education, training, employment and social services	1.1	4.0	5.1
Commerce and Transportation	6.3	4.6	3.9
Natural resources, environment, and energy	2.1	2.0	4.2
International Affairs	3.1	1.8	1.8

(Source: *Statistical Abstract of the United States,* 1977.)

The Pentagon, headquarters for the U.S. military.

area. The ultimate enforcer of all state policies is the military. Likewise, it is control over the military that is the acid test of control over the state.

The primary function of the military in every society is the defense of the interests of the ruling class, both from insurrection at home and from competing ruling classes abroad. This latter aspect includes both the defense of the geographic boundaries from any external enemies and the expansion of the areas under the political control of the state.

The military, though its "requirement" for ever-changing and more expensive weapons systems, serves the important function of allowing the state to generate economic demand, thus maintaining a high level of corporate profits. The military also operates to instill patriotism and discipline in the working class. The effect of two or more years in the armed services may be to reinforce authoritarianism, the sense of discipline, and feelings of inadequacy, thus making people better workers. It also gives working people (who disproportionately tend to be the people who in fact serve in the military) a sense of personal involvement in implementing "their" country's policies, thereby building feelings of patriotism and consequently increasing the willingness of workers to do the bidding of the upper class which controls the state.

The military is tightly under the control of the corporation-based upper class in

all developed capitalist countries. In the United States the military is closely supervised by civilian representatives of the corporate rich. The secretary of Defense and
quite a number of levels of positions under him must by law be assigned to civilians
appointed by the President (of course, on the recommendations of such groups as the
Council on Foreign Relations). The National Security Council (the on-again-off-again
top military policy-making body) excludes military officials from full participation.
Defense Department civilians pass on all promotions in the services. The Secretary of
Defense and the secretaries of the various services as well as the under secretaries
are normally either members of the upper class or come from the top levels of institutions controlled by them (such as McNamara of the Ford Motor Company). Very few
top officers in any of the services are in the upper class (4 percent of top Navy officers, 3 percent of top Army officers, and no top Air Force officers are listed in the
Social Register). Instead of the military being controlled by the ruling class through
its top officers (as has historically been the case in pre-monopoly capitalist societies),
the contemporary military is lead by qualified experts in warfare who have been
trained and promoted for their skills, inculcated with professionalism, discouraged
from developing political consciousness, and closely controlled through the Defense
Department.

Manipulating Public Opinion

In order to maintain the massive military establishment, it has been necessary to institute and maintain popular support for the military's recruitment policies and the
extraordinary level of taxation necessary to support the military. It took quite a bit of
work to turn U.S. public opinion around after World War II to come to think of the
Soviet Union as *the* enemy (after four years of war propaganda designed to convince
the people that the Russians were our friends). As part of the effort to justify massive
military spending and the draft during peacetime (to prop up the economy and maintain the new, informal U.S. empire), it was necessary to have an enemy that could
realistically be billed as a threat to the United States. In spite of its conservative and
defensive foreign policy, as well as its virtual prostration as a result of World War II,
the Soviet Union was made to play the role needed, and the Cold War was created.
Newsreels, speakers, conferences, radio advertisements, magazine articles, news
stories, textbooks, comic books, and even bubble gum cards, painted the Soviet
Union as another Nazi Germany. The thrust of this campaign was the attainment of
support for a massive and aggressive U.S. military establishment. In 1951 there were
2,235 military men and 787 full-time civilians in the Pentagon working only on public
relations for the military. The Korean war and the associated war hysteria completed
the campaign to convince the public of the need for a massive military establishment.

A similar campaign was mounted to assure public support for the Vietnam war
effort. Congress was manipulated, through phony intelligence information, into pass-

ing the Gulf of Tonkin resolution, which gave the executive branch a free hand in escalating the war. Lyndon Johnson ran for President in 1964 against Barry Goldwater on a platform of not sending American "boys" to fight a war for Asians, all the time knowing full well that he would probably do exactly that as soon as the election was over. Opposition to the war became a significant factor only after it became apparent that the United States was bogged down in a no-win situation. When the blacks in the major cities started rioting, the campuses rose in revolt, and discipline in the military itself began to collapse, the ruling class finally recognized that it could not afford to continue the war.

CONTRADICTIONS AND CHANGE IN THE CAPITALIST STATE

Under monopoly capitalism, the state has become an ever stronger element in society. There are many advantages for the capitalists in this situation; indeed, it is unlikely that monopoly capitalism could function without a very strong state. But social reality is contradictory. The strengthening of the state which is necessary for monopoly capitalism is also a threat to it. The state which is used to placate and buy off the working class creates new problems and demands.

The monopoly capitalist state creates expectations in the working class that are difficult to meet. While under competitive capitalism the state was not considered to be responsible for fluctuations in the economy, today Americans hold the President responsible for recessions, inflation, unemployment, and other economic ills. Presidents who fail to produce a satisfactory economic performance are not likely to be reelected, and are threatened by new politicians who promise more liberal economic policies. The monopoly capitalist state has expanded educational opportunities in order to give everyone the feeling of a fair chance of obtaining middle-class jobs. But there is no way it can provide enough jobs for everyone. Cutting back educational opportunities is difficult, but so is educating people with expectations that cannot be met.

The modern capitalist state promises everyone a chance to participate in decision making. It must do this in order to keep the population happy and assure a tranquil and cooperative work force. But people who are promised a chance to participate in their government are likely to try to take advantage of it. Consumer groups are formed to demand safer cars and a cleaner environment. Labor groups pressure for higher wages and better labor legislation. Women and minorities pressure for equal treatment in the labor market. The unemployed pressure for jobs. Monopoly capitalism tries to meet these demands, since failing to do so would undermine its pretense of democracy. But meeting them is difficult and expensive, sometimes so much so that it cannot be done without compromising the interests of the corporations themselves.

The capacity of the monopoly capitalist state to deal with these contradictions is relatively great, much more so than that of the competitive capitalist state of Marx's time. But there are limits. Deficit spending can be used only up to a point before inflation becomes too serious a problem. Only a limited number of nonproductive middle-class jobs can be paid for without raising taxes so high that the workers rebel against them.

Radicals are exploring different strategies for using the contradictions of the capitalist state as pressure points for change. Some believe that the best strategy is to join with liberal groups in pressuring for specific reforms. By doing so they hope to win significant benefits for working people, while also increasing demands for the system to be restructured in a more radical way. In this way, they hope to further the inherent tendency for democratic political systems to move gradually to the left as they accede to pressures from the working classes. The risk of this approach is that workers may be misled into believing that qualitative change in their condition is possible in a piecemeal fashion, when actually the capitalist system cannot allow such a degree of change.

Other radicals believe that working for such reformist measures not only is not viable but only helps to shore up the system and to delay its eventual collapse. They believe that the best strategy for radicals is to use propaganda and educational measures to undermine the ideological hegemony of the capitalist class, while working to build revolutionary workers' organizations that will be ready to fill the void when the system develops a serious crisis. The risk of this approach is that there may be no such dramatic crisis of the system, or if there is, the forces of the right may prove to be stronger than those of the left.

The capitalist state is strong, but it is not all powerful. At various points in history it has been forced to make concessions to the working class in order to sustain its control over society. It could not suppress the labor movement in the 1930s, or expand the Vietnam war into a major conflict with China. Organized mass movements, with a substantial basis of support in the working population, can mount a significant threat to the power of the capitalist state. Chapter 14 will discuss the ways in which social movements may develop.

Summary

Primitive, classless societies had no need for a state with a monopoly on the legitimate use of violence. When social classes developed, the dominant class needed a state to enforce their interest on the rest of the population. While liberals view the contemporary democratic state as representing the interests of diverse groups within the population as a whole, radicals argue that the contemporary state essentially represents the interest of the capitalist class. Parliamentary democracy developed historically as the best way of representing the diversity of interests *within* a competitive capitalist class. Parliamentary democracy survives only so long as it is able to successfully co-opt or ignore pressures from the working class without fundamentally compromising the interests of the capitalists.

With the growth of monopoly capitalism, the state assumed greater control of the economy in order to insure the stability needed by the capitalist class. Regulatory commissions were created and social security and labor legislation was passed in order to protect against the worst abuses of the system while avoiding basic change in the relations of production. Capitalists retained control of the state through a number of mechanisms, such as lobbying by special-interest groups, financial and other help to candidates for office, use of foundations and commissions to shape policy, and through the mechanisms of ideological control over public opinion. Elections serve to settle disputes within the elite and as a barometer of public discontent. State spending is used to shore up the economy and maintain profits for the corporations.

While the monopoly capitalist state has been effective in many ways, there are contradictions within it, and radicals are exploring different tactics for challenging the power of the state.

Review Questions

1. When and why did the state first emerge in human history?
2. How do liberal and radical theories of the state differ?
3. When and why did parliamentary democracy first come about?
4. How do state policies under monopoly capitalism differ from those under competitive capitalism?
5. Describe the four mechanisms that the capitalist class uses to control the state.
6. What are the three functions of elections in a capitalist political system?
7. When may capitalist countries abandon democratic institutions and turn to fascism?
8. What is the relationship between the national upper-class and the regional upper-class groups in exercising national power?
9. What are some antagonisms between different upper-class groups which the state must resolve?
10. Why has the proportion of the state budget allocated to the military declined in recent years?
11. How successful has the upper class been in persuading the public to support its foreign policy decisions?
12. What are some of the contradictions of the monopoly capitalist state?

Suggestions for Further Study

1. Visit the local office of your congressperson. Ask the person with whom you are able to speak to explain the congressperson's ideas about what are the major

problems confronting American society today. Ask what solutions he or she proposes for these problems. How does the congressperson's analysis differ from the one presented in this book, or from your own ideas? What issues are stressed which are unimportant in your view, or what important issues are ignored or misunderstood? What do the congressperson's views tell you about his or her political ideology?

2. Choose a major decision that you feel has had a strong influence in shaping your life or the society in which you live. Some possibilities might include the decisions to go to war in Vietnam, suspend the draft, build a nuclear power plant, build the Alaska pipeline, pass affirmative action legislation, increase tuition at the local state university, or build a freeway. Or you may choose a decision that was not made, e.g., to pass effective legislation to end unemployment. Try to find out as much as you can about how this decision was made and by whom, either through library research or, if possible, through interviews with decision makers. Examine how public opinion on the issue was shaped prior to the formal decision making and how the general policies were formulated which shaped the final decision.

3. Investigate the power structure of the community in which you live, work, or go to school. The best way to do this is to interview people who know the political life of the community well, finding out who they feel has power and how important decisions are made. In what way are important decisions in the community influenced by powerful interests on the national level, such as corporations that may consider building factories in the area?

Selected Readings

Alexander, Herbert. *Financing the 1968 Election.* Lexington, Mass.: Heath, 1971.

Andreski, Stanislav. *Military Organization and Society.* Berkeley: U. of California Press, 1968 (1954).

Beard, Charles. *An Economic Interpretation of the Constitution of the United States.* New York: Free Press, 1965 (1913).

Brady, Robert. *Business as a System of Power.* New York: Columbia U. Press, 1941.

Chakotin, Sergei. *The Rape of the Masses.* New York: Alliance Press, 1940.

Chorley, Katherine. *Armies and the Art of Revolution.* Boston: Beacon, 1977 (1943).

Domhoff, G. William. *Fat Cats and Democrats.* Englewood Cliffs, N.J.: Prentice-Hall, 1972.

————. *The Higher Circles.* New York: Random House, 1970.

————. "New Directions in Power Structure Research." *The Insurgent Sociologist* 5 (Spring 1975), 3.

————. *Who Rules America?* Englewood Cliffs, N.J.: Prentice-Hall, 1967.

Duverger, Maurice. *Political Parties.* New York: Wiley, 1954.

Engels, Frederick. *The Origin of the Family, Private Property and the State.* New York: International, 1972 (1884).

Engler, Robert. *The Politics of Oil.* Chicago: U. of Chicago Press, 1967.

Fellmeth, Robert. *The Interstate Commerce Commission.* New York: Grossman, 1970.

Glazer, Nathan. *The Social Basis of American Communism.* New York: Harcourt, Brace & World, 1961.

Goertzel, Ted. *Political Society.* Chicago: Rand McNally, 1976.

Guerin, Daniel. *Fascism and Big Business.* New York: Monad Press, 1973 (1939).

Hamilton, Richard. *Affluence and the French Worker.* Princeton, N.J.: Princeton U. Press, 1967.

————. *Class and Politics in the United States.* New York: Wiley, 1972.

————. *Restraining Myths.* New York: Wiley, 1975.

Kariel, Gabriel. *The Decline of American Pluralism.* Stanford, Calif.: Stanford U. Press, 1961.

Lenin, V. I. *The State and Revolution.* New York: International, 1932 (1916).

Linz, Juan, and Lipset, Seymour Martin. *The Social Bases of Political Diversity in Western Democracy.* Mimeographed. Stanford, Calif.: Center for Advanced Study in the Behavioral Sciences, 1956.

————. *Political Man.* New York: Doubleday, 1959.

Lipset, Seymour Martin, and Raab, Earl. *The Politics of Unreason.* New York: Harper & Row, 1970.

Marcuse, Herbert. *One Dimensional Man.* Boston: Beacon, 1964.

Marx, Karl. *The 18th Brumaire.* New York: International, 1963.

Melman, Seymour. *Pentagon Capitalism.* New York: McGraw-Hill, 1970.

Milliband, Ralph. *The State in Capitalist Society.* New York: Basic Books, 1969.

Mills, C. Wright. *The Power Elite.* New York: Oxford, 1959.

Mintz, Morton, and Cohen, Jerry. *America, Inc.* New York: Dell, 1971.

Mosca, Gaetano. *The Ruling Class.* New York: McGraw-Hill, 1939.

Neumann, Franz. *Behemoth: The Structure and Practice of National Socialism.* New York: Oxford U. Press, 1944.

O'Connor, James. *The Corporations and the State.* New York: Harper & Row, 1974.

————. *The Fiscal Crises of the State.* New York: St. Martin's Press, 1973.

Pareto, Vilfredo. *Mind and Society.* New York: Dover, 1935.

Perlo, Victor. *The Empire of High Finance.* New York: International, 1957.

————. *Militarism and Industry.* New York: International, 1963.

Piven, Frances Fox, and Cloward, Richard. *Regulating the Poor.* New York: Vintage, 1971.

Poulantzas, Nicos. *Political Power and Social Classes.* London: New Left Books, 1973.

Reich, Wilhelm. *The Mass Psychology of Fascism.* New York: Farrar, Straus & Giroux, 1970 (1945).

Rose, Richard (ed.). *Electoral Behavior*. New York: Free Press, 1974.

Rowbotham, Sheila, *Woman's Consciousness, Man's World*. Baltimore: Penguin, 1974.

Sale, Kirkpatrick. *Power Shift: The Rise of the Southern Rim and Its Challenge to the Eastern Establishment*. New York: Vintage, 1975.

Schweitzer, Arthur. *Big Business in the Third Reich*. Bloomington: Indiana U. Press, 1964.

Stern, Philip. *The Rape of the Taxpayer*. New York: Random House, 1973.

Sweezy, Paul, and Baran, Paul. *Monopoly Capital*. New York: Monthly Review, 1967.

Szymanski, Albert. *The Capitalist State and the Politics of Class*. Boston: Winthrop, 1978.

Tasca, Angelo. *The Rise of Italian Fascism*. New York: Fertig, 1966 (1938).

Thayer, George. *Who Shakes the Money Tree: American Campaign Financing Practices*. New York: Simon & Schuster, 1974.

Vagts, Alfred. *A History of Militarism*. New York: Free Press, 1967 (1937).

Weinstein, James. *The Corporate Ideal in the Liberal State*. Boston: Beacon, 1969.

Wolfe, Alan. *The Seamy Side of Democracy: Repression in America*. New York: McKay, 1973.

Yarmolinsky, Adam. *The Military Establishment*. New York: Harper & Row, 1971.

Chapter 9

Crime and
the State

by Drew Humphries

Crime is pervasive in American society. It is a political issue, a news item, a popular subject for the entertainment and media industries, a personal fear, and a reality for many. Criminologists and sociologists are frequently called upon to study the behavior of criminals or to make recommendations about how to deal with the crime problem. Each of the main paradigms in sociology has a different approach for studying crime. The conservative tradition understands crime as the failure of the individual to conform to the norms of society. This comes about because of conflicts or inconsistencies in the norms or because of weakness in the socialization process whereby individuals are taught how to behave. Conservative studies of crime focus on inadequate socializing agents such as the single-parent family where divorce, desertion, or death are identified as the causes of incomplete socialization and consequent wrongdoing on the part of children and teenagers. The conservative tradition emphasizes structurally repressive remedies for these weaknesses. One strategy is to bolster socializing agencies—like the family, the school, and the church—by integrating them with policing agencies. The Police Athletic League, for example, illustrates the conservative response because police sponsorship of and participation in recreation activities with youths from low-income families are intended to compensate for the socialization received in the home which is assumed to be inadequate. Overall, the conservative tradition seeks to reintegrate society by reinforcing the value consensus upon which it is assumed to rest.

The liberal tradition in criminology reveals more diversity in the study of crime than does the conservative approach. Liberal criminologists are also concerned with values but attribute criminal behavior to value distortions, suggesting, for example, that the overemphasis on material rewards in American society together with discrimination contribute to high rates of deviance and crime. Liberals also attribute crime to conflicts within society. Liberals define society as a system of competing groups each pursuing specific interests. This conception is called "pluralism" and accounts for crime by holding that an interest group which succeeds in enacting criminal legislation has the power to impose criminal and/or deviant labels on less powerful groups. This generalization is referred to as "labeling theory" and has opened up a new line of inquiry for liberal criminologists: the contribution of the criminal justice system itself to the generation of crime. The argument is not complex: creation of deviant labels is the product of political conflict and the application of these labels sustains deviant behavior by informing an audience how to react to the labeled individual.

The shortcomings of both conservative and liberal criminology have been noted by radicals. The focus on agencies of social control fails to raise moral and social questions about the nature of society. Conservatives assume that consensus over cultural values integrates and holds society together. Liberals assume that interest group conflict defines society. Neither tradition questions these assumptions. Consequently, each holds that it is possible to create a well-regulated and fair system of justice under the present economic and political conditions.

Marxist criminology offers a different analysis of crime. Radicals see crime as a legal category created by the state and used by the economically dominant social class for its own purposes. As we saw in the last chapter, the radical analysis of the state argues that its chief function is to defend the interests of the ruling class against the exploited class in society. Much of the information we have about crime confirms this analysis. For example, self-reported studies of crime show that most people have committed an act for which they could be criminally prosecuted at some time during their lives. This is true for all social classes, all races, and all ethnic groups. However, when we examine statistics to see who is arrested, prosecuted, and convicted by the state for crimes, we find that it is primarily young, black, men living in urban low-income areas. Thus, our criminal justice system does not enforce the norms of society equally against everyone. It enforces them selectively against groups on the bottom of society. Unlike conservative and liberal traditions, the radical approach to crime questions not only the agencies of social control but the society in which they function. Moral and political questions are at the heart of Marxist criminology and lead us to an understanding of crime that his historical and structural in the broadest sense. In this chapter, we will be exploring these questions. We will trace the origins of crime and its historical relation to the state in class societies. We will examine in particular the role of criminal justice in contemporary society. We will look at crime as a business and at crime as it is committed by the poorest and most marginalized classes in American society. We will consider the relationship between the destruction of

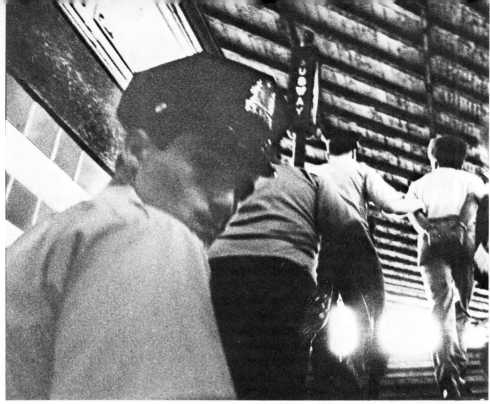

An individual under arrest.

productive life and the application of the penal sanction. And, finally, we will consider the question of the reform of the criminal justice system in America.

HISTORY OF CRIME AND THE STATE

Any analysis begins with a definition and the study of crime is no exception. Liberal and conservative criminologists define crime as a legal category and also incorporate the values underlying the law as part of their analyses. If the law condemns certain behavior and if law-enforcement officials pursue its suppression, then often the work of liberal and conservative criminologists contains the same moral bias. Marxists begin with the same legal definition of crime but analyze it critically, that is, they do not accept its moral bias. Crime is taken as nothing more than an instrument through which the state uses violence and coercion to impose legitimately the conditions of order. It spells out a set of procedures that compel the state to move against those who violate the law and require punishment upon conviction. It also lists the acts and omissions to act that the state deems sufficiently damaging to necessitate punishment. Marxists begin with the legal definition of crime in order to examine the conditions under which activity comes to be defined as socially injurious and therefore properly subject to the criminal sanction within the moral framework of the state. Here, the moral bias of law is an object of sociological investigation. In a very general sense; we can identify three conditions under which an activity becomes a crime: (1) a state exercising jurisdiction over a given territory, (2) a dominant social class affecting the development of criminal law, and (3) a pool of uprooted individuals bearing no legal relation to the means of production. Historically, these conditions came into being at different times and we turn now to an examination of these developments.

While people have had disputes throughout human history, and people have violated norms held by others in all types of societies, crime as a legally defined set of behaviors prohibited by the state is a relatively recent event. In primitive societies, disputes were settled between family or clan groups. There might have been a leader or clan head to whom complaints could be referred but there was no state to define behavior as criminal. Often disputes were settled informally without the mediation of leaders. In Oriental despotic society, people could be punished at the discretion of the rulers. There was often no code of laws defining what was criminal and what was not. It was only with the development of feudalism in the thirteenth century that crime came to be formally defined in English law.

Anglo-Saxon law remained weak prior to the Norman invasion in 1066 because the kings possessed no means to compel litigants to appear before the court. The customary blood feud, a form of private vengeance, settled most disputes under these circumstances. Personal injury and cattle theft provoked private war between the kindred of a wrongdoer and the kindred of the person wronged. The feud, however, could be forestalled by compensation: the amount was fixed by custom and was used to determine the value of a man's life and the measure of his fine. Those who refused to provide compensation denied justice and were considered to be outlaws. In prefeudal England, society was agrarian and composed of a large portion of freemen each residing in homesteads and answerable for his own "fense."

Norman law identified crime for the first time and defined it as a legal instrumentality of the feudal state. William the Conqueror exacted an oath of fealty from all freemen and lords, made criminal law turn on the violation of the king's peace, and did away with the compensation system. Henry II (twelfth century) centralized English law by instituting a permanent court of professional judges as well as by sending itinerant judges throughout the land and by introducing the inquest and the writ as normal parts of the justice system. Jurist Ranulf de Glanville (twelfth century) distinguished civil wrongs from crimes and defined treason (the slaying of the king or betrayal of his person, realm, or army), concealment of treasure, breach of the king's peace, homicide, arson, robbery, rape, and forgery as crimes. By the end of Henry III's reign (thirteenth century) the Magna Carta brought the sovereign under the rule of the law and completed the main outlines of the modern state. Historically, then, crime emerged as a set of institutions properly imposing punishment and corresponded to the consolidation of the state.

Such a development rarely occurs, however, without a clash between the rights and obligations defined by custom and those newly identified in central law. Many of the behaviors that were considered criminal by the feudal state of the time were things the peasants had done for generations and that they always considered to be appropriate and morally correct. The criminal code was used to enforce the will of the feudal nobility against the peasants. Norman law defined the parties to a dispute not as equal clan members as under Anglo-Saxon law but as propertied individuals. Norman law criminalized the Anglo-Saxon system of compensation and the right to private war. The clash between customary and central law produces a special type of criminal, the social bandit, who like Robin Hood, followed custom and became an outlaw in relation to the Norman crown. The social bandit, however, provided some inspiration for the peasantry being forced to conform to the Norman law through the sheriffs, the itinerant judges, and the local lords. Thus, the criminal justice system originated as part of the structure of class domination in feudal society. And, as society changed, the nature of the criminal code and the criminal justice system had to change to reflect the needs of the changing class structure.

Historically, the economically dominant social class has used the penal sanction to its advantage. By the fifteenth century, English wealth was no longer measured simply in land but increasingly by the goods produced in one nation for exchange in another. The mercantilists, the producers of movable and exchangeable products, represented a social class that prospered from the increase in commerce but that suffered from the restrictions still imposed by feudal law. One restriction was the feudal law of theft, which held that no servant could steal property from his master on the grounds that the servant belonged to the master. When a master turned over property to a servant, the master transferred custody and not possession, since both the property and the servant remained in the possession of the master. As the mercantile relation between buyer and seller replaced the feudal relation between master and servant, the law of theft inhibited buying and selling to a degree that made commercial transactions dependent on feudal bonds of loyalty. This contradiction was resolved by the Carrier Case, which revolutionized the law of theft in the fifteenth century. The facts of the case are straightforward: an Italian merchant hired an English carrier to transport merchandise to South Hampton for shipment to Italy. The carrier took the bales of cotton, broke them open in transit, and apparently disposed of the contents to his own advantage. After much deliberation the judges held that the carrier in breaking open the bales illegally converted his legitimate custody to possession and was therefore guilty of larceny. What this decision did was encourage trade by exonerating merchants from the feudal responsibility of watching over the transporters of goods. The judges were influenced in this decision by the mercantile interests of the king himself, by the credit arrangements that obligated the English crown to Italian mercantilists, and by the rising importance of the mercantile class. The favorable decision represents the role played by an economically dominant social class in the exercise of state power and in particular in the formulation of criminal law, that is, in defining the circumstances under which the monopoly over the use of coercion would be imposed in commercial life.

Marginalization

Crime as an instrument of the state is shaped by underlying processes of marginalization. Marginalization refers to the destruction of a class or class fragment's relation to the means of sustaining and reproducing social life. As we know, an economic class is defined in relation to the means of production. All persons who live by tilling the land and by consuming its produce are peasants. All persons who live by selling their labor to another in exchange for a wage are proletarians. In this context, the relation to the means of production identifies the way in which an entire class acquires the resources to live from day to day and from generation to generation. Under certain conditions, this vital link can be broken and when it is the social class in question is left without the materials to create a livelihood.

This process of marginalization occurs for many different reasons. Historically, European peasants were subjected to marginalization when the enclosure laws defined commonly held lands to be the private property of the nobility and when the state forcibly expelled the peasantry from the land. The enclosure laws assisted in the expropriation of common lands by the nobility, that is, in the theft of peasant lands. In addition, the state and factory owners assisted in the deployment of marginalized peasants by imprisonment and transportation to penal colonies, as well as by offering wage labor as a substitute livelihood. The relation between crime and marginalization is complex and is best illustrated by historical example.

In the eighteenth century the administration of justice reflected social class inequities based on title and tenure to land. English peasants and prosperous freemen claimed pasture rights to common lands, while local lords exercised land tenure including title to game and vegetation. The chase was a symbol of wealth and privilege, for the crime of poaching restricted the hunt to those lords earning substantial incomes from their estates. Less affluent lords, merchants, miners, and free as well as peasant farmers risked fine, imprisonment, and transportation for poaching and they justified it by customary claim to the game as well as by hatred for the gamekeepers and lords. That poaching was already a crime signifies that this customary right had already been appropriated and taken over by the lords as a private privilege. In addition, the crime of poaching was used to appropriate one of the last customary rights: the claim to common pasturage on the landed estates. Local lords closed off the common pasture lands for use in producing game animals for the commercial meat market. The enclosure was contested by merchants and free farmers who pursued the matter through the courts and organized destruction of the game animals in order to clear the common lands for pasturing their own herds. Poaching became a tactic in the fight to impose expropriation: those who resisted the enclosure by killing game animals were charged with poaching. The King's court upheld the lords' action and the penal institutions absorbed marginalized producers.

The struggle to retain material resources in the face of impending factory work can be seen by examining the situation in Germany in the 1840s. The theft of wood in the Rhineland represented an effort to maintain and increase the ability of agricultural producers to survive independently of the wage. On the one hand, the price of timber appreciated over the 1800s and corresponded to the Prussian state's move to preserve forest acres for private and state profit. On the other hand, the parceling of land in agricultural districts reduced the resources available to small farmers and peasants, making them dependent on the smallest rises in prices. Price increases threw peasants into the situation where exercising customary rights to forest products was their only means of survival. The expropriation of forest lands by the state was part of the destruction of communal norms that had begun in the sixteenth century. By the 1840s, however, this movement jeopardized the livelihood of an entire class in the Rhineland. Peasant usage of forest products—fodder for cattle, wood for building and fuel—was made punishable by fine and imprisonment. The peasant movement to continue use of forest products represented a struggle against the legal expropriation of forest products and against the conditions that otherwise would have forced the peasantry into factory work. The state intervened in this process and thereby underwrote the deployment of workers into the factory by criminalizing customary relation to forest products: wood gathering became a crime.

This brief historical overview has shown that crime is not only a legal instrumentality dependent on the creation of the state and a ruling class but also that application of the criminal law is tied to the existence of marginalized classes. Revision of the English law of theft advanced mercantile interests by removing feudal obligations from commercial relations. The poaching laws signal the penetration of capital into agriculture and the resulting pressures to utilize even common lands for the purpose of commercial trade. The wood theft laws of Germany outlawed a means of subsistence and forced marginalized peasants onto the wage and into factory work. In the course of further developments, crime and criminals take on more modern features as wage labor and capital define the major class divisions in society.

CRIME IN AMERICA

In capitalist society, the capitalist owns or controls the means of production and the workers sell their labor in exchange for a wage. The wage-labor exchange is the source of antagonism between the capitalist and the working class: workers receive a wage in exchange for the value they produce for the capitalist; the wage is determined by the amount of time it takes to produce a commodity; and its value is determined by the creativity and energy of the worker. The difference between the value conferred on a commodity by labor and the amount of wage received by the worker is the source of profits in a capitalist society. Part of the value created by the working class is legally appropriated—taken over—in the form of profits by the capitalist class. Crime as a legal instrument sustains this relationship by imposing the conditions of wage labor and by mediating the resulting class contradictions. The state invokes the penal sanction against those who would jeopardize order based upon fundamental class differences by challenging the wage-labor exchange itself and/or by reproducing the conditions of life outside the limits set by wage labor. This, however, is only one side of the coin. The penal sanction ignores much of the wrongdoing of the capitalist class. Socially injurious behavior traceable to the capitalist class is often not proscribed by the criminal code. Starvation stems not from the difficulties of agricultural production but from the production and distribution of foodstuffs for profits: if production is unprofitable, then the resulting food shortages are not criminal; they are simply good business. Moreover, when the capitalist class is subject to legal action, it faces civil litigation involving *negotiations* to determine if a wrong did occur, and if damage is demonstrated the remedy is fine and/or compensation. Only in cases where wrongdoing is blatant is the capitalist class subject to the penal sanctions, as in Watergate or in the Patty Hearst trial where failure to prosecute would substantiate charges of class bias.

Under these conditions, the state confronts the problem of mediating class antagonisms, that is, the problem of persuasively securing broad-based consent for its capitalist conception of order. The judicial system mediates by formally guaranteeing the norm of equality under the law. The police, the courts, and prisons do protect the life and property of all individuals by apprehending, prosecuting, and convicting some portion—albeit a class-biased portion—of those who commit crime. All classes and races are protected formally, even though the equal treatment standard is routinely violated in applying the penal sanction. In addition, the mass media serve to mediate class antagonisms. Prime-time television, for instance, glorifies policing and fans the relentless war on criminals. Criminals are frequently portrayed as vicious, dangerous, and psychologically deranged. The media obscures the relation between marginalization and crime by emphasizing only the tie between emotional disturbance expressed as violence and the ability of the police to suppress it.

The most important way that the state mediates class antagonisms is by responding to the real increase in crime. In America all measures show that crime is on the increase. The Federal Bureau of Investigation measures crime by the number of offenses known to the police and by the number of arrests made annually. These measures are based on data for the seven index offenses of homicide, forcible rape, aggravated assault, robbery, grand larceny, and auto theft. The Uniform Crime Report publishes the annual crime rate based on the index offenses and it shows a steady increase in crime over the last several decades and a sharper increase since 1970. This relation holds true when the crime measures are reported as a rate per 100,000 population: the seven index offenses increased by about a third from 1970 to 1975. This increase holds true for property crimes and personally violent crimes. It is highlighted by findings from victimization surveys sponsored by the U.S. Department of Justice: when citizens are questioned directly about the type and frequency of criminal victimization the resulting estimate of crime far exceeds the rate reported by the Uniform Crime Report. When the state responds to crime with prevention

Ted Goertzel

Alcatraz prison, a foreboding symbol of the criminal justice system.

and/or control programs, it addresses the real issue of victimization for which there is deep concern.

Crime in America is even more complex an issue than this, however. As a legitimate instrument of coercion, it imposes the conditions of capitalist wage labor. As a feature of ideology, it organizes broad support for the state's programs. In addition, the process of marginalization operates to sever class connections to the means of production, while the penal sanction anticipates that some potential for resistance—organized or not—exists amid the forces making up society. We will take a closer look at syndicated crime and street crime, which illustrate the complex reality of the crime problem in America, by grouping together legally defined crimes in two recognizable patterns. These crimes were selected over others because they tie together upper-class and lower-class crime within the same framework.

Syndicated Crime

Syndicated crime illustrates how some crime is tolerated when it is useful to the capitalist class. Syndicated crime refers to (1) the monopolization of vice together with its black-market organization and (2) to both industrial and labor racketeering. Crime syndicates organize in the illegal marketplace supplying illicit commodities and services to fulfill consumer demand. They also provide management with the means of preventing unionization and controlling labor. In many countries of the world, the relation between the black market and the syndicate's suppression of labor is quite obvious. In France, after World War II, Marseilles gangsters monopolized prostitution and gambling under municipal protection, and in return brutally suppressed Communist strikes in the city. In Saigon, during the later part of the Vietnamese war, high-ranking government officials organized the heroin trade as a means of financing urban counterinsurgency programs that required constant payoffs for the citywide network of informers and agents. In the United States, the relationships between the black markets and labor, between syndicated crime and governmental authority, resemble the situation in other countries.

The conditions that make black markets and racketeering possible in this country are *structural* and are only related to special ethnic groups insofar as each has occupied such positions. The Irish, Jews, and Italians, as well as native Protestants, have all organized prostitution, drugs, alcohol, and gambling, and also been involved in racketeering. Such organization requires the existence of four conditions: (1) a market ethic supporting an exploitable demand for illegal services and commodities, (2) a political system hostile to the emergence of a left-wing labor movement, (3) decentralized government vulnerable to local graft and corruption, and (4) a ruling class that is not threatened by organized crime and that benefits from its continued existence. Syndicated crime's ability to suppress labor is consistent with the attempts on the part of the ruling class state personnel to mediate fundamental class antagonisms. Syndicates purchase municipal protection for vice by providing extralegal policing power for the state. The ruling class and the state purchase class harmony in exchange for illegally franchising vice.

Syndicated crime figures have typically specialized in one of the vices: Al Capone organized beer-running in Chicago during Prohibition, Lucky Luciano enlarged the scale on which prostitution had been organized previously and introduced heroin into the trade. These monopolies existed by virtue of the political influence wielded by the syndicated crime leaders. This influence, however, has both political and economic qualifications. It stems from the more conservative tendencies within an ethnic working-class community and historically has been used to oppose the militancy of immigrant workers from these same communities. In 1926, for example, when Mussolini's goodwill ambassador landed on Lake Michigan, Al Capone was on the welcoming committee to quell the potential for Italian working-class antifascist riots. Capone himself claimed repeatedly that he was not a radical and that he wanted to preserve the American system.

The amount of political influence wielded by syndicated crime depends on the kind of resources it possesses. Resources available to organized crime through the vice rackets and services are substantially less than the resources available to the ruling class with its access to manufacturing and construction profits. In addition to vice revenues, syndicated crime derives financial support from racketeering in the competitive service sector. Here racketeering has been known to stabilize the market by guaranteeing predictable labor relations and an absence of competition in services like car towing, garbage hauling, and bakery products. Nonetheless, these resources are small in relation to those of large-scale manufacturing. In this sense, the influence of the syndicate is limited by the monopoly capitalist class. The downfall of Al Capone illustrates this relationship. When prominent Chicago Republicans began to see that racketeering was no longer in their interests, they secured President Hoover's intervention, thereby bringing federal proceedings against Capone. Within three years,

Capone was serving a ten-year sentence for income tax evasion. There was no doubt as to who controlled Chicago.

Syndicated crime is not only politically conservative and subservient to the ruling class, it is one instrument through which the ruling class has attacked the labor movement. Prior to the 1935 Wagner Act, which recognized unions and collective bargaining, gangsters had been used to stop unionization. With legitimate unions, gangsters shifted grounds and worked to suppress wages and to control the labor movement. Syndicated crime was able to suppress wages by forming paper locals (locals with no rank and file control) and then negotiating "sweetheart" contracts with management in the service sector. In transportation and manufacturing, gangsters suppressed militant tendencies in various unions by murder, intimidations, and terrorism, and thereby assisted in creating an essentially conservative labor movement in the United States, that is, a labor movement whose concern was with the improvement of wage conditions and not the capitalist system itself. The no-strike agreement during World War II and the McCarthy period completed the suppression of militant tendencies in the labor movement and assured capital of a stable and predictable labor force.

Street Crime

Street crime illustrates how the criminal justice system is used to maintain control over people who are victims of the marginalization process. Street crime refers to the personally violent offenses including homicide, aggravated assault, robbery, and forcible rape, as well as that portion of property crime organized around street life. Personally violent street crimes involve intraclass patterns of victimization, where both the assailant and victim are poor or working class. These are crimes of spontaneous violence committed by recently marginalized populations that in turn have been concentrated in American ghettos. Southern blacks and poor whites were pushed off the land by drought, forced land sales, and Jim Crow laws, and were then redeployed to the industrial North by the demand for labor and high wages during the first and second world wars. When the demand for surplus labor collapsed after World War II, black and other minority workers lost the wage and suffered chronic unemployment and underemployment. These events reveal that capitalism cannot sustain the conditions of full employment in an expanding labor market. They also demonstrate the impact of a racially segmented labor market on the process of marginalization. Black and other minority workers are most vulnerable because of placement in unstable, low-paying jobs. Marginalization concentrated those who no longer possessed a relation to productive life in the ghetto and the state legitimated this concentration by the provision of welfare, income maintenance, and other programs.

The ghetto and its street life mark the destruction of an entire class's relation to productive life. The brutalization and the exploitation of the street result from the

absolute deterioration of social life and the destruction of the essentially social character of consciousness. Such deterioration occurs when the productive foundations un-
derpinning social life are destroyed; it is revealed by the spontaneous pattern of violence and intraclass victimization associated with street crime. Homicides often begin
as aggravated assaults and frequently start as spontaneous quarrels between people
who know each other, such as drinking partners, neighbors, and family members.
Quarrels occur in the home about as frequently as they occur in downtown bars and
on inner-city streets where marginalized groups are concentrated.

Young black males are overrpresented both as assailants and as victims in
murders and in aggravated assault cases. Aggravated assault victims are most
frequently young males from nonwhite low-income groups; the assailants are predominantly black or Latin. The typical assault involves black males and this situation is
only slightly more frequent than black males assaulting black women. Recent evidence suggests that male-female assaults are substantially underreported for all races
and social classes and that they are more likely to surface in hospital emergency
rooms as accidents than in arrest reports. Closely associated with male-female assaults
is rape. Rape is not the result of provocation or enticement on the part of the victim;
nor is it related to the victim's character or reputation. Rape is an act of sexual aggression in which the primary goal is the conquest and degradation of the victim. Surveys
indicate that rape is both an intraclass and intrarace crime: the most frequent rape situation involves a black man and a black woman coming from low-income areas. This
suggests how patriarchy affects already high rates of victimization in low-income areas.

Heroin addiction also contributes to the deterioration of life in the ghetto by intensifying intraclass and intrarace patterns of victimization. Studies of addicts un-
dergoing methadone treatment suggest that most addicts have been arrested for
property crime prior to the onset of addiction. Its effect is to increase the frequency
of arrests and of victimization. Again, most robberies and burglaries victimize low-income, nonwhite communities. This pattern links marginals with syndicated crime at
two levels. First, heroin syndicates are reluctant to enter into the retail distribution of
the drug: black and Latin narcotics entrepreneurs drawn from marginal populations
now distribute heroin at the street level. Second, heroin syndicates are dependent on
an active consumer demand and consequently on the exploitation of social deterioration in the ghetto. Both levels provide justification for increased police surveillance
programs, including undercover teams and networks of police informers, thereby increasing the level of police repression in the ghetto.

SOCIAL JUSTICE

Anticrime programs have failed to reduce the inordinately high rates of victimization
that characterize American cities. Intensified police patrols do not affect the incidence
of crime. Pretrial diversion programs and plea bargaining only circumvent the right

to trial and redirect the defendants to minimal security programs. The effect of longer sentences and even the effect of the death penalty are largely undetermined in relation to the incidence of crime. Rehabilitation programs produce only minor effects in preventing future crimes because far too many ex-inmates continue to commit crimes and to be returned to prison. The criminal justice system has failed to reduce crime. Recognition of this failure has produced several different reactions among criminologists and criminal justice practitioners.

The New Realism

On many issues conservatives and liberals tend to agree with what has been called the New Realism. The New Realism is a reform strategy designed to reconcile class antagonisms by imposing harsher measures on offenders and by upholding the formal standard of equality under the law. The logic of the position is clear: if the state is granted the necessary authority to suppress marginalized classes, then the state can fulfill its obligation to protect all citizens from victimization. In policing, the New Realism includes several developments. Police discretion has been increased by recent Supreme Court decisions; civilian auxiliary units accountable to police precincts now patrol urban neighborhoods; the image of the police has been improved by the more balanced race and sex composition of the force. This new image of police-community integration overlays the real change: the increased freedom with which the police patrols now deal with the problem of containing marginal groups and the increased organized support the police have for carrying out this activity. In corrections, advocates of the New Realism have modified sentencing law in several states. The new sentences are longer and fixed by statute so that judges cannot alter the length of imprisonment. In addition, state and federal prison construction programs have resumed, indicating that the state is prepared to allocate scarce resources to control institutions even in times of economic crisis. Consequently, those convicted are to face longer sentences, the expected increase in the prison population is to be absorbed into the newly constructed prisons, and if resistance to the conditions of incarceration arises, the death penalty exists to guarantee order.

The problem with the New Realism stems from its most basic assumption, namely that it is possible to reconcile the class antagonisms at the heart of crime through the increased use of coercion. Repression will not noticeably affect the victimization rate because it fails to recognize the underlying causes of crime. The New Realism simply relies on the organization of support among the criminally victimized to legitimate repressive measures against those who victimize. It provides no remedy for those who are marginalized because these programs ignore the role of productive life in creating constructive social life. And it discourages community democracy because citizen participation is limited to police programming instead of extended to autonomous community organizations where practical equality defines the goal.

Meaning of Crime

Anticrime programs must be developed with the recognition that the causes of community destruction are rooted in capitalism and that the fight to reduce crime must represent a struggle against the destruction of productive and social life that must also foster democratic social relations within and between communities. Some Marxist criminologists have outlined specific measures for reducing crime. For the immediate situation, there are reforms recommended by the state's agencies of social control which might reduce crime without pitting the working class against itself—better street lighting, escort services for the elderly, victim compensation programs. These reforms provide some protection for the victim without intensifying and legitimating the process of marginalization. In addition, community crime control programs must be explored. These programs must remain independent of the criminal justice system and involve community members in social defense efforts at the same time that they explore how race and sex divide the working class. Women have organized against rape, for instance, and black political groups have organized against police harassment and brutality; such examples suggest that the fight against crime is only part of a much larger contest. At a minimum this contest is for the achievement of full economic rights in the United States, including the right to work, the right to health, the right to housing, and the right to recreative activity. This is a fight against the conditions imposed by the wage, the process of marginalization, and the effects of a racially segmented labor market.

This larger fight has been won in countries where socialist revolutions have taken place and one result of revolution has been a drastic change in the meaning of crime and the methods for dealing with it. In Cuba, for example, crimes are defined as activities that endanger the goal of the revolution. The power of the state to impose punishment is used to foster socialist and democratic relations. It is a crime, for example, for a husband to rape his wife on the grounds that in socialist societies equality in the family is a primary goal of the revolution. It should be noted that in the United States forcible intercourse between marriage partners is not a crime. While the incidence and distribution of crime in Cuba is not known, the method for dealing with it is. Popular tribunals organized on a neighborhood basis and peopled by nonprofessional community members represent one important institution of justice in Cuba. Those in a community define the terms of their own justice system by direct participation. The people decide whether a crime has been committed and what to do about it. Underlying this participation, however, is a network of mass organizations where community members discuss and study the principles of socialism. These mass organizations furnish the guidelines and generate the skills necessary to participate effectively and responsibly in the popular tribunals. Thus, these tribunals are not examples of vigilante justice where personal interest or private passion determine the outcome. The popular tribunals grow out of and remain democratic to the extent that they are related to Cuba's mass organizations.

The organization of society, then, determines whether the fight against crime can be waged democratically as in Cuba or whether it is waged repressively as in the United States. As we have pointed out, the New Realism is a philosophy that would criminalize marginals to the extent that the state personnel and criminal justice experts can secure the necessary popular consent. This philosophy does not address the underlying antagonisms of social class; nor can it do so. These antagonisms, as we have noted, were based on the wage-labor exchange that characterizes capitalism. In this exchange, proletarian advantage would jeopardize the economic dominance of the capitalist class. Capitalist dominance, however, means an organization of society that continually subjects workers to marginalization simply because the economy cannot sustain the conditions of full employment when the labor pool is expanding. In this respect, the wage-labor exchange is also the condition for the process of marginalization and the penal sanction not only imposes the conditions of wage labor but also punishes attempts to exist outside the wage. Thus, labor militancy as well as other forms of militancy are suppressed to the same extent that street violence is. Criminal syndicates together with their exploitative effects in the ghetto are permitted to operate as long as their criminal activities contribute to suppression of militancy. These relations account for the face of crime in America. Modern crime, it must be recalled, is the product of previous historical developments, including the creation of a wage-labor class by process of marginalization, the development of the modern state complete with specialized justice institutions, and, finally, the division of society into economically defined classes.

Summary

A definition of crime represents the legal conditions under which the state, as an instrument of an economically dominant class, exercises its power to punish. The body of criminal law presupposes a class-based state with a territorial jurisdiction. This condition occurred only toward the end of the thirteenth century in England. Historically, the English criminal law paralleled the transformation of the feudal mode to the capitalist mode of production, where, for example, the expansion of commerce redefined the law of larceny and the enclosure laws forced the peasantry off the land and eventually into the factory as wage-labor. Crime under contemporary American capitalism also represents the coercive power of the state and further indicates marginalization of workers, that is, the expulsion of older workers from and the inability to employ new workers in the productive world. Under these conditions, organized crime illustrates how marginal as well as productive workers are implicated in the criminal underworld. Vice and labor racketeering can be seen as protected but illegal monopolies where the capitalist class purchases labor peace at the expense of marginalized workers. Workers, marginalized from productive labor, congregated in northern ghettos where the quality of social life, especially its violence, followed collapse of the job market for national minorities. The illegal markets created by vice racketeering contributed to the absolute deterioration of social life by introducing heroin and reorganizing prostitution and generally transforming marginals into consumers of illegal and debilitating commodities. The prevalence of crime need not contribute to such deterioration, and this is evidenced in socialist countries where crime as the coercive power of the state is used to further the aims of the revolution. Here, punishment is imposed on practices and activities that violate principles of equality, whether racial, sexual, or class, and is the outcome of popular tribunals as in Cuba, where nonprofessional citizens participate in the creation of justice on a collective basis.

Review Questions

1. Why is crime a modern concept?
2. What is the legal definition of crime?
3. What role does crime play in the development of capitalism?
4. In what sense does the state create crime?
5. How does the violence of street crime contribute to the stability of capitalist society?
6. How does crime describe a relationship between marginalized and productive labor?
7. Why is syndicated crime subordinated to capitalist activity?
8. What role does the legal definition of crime play in socialist societies?
9. How does the socialist definition of crime differ from the capitalist definition of crime?
10. What differences would you expect to find in the social characteristics of prison populations in the United States as opposed to Cuba?
11. How does liberal criminology differ from radical criminology?
12. How does conservative criminology differ from radical criminology?

Suggestions for Further Study

1. American justice is often criticized for its racial and class inequities. One way of studying this process is to attend regularly the proceedings of your local criminal court and to record systematically the process that you observe. Your own find-

ings can be compared with official information on the disposition of cases over the course of a year to see how sex, race, age, and class affect the sentences received by offenders.

2. Crime pays, in the sense that movies, television, magazines, and newspapers that feature "crime" are often profitable ventures. Select one type of media for systematic study of the presentation of crime. Select a set of items that are appropriate for the study of your media; these might include the type of crime involved, demographic data on the victims, offenders, and policing agents. And then try to identify the media "image" of crime.

3. Street crime inspires fear. Review recent victimization surveys on determinants of the fear of crime and then compare these findings with results of questions that you have asked your own sample of respondents.

4. Reconstruct the social history of a particular crime according to the method of analysis used in this chapter. There are many sources, including histories of the common law, of legislative debate and intent, and monographs on social histories of particular crimes.

5. Crime is a political term and the views that people have of it are also political. Select a sample of people for in-depth interviews aiming at the meanings that your respondents attach to crime. Categorize these meanings according to whether each is liberal, conservative, or radical, following the use of these terms in the text.

Selected Readings

American Friends Service Committee. *Struggle for Justice.* New York: Hill & Wang, 1971.

Cantor, Robert. "New Laws for a New Society." *Crime and Social Justice* 2 (1974):12–23.

Center for Research on Criminal Justice. *The Iron Fist and Velvet Glove: An Analysis of the U.S. Police.* Berkeley: Center for Research on Criminal Justice, 1977.

Cleaver, Eldridge. *Soul on Ice.* New York: McGraw-Hill, 1968.

Crime and Social Justice Collective. "The Politics of Street Crime." *Crime and Social Justice* 5 (1976):1–4.

Davis, Angela. *If They Come in the Morning.* New York: Signet, 1971.

Hall, Jerome. *Theft, Law and Society.* Boston: Little, Brown, 1935.

Hay, Douglas, et al. *Albion's Fatal Tree: Crime and Society in Eighteenth-Century England.* New York: Pantheon, 1975.

Hobsbawn, E. J. *Primitive Rebels: Studies in Archaic Forms of Social Movements in the 19th and 20th Centuries.* New York: Norton, 1959.

Jackson, George. *Soledad Brother: The Prison Letters of George Jackson*. New York: Coward-McCann, 1970.

Klein, Dorie, and June Kress. "Any Woman's Blues: A Critical Overview of Women, Crime, and the Criminal Justice System." *Crime and Social Justice* 5 (1976):34–49.

Linebaugh, Peter. "Karl Marx, the Theft of Wood, and Working Class Composition: A Contribution to the Current Debate." *Crime and Social Justice* 6 (1976):5–15.

Malcolm X. *The Autobiography of Malcolm X*. New York: Grove, 1964.

Melossi, Dario. "The Penal Question in Capital." *Crime and Social Justice* 5 (1976):26–33.

Pearce, Frank. *Crimes of the Powerful: Marxism, Crime and Deviance*. London: Pluto Press, 1976.

Platt, Tony. "Prospects for Radical Criminology." *Crime and Social Justice* 1 (1974):2–9.

Quinney, Richard. *Class, State and Crime: On the Theory and Practice of Criminal Justice*. New York: McKay, 1977.

Rusche, George, and Otto Kirchheimer. *Punishment and Social Structure*. New York: Russell and Russell, 1968.

Schwendinger, Herman, and Julia Schwendinger. "Social Class and the Definition of Crime." *Crime and Social Justice* 7 (1977):4–13.

———. "Delinquency and the Collective Varieties of Youth." *Crime and Social Justice* 5 (1976):8–25.

———. "Rape Myths: In Legal, Theoretical, and Everyday Practice." *Crime and Social Justice* 1(1974):18–26.

Chapter 10

Imperialism and Development

By imperialism is meant the political, social, and economic domination of one nation by another, normally in the interests of the ruling group in the dominant nation. Imperialist policies have often been pursued by class societies. Societies in which slavery existed as a relationship of production often engaged in imperial wars in order to capture people who could be exploited as slaves and land to be worked by them. Oriental despotic societies engaged in imperialism primarily in order to exact tribute from conquered states. Often, the warrior groups in a nation have encouraged imperialist policies in order to secure the prizes of war for themselves.

When capitalism first developed, early sociologists such as Auguste Comte and Herbert Spencer thought that it would bring an end to imperialist warfare. They thought that capitalists would find it more profitable to remain at home and produce wealth through their control of factories, banks, and commercial enterprises. They favored trade with other nations, but believed that this would be done on a mutually beneficial basis without the need for compulsion through imperialist policies.

Unfortunately for the peoples of the world, the early optimistic forecasts proved erroneous. Capitalist nations used their mastery of superior military technology to embark on wars of imperialist expansion that covered the globe. Under capitalism, we have had two world wars which caused millions of casualties. With the development of nuclear bombs and ballistic missiles, world war between major powers has become too horrible for even the strongest capitalist power to seriously contemplate initiating, at least so long as no defense exists against nuclear retaliation. But this has not kept capitalist powers from waging wars against militarily weaker Third World nations which do not have the capability of retaliation.

The United States has been engaging in imperial ventures since its independence. The primitive societies that occupied North America before European settlement were driven off the land, exterminated, or placed in reservations. The slave-owning aristocrats in the South were particularly militant in demanding imperialist expansion into the West in order to obtain more land for their plantations. A war was fought with Mexico which resulted in one half of its territory being annexed into the southern half of the United States. The slave lords' designs on Cuba and Central America were frustrated only by their defeat in the Civil War.

In the generation after the Civil War, with the maturation of industrial capitalism and monopoly corporations, new forces began operating on the state to lead it into a new era of imperialism in Latin America and the Pacific basin. In this case, the economic contradictions of monopoly capitalism were the origin of imperialist policies. Capitalist societies engage in imperialism for several reasons. One is to assure a source of raw materials and other primary products at low prices. Another is to justify high military spending which results in huge profits for the largest corporations. A third, and for monopoly capitalism, especially, the most important, is to find a secure place to invest profits abroad. Monopoly corporations tend to make very high profits. Since they are extracting such high profits from their own societies, the people in their societies do not have enough money (from their wages) to purchase the products that the corporations produce. This causes stagnation and depression if no outlet for excess capital can be found. Imperialism ensures that other nations which receive this capital provide protection for the interests of foreign capitalist investors. A fourth motive force for imperialism is the need for export markets, i.e., for areas of the world that can be induced to purchase the products of the capital-intensive industries of the advanced countries, products which otherwise could not profitably be sold.

During the period of the consolidation of monopoly capitalism (1890–1917) the United States engaged in a war with Spain which deprived that country of all of its remaining colonies in Latin America (Cuba and Puerto Rico) and the Pacific rim (the Philippines and Guam). Hawaii and Samoa were annexed at the same time. During the same period the United States pursued an active policy of intervention in the Caribbean and in Central America, frequently sending Marines and Naval forces into countries whose governments threatened not to do the bidding of the United States. This expansion was similar to that engaged in by European monopoly capitalist powers, although often these powers already had colonies obtained during the period of mercantile capitalism.

The imperialist ventures of the U.S. government and corporations were pretty much restricted to northern Latin America and the Pacific rim until World War II. A conflict with Japan over economic and political supremacy in the Pacific rim, and especially in China, led to a war which also involved the defeat of German aspirations

Ted Goertzel

Street markets in Latin America.

to become the leading capitalist power. World War II resulted in the world hegemony of the United States both economically and militarily. With economic and political interests everywhere outside of the Communist countries, the United States defined itself as the policeman of the world. It intervened wherever necessary in order to preserve and advance its newly established informal world empire.

The period after World War II also saw the growth of anti-imperialist movements throughout the Third World. As these movements increased in strength, it became too costly for the European powers to retain colonies throughout the world. Where possible, the European powers tried to turn power over to local elites who had been educated in European countries and indoctrinated into accepting the benefits of setting themselves up as local representatives of the imperialist powers. Independence was resisted in countries such as Vietnam, where Communist movements were strong, or such as Algeria, where there were large settler populations to contend with.

The United States, most particularly through its Central Intelligence Agency (CIA), became the leading exponent of this form of indirect imperialism. It used a combination of open and clandestine methods to assure that governments subservient to its interests remained in power in Third World countries. In some cases, grants of aid to corporations controlled by local elites, bribes to local politicians, manipulation of news media for ideological purposes, and other relatively subtle methods were sufficient. When things got out of hand, as under the Mossadegh government in Iran or the Arbenez government in Guatemala, direct intervention by CIA agents was used. In the case of Chile under the Allende government, economic boycotts combined with clandestine aid to fascist groups in the country eventually brought down the elected government and replaced it with a pro-American fascist dictatorship.

The small country of Vietnam proved to be a major obstacle to American imperialism. While the United States had no significant economic interests in Vietnam itself, policy makers felt it necessary to maintain an anti-Communist regime there because they feared that not doing so would set a precedent for similar movements in other countries. The heroic struggle of the Vietnamese people, led by a highly disciplined Communist Party, finally succeeded in wearing down the American military and economy to the point that Americans lost patience with the war and demanded its end. As a consequence, Americans today are reluctant to support imperialist ventures. While the capitalist class still does its best to support anti-Communist regimes throughout the world, it is somewhat restricted in the means that it can use to do so. Congress has, for example, ended direct military aid to Chile. It would be difficult for the administration to persuade Congress to authorize the sending of American troops to suppress a rebellion anywhere in the Third World today.

Since we are in a period of re-examination of imperialist policies, it is important for Americans to inform themselves about the causes of imperialism and about the forms it is likely to take in the future. While the vast majority of the American people have no interest in exploiting Third World countries, there are powerful forces that do. These forces have much at stake, while the average American has relatively little interest in foreign policy. Too often, Americans become concerned only when it is too late—when the oil companies have already doubled gasoline prices, or when the United States is already involved in a military action, or when an American factory is closed because its owners have found it more profitable to invest in a dictatorial Third World country. Modern capitalism is a worldwide system, and we cannot avoid being affected by events throughout the world.

MECHANISMS OF CONTROL

The countries subject to imperialism are not autonomous societies that have real control over their own economies, states, and cultures. The fundamentals of their social relations and culture are in large part determined by the structure of the imperialist-satellite relations in which they are enmeshed.

Manipulation of Local Ruling Groups

The earlier forms of direct rule have been replaced by methods that rely less on direct military force and more on manipulation of local ruling groups.

As the period of direct rule wore on, resistance movements tended to become more and more powerful and the costs of maintaining the formal empires skyrocketed while profits declined as a result of increasing civil disorders. The granting of formal independence confused the people and minimized opposition to imperial power by channeling its exercise through the local ruling groups. The basis of this arrangement lies in the convergence of the interests of the local dominant interests with that of the metropolitan countries. Neocolonial regimes were established virtually everywhere as successor states to the old colonial regimes. Based on a coalition of landlords, monopolists, and merchants who all opposed industrialization policies that would undermine their class position, these regimes saw their best hope for longterm survival in a symbiotic relationship with the imperialist countries. Afraid of revolutionary forces among their own people that would sweep them away, they accepted the guarantees of the imperialist countries to support their regimes economically and militarily in exchange for compliance with the political and economic interests of the imperial powers. Both parties gained from this arrangement.

Of course, the losers are the workers and peasants of Third World countries whose labor goes to produce an economic surplus shared by the local ruling group and the foreign imperialists. These groups are willing to sacrifice the economic development of their own countries, as well as the lives of their own people, in return for a guarantee that their extraordinary privileges will be protected by the United States and other imperialist countries.

Economic Power

Power is exercised over Third World countries through a combination of economic, military, and ideological forces (these in addition to the factor of the convergence of interests between the local and imperialist ruling groups). Economic power is exercised through trade, foreign investment, foreign lending, and foreign assistance. Third World countries often specialize in the production and export of only one or a few raw material exports, while they require a wide range of manufactured imports. This peculiar trade pattern often puts the Third World countries in a weak position vis-à-vis the buyers of its exports and the suppliers of its manufactured goods. The greater the percentage of its exports concentrated in one commodity, the more susceptible the country is to influence stemming from the buyers of that one commodity who can manipulate the market to secure political and economic advantage for themselves. Likewise, the higher the percentage of a country's exports that go to *one* advanced country, the greater the power that the advanced country can exert over it. The industrial countries have highly diversified imports and exports, as well as highly diversified trading partners. The Third World countries, which have neither, have a great deal of power exerted over them through trade. This dependence is aggravated by a higher reliance on exports and imports than is the case with industrialized countries, because of the lack of significant capital goods industries in the Third World. A developed country, such as Germany in both world wars, can adequately compensate for whatever goods it might be cut off from because its advanced technology gives it an ability to develop substitute products. Because of their technological backwardness, Third World countries, when deprived of export markets or imports, have great difficulty converting their economies to produce something else either for export or for local consumption-goods production.

Power is also exerted through foreign investment. Large segments of the most central sectors of Third World economies are owned or controlled by corporations based in the advanced capitalist countries. These firms are integrated on an international basis and make decisions on imports, exports, investment, prices, what to produce, what wages to pay, etc., on the basis of long-term profit maximization of their world holdings as a whole. Decisions are thus taken out of the hands of local forces. In addition, these international giants, many of whose annual sales are greater than the GNPs of the countries in which they invest, exert great political power indirectly through their influence on U.S. foreign policy as well as directly on the local governments.

Economic assistance is used by imperialist countries to control their satellites. Aid is given on the condition that the recipient countries follow political, social, and economic policies that are in the interests of U.S. corporations; for example, on the condition that local governments favor raw material production over industry (so as not to compete with U.S. corporations that specialize in industrial production), encourage private enterprise, favor foreign corporations, keep wages, taxes, and tariffs low and profits high, and avoid exchange controls (so profits can be repatriated at will). In addition to enforcing an open-door policy for U.S. corporations, hindering the development of locally controlled industry, and minimizing state interference with the foreign corporations, foreign assistance is also used to secure worldwide military and political support for the policies of the imperialist countries and to directly subsidize U.S. corporations. Foreign aid funds are usually repayable to the metropolitan countries in their own currency with interest. Furthermore, most aid money never leaves the metropolitan countries. Foreign assistance is granted in trade credits to the Third World countries. They are provided with a list of goods on which they must use this credit. And this list is comprised of goods metropolitan corporations want to sell overseas (generally goods they could not sell profitably in the free market because the goods are produced cheaper by other metropolitan countries). Thus, virtually all foreign aid is a subsidy to U.S. corporations for their exports. In addition to this, much of "foreign aid" is in the form of export credits, not to the Third World states or to locally owned businesses in Third World countries, but rather to U.S.-owned and -operated businesses in the Third World.

Military Power

Great military power is also applied to Third World countries. In spite of their nominal independence, there is a constant threat of direct military intervention by the leading metropolitan countries or their representatives in the event that metro-politan economic interests are threatened by the local regimes, or that the regimes themselves are threatened by anti-imperialist movements (whether nationalist, social-ist, or Communist). There does not have to be an actual military intervention for con-trol to be exercised in this fashion. An occasional intervention is enough to terrorize the world. This was the significance of Vietnam. The tremendous cost of this war must be evaluated against the great potential profits incumbent on the intimidation of na-tionalist, socialist, and Communist forces throughout the world.

In addition to military power exerted through direct intervention and the threat thereof, it is also exerted through the support of local military institutions and the resultant gratitude of their officer corps. The local military establishments frequently are willing to support the imperialists against their own people. Metropolitan coun-tries train the officers of Third World armies, either in the metropolitan countries (the top officers), or in Third World countries (lower-level officers). They provide mil-itary advisers at all levels of the chain of command, and they provide the modern weapons of war—airplanes, tanks, artillery, etc.—on which the Third World armies are totally dependent.

Ideological Power

In addition to economic and military power, ideological power is also exerted on Third World countries. Educational institutions, churches, labor unions, and the mass media participate in the control of Third World countries. Leading students from Third World countries are trained in the imperialist countries, which inculcate in them metropolitan values and ideology as well as provide them with the skills that the metropolis desires them to have. Teachers from the imperialist countries are sent to the Third World countries; local universities are financed and educational minis-tries have metropolitan advisers attached to them. These activities are designed to restructure local education in the image of the imperialist country's schools so that students will both accept proimperialist values and have the skills needed by the im-perialist-controlled economy.

Great power is exercised by molding the local culture through metropolitan-owned magazines, books written by metropolitans, films from the metropolitan coun-tries, and news supplied through metropolitan-controlled news services. Consider-able influence over local radio and TV programming comes from metropolitan pro-duction of programs. Religious institutions are greatly influenced by the metropolitan training of their clergy, missionaries, and the financing of local religious institutions. Labor unions are likewise controlled through the training of labor leaders in the met-ropolitan countries and the financing of local unions.

CAUSES OF IMPERIALISM

Radical economists and social scientists have engaged in a lively debate for many years over the causes of imperialism. This debate is important for two reasons. First, those who want to join in a struggle to end imperialism must have a clear understanding of its causes so they will know which groups in society have an interest in it and how and why they are likely to defend it. Second, it is important to know what effect imperialism has on events in our own country. Does it enrich everyone in our society, at the expense of people in exploited societies? Or does it benefit only the corporate upper class? This, of course, has significant political implications since people who do not benefit from imperialism are more likely to be willing to oppose it.

European countries were engaged in imperialist adventures around the world long before the United States became the major imperialist power. Not surprisingly, the debate about imperialism took place first in Europe. English social-democrat J. A. Hobson published an influential critique of imperialism in 1902. After carefully reviewing the evidence, he concluded that the main reason for imperialism was not trade or the need for raw materials but rather an outlet for the investment of surplus capital. Capitalists found that there were insufficient opportunities for profitable investment in England, largely because their own low wage policies meant that people didn't have enough money to buy the goods that new industries might produce. Consequently, they sought investment opportunities in less developed countries where there were not yet large capitalist corporations that monopolized the profitable areas of production. It was these groups that urged the British government to undertake an imperialist foreign policy which required it to send troops, civil servants, and missionaries around the world to conquer and rule poor societies. Hobson argued, on the basis of his data, that the vast majority of the British people did not profit from imperialism. Quite the contrary, they paid taxes to the government to support its imperialist wars, which benefited only big business. He favored social and economic reforms within Britain which would redistribute income and force the capitalists to invest their money at home.

More radical writers, such as V. I. Lenin and Rosa Luxemburg, accepted Hobson's central point about the need for investment outlets for surplus capital being the major cause of imperialism. However, they criticized Hobson's argument that this problem could be solved through social reforms. They argued instead that imperialism was absolutely necessary for the survival of the monopoly capitalist system. They felt that capitalists could not tolerate reforms that would raise wages and hence cut their profits. They noted that profit rates were already lower in the advanced countries and argued that attempting to keep all the capital within the advanced countries would lead to an eventual collapse of the system because of the lack of any profitable investment possibilities.

As the wealthy countries invested capital abroad, one might naturally expect that it would stimulate rapid economic growth in those countries. This was, in-

By Ross Koppel

Dependency theorists argue that there is a flow of wealth away from the less developed countries.

deed, the expectation of Marx, Lenin, and Luxemburg. They felt that the spread of imperialism throughout the world would cause the entire world to go through a process of capitalist development similar to that first experienced by the European countries. And it is true that imperialist penetration did begin a process of industrial development in many countries. The contradiction in this process became apparent, however, when the capitalists began to make huge profits on their investments in the poor countries. They then brought these profits home to their own countries. It became apparent that more money was flowing from the underdeveloped countries to the developed ones than vice versa. While the initial impetus for modern imperialism was a surplus of capital, imperialism generated more capital of its own!

With this new data in hand, Marxist authors such as Paul Baran, Paul Sweezy, Harry Magdoff, and André Gunder Frank formulated a new theory of imperialism. This theory, which came to be know as "dependency theory," arose from the fact that the flow of capital was from the *less* developed to the *more* developed countries. Dependency theorists argued that the wealthy countries, which constituted the core of the world capitalist economic system, were able to take advantage of their monopoly of advanced industrial technology, and of the capital needed to use it, in order to charge the poor countries high prices for industrial goods while paying them low prices for raw materials and the agricultural products they produced. While most earlier writers had placed greatest emphasis on investment, some of these theorists and others, such as Samir Amin and Arghiri Emmanuel, argued that unequal trade relationships were the most important method by which the capitalists exploited the poor nations.

This argument has also been quite popular among nationalist intellectuals in the Third World countries who felt that the poverty of their countries was largely due to foreign exploitation. Trade statistics available to them at least until recently seemed to show that the trends in prices were against them. Prices of raw materials and agricultural products seemed to drop relative to prices of industrial goods their countries had to export. Also, statistics showed that the economic gap between their countries and the wealthy countries was increasing. The rich were getting richer and the poor were getting poorer. This was blamed on both the expatriation of profits from foreign investment and on unequal trade relationships.

This debate provides an excellent example of how alternative theories can be advanced within a common paradigm. As the world situation changes, and new data becomes available, different authors use different elements of the Marxist paradigm in attempts to explain what is going on and, more importantly, to determine what can be done about it politically. The debate on imperialism and underdevelopment has serious political implications. If the rich countries are getting richer and the poor countries poorer, then we would expect the major polarization in the world to be between these two blocs of countries. We would expect the next major socialist revolutions to break out in the poor countries. Radicals in the rich countries would then focus their efforts on supporting movements in these countries, but would find little support for socialist movements among the relatively affluent workers in the wealthier countries. This perspective was adopted by some radical groups in the 1960s who focused their energies on opposing the Vietnam war but were pessimistic about domestic political issues. At the same time, radical groups in Latin America and other Third World countries launched guerrilla movements in the hope of toppling governments they felt would be decaying as a consequence of the weakening of their economic base caused by imperialism.

These debates within the Marxist paradigm cannot be solved by theoretical argument, or by reference to the works of Marx. The question is one of using and, if necessary, modifying theory to best explain actual empirical trends. It requires careful examination of the data on the role of imperialism in the economies of the advanced countries, on its effects in the Third World countries, and on the relationships between the two groups. This is a difficult task, especially since patterns in both the developed and underdeveloped countries are constantly changing. Different writers, using different bodies of data, have come up with different conclusions. However, as more research is done, and as trends become clearer as they develop through time, we can develop a more adequate picture of the true situation.

ROLE OF IMPERIALISM IN THE U.S. ECONOMY

It is clear that the net flow of funds is from the underdeveloped to the developed countries. Nevertheless, industrial capital, often in the form of whole factories, continues to be exported to the less-developed countries where wages are low and dictatorial regimes keep the workers compliant. Capitalists invest abroad because they can make more money there, whether or not there is a capital surplus at home.

Costs of Imperialism to the Taxpayers

While in terms of capital flow the United States gains more than it loses from Third World countries, this does not mean that American society as a whole is richer because of this exploitation. Maintaining the imperialist system requires that the United States maintain a large military force capable of protecting its investments in countries throughout the world. These armed forces are extremely expensive, particularly when we become involved in a war such as that in Vietnam. If we look at the figures for the years 1968–1969, when military expenditures were quite high, we find that the United States was spending far more on keeping its war machine going than it was taking in through investments and unequal trade relations.

In that year, the United States was spending $205 billion for direct and indirect military expenses. The other major capitalist powers spent only one-third as much as the U.S., despite the fact that they are geographically less secure than the U.S. We can thus assume that two-thirds of American military expenditure were not needed to defend the U.S., but were excess needed to maintain the empire. This excess expense can be roughly estimated at $137 billion. If we add up the total gains from imperialist investments and unequal trade relationships with the Third World, they come to approximately $19 billion (for data and sources, see Szymanski, 1973). This means a net loss of $118 billion, or $581 for each of the 203 million people living in the U.S. in 1969.

Of course, this does not mean that every man, woman, and child in the country paid the same amount of the cost. As we know from Chapter 5, our tax system is quite inequitable in allowing wealthy Americans to avoid much of the burden of sustaining it. The benefits of the imperialist system, however, go primarily to the capitalist class, which owns the major corporations with holdings abroad. Thus, imperialism continues because it is in the interest of this capitalist class, even though it is costly for the society as a whole.

Benefits of Imperialism for the Corporations

Capitalist corporations have six major motivations for maintaining the imperialist system (although all of them reduce to the drive for profits): (1) the need for cheap and secure raw materials, (2) their need for overseas markets for manufactured goods that they cannot sell profitably at home, (3) the extra profits to be made in industrial investment in the Third World, where the workers work for much less than at home, (4) the huge profits to be made in war contracts, (5) the containment of socialist,

Communist, and nationalist threats to profit opportunities, and (6) the domestic tranquilizing effect that overseas adventures have on the working class who are led to identify with them.

An increasing percentage of the raw materials used by the giant corporations must be imported. In the two-decade period from 1900 to 1920 the United States exported more raw materials than it imported, in the period from 1940 to 1950 net imports of raw materials accounted for 5 percent of U.S. raw material consumption, and in the 1950s for about 15 percent. In the 1960s, imports of raw materials as a percentage of domestic production stood at 43 percent for iron, 18 percent for copper, 131 percent for lead, 140 percent for zinc, 636 percent for bauxite, and 31 percent for petroleum. The range of raw materials required by the corporations has expanded enormously. Of the 62 materials listed as strategic and critical materials by the Defense Department, 80 to 100 percent of 38 of them must be imported. A high percentage of these materials are imported from Third World countries. It is the necessity not only of acquiring such materials that is an important motivating force for U.S. imperialism but of acquiring them cheaply and having the insurance that their supply will be continuous and not become an instrument of power to be exerted against the corporations or the U.S. by a Third World country. Direct ownership or at least control over the sources of raw material products provides both continuity in delivery and a low cost.

The tendency for the surplus to increase in monopoly capitalist society means that the corporations have increasingly greater difficulty in selling their goods (see Chapter 4 for a discussion of this tendency). This is the force that caused the first modern wave of U.S. expansionism in the 1890s into the Far East and Latin America, and which today compels the search for markets for goods difficult to sell at home. Not only do firms seek out overseas markets for goods produced in the United States but they also invest in overseas plants that are geared to production for overseas markets. Overseas industrial production has the great advantage of bypassing local tariff barriers as well as enabling U.S. firms to mobilize local capital. U.S. exports amount to about $50 billion a year (most of this is, however, to other industrial capitalist countries). The production of U.S. firms abroad averages about six times the level of U.S. exports (about 30 percent of the GNP of the U.S., or about two thirds the value of the GNP of the Soviet Union).

The rate of profit on U.S. overseas investments is approximately twice that on U.S. domestic investments. Although U.S. investments in the Third World total only 30 percent of all U.S. overseas investments, they account for 50 percent of all overseas earnings, and 60 percent of all overseas repatriated profits. The rate of profit on U.S. investments overseas is approximately 19 percent on invested value. In recent years the United States has been repatriating over three times more profits from Third World countries than it has been investing there (in the late 1960s, about $3 billion a year was repatriated and only $1 billion a year invested). The value of U.S. direct investment overseas increased tenfold from 1946 to 1970. The great bulk of

U.S. overseas investment is concentrated in a few corporations. Forty-five firms own about 57 percent of all U.S. overseas investments—the concentration of investment in the Third World is even greater than this. Great profits are to be made in both the extraction and processing of the raw materials of the Third World and in local manufacturing industries that utilize very cheap labor (frequently people work for $2 a day on the same machines as American workers who receive over $40 a day). These highly profitable operations, in East Asia particularly, produce not only goods for local consumption but also goods for import back into the United States. Labor is so much cheaper in East Asia that most simple electronic goods are now produced there for import into the U.S.

Defending the Empire

Perhaps the most lucrative aspect of imperialism is not the profits to be made overseas but rather the profits to be made in the production of weapons for the maintenance of the empire. Already we have seen how monopoly capitalist society solves the problem of absorbing the economic surplus through military spending. This is not only convenient for the system but it also is highly profitable for the giant corporations, many of whom profit immensely from the very generously administered defense contracts that are extremely important to a number of large and powerful corporations such as G.E., Westinghouse, General Dynamics, and most aircraft and electronics companies. It has been estimated that an average of 35 percent of the output of the largest corporations in the United States is either exported or goes to the military. The defense budget in the late 1960s and early 1970s allocated approximately $50 billion per year to the corporations in the form of defense contracts—a very substantial subsidy.

If the great profits and profit opportunities obtained through these imperialist processes are to be protected, then the world empire must be both defended from all instrusions that would interfere with its profitability, and a militarist policy of containment of socialist, Communist, and nationalist regimes must be pursued. U.S. foreign and military policy must stress the preservation of submissive regimes throughout the world. Nationalists that threaten to expropriate U.S. interests and turn them over to local capitalists are as dangerous as socialists and Communists who would turn them over to local workers or the state. All three alternatives threaten the profitability of the corporations and therefore all are systematically opposed by the U.S. government. Not only Communist regimes have been attacked by the United States but also such nationalist regimes as that of Mossadegh in Iran, Arbenz in Guatemala, Juan Bosch in Santo Domingo, and Goulart in Brazil have been overthrown directly or indirectly by the United States, which groomed local oppositional elements to make coups d'etat that had the complete support of the U.S.

The necessity of containing threats to the system results in a foreign policy directed, not in a shortsighted fashion, to merely defending the specific economic interests of the corporations, but rather in defending the integrity of the American imperial system as a whole. Thus the United States will respond to anti-imperialist movements anywhere, regardless of whether or not it has any significant investments, markets, or raw material supplies in a given area. The system is defended at its weakest points, not where the stake is greatest. The U.S. ruling class views the world just as it views the U.S. If an insurrection broke out in New Mexico, which then declared itself to be an independent country, in spite of the fact that this area might hypothetically cost the corporations more to maintain in welfare costs than the economic benefit they derive from it, the ruling class would stop at nothing to suppress the secession. It is not the profits gained or lost in New Mexico that would motivate this repression but rather the potential repercussions of a successful secession on the rest of the country where the real profits lie. Likewise in the world system, the United States before 1960 had no significant investments, markets, or raw material supplies in Vietnam. Nevertheless, it committed itself totally over a very extensive period to prevent either Communists or genuine nationalists from forming a government there. U.S. Vietnam policies were designed not primarily to maintain or secure profit opportunities but rather to prevent the reverberation of a successful revolution from resonating throughout the Third World and inspiring attempts to destroy the whole informal U.S. empire. Of course, the involvement in Vietnam also greatly benefited the corporations by providing an occasion to justify the vast sums the government was allocating to them.

The pursuit of an aggressive foreign policy, provided the domestic suffering in terms of taxes and lives lost does not reach a critical point, has traditionally resulted in popular identification with imperial policies. This is because the schools and media function to channel the frustrations and aggressiveness that originate in people's daily lives into identification with their rulers' adventures. Patriotism, discipline, respect for law and order, and reverence for the capitalist system in general are instilled in the masses, as we have seen. The militarist crusade against Communism engenders blind respect for authority and conformity, as well as an undercutting of domestic opposition by identifying it with an external enemy (Communism).

Stirring up anti-Communist feelings can be a dangerous policy for the ruling class, however. It was the commitment to protect the entire world against Communism that led the United States into the futile attempt to suppress the Vietnamese socialist revolution. While people supported this war at first, when they were promised a quick victory against a distant enemy at little cost, their support lessened and turned to opposition as the war dragged on year after year with every indication that the Vietnamese on the other side were fighting better than "our Vietnamese." The social and economic costs of this war were very great, leading the ruling class to reverse its policy and abandon the effort in an attempt to cut their losses.

Imperialism is profitable for monopoly corporations so long as they can get the rest of us to cheerfully pay the military costs, or so long as they can get their capitalist allies within the Third World countries to police their own citizens. Whatever their protestations of belief in democracy and freedom, capitalist corporations will invest in South Africa, Chile, or any other country that guarantees super-profits. Imperialism is a natural product of the capitalist pursuit of profits by seeking the best return on their money. This does not mean, however, that capitalists will necessarily pursue neocolonial policies if the costs come to exceed the gains, or that if they are denied opportunities for imperialist exploitation they will not find some way to extract their profits from people in their own countries.

EFFECTS OF IMPERIALISM ON THIRD WORLD COUNTRIES

Just as there has been disagreement among Marxist writers about the causes of imperialist behavior on the part of advanced capitalist countries, so too has there been disagreement about its effects on the Third World countries that experience imperialist intervention. Marxists recognize that imperialists go into these countries in order to make money, whatever their rhetoric about bringing civilization and economic development to the poor of the world. Capitalist exploitation in the Third World has basically the same motivation as that in the home countries: to make profits. The consequences of profit-oriented enterprise can vary greatly, however, depending on the level of economic development in a country and how it fits into the world economic system.

Marx was perhaps the most vigorous critic of the exploitative nature of early capitalism in Europe. Despite his moral outrage, however, he was sufficiently objective as a scientist to recognize that the early capitalists played a progressive role in history by breaking down feudal social institutions and building the economic base needed for advanced capitalism and eventually for a transition to socialism. By taking part of the value produced by the workers as profits, and reinvesting it in capital goods to increase future production, they increased the total productivity of their societies.

Marx thought that capitalists might play a similar role in the Third World countries by extracting wealth and investing it in industry, as well as by investing capital that had been taken from the workers in the advanced countries. Thus, he felt that if imperialist capitalists broke down feudal or Oriental despotic power structures in poor countries, and developed even the minimal industrial facilities necessary to build railroads and other facilities needed for their own exploitative activities, this might serve to get the process of economic development going in such countries.

Views of the Dependency Theorists

Marxist writers such as Lenin and Luxemburg felt that the chief function of imperialism for the developed countries was as an outlet for surplus capital. If this were cor-

rect, and if the consequent flow of capital was from the developed to the underdeveloped countries, then that flow of capital would be expected to stimulate economic
growth. The dependency theorists, on the other hand, noted that the data appeared
to show that the real flow of capital was from the poor countries to the rich countries.
They argued that the United States and other metropolitan countries used their domination of the political and social systems in these countries to impose disadvan-
tageous economic conditions that drained the poor countries of their limited capital.
They argued that through private and public loans which had to be repaid, through
repatriation of profits, through various "service charges" for things such as insurance, freight, royalties, patents, rents, etc., and through manipulations of the prices
paid for goods produced in the Third World Countries, the large imperialist corporations took so much capital from the Third World that rapid economic growth was
impossible there.

The dependency theorists found a great deal of evidence from history to support
their arguments. They found that a great deal of the capital used to finance metropolitan investments came not from the imperialist countries, but rather from local landlords, merchants, and banks. In earlier times, very frequently only a token investment was made in order to secure raw material rights through bribes or other shady
deals. For example, the petroleum rights of the metropolitan oil companies in Vene-
zuela were initially secured through personal favors to the dictator of that country,
which were analogous to the trinkets and beads offered to the Indians in exchange for
Manhattan Island. Control over the nitrate deposits in Chile was obtained by British
business interests through speculation in the stock of Peruvian nitrate companies
thought to be worthless after Chile conquered that part of Peru where the deposits
were located. Because of the resultant pressure exercised by the British government
on Chile to respect the property rights of its subjects, Chile honored the stock certifi-
cates that British citizens had bought up in Peru for next to nothing.

In its earliest stages, imperialism was almost purely exploitative. This was the
"mercantilist" period when Europe first expanded into America, Asia, and Africa, in
order to plunder their empires and steal their wealth. The development that took
place once the initial plundering was over was in the organization of the local populations—or the importation of African slaves—into plantations that produced agricultural products for export. Workers on these plantations received nothing more than
the bare minimum needed to keep them alive.

In the nineteenth century, competitive industrial capitalism became the dominant system in Western Europe. As the advanced countries became increasingly industrialized, they became more interested in a sustained and extensive supply of raw
materials for their growing factories, and in mass markets for the export of their manufactured goods. The close of this period saw the virtually complete division of the
world by the European states in their competition with one another to grab as much
as possible before someone else got it first. In the most recent phase of imperialism,
that of monopoly capitalism, the focus of imperial policies has increasingly been the

export of capital overseas to build up industries in the Third World countries which both take advantage of cheap local labor and dominate local markets, while frequently providing exports back to the home market.

The forms of political relationships between the imperialist and the colonized countries have also gone through historical phases. During the earliest period, the imperialist countries normally set up trading posts or engaged in raiding expeditions. This was often supplemented by the colonization and settlement of limited areas that were exploited either by the monopolistic trade arrangements of mercantilism or through the establishment of plantations or mines geared to European export that exploited unfree labor for great profit. In the period of late competitive capitalism and in the early period of monopoly capitalism, these forms gave way to the overt political control of virtually all Third World countries, in order to establish sanctuaries for the privileged use of an imperialist country's own export and investment interests. In the mature form of monopoly capitalism, direct control over Third World countries has been supplanted by neocolonialism, or indirect rule in collaboration with local ruling groups with interests compatible with those of the imperialist powers.

The basis of the monopoly position of the metropolitan countries has always rested in their technological superiority. It was their superiority in navigation and military technology that allowed them to plunder the seacoasts of the world during the period of mercantilism. It was their continuing technological superiority that allowed them to conquer the world during the period of the transition from competitive to monopoly capitalism. And it has been their monopoly on advanced technology that has allowed them to dominate much of it ever since. The technological sophistication of the metropolitan countries has been the basis of their monopoly position in trade as well as the investments of their corporations. While the Third World specialized in such raw materials as cotton, sugar, and tea, the basis of the monopoly position of Europe was textiles. When the advanced capitalist countries moved to heavy industries like steel, the Third World countries were then allowed, if not encouraged, to produce textiles (which as labor-intensive commodities could take advantage of the very low prices of labor in these countries). When the technological leading edge in the advanced countries moved to sophisticated electronics, machine tools, airplanes, and chemicals, the Third World began producing simple industrial goods such as steel. The superior trade position of the leading capitalist countries is today based on such highly sophisticated goods, rather than on its export of steel and locomotives, as it was during the early phase of monopoly capitalism. Although most exports from the Third World are still raw materials, increasingly these countries are exporting simple and labor-intensive manufactured goods to the developed countries and are producing such basic goods as steel domestically. The development of relatively labor-intensive basic industrial capacity in Third World countries is normally spearheaded and controlled by capital from the metropolitan countries, which is invested in the relatively modern manufacturing sectors to take advantage of cheap labor and hence make super-profits. Metropolitan investors do not invest locally in manufacturing

Housing for sugar plantation workers in Brazil.

until it is more profitable for them to produce locally than it is for them to produce at home and export to the Third World countries.

These recent economic trends have changed the economic relationships between the developed and less-developed countries. In the early days, imperialists were primarily interested in bringing wealth back to their home countries. Today's imperialists, however, are more multinational. They are willing to invest their profits wherever the most money can be made. Thus, when the Arab and other oil-producing countries raised the price of oil to American consumers, the international oil monopolies encouraged and assisted them. Although these companies are controlled by capitalists in the United States and Western Europe, they are just as willing to make super-profits from consumers in the United States as they are from workers in the Third World.

The dependency theorists have played a useful role in exposing much of the exploitation inherent in the imperialist system. They were wrong, however, in assuming that this exploitation meant that economic growth could not take place in the Third World countries. Certainly, these countries could have developed much more rapidly if they had adopted socialist relations of production. On the other hand, it is also true that countries such as China and India experienced many years of economic stagnation prior to their discovery by Europeans. Economic growth was eventually accelerated in these countries because the Europeans weakened or destroyed local Oriental despotisms that were retarding growth.

Dependency theorists such as André Gunder Frank have been proven wrong in their prediction that as long as the imperialist system continued the gap between the poor and the rich nations would necessarily grow larger and larger, and that underdevelopment would become worse and worse. When an American-supported right-wing military dictatorship took power in Brazil in 1964, for example, dependency theorists predicted that this would mean an end to any hope of rapid economic growth. They thought that the new political leaders would be subservient to American imperialist interest, and would consequently repress local economic development in order to export capital to the United States.

The dependency theorists, and other Marxist critics, were correct about the new Brazilian government's close ties to United States and European imperialism. However, they failed to recognize that under the advanced monopoly stage of imperialism, capitalists find it more profitable to invest in Third World countries where labor costs are low, where raw materials are cheap, and where there are few restrictions on polluting the environment. The Brazilian coup of 1964 paved the way for a period of rapid economic growth based on low wages and repressive working conditions. This growth was to the benefit of both Brazilian and metropolitan capitalists.

Current Trends in Third World Countries

The current stage of imperialism is largely based on the same pattern as that in Brazil. Similar repressive governments have been established in most Latin-American countries, in Asian countries such as South Korea, the Philippines, and Taiwan, and in many African countries. These governments encourage international corporations to come in and exploit their citizens by paying them extremely low wages in factories that produce goods which can be sold back to the American market. Any student who wants to check how far this process has gone needs only visit any discount department store where American working people buy their clothing and other necessities. Check the labels on a random selection of goods, and see what percentage come from underdeveloped countries where repressive American-supported governments keep wages low and labor docile.

This flow of investment money into the Third World countries has made changes in the economic picture which the dependency theorists noted in the early 1960s. The data in Table 10-1 document these changes. They show the average annual growth rates for the developed and underdeveloped countries for the period from 1960 to 1975. During the period from 1960 to 1968 the developed capitalist countries were growing more quickly than the underdeveloped ones. During the period from 1968 to 1975, however, the pattern was reversed. The underdeveloped countries increased their rate of growth, while the developed capitalist countries slowed down.

TABLE 10-1. Average Annual Rates of Per Capita Economic Growth, 1960–1975

Group	AVERAGE RATES BY PERIOD		
	1960–1968	1968–1975	1960–1975
Less developed Capitalist countries	2.4%	3.5%	3.1%
Developed Capitalist countries	4.1	2.5	3.5
Communist countries	5.5	5.5	5.7

(The figures in the table are computed as average annual geometric rates of growth expressed in percentage terms for the periods indicated. For the capitalist countries, the data are for gross domestic product per capita. For the Communist countries, the data are for the net material product per capita (excluding services, government, and defense). For technical details consult the source: United Nations, *Yearbook of National Account Statistics*, 1976, Vol. II.)

There are many factors which affect these economic trends, and we can expect further fluctuations in the future. One factor is the flight of investment, and jobs, from the high-labor-cost areas in the advanced countries to the low-labor-cost Third World nations. Another is the efforts of many Third World countries that produce mineral and agricultural products to band together into monopolies in order to counter the industrial monopolies of the wealthy countries. Oil-producing countries, in particular, were able to greatly increase the prices obtained for their oil by uniting in a monopoly to maintain a high price. (The multinational oil companies encouraged and profited from this price increase.) Thus, in recent years, some Third World countries have grown rapidly by raising the prices of their products. Others, without valuable raw materials to sell, have continued to stagnate economically.

As Table 10-1 shows, the growth rate has been consistently higher in the Communist countries than in either the developed or the underdeveloped capitalist countries. Economists are agreed that this is a true indication of the economic trends in these countries, although their methods of measuring economic growth are somewhat different. Communist countries are able to sustain high growth rates by importing technology at the lowest prices possible and building their own industries which are coordinated by a central plan designed to maximize growth. By not accepting the supposed benefits of foreign investment, they retain the profits of their enterprises for their own use. Somewhat the same pattern of rapid economic growth took place in Japan, for many of the same reasons. Japan was fortunate in being remote enough and poor enough that it was not worthwhile for any imperialist power to make the effort necessary to colonize it. By retaining control of the economy in a local ruling class which recognized the necessity of rapid economic growth in order to maintain military strength, Japan managed to industrialize rapidly and is today one of the developed countries.

CONCLUSIONS

The most recent data show that it is possible for Third World countries to industrialize and grow economically even though they are under the economic domination of imperialist powers. This growth is not usually as quick as it would be in a well-organized socialist economy. More significantly, however, it is a form of economic growth that depends on maintaining extremely high rates of exploitation of the domestic working class. This requires repressive governments, usually military dictatorships. Truly popular governments, such as the Allende government in Chile, which depend on the support of the masses of their people, will naturally demand that the fruits of their labor be retained for their own use. This is why the United States, through the CIA and through its great economic power, did everything it could to bring that government down.

The United States and other imperialist powers use a variety of means, open and covert, legal and illegal, to assure that Third World countries have conservative governments that impose "austerity" on their own people, give good terms to foreign investment, and permit multinational corporations to extract super-profits from their workers. These governments routinely engage in torture and political assassinations as a means of keeping their people down. While the American government pretends to be deeply concerned with "human rights," it maintains academies to train foreign military and police officers in the latest torture techniques. While economic growth is possible under these governments, it is growth which benefits the few at the expense of the many.

Imperialism requires a large military establishment which drains away resources that could be used for social purposes. It puts American workers on the unemployment rolls when their jobs are exported to countries with cheaper labor. It depends on racist, authoritarian, political ideologies which encourage fear and hatred of peoples with differing social systems. Capitalism might be able to survive in the United States without imperialism, but it would have to change its nature in order to do so. It would no longer require a huge military budget, so it would have to find some other way to stimulate the economy. It would no longer win people's support by inciting the fear of Communism or some other foreign enemy, so it would have to gain support by reducing unemployment and providing more jobs at decent pay. Having no foreign outlets for its capital, and no profits from foreign operations to cover its losses at home, it would be forced to attempt to maintain a functioning industrial system in the United States. For a capitalist system to accomplish all these things, however, it would have to modify its basic principle of profit maximization so far that it is questionable whether it would be viable. As long as capitalists are free to seek the highest profit wherever they can find it, imperialism will survive.

Summary

Imperialism results when the ruling classes in class societies attempt to increase their wealth and power by exploiting not only the workers of their own country but also the working people of other countries. They may do this by direct conquest and colonialization or through indirect means, such as corruption of local elites, subversion by clandestine agencies, and propaganda. Monopoly capitalists use imperialism largely as a mechanism for making large profits based on the low costs of labor in poor countries. Imperialism also provides sources of cheap and secure raw materials, as well as justifying high military expenditures in the home country.

There has been considerable controversy about the causes of imperialism and its consequences for both the imperialist countries and their victims. The data show that the net flow of money is from the poor countries to the rich ones. In good part because of this, the economic development of countries suffering from imperialist control is slower than it could be under socialist development policies. It is possible, however, for countries to grow fairly rapidly under imperialism if they adopt rigidly authoritarian political systems that enable them to keep the wages paid to their citizens down to a bare minimum. The workers can then produce enough wealth for both the imperialists and their own local capitalists.

Imperialism is not to the benefit of the American people. The costs of maintaining the system are higher than the benefits obtained. It is, however, highly profitable for the monopoly corporations who reap the rewards of the system while getting the taxpayer to absorb the costs.

Review Questions

1. What role has imperialism played in American history?
2. Why do corporations in monopoly capitalist countries find it desirable to invest money in poorer countries?
3. What methods do the United States and other imperialist powers use to control the politics of poor countries?
4. What did Hobson find was the chief motivation for English imperialism?
5. How did dependency theory differ from the older theories of Hobson and Lenin in its explanation of the basic cause of imperialism?

6. In which direction is the predominant flow of funds between the rich and poor nations of the world?

7. Does the American economy as a whole gain from imperialism?

8. How do profit rates in the poor countries compare with those in the United States?

9. What was the primary reason for the United States government's decision to commit itself to the Vietnam war?

10. What effect did Marx expect imperialism might have on the economies of developing nations?

11. How has the nature of imperialist policies in poor countries changed to reflect the changing needs of the imperialist countries' economies?

12. Were the dependency theorists correct in predicting that imperialism would prevent the poor countries from growing economically?

13. What effect does the pattern of development chosen by Brazil since 1964 have on the workers in Brazil and other countries whose ruling classes have chosen this strategy?

14. How has the rate of economic growth in the socialist countries compared with that in the capitalist countries?

Suggestions for Further Study

1. Visit a local department store that sells consumer goods to American workers. Visit a selection of departments, such as clothing departments, where labels indicate the country in which an item was manufactured. Keep a tally of where items were manufactured and of the company that produced them. What percentage of the items are produced in poor countries where low labor costs are maintained by repressive governments supported by the United States?

2. Choose a particular imported commodity that is either sold to American consumers or used as a raw material in manufacturing in the United States. Find out where this commodity comes from, and which corporations control its production and distribution. How are prices set and maintained? What kind of wages are paid to the workers who produce the goods in the poor countries? Commodities you might choose include oil, coffee, copper, tin, cocoa, sugar, diamonds, sisal, bauxite.

3. Choose a particular country in Asia, Africa, or Latin America. Find out what are its major industries and major export products. Which American, European, or Japanese corporations have a predominant role in the economy? See what you can find out about how they manipulate prices, profits, and working conditions.

Selected Readings

Aberle, Kathleen Gough, and Sharma, Hari. *Imperialism and Revolution in South Asia.* New York: Monthly Review, 1973.

Amin, Samir. *Accumulation on a World Scale.* New York: Monthly Review, 1974.

———. *Uneven Development.* New York: Monthly Review, 1976.

Baran, Paul. *Political Economy of Growth.* New York: Monthly Review, 1957.

Barnet, Richard, and Muller, Ronald. *Global Reach.* New York: Simon & Schuster, 1974.

Brown, Michael Barratt. *The Economics of Imperialism.* Baltimore: Penguin, 1974.

Chilcote, Ronald. "Dependency: A Critical Synthesis of the Literature." *Latin American Perspectives* 1:1 (Spring 1974).

Davidson, Basil. *The African Slave Trade.* Boston: Little, Brown, 1961.

Dobb, Maurice. *Economic Growth and the Underdeveloped Countries.* New York: International, 1963.

Emmanuel, Arghiri. *Unequal Exchange: A Study of the Imperialism of Trade.* Appendix by Charles Bettelheim. New York: Monthly Review, 1972.

Fann, K. T., and Hodges, Donald, eds. *Readings in U.S. Imperialism.* Boston: Porter Sargent, 1971.

Fanon, Frantz. *The Wretched of the Earth.* New York: Grove, 1966.

Fernandez, Paul A., and O'Campo, José F. "The Latin American Revolution: A Theory of Imperialism, Not Dependency." *Latin American Perspectives* 1:1 (Spring 1974).

Ferrer, Aldo. *The Argentine Economy.* Berkeley: U. of California Press, 1967.

Frank, André Gunder. *Capitalism and Underdevelopment in Latin America.* New York: Monthly Review Press, 1967.

———. *Latin America: Underdevelopment or Revolution.* New York: Monthly Review Press, 1969.

Furtado, Celso. *Diagnosis of the Brazilian Crisis.* Berkeley: U. of California Press, 1965.

———. *Economic Development of Latin America.* New York: Cambridge U. Press, 1970.

Geertz, Clifford. *Agricultural Involution.* Berkeley: U. of California Press, 1970.

Guerra y Sanchez, Ramiro. *Sugar and Society in the Caribbean.* New Haven: Yale U. Press, 1964.

Gutkind, Peter, and Waterman, Peter. *African Social Studies: A Radical Reader.* New York: Monthly Review, 1977.

Hobson, John A. *Imperialism.* Ann Arbor: U. of Michigan Press, 1965 (1902).

Horowitz, David (ed.). *Corporations and the Cold War.* New York: Monthly Review Press, 1970.

Horowitz, Irving L. *Three Worlds of Development.* New York: Oxford, 1972.

Hussein, Mahmoud. *Class Conflict in Egypt*. New York: Monthly Review Press, 1973.

The Insurgent Sociologist. *Imperialism and the State*. Special Issue 7:2 (Spring 1977).

Jacoby, Erich. *Agrarian Unrest in South East Asia*. New York: Columbia U. Press, 1949.

Kay, Geoffrey. *Development and Underdevelopment: A Marxist Analysis*. New York: St. Martin's, 1975.

Klare, Michael. "The Nixon-Kissinger Doctrine and America's Pacific Base Strategy." *Bulletin of Concerned Asian Scholars* (April–June 1975).

Kolko, Gabriel. *The Politics of War*. New York: Random House, 1968.

———. *The Roots of American Foreign Policy*. Boston: Beacon, 1969.

Kolko, Joyce and Kolko, Gabriel. *The Limits of Power*. New York: Harper & Row, 1972.

Kolko, Joyce. *America and the Crisis of World Capitalism*. Boston: Beacon, 1974.

Laclau, Ernesto. "Feudalism and Capitalism in Latin America." *New Left Review* 67 (May–June, 1971).

Lenin, V. I. "Imperialism: The Highest Stage of Capitalism," in *Selected Works*, Vol. I. Moscow: Foreign Languages Publishing House, 1967 (1917).

———. "Preliminary Draft of Theses on the National and Colonial Questions," *Selected Works*, Vol. III. Moscow: Foreign Languages Publishing House, 1967.

McBride, George. *Chile: Land and Society*. New York: Octagon, 1971 (1936).

———. *The Land Systems of Mexico*. New York: American Geographic Society, 1923.

Magdoff, Harry. *The Age of Imperialism*. New York: Monthly Review Press, 1969.

Mamdani, Mahmoud. *Politics and Class Formation in Uganda*. New York: Monthly Review Press, 1976.

Mandel, Ernest. *Europe versus America*. New York: Monthly Review Press, 1970.

Marx, Karl. *On Colonialism and Modernization*. Edited by Shlomo Avineri. Garden City, N.Y.: Doubleday, 1969.

Marx, Karl, and Engels, Frederick. *On Colonialism*. Moscow: Progress Publishers, 1968.

Owen, Roger, and Sutcliff, Bob. *Studies in the Theory of Imperialism*. Bristol, Eng.: Longmans, 1972.

Perlo, Victor. *Militarism and Industry*. New York: International, 1963.

Petras, James. *Politics and Social Structure in Latin America*. New York: Monthly Review Press, 1970.

Radice, Hugo (ed.). *International Firms and Modern Imperialism*. Baltimore: Penguin, 1975.

Stavenhagen, Rudolfo. *Social Classes in Agrarian Societies*. Garden City, N.Y.: Doubleday, 1975.

Stork, Joe. *Middle East Oil and the Energy Crisis*. New York: Monthly Review Press, 1975.

Szymanski, Albert. "Capital Accumulation on a World Scale and the Necessity of Imperialism." *The Insurgent Sociologist* VII:2 (Spring 1977).

———. "The Decline of the American Eagle." *Social Policy* 4:5 (March 1974).

———. "Dependence, Exploitation and Economic Growth." *Journal of Political and Military Sociology* 4:1 (Spring 1976).

———. "Economic Development and Population." *Studies in Comparative International Development* 9:2 (Summer 1974).

———. "Marxist Theory and International Capital Flows. *Review of Radical Political Economics* 6:3 (Fall 1974).

———. "U.S. Imperialism and the U.S. People." *Social Praxis* 1:1 (Summer 1973).

Warren, Bill. "Imperialism and Capitalist Industrialization." *New Left Review* 81 (September–October 1972).

Weissman, Steve. *The Trojan Horse.* San Francisco: Ramparts, 1974.

Williams, Eric. *Capitalism and Slavery.* New York: Putnam, 1966 (1944).

Woodis, Jack. *Africa: The Roots of Revolt.* New York: International, 1960.

Zeitlin, Maurice, and Petras, James. *Latin America: Reform or Revolution?* Greenwich, Conn.: Fawcett, 1960.

Chapter 11

Racism and Capitalism

Racism is the use of real or imagined biological or cultural differences to justify treating a group of people as less than fully human. Racism is not limited to economic life. The systematic humiliation and degradation of racial oppression permeates the full range of social life—production, consumption, recreation, politics, religion, the military, education, and interpersonal relationships. In recent U.S. history it has been black people who have been the principal objects of racial oppression. Blacks have been systematically dehumanized and brutalized both by the institutions of capitalist society and by prejudices encountered in their interpersonal relationships with white people of all classes. Descriptions of the oppression of blacks and other racially oppressed groups in the United States abound. The white student not familiar with any of these accounts, written by black people themselves, should read them since only in this way can one begin to get a feeling for what it is to be racially oppressed.

Our purpose in this chapter is not to summarize this descriptive literature. Doing so in a useful way would require greater literary skills than one is likely to find among white sociologists. And even if we could, it would serve primarily to draw attention to the psychological dimensions of racism. It may be that the humiliation of racism in interpersonal and institutional relations with whites is more vicious and destructive than economic discrimination. But this does not mean that racism is *caused* by interpersonal discrimination. Our goal in this chapter is to explore the causes of racism. While liberal sociologists often stress the importance of psychological prejudices in race relations, radical sociology asserts that the fundamental cause of racial discrimination is economic. The way in which racial groups are oppressed varies according to the needs of the economic system. Racism persists so long as it plays a useful function for the dominant economic system in a society. Change in race relations is necessarily linked to changes in the economic and class systems of society.

Origins of Racism

While racists insist that races are biological groups, in fact the very definition of so-called "races" is determined by society. The same individual may be considered white in Brazil but black in the United States. Jews were considered to be a "race" by the German Nazis, who prepared an elaborate literature attempting to prove that "Aryans" were a distinct "race." They placed great stress on minor physical traits, such as the shape of the nose, which supposedly identified members of the Jewish "race." In India, a whole elaborate system of "castes" exists, based in part on biological differences that would never be noticed by an American observer, if indeed they are distinguishable by the Indians themselves.

A group gets defined as belonging to a distinctive "race" when its economic role becomes highly distinct and inheritable from generation to generation. Socially irrelevant biological differences (such as skin color differences between blacks, yellows, reds, browns, and whites), or geographical and cultural differences (as between Germans and Slavs), or religious differences (as between Jews and Christians in Germany or Catholics and Protestants in Ireland) are used to justify this economic segregation. Whatever cultural differences exist between the groups are maintained and reinforced by their different economic experiences and their segregation into separate communities.

FUNCTIONS OF RACISM

Racial discrimination plays two basic functions in a capitalist economy. The first is to provide a supply of workers who have no alternative but to accept dirty, unpleasant, and low-paying jobs. The second is to divide the working class, preventing it from uniting against the capitalist class. When the least desirable jobs in a society are filled by members of a racial minority, the white working-class people can often be led to direct their frustrations against this minority. Members of the minority may accept and internalize the racist ideology, believing themselves to be inferior. Or if they overcome this, they may direct their hostilities against white people as a group, often coming into the most immediate conflict with working-class white people who live close to them.

The existence of a relatively helpless group against whom frustrations can be vented provides a sort of cheap psychological compensation for the miserable lives led by poorer whites. No matter how oppressed whites may be, they feel that at least they have their "white" skin—"all whites are better than all blacks." Class society is stabilized by racism. A group's deep-rooted need to compensate for its feelings of inferiority towards those "above" it is manifested in an attitude of superiority to those "below." Blacks provide a convenient scapegoat for the white working class. Because criticism is deflected from the system, capitalism is strengthened. It has been shown that the number of lynchings in the U.S. South has varied with the rate of unemployment of whites. The more the white working class is systematically frustrated by the system, the more its frustrated energies are channeled (harmlessly for the system) onto relatively defenseless minority peoples. The positive relationship between economic and political troubles and racism does not come about solely through unconscious mechanisms. It has historically been very common for the ruling class of a society to stir up racism in times of crisis in order to deflect attacks from themselves (the czarist pogroms around 1905, Nazi anti-Semitism in the 1930s, the Jim Crow movement in the U.S. South in the 1890s). The scapegoating of blacks undermines the possibilities of class solidarity. Strong unions, working-class political parties, joint economic and political actions all become virtual impossibilities because of the divisiveness of racism. Only the corporations benefit from this hostility and disunity.

While racism plays useful functions for capitalism, it also has disadvantages. The extent to which racism is encouraged in a capitalist society depends on the extent to which the advantages outweigh the disadvantages. One obvious disadvantage is that members of oppressed racial groups frequently rebel against their condition. Their basic human drives cannot be fulfilled in a racist society that denies them dignity and respect. Rebellions among oppressed racial groups are consequently endemic in racist societies, although they reach massive proportions only when there is some prospect of success. Members of oppressed racial minorities naturally do not tend to make highly motivated or responsible workers. There is no reason why they should be highly motivated to work for an oppressive boss who does not recognize their humanity, and who does not reward them properly for their labors.

If the racially oppressed group is large and potentially powerful, as in South Africa where blacks are the vast majority of the population, it may be necessary for capitalists to pay premium wages to white workers in order to assure their loyalty to the system. In any case, denying blacks access to the more highly skilled or responsible jobs cuts down the available labor force and may consequently drive wages up or give the white workers greater bargaining power in labor negotiations.

Racism is most useful in those capitalist economies which require large amounts of tedious, repetitive, and easily supervised labor. This is particularly true in plantation agriculture, where large numbers of fieldhands are required to do back-breaking work for long hours at low pay. Racism is also essential in highly competitive and labor-intensive sectors of more advanced capitalist economies. Establishments such as restaurants, hotels, supermarkets, hospitals, small factories, and the like require low-paid labor forces if they are to survive against their competitors.

Large monopoly corporations are often in a position to pay better wages. They

A Civil Rights demonstration.

also require workers who are sufficiently committed to their jobs not to sabotage industrial equipment or to do unacceptably sloppy work. Owners of these corporations can afford to take a fairly broad view of societal problems, and may feel that it is necessary to integrate minorities into the working class in order to prevent mass disruption. Thus, when mass rioting broke out among the black population in Detroit, the major auto companies quickly accepted the need to integrate black workers into the higher-paying assembly-line jobs.

The treatment of racial minorities in the United States has varied according to the needs of the economy in different regions and during different historical epochs. Members of the ruling class have differed in their opinions as to how minorities should be treated, because their economic interests have differed. As long as minorities remain quiet and uncomplaining, only small numbers of white people have concerned themselves about their fate. When minorities organize to demand changes, however, the response of the white community has varied depending on economic and social interests. To fully understand the role of racism in American society we must examine its history.

Blacks in Industrial Capitalism

The growth of industrial capitalism led to major changes in the position of black people. Industrial capitalist firms required industrial workers, not fieldhands. Black people were first integrated into these positions in large numbers during the two world wars when there was a severe labor shortage. Even when the nation was not at war, they were often used as a reserve labor force. Thus, they were called into production during periods of relative boom in the economy, and sent home during periods of depression. Through discrimination, they were forced to endure disproportionately the hardship of the capitalist business cycle.

While black people continued to be discriminated against relative to whites, their position improved relative to what it had been before. Gradually, black people established themselves as industrial workers and began to make claims for more equal treatment. The civil rights movement that developed in the mid-1950s in the American South was a response to gradually improving conditions brought about by industrial capitalism. As black people became more and more militant, the more enlightened members of the upper class recognized that social stability required that blacks be integrated into American society.

Table 11-1 helps us to assess the trends in the role of black people in the American economy since that period. The table compares the percentage of whites and non-whites in each occupational category in the years 1960, 1970, and 1975. (The

TABLE 11-1. Race and Occupation in the United States

Occupation	1960			1970			1976		
	White	Non-white	NW/W*	White	Non-white	NW/W	White	Non-white	NW/W
Professional and technical	12.1%	4.8%	.40	14.8%	9.1%	.61	15.7%	11.7%	.74
Managers, administrators	11.7	2.6	.22	11.4	3.5	.31	11.4	4.4	.39
Salesworkers	7.0	1.5	.21	6.7	2.1	.31	6.7	2.5	.37
Clerical workers	15.7	7.3	.46	18.0	13.2	.73	18.0	16.1	.89
Craft and kindred workers	13.8	6.0	.43	13.5	8.2	.61	13.4	8.7	.65
Operatives	17.9	20.4	1.14	17.0	23.7	1.39	14.6	20.5	1.41
Nonfarm laborers	4.4	13.7	3.11	4.1	10.3	2.51	4.5	8.3	1.84
Private household workers	1.7	14.2	8.35	1.3	7.7	5.92	.9	4.4	4.89
Service workers, non-household	8.2	17.5	2.13	9.4	18.3	1.95	11.4	21.0	1.84
Farmers and farm-workers	7.4	12.1	1.64	4.0	3.9	.98	3.3	2.3	.70

(Source: U.S. Bureau of the Census, *Statistical Abstract for 1977*, p. 373.)

*The ratio NW/W indicates the overrepresentation or underrepresentation of non-whites in a category. Numbers larger than 1 signify overrepresentation. Numbers smaller than 1 signify underrepresentation.

non-white category used by the Census Bureau includes American Indians and some Orientals; however, 89 percent of the non-whites are blacks.) The table shows that occupational discrimination decreased consistently during the period from 1960 to 1975. The percentage of black people who were professionals, managers, clerical or sales workers, and service workers increased. The percentage who were laborers, household workers, and farm workers decreased. While significant discrimination remains, with white people holding more than their share of the most desirable jobs, the gap between white people and non-whites has been lessening.

As a consequence of these trends, black people have become a heavily working class group. They are heavily represented in the key industrial occupations that provide the core of the manual working class. They occupy a central role in the economy which gives them great potential power. While their incomes are not yet equal to those of white people, the gap in income between white and non-white populations is also slowly decreasing. There is a clear trend for economic discrimination against non-whites to diminish, as vicious as its remaining manifestations may be.

DEVELOPMENT OF RACE RELATIONS IN THE UNITED STATES

The condition of the black people has always been a product of their economic role in American society as a group, subject not only to special economic exploitation but also to the degradation necessary to keep the white working class loyal to the system. What black people, and other minorities, are is very much a product of U.S. capitalism—the needs of both the early plantation system and the giant corporations for a certain kind of labor. Blacks were largely robbed of their African culture, language, and customs, and shaped into what they have become by the economic requirements of U.S. economic institutions. Racial prejudice, discrimination, and popular conceptions that blacks are inferior to whites are justifications for the economic exploitation and degraded position of the blacks.

Plantation Slavery

The plantation system in the antebellum American South needed cheap labor that it could exploit to the hilt. It first tried Indians and white indentured servants, but eventually came to settle on the use of blacks as most profitable. The institution of chattel slavery had to be redeveloped over the course of the seventeenth and early eighteenth centuries to suit the needs of the system. The first blacks sold in the colonies were treated exactly like the whites indentured in the British Isles for definite terms (often seven years) after which they were freed. Only gradually did the system of lifetime servitude, with the extension of servitude to all children born of black women, develop to suit the insatiable need for labor of the growing plantation system. In parts of the lower South the average work life of the slave was seven years. It was profitable to work the slaves to death and then replace them with new ones. To justify this kind of super-exploitation, an ideology had to be developed which claimed that blacks were less than human. People could not treat others whom they considered to be like themselves in this manner. The notion and reality of "race" and racism developed with the world expansion of the commercial system in the sixteenth, seventeenth, and eighteenth centuries.

Slavery was adopted as the chief relation of production in the areas around the Caribbean because of the plantation system's need for a large group of unskilled laborers. In a commercial system unfree labor is preferred to free labor only when there is no other way of obtaining cheap labor power and when the necessary tasks are simple and routine. Blacks were chosen for the role of slaves everywhere in the New World after Indians failed to perform properly. It was said that one black was worth four Indians as slave laborers. Blacks, unlike most Indians, came from a rather developed class society. They adapted much better to slavery in the New World because they had aleady been broken to menial labor and submissiveness in Africa. The slaves were obtained largely through trade with the powerful African kingdoms along the coasts of Africa that traded their war captives for European guns and consumer goods. The ruling classes of Africa sold African peasants, menial laborers, and slaves to the Europeans in exchange for goods they did not themselves produce.

Emancipation and Economic Competition

After the formal emancipation of slaves in the United States, the economic condition of black people stayed essentially the same. They continued as a caste whose economic function was to perform the most degrading and least remunerated jobs in the society, especially as sharecroppers in the South, but also as domestics and service workers. The need for racism as a legitimating ideology continued.

The prejudice against blacks has by no means been unique in U.S. history. A similar prejudice has developed in turn against each major group of immigrant workers to the North since the massive migration of the Irish. The Irish were forced to migrate in large numbers to the United States because of the English-owned export-oriented plantation system in Ireland which produced mass famines. The Irish, forced by hunger to leave their native country, were willing to work in the U.S. for almost nothing. Because they worked so cheaply, great hostility developed against them among the rest of the working class. In the next generation the same phenomena occurred all over again with the Poles, the Italians, and various Eastern European groups. The Irish, who a generation before had borne the brunt of great hostility, felt the same kind of hostility towards the latter-day immigrants who were now in the same position that the Irish had been in earlier. The blacks were the last of the major immigrant groups (except for Latin Americans in many areas). They migrated into the

North after European migration had been closed off by World War I and the consequent Red scares. As we have seen, the great demand for industrial labor during the two world wars was the main stimulus for this migration. In the course of fifty years blacks were transformed from a predominantly rural group of sharecroppers into a predominantly urban group of unskilled workers. In 1910, 75 percent of all blacks were rural, but by 1960, 75 percent were urban. On the one hand, they were pushed off the land in the South by the mechanization of agriculture, and on the other hand they were attracted to the North by the rapidly expanded industrial system's need for labor. Blacks have been transformed from a semi enslaved peasantry into an urban proletariat.

The initial antagonism between white and black working people originated during slavery. In southern cities slaves were employed to some degree in just about every industry by their masters. The resultant competition between free white labor and black unfree labor led to great hostility on the part of the whites to the blacks who were underselling them. The resentment of the poor whites against this unfair competition was often directed against the slaves themselves rather than against the slave owners who dominated the society. After emancipation the freedmen continued to be willing to work for less than whites (even less than Irishmen) both because their customary living standard was less and because they were more desperate. To defend themselves against black workers who were willing to work for less, white workers began discriminating against black workers in their unions. Since they were prohibited from joining the white-controlled unions, blacks sometimes acted as scabs on the strikes of white workers. Blacks thus came to acquire a reputation as strikebreakers and frequently came to be systematically used as such by northern capitalists. Their use as strikebreakers resulted in increasing hostility on the part of whites, which increased the resolve of blacks to scab, and so on.

The historical hostility between white and black workers proved very profitable to the corporations, which played one group off against the other, just as they played one nationality off against the other. When white workers threatened a strike, the boss would threaten to bring in black scabs. This same process worked with other groups in earlier times. Anglo-Saxon workers who went on strike were similarly threatened with Irish scabs. Later the Irish were threatened with Italians and Poles. In general, probably more than any other single factor, racism has prevented the American working class from effectively getting itself together for class actions. The greater emphasis in people's minds on nationality or race over class has stymied the development of class consciousness and accounts for the lack of the development of working-class socialism in the United States. Probably for similar reasons mass unions of the unskilled and semiskilled did not take root in the United States until the 1930s with the development of the Congress of Industrial Organizations (CIO), which worked rather hard on the race issue. To this day it is much more difficult for unions to organize in the South than in the North because of the greater saliency of the race question there. The apparent "white skin privilege" which working class whites believe they have, particularly in the South, has hindered them from understanding the basic class situation they have in common with working class blacks.

Disenfranchisement

Even though the federal army was withdrawn from the South in 1877, blacks did not lose the right to vote in the South until around the turn of the century. During this period the black vote was manipulated by the old plantation lords (who were the owners of the land the blacks worked as sharecroppers) to keep themselves in power over the poor white farmers. Just as the blacks were used in the North by industrial capitalists to split the working class, they were used in the South by the plantation lords to keep the radical-leaning poor white farmers in line. The alliance formed in 1877 between the northern industrialists and the plantation lords was very unpopular with the poor whites. To maintain themselves in power in the South, the plantation lords greatly flattered the black vote. Blacks were appointed to office, given welfare benefits, and otherwise manipulated into voting for the ruling group. If blacks did not willingly vote for their masters, the votes of the black areas were generally counted for the candidates of the plantation lords anyway.

Beginning in the 1880s a wave of agrarian radicalism swept the West and the South. The Populist or People's Party was formed as an alliance between the farmers of these two areas against the railways and banks that were exploiting them. In the South, the Populist Party organized both the white and black poor farmers (although they had more success in organizing whites than the somewhat more suspicious blacks). The Populists were motivated by the egalitarianism created by want and poverty and by their grievances against a common oppressor. Their moderate success in uniting poor blacks and whites created a great fear in the southern ruling class, which temporarily lost control of a few southern states and came very close to losing control in the rest.

To beat back the threat of Populism, the plantation lords stepped up their efforts to use the black vote to maintain their rule. Increasingly, it turned to intimidation, terror, and ballot box stuffing to secure great majorities in the black-belt counties to balance the great majorities that the Populists were winning in the predominantly white up-country areas. In most cases this strategy was successful, i.e., the black vote was used to save white supremacy, and as a result Populism was defeated. However, the manner of its defeat created great resentment among white farmers who felt they had been betrayed by the blacks. The white farmers who were otherwise progressive thus became enthusiastic supporters of the disenfranchisement of the blacks as an election reform to prevent electoral corruption and thereby undermine the basis of the rule of the plantation lords. The plantation lords, on the other hand, frightened by the specter of a Populist success at uniting blacks and whites, also supported the move to disenfranchise the blacks. The plantation lords were responsible for instituting the Jim Crow system of systematic discrimination against blacks through their control over the local legislatures and media. Jim Crow was invented as part of a ruling-class strategy of splitting poor whites from poor blacks. It became the new support of the rule of the plantation lords in the South (replacing the unstable reliance on a manipulated black vote). It was the necessary corollary of black disenfranchisement and the basis on which to secure the poor white vote. White skin privilege became the new cement for the system. Whites were convinced that no matter how bad off economically they might be, at least they had the same color skin as the ruling class. What they had in common with their exploiters thus became more important in their minds than the common class position they shared with blacks. This system, institutionalized in the late 1890s to prevent the rebirth of radical populism, has worked very well down to the present day. The South, in spite of its being the poorest area of the country, remains the most conservative.

Contradictory Role of Racism

All the major developed capitalist countries, not just the United States, are racist. Each imports workers of another "race" to perform the most menial and lowest-paid jobs in the society. The northern Europeans import southern Italians, Greeks, Portuguese, Spaniards, Turks, Arabs, and Africans. Great Britain imports both West and East Indians and Japan imports Koreans. Each treats their menial workers more or less like black and Latin peoples are treated in the United States and for the same reasons.

Looking at the problem in comparative perspective, we can once again see that discrimination and prejudice have absolutely nothing to do with skin color or national origins, but rather are a product of the economic system's need for labor and the need for an ideology that justifies its exploitation. For example, in the British West Indies, which originally had essentially the same social structure as the U.S. South, upon emancipation the blacks generally refused to continue as cheap manual labor. East Indians were thus imported in large numbers to do the menial agricultural labor in these areas. As a consequence, the blacks became a sort of middle class of relatively privileged people, while the East Indians came to form the lowest economic group upon whom the blacks looked down. Many of the basic conflicts today in areas such as Trinidad, Jamaica, and, above all, Guyana, are based on the division of these societies between the better-off blacks and the especially exploited East Indians.

The corporations have a definite interest in the integration of blacks into the U.S. working class. Their greatest profit is realized by creating the largest possible pool of mutually substitutable employees. Such a large pool of workers provides maximum flexibility to the corporations in the increase and decrease in, and allocation of, their labor force. It also, by enlarging the reserve army of the unemployed, puts maximum pressure on those workers who are holding relatively well-paying jobs, thus

Black people are heavily represented in the industrial jobs at the core of the working class.

keeping wages at a minimum and submissiveness at a maximum. The larger the pool of mutually substitutable potential employees, especially those without jobs or with jobs at low rates of pay, the more threatened are the workers with comparable skills who are employed. To restrict blacks to their traditionally more menial and peripheral jobs, especially in light of their growing militance and disruptive potential, makes no economic sense.

This process is most clearly shown by the example of the construction companies that are in alliance with the blacks who are trying to integrate the construction unions. A massive influx of non-whites into the construction trade will send the level of wages down significantly by breaking up the unions' monopoly on the entrance into these occupations (which is the source of their high prevailing wages). Likewise, the contemporary policy shift towards blacks is indicated by the practices of key foundations. Many of the major foundations, especially the Ford and Rockefeller Foundations, have in recent years been focusing their domestic efforts on job training and improving the living conditions of blacks.

This process is not without its contradictions, however. The gradual elimination by the logic of capitalism itself of the divisive racial differentiation of the working class would bring down one of the major if not the single greatest obstacle to the creation of a working-class consciousness in the U.S. proletariat. A consequence of a decreasing saliency of racial discrimination is the increasing saliency of class position. An increasingly homogeneous working class would be more able to achieve a class consciousness that interprets oppression not as a product of one's color but rather as a product of the capitalist system.

SOUTH AMERICANS: THE NEW CHEAP LABOR

The gradual elimination of the material basis for antiblack racism does not mean that capitalist society is any less racist. It only means that black people, like the Irish, Poles, and Italians before them, are gradually being integrated into the mainstream of the working class as new groups of immigrants from the more rural backward areas of the world come into the industrial areas to replace them as capitalism's menial workers. Racism, just as it was redirected from the Irish to the Poles and Italians, and from them to the blacks, is now being redirected to the new immigrants from Third World countries—mainly Spanish speaking and other peoples from Central and South America.

Racism must be viewed dynamically. No group remains the victim forever. New groups are constantly needed as the older groups gradually learn to deal with their industrial environment, organize themselves, and begin effectively resisting their humiliation. This happened in turn with each of the major groups of immigrants from the backward areas to the industries of the United States—the Irish in the 1840s through the 1870s, the Eastern Europeans and Southern Italians from the 1870s to the 1910s, and it is now happening to the blacks who began their migration in large numbers to the industrial areas of the United States with the closure of European migration in 1914. Southern blacks provided the largest pool of immigrants for the industrial areas of the United States from this date until the mid 1960s, when they were surpassed by Central and South Americans.

The growing influx of Central and South Americans into the United States is resulting in people of Spanish origin (plus others from the West Indies) displacing blacks from the more menial dirty work occupations in the U.S. economy. If dirty work occupations are defined as including all of the U.S. census categories of operatives, non-farm laborers, farm laborers, service workers, and domestics, in 1950 Mexicans and Puerto Ricans (the two largest single categories of Central and South Americans) represented only 40 percent as many menial workers as non-Southern black males and only 20 percent as many as non-Southern black females. By 1970, however, these figures rose to 57 percent and 39 percent, respectively.

Blacks outside of the South are in somewhat better jobs than Puerto Ricans and first- and second-generation Mexicans (the comparable group to Puerto Ricans and non-Southern blacks). A higher percentage of all blacks are in professional jobs and a smaller percentage are in dirty work occupations. Non-Southern blacks also make more than Mexicans or Puerto Ricans. For example, in 1969 the median income of black males outside of the South was $5,587 a year, while that of Puerto Rican males was $5,156 and Mexican males, $4,839.

Not only are black people outside of the South in a better economic position than the new immigrants from Central and South America, but blacks are improving their economic position more rapidly than the Latins. Blacks in 1970 were relatively less likely than Latins to be menial workers than they were in 1950. Likewise blacks increased their income more rapidly than Latins in the period from 1950 to 1970.

The gradual displacement of blacks by Latins is only the most recent example of this phenomenon. Capitalism continues to generate racism because it is functionally necessary for its profitable operation. Only the color of the faces changes. The institution of racism persists. It is very difficult, if not impossible, for capitalism to permanently assign any one group to be its menial workers, since the costs of maintaining a group in this position escalate over time. When a group is first imported from a backward rural area it is grateful to have steady work at what, at the time, appears to be a high rate of pay. It is, consequently, generally willing to put up with terrible living and working conditions. But after a generation or so, the group of menial workers no longer are grateful for what now appears to be low pay and terrible working and living conditions (since they are now comparing themselves to other urban workers rather than their own earlier experience in rural areas). They no longer are willing to suffer the humiliations of racism. As they gain urban and industrial experience they develop organizations and forms of resistance to their oppression. They increasingly resist their social role as capitalism's dirty workers. The easiest response of capitalism to the growing demands of its menial workers for treatment as human beings is not to repress them but to import new groups of people from other backward rural areas of the world. Groups that will not (at least for some time) cause the difficulties that the older groups of menial workers cause. Importing illegal workers is ideal for this purpose, since they cannot risk complaining of ill treatment. This is why businessmen have resisted controls on illegal immigration.

EFFECT OF ECONOMIC DISCRIMINATION ON WHITE WORKERS

While it is true by definition that the greater the economic discrimination against blacks the more whites make relative to blacks, it does not follow that white workers benefit economically from economic discrimination against blacks. For such to be the case whites in those areas and occupations where discrimination is the greatest would have to earn more than whites in those areas and occupations where discrimination is the least. That whites do not in fact benefit from economic discrimination against blacks is demonstrated in Table 11-2.

Table 11-2 shows that whites earn about $800 a year more in those states where discrimination against blacks is the least. This is true because the states with the most racism are also the states with the lowest overall level of economic development, the smallest percentage of the labor force in unions, and the lowest overall wage rates.

TABLE 11-2.   Relationship Between Black and White Male Earnings and White Male Income Levels

Groups of States	Ratio of Black/White Male Earnings	Average Earnings of White Males
25 states with least inequality between white and black males	.78	$8453
25 states with most inequality between white and black males	.61	$7651

(Source: *U.S. Census of Population, 1970. Detailed Characteristics.*)

Without racism to provide them with cheap laborers, capitalists are forced to increase productivity if they want to maintain their profit rates.

Racism also has a divisive effect, preventing workers from uniting effectively to demand higher wages. The existence of a pool of poorly paid black workers weakens the bargaining position of the whites. Both whites and blacks lose economically by racism. Racism functions to prevent the development of a class consciousness, to make militant unions impossible, to undermine effective political and economic action of all kinds designed to improve the position of the working class. By dividing the working class and channeling the hostility of both white and black workers against one another it greatly strengthens the position of the capitalist class while more or less neutralizing the power of the working class to advance its common interest. Where racism is the strongest, there the working class and its economic and political strength is the weakest. And there, consequently, the level of wages and benefits is the lowest for everyone. This is obscured by the fact that however low white wages may be, it looks as if white workers are getting a good deal because blacks are worse off. But in Bob Dylan's words, "They are only pawns in their games." Socialist sociologists must go deeper than the myths perpetrated by the capitalist class to keep the races divided and understand that racism benefits neither black nor white working people.

Racism is a contradictory phenomenon for capitalism. It offers benefits in providing a cheap labor force for unskilled and undesirable work. But it cuts down on the available labor force for more essential industrial jobs, while it provides a potential for disruptive conflict and disorder. It is for this reason that we see the capitalist system behaving in contradictory ways. Capitalists move to reduce racial discrimination, integrating black people into the industrial labor force. At the same time, they import new minority workers, mostly from Spanish-speaking countries, in the hopes that these workers will provide a complacent, cheap work force. The contradictions of capitalism are such that capitalists can be expected to continue behaving in such contradictory ways, trying to maintain a balance between having too much racism (leading to instability and restricted skilled-labor supplies) or too little (leading to unavailability of menial workers).

Summary

Racism is a systematically dehumanizing form of oppression which pervades all aspects of the social and personal lives of its victims. Racism develops when socially irrelevant biological, cultural, or religious differences are used to justify subjecting a group to discriminatory and exploitative treatment. In a capitalist economy, racism plays two basic functions. First, it provides a supply of workers who are forced to accept low-paying jobs. Second, it helps to divide the working class by providing a helpless group against which the frustrations of workers can be vented.

Members of oppressed groups do not voluntarily accept racial oppression. When provided with any reasonable opportunity for success, they struggle to change conditions so that their basic human needs can be fulfilled. Once this struggle occurs, it is often advantageous for the ruling class to make concessions to the minority that is protesting. The costs of keeping the minority in oppression come to be greater than the advantages that can be obtained. The position of black people in the United States, for example, has improved steadily since the civil rights movement of the 1950s and 1960s.

While it is difficult to keep an oppressed minority down for an extended period of time, it is also difficult for capitalism to survive without a supply of cheap labor. Consequently, as soon as one minority establishes itself within the dominant society, another group is typically sought to take their place. In the United States today, Latin-American and Caribbean immigrants are currently being recruited into the lowest-paying jobs. European capitalist countries, also, depend on cheap labor imported from poorer countries.

Review Questions

1. When does a social group come to be defined as a "race"?
2. What are the two key functions of racism in a capitalist economy?
3. What are some of the negative functions of racism for a capitalist economy?
4. How has the economic and social situation of black people changed since the early days of the civil rights movement?
5. How was racism useful for the slave economy of the American South?
6. How has racism been used by employers to undermine the labor movement?
7. When and why was the Jim Crow system established in the South?

8. Why have South Americans been brought into the lowest levels of the American economy?

9. Do white workers gain economically from racial discrimination?

10. Why is racism a contradictory phenomenon for capitalists?

Suggestions for Further Study

1. Obtain a recent copy of a popular illustrated magazine. Make a note of all instances where a non-white person is shown in a photograph. What is implied about the person by the situation he or she is in, the clothing worn, the caption for the photograph? Include both advertising and editorial photographs. Go to a library and find the issue of the same journal published twenty years previously. Make a similar search for photographs of non-white persons and compare your findings.

2. Obtain a copy of an autobiographical work by a black author such as Richard Wright or Malcolm X. How do the experiences of the author compare with your own experiences at a similar age? How would the experiences of a young black person today differ from those portrayed in the book? Black students may prefer to compare their own experiences with those described by a white author.

3. Visit a large department store, government office, or other place of employment that is open to the public. Observe as many employees as you can, and note their race (as well as you can determine) and the type of work they are doing. Construct a table indicating the percentages of whites, blacks, and Hispanics in each of the major occupational categories present.

Selected Readings

Allen, Robert. *Black Awakening in Capitalist America*. Garden City, N.Y.: Doubleday, 1964.

Baran, Paul, and Sweezy, Paul. *Monopoly Capital*. New York: Monthly Review, 1966.

Bracey, John; Meier, August; and Rudwick, Elliott. *Black Workers and Organized Labor*. Belmont, Calif.: Wadsworth, 1971.

Castles, Steven, and Kosack, Godula. *Immigrant Workers and Class Structure in Western Europe*. New York: Cambridge U. Press, 1971.

Cox, Oliver. *Class, Caste and Race*. New York: Monthly Review, 1959.

Davidson, Basil. *The African Slave Trade*. Boston: Atlantic-Little-Brown, 1961.

Davis, Allison, et al. *Deep South*. Chicago: U. of Chicago Press, 1941.

Dollard, John. *Class and Caste in a Southern Town*. New York: Oxford U. Press, 1937.

Fanon, Frantz. *The Wretched of the Earth*. New York: Grove, 1966.

Foster, William Z. *The Negro People in American History*. New York: International, 1954.

Hiro, Dilip. *Black British, White British*. New York: Monthly Review, 1973.

Leggett, John. *Class, Race and Labor*. New York: Oxford U. Press, 1968.

Lipset, Seymour Martin, and Raab, Earl. *The Politics of Unreason*. New York: Harper & Row, 1970.

McWilliams, Carey. *Factories in the Field*. Santa Barbara, Calif.: Peregrine, 1971 (1935).

Marx, Karl, and Engels, Frederick. *Ireland and the Irish Question*. New York: International, 1972.

Massing, Paul. *Rehearsal for Destruction*. New York: Harper & Row, 1949.

Perlo, Victor. *Economics of Racism U.S.A.* New York: International, 1975.

Philadelphia Workers' Organizing Committee. *Black Liberation Today*. Philadelphia: Philadelphia Workers' Organizing Committee, c.1975.

Reich, Michael. "The Economics of Racism," in David M. Gordon (ed.) *Problems in Political Economy*. Lexington, Mass.: D. C. Heath, 1971.

Reich, Wilhelm. *The Mass Psychology of Fascism*. New York: Farrar, Straus & Giroux, 1970 (1945).

Rudwick, Elliott. *Race Riot at East St. Louis*. Carbondale, Ill.: Southern Illinois U. Press, 1964.

Spero, Sterling, and Harris, Abram. *The Black Worker*. New York: Atheneum, 1968.

Stalin, Joseph. *Marxism and the National Question*. New York: International, 1940 (1913).

Szymanski, Albert. "Racial Discrimination and White Gain." *The American Sociological Review* 41:3 (June 1976).

———. "Racism and Sexism as Functional Substitutes in the Labor Market." *The Sociological Quarterly* 17:1 (Winter 1976).

———. "Trends in Racial Discrimination in the U.S." *The Review of Radical Political Economics* 7:3 (Winter 1976).

Taub, William. *Political Economy of the Black Ghetto*. New York: Norton, 1970.

Wagley, Charles, and Harris, Marvin. *Minorities in the New World*. New York: Columbia U. Press, 1958.

Woodward, C. Vann. *The Strange Career of Jim Crow*. New York: Oxford U. Press, 1974.

Chapter

12

Family,
Sex,
and Society

In some ways, sexism and racism are similar phenomena. Any form of discrimination that enables capitalists to pay lower wages helps to raise profit rates. If women are disriminated against, they may be forced to accept undesirable jobs, or they can be hired when there is a shortage of labor and then let go when conditions change. Discrimination against women also carries many of the same disadvantages for capitalists as does racial discrimination. Excluding women from certain professions and occupations may create labor shortages and drive the cost of male labor up. And women may react against discrimination, causing social unrest and agitating for change.

Despite these similarities, there are also fundamental differences between sexism and racism. While racial minorities are frequently segregated in distinct communities from the dominant society, women (in most cases) live together with men in intimate family relationships. Their social class position is very heavily influenced, if not determined by, the class position of their fathers and husbands.

ORIGINS OF SEXISM

The division of labor between men and women first arose because of biological differences between the sexes. Men are somewhat stronger than women, and hence

285

were more effective as hunters of large animals and as warriors in the days before the development of modern weapons. More importantly, because of high death rates before the development of modern medicine, it was necessary for women to be pregnant or nursing small children during most of their fertile years. Thus, as we have seen, in most if not all hunting and gathering societies, the men specialized in hunting large animals while the women remained close to the base camp and spent their time gathering plant products, hunting small game, caring for children, and doing other chores close to home.

While there is some controversy among anthropologists about the nature of these early societies, it appears to be true that in at least most of them, women were essentially equal to men in power and status. Women's activities in gathering vegetables and fruits and hunting small animals were at least as essential to the survival of the group as the men's hunting of large animals. Family ties were frequently traced along the female line, especially since some primitive peoples were uncertain of the link between sexual intercourse and pregnancy. Sexual norms often tended to be relaxed, with women enjoying as much freedom in this regard as men.

With the development of more advanced societies, women's direct role in the productive process became less central. In herding societies, men were best able to care for large numbers of animals. In early horticultural societies, women continued to play a central role. However, with the development of the plow and the use of animals in the fields, men's traditional control over large animals gave them an advantage in agricultural societies.

Thus, with technological development and the growth of classes in society, women's position in the productive process became less central. Women became increasingly dependent on men for food and shelter. Of course, they played a central and necessary social function in child raising and in food preparation and other handicrafts that could be done in the home. But this work did not give them a position of power against husbands who came to more or less monopolize direct access to the means of production. Indeed, their involvement with small children tended to make them even more dependent on their husbands in order to secure the necessities of life.

Among the wealthier classes, women came to be treated as luxury objects. A great deal of money might be spent on their clothing and adornments, and on teaching them social refinements, but they were usually denied a major role in the running of society. Furthermore, their sexual lives were severely restricted in order to guarantee that their husbands had legitimate offspring (preferably sons) to whom they could pass on their wealth and social positions. Often, wealthy men had a number of wives, and a wife who was barren was easily rejected. Wealthy men also enjoyed freer sexual lives, usually at the expense of poor women who were forced into prostitution and concubinage.

Working men could not afford to use their wives as objects of conspicuous consumption. If they could afford a wife at all, they worked her to the bone in order to stretch their meager incomes into enough to feed a family. If their relationship with their wife was good, they might find that they could meet some of their needs for affection, intimacy, and dignity in the family situation. Needs that were systematically frustrated in their working lives in slave, Oriental despotic, or feudal societies. If their relationship was not so good, at least the wife could serve as an outlet for their frustrations.

In all human societies, men and women have lived closely together. While kinship systems have varied significantly from one society to another, in most if not all societies the vast majority of adults have lived in heterosexual couples.

Changes that have taken place in the position of women in society have not been due to biological change. Men and women have not changed biologically since the days of hunting and gathering societies, but their social positions have varied tremendously. These changes have reflected changes in the ways in which societies are organized to produce goods. We are going through a period of very rapid change in the social position of women. Women today enjoy most of the formal legal and political rights that men have. Women still bear children, but they have fewer of them and are able to enjoy sex without fear of unwanted pregnancy. Women are increasingly integrated into the labor market, so that today the large majority of women work outside the home for at least a substantial part of their adult lives.

These changes have come about because of the transformation that modern capitalism has produced in the social system. Women today are less closely dependent on their husbands, but more dependent on the capitalist economic system. They increasingly face all of the same problems that men of their class do in seeking employment and in dealing with the job situation once they become employed. This change in women's roles has important consequences for both men and women. If we are to understand these trends, we must look beyond biology and psychology. We must analyze the nature of the capitalist system as it relates to sexual differences.

TRANSFORMATION OF HOUSEWORK

In agricultural societies, most economic production takes place on land that is close to the home where the farm family lives. In farming families, husband and wife work closely together on related tasks. In the earliest days of capitalism, much economic production was still done in the home under contract to capitalists who marketed the goods. With the development of the factory system, however, economic production was systematically separated from the home. Men, women, and children left the home to work in factories for long hours, returning home for a few hours to eat and sleep.

The use of children in factories led to protest from working-class and reformist middle-class movements. These movements insisted that the children of working-class people needed to be kept home during their earliest years and then sent to school for at least part of the day. Consequently, a pattern developed where the men left the home to work in the factories and the women stayed home to care for children. Working men insisted on receiving adequate wages to support their wives and children. Women spent their time on housekeeping, sewing, landry, food preparation, and other chores that could be done in the home.

Under relatively primitive technological conditions, it is doubtful whether the working class could have survived without a system that permitted women to remain at home. Since death rates were quite high, it was necessary for women to be pregnant or caring for young children for most of their fertile years. And the work that had to be done to feed, clothe, and otherwise care for a family was so burdensome that it could not adequately be done by parents who both had to work 12 or more hours a day in factories.

With technological developments, however, the burden of housework became lighter. Machines were invented to help with chores such as sewing, washing, and cleaning. Prepared foods and cheap, ready-made clothes became available in the stores. Refrigerators and freezers made it possible to store larger amounts of food in the home rather than shopping every day. Scientific methods of birth control and modern public health measures combined to make it necessary for women to give birth to fewer children. Small children still required a great deal of attention, but even this could be reduced through the use of diaper services, formula feeding, and nursery schools.

These changes, together with the shorter working day demanded by the labor movement, have made it possible for women to once again go out of the home and work, especially once their children are old enough to go to school. Of course, not all women are eager to do so. The nature of housework is such that it can fill as much time as the individual wishes to devote to it. Many men and women felt that it was a disgrace for a wife to have to work, and took pride in their well-kept homes. Today, women who work outside the home spend less than half as many hours on housework as do women who do not have jobs. Working women have been shown to average about 25 hours a week doing housework compared to about 55 hours for non-working women. While employed women average 3½ hours a day on housework during the week and 5 hours a day on weekends, non-employed women average 8½ hours on weekdays and 6 hours on weekends (see Vaneck, 1974).

These figures suggest that working women are doing the minimum amount of housework necessary to sustain themselves and their families. They also get somewhat more help from their husbands. Non-working women tend to raise their standards of housekeeping and to spend time on activities that improve their living standards and give them a sense of fulfillment but that are not strictly essential. They continue to spend as much time on housework as they did in the 1920s, despite the great advances in household technology since that time.

Economic conditions today are such that relatively few families can afford a non-working wife, at least beyond the years when their children are very small. The supposedly "typical" family, with the husband working and wife and children at home, represents no more than one fifth of American households today. While traditional attitudes demanding that women be responsible for housework persist in many cases, they are gradually changing to fit the new objective conditions. A 1965–66 Department of Labor study showed that on the average married working women spent 71.4 hours a week on paid jobs, commuting to work, and housework. Their husbands averaged 66.5 hours a week (with a higher percentage on working and commuting). Thus, while women spent a few more hours overall than men, the difference was not terribly great. At least in terms of time, working women do not perform the equivalent of two jobs while their husbands do only one.

WOMEN IN THE LABOR FORCE

With the development of modern capitalism, the percentage of women in the labor force has steadily increased. Whereas in 1890, women represented only 17 percent of the labor force, Census Bureau statistics show that the percentage increased to one fourth by 1940 and reached close to 40 percent by the mid 1970s. This has been a steady, incremental change, and if it continues at approximately the same rate, women will be approximately one half the American labor force by about the year 2000. Meanwhile, the percentage of men who participate in the labor force has declined slightly. Thus, people who are now in their twenties can expect to live to see the day when men and women will participate equally in labor outside the home.

While in the past the majority of working women were single, today the majority are married. Furthermore, many have children. While only about a third of women with children under six work outside the home, slightly over half of those with children six to seventeen work outside the home. This percentage is even higher than that for married women without children under eighteen (43 percent of whom work outside the home). The fact that mothers of older children have a higher rate of labor force participation than women whose children have grown up (or without children at all) suggests that a major reason why women work outside the home is economic necessity rather than escape from the tedium of housework.

Women's participation in the labor force is relatively stable from year to year. It does not increase or decrease greatly with fluctuations in the business cycle. While some women may find it necessary to seek work when their husbands become unemployed during a depression, others may become discouraged during depressions and give up trying to find work themselves. Similarly, during boom periods, some may not find it necessary to work, but others may choose to do so. Women's labor is not marginal to the economy. Rather, women fill central positions necessary to the maintenance of the system. Their stability of employment tends to be similar to that of men, and to respond to similar fluctuations in economic conditions.

The fact that so many women are working has had an inevitable effect on rela-

Women at work.

tionships between husbands and wives. Even women who are not employed at a given time know that the alternative is open to them. They are no longer so dependent on their husbands as they were in an era when it was difficult for women to support themselves. This economic alternative gives women the opportunity to demand greater equality with their husbands, or to break up marriage relationships that they find to be unsatisfactory. Divorce rates have been steadily increasing throughout this century. In the late 1970s, there have been almost half as many divorces recorded each year as marriages. This does not, however, reflect a decline in heterosexual coupling, since the majority of those divorced remarry and many people live together in couples without being formally married. People seem to need the emotional and physical intimacy of marriage as much as ever. However, people find it difficult to sustain stable, long-term relationships during a period of rapid change in attitudes and social conditions. As both men and women struggle to hold jobs in highly competitive capitalist labor markets, very often the strain is taken out on the marriage relationship. As their possibilities for economic independence grow, women are becoming less likely to remain in unhappy marriages.

SEXISM AND WOMEN'S WORK

While women are participating in the labor force in numbers that approach those of men, their participation is not distributed equally throughout the occupational struc-

Courtesy DuPont Company

ture. Employers tend to prefer women for certain types of occupations and men for others. Women are preferred for clerical, sales, and service work, while men are favored for blue-collar and managerial work. While women's participation in the professions is about equal to that of men, here too they are concentrated in certain fields. Women tend to predominate in fields such as teaching, social work, and nursing, which involve caring for people at relatively low rates of pay.

In industry, women are often assigned to the most monotonous, menial, and low-paying jobs. Sexism thus allows capitalism to get these tasks done with a minimum amount of resistance and at a lower rate of pay than most men would accept. The ideology of sexism, with its stress on women's passivity and submissiveness, leads women to accept humiliating economic treatment. Consequently, larger profits can often be made from the exploitation of women than from men. Not only are women concentrated in the worst-paying jobs, but when they do jobs equivalent to those done by men, they are often paid less for the same work. Women are often hired by industries that are not highly mechanized and that consequently require a great deal of low-paid labor in order to make acceptable profits.

The figures in Table 12-1 (p. 292) show the trends in the percentage of workers in each occupational category who are female. While the percentage of the labor force that is female has doubled since 1900, women are still only a small percentage of the "craftsmen" and of the non-farm laborers. Women are a smaller percentage of the operatives (manual workers in industry) than they were in 1900. They continue to be

TABLE 12-1. Concentration of Women in Occupations

	% OF WOMEN IN EACH OCCUPATION		
	1900	1940	1976
Professionals	35.2	41.3	42.7
Managers	5.2	6.3	22.3
Clerical and Sales	20.0	43.0	69.5
Craftsmen	2.5	2.2	5.1
Operatives	34.0	25.7	31.1
Laborers	3.8	2.7	9.4
Service	71.8	61.0	61.5
Total Economy	18.5	24.4	40.4

(Sources: *Historical Statistics of the U.S., Statistical Abstract of the U.S.,* 1977.)

a majority of the workers in service jobs. The most remarkable change, however, is in the clerical and sales category. In 1900, these occupations were predominately male. It was not until the 1940s that women came to predominate in them. By 1970, two-thirds of all clerical and sales workers were female. Given the great number of such jobs, it appears that the rapid expansion of women in the labor force has been largely absorbed by clerical and sales work. As Table 12-2 shows, over 40 percent of working women are employed in this sort of job.

Jobs in the American economy are highly sex-typed. Of 250 job categories listed by the U.S. Bureau of the Census in 1969, one half of all women workers were con-

TABLE 12-2. Women's Occupations

	% OF ALL EMPLOYED WOMEN		
	1900	1940	1976
Professionals	8.1	12.8	16.1
Managers	7.3	4.5	5.7
Clerical and Sales	8.2	28.8	41.8
Service	35.5	29.4	20.8
Craftsmen	1.5	1.1	1.6
Operatives	23.8	19.5	11.7
Non-farm Laborers	2.6	1.1	1.1
Farm Workers	13.1	2.8	1.2

(Sources: *Historical Statistics of the U.S., Statistical Abstract of the U.S.,* 1977.)

centrated in just 21 types of jobs (one half of all men were in 65 types of jobs). One fourth of all women were in just 5 types of jobs, those of secretary, paid domestic worker, bookkeeper, elementary-school teacher, and waitress. In 1973 three-fourths of women employed were employed in 57 occupations. Table 12-1 shows that this sorting of women into specific occupational categories has not decreased significantly since 1900.

When we look at the trends in the incomes of full-time, year-around women workers as compared to men in similar conditions, we see that not only has there been no improvement in the position of women workers, but there has actually been a deterioration of their position relative to men. Full-time working women as a whole made 72 percent of what full-time male workers made in 1939, but only 57 percent as much in 1973. Women in every occupational category but managers earned less relative to men in the latter year than they did in the former. Sexual discrimination in the labor market is not disappearing in the capitalist economy.

This is one way in which the trends for women differ from those for any given racial or ethnic minority. As we have seen, the tendency is for a minority to improve its position as it becomes more established in American society. It is then replaced by a new minority which occupies the least desirable jobs. Women, of course, cannot be replaced by a third sex which would be willing to perform their jobs at low pay. Thus, capitalists continue to recruit women into these occupations and to keep them working under oppressive conditions.

Sexism and racism can, however, be functional substitutes for one another. White women are often used in place of minority men and women in a wide range of menial and low-paying jobs. Whenever there is an insufficient number of blacks or other minority peoples, or whenever economic discrimination against these groups is lessened for higher-paying work, white women are called upon to help fill the jobs. Black and other minority women, of course, suffer from both types of discrimination and have the worst jobs and lowest pay.

Although women and minorities do not compete with one another for the entire range of low-paying menial jobs, they do compete for a very wide range of them. Most categories of service work, for example, are equally available to minority men and to white women, as well as of course to minority women. The major occupation from which women are pretty much excluded is non-farm labor, while the major occupation from which minority men are largely excluded is lower-level clerical and sales work. With these major exceptions, it seems to be true that when minorities are available for the dirty-work jobs they are used. When they are unavailable, white women are recruited to fill them.

Occupational Sex Typing

Women's labor is increasingly necessary for advanced capitalism, since it requires large numbers of clerical and sales workers to keep the bureaucracies and retail establishments running. The sex typing of occupations and the relatively low pay of women provide strong motives for the corporate capitalist class to reproduce sexism both on the job and in society at large. One way in which they do this is by pressures placed on women by their employers directly. An equally important way is through their control of the means of mental production: the schools, the mass media, and the other cultural institutions. These institutions are used to reinforce traditional conceptions of women as passive and unassertive, while men are portrayed as assertive and competitive.

The corporations use these traditional personality differences to motivate both men and women to perform well in different types of jobs. The socially conditioned meekness, compliance, and subordination of women are especially preferred in the tasks that are the nervous system of advanced capitalism. The file clerks, typists, secretaries, etc., of the modern corporations have access to all the information possessed by the firms and often interact on a personal level with corporate executives and their customers. These occupations, as well as most sales jobs, require the greatest loyalty from employees and the greatest subordination to management and customers. But in a great number of manual jobs, in which men specialize, strength, virility, risk taking, and independence are especially desirable traits. Such jobs include police work, work in the construction, steel, lumber, mining industries, and the like.

Because the corporations need a labor force that is differentiated by character traits, they have a major stake in perpetuating the masculine-feminine distinction, i.e., in encouraging meekness and subordination in women while encouraging virility and assertiveness in many categories of male workers. These supposedly "masculine" and "feminine" personality traits are not biologically determined. Many men have feminine character traits and many women have masculine character traits. There is no innate, biological association of masculine traits with men or of feminine traits with women. The association is purely historical and socially determined.

These traits are reinforced most effectively through the mass media and the educational system. The capitalist class controls the universities and the mass media—the TV and radio networks, the newswires, the major newspaper chains, and the major magazines. The smaller capitalists control the smaller newspapers, local radio stations, and local schools. Through ownership, control, and advertising, capital is able to determine the basic content of almost all the mass media and of much of education. The ideal that is portrayed is of a woman who is passive, sexy, compliant, warm, and supportive, while that of a man remains virile, aggressive, fearless, and hard. These images permeate the lives of virtually every boy and girl, man and woman, in the United States. The ideal norms of behavior learned by both sexes come to correspond in good part with the sexist images propagated by the bourgeois media and schools—images propagated not because they are traditional but because they are profitable.

The major exceptions to these trends would seem to be the elite universities and colleges, and magazines and other media directed at the professional and managerial strata of society. These institutions were just as sexist as any others until the growth of the feminist movement in the 1960s. The feminist movement had its major influence among college-educated women from middle-class family backgrounds. These women rejected the traditional sexist ideology and demanded professional and managerial jobs consistent with their education and status in society. Once confronted with this rebellion, government and business leaders found it most expedient to make concessions and open up more of these positions to women with anti-discrimination and affirmative action legislation.

While many highly educated middle-class women are questioning sex role discrimination, sexist ideas remain strong in a large proportion of the population—both male and female. This is not the result of a small conspiratorial elite who really know that sexist ideals are false but who cynically push them on the masses of people in order to profit thereby. On the contrary, the masters of the media and education for the most part really believe the ideas they are responsible for, because they correspond to their own experiences, which in turn are structured by the needs of capital. The need to oppress women on the job, a requirement of profitability, thus transforms itself, without conscious malintent, into the ideological dominance of sexist values.

Of course, the relationships between the sexes that are part of the capitalist occupational structure do not begin at 9 o'clock in the morning and end at 5 o'clock in the afternoon. For these sexist character traits to be effective, they must be firmly established in people's personalities. They must permeate all aspects of the male-female relationship in the home, at play, and in bed. Many women, particularly those with relatively satisfying professional or managerial jobs, find personal degradation and sexual humiliations outside the job situation to be more oppressive than low pay or menial working conditions. But these interpersonal manifestations of sexism, however vivid and immediate in people's experience, must not be considered to be the cause of sexism in advanced capitalist societies. The basic trend in modern capitalism is to weaken the power of individual men over the women in their personal lives but to increase the power of employers over women as workers. While it is true that most employers are men, it is their position in the occupational structure, not their sex, that gives them power. The situation is not essentially different when women are promoted to managerial positions. In order to carry out these positions effectively they must exploit the labor of their female—and male—subordinates in the same way as a man would.

CLASS AND WOMEN'S OPPRESSION

The ways in which women experience sexism in their lives differ according to their position in the class system. Many women at the very lowest level of society obtain their incomes from the welfare system rather than from their own employment or from their husbands. Given the nature of welfare regulations, it is often most advantageous for them not to have a man in the house. They are then able to qualify more or less automatically for "aid to families with dependent children" since mothers with small children are usually not expected to be able to work. Thus, among this *lumpenproletarian* stratum, women tend to be financially independent of men. The treatment they receive from the welfare department, however inadequate the benefits, is no worse and in some ways better than that accorded to men.

Women in the working class are more likely to work than are middle-class or *lumpenproletarian* women. As Table 12-3 shows, women whose husbands earned low wages—between $2,000 and $8,000 in 1968 dollars—are the most likely to work outside the home. Women whose husbands earn more, or less, are less likely to be in the labor force. These working-class women need to work in order to bring in an adequate income for their families. The jobs they take are generally in the manual labor or clerical and sales categories. These are not occupations that offer great possibilities for creative fulfillment. In any event, they are quite similar to the type of jobs held by their husbands. As Table 12-4 shows, there is a strong correlation between the categories of jobs held by husbands and wives.

While working-class women experience more oppression on the job, they seem to have more equality relative to their husbands. Their independent source of income gives them the material basis to resist the sexist demands their husbands may make. Middle-class husbands have been shown to have more power relative to their wives

TABLE 12-3. Labor Force Participation of Wives in March 1969, by Earnings of Husbands in 1968

Earnings of Husbands	Percent of All Wives in Labor Force
$ 0– 999 (or less)	33
1,000– 1,999	38
2,000– 2,999	42
3,000– 3,999	44
4,000– 4,999	45
5,000– 5,999	47
6,000– 6,999	47
7,000– 7,999	45
8,000– 9,999	41
10,000–14,999	35
15,000–24,999	26
25,000 and over	18

(Source: Krebs, Juanita. *Sex in the Marketplace: American Women at Work.* Baltimore: Johns Hopkins Press, 1971.)

TABLE 12-4. Correlation between Wife's Occupation and Occupation of Husband, 1974

Wife's Occupation	HUSBAND'S OCCUPATION				
	Professional-Managerial	Clerical-Sales	Manual Workers*	Farmers	Total
Professional-Managerial	56.0%	13.3%	28.2%	2.4%	100%
Clerical-Sales	34.1	17.8	46.6	1.5	100
Manual Workers*	15.9	9.2	72.9	2.0	100
Industrial	13.7	8.2	76.4	1.8	100
Service	17.9	10.0	69.8	2.2	100
All Working Women	32.4	13.6	51.1	2.9	100

(Source: U.S. Bureau of Labor Statistics, *Special Labor Force Report; Marital and Family Characteristics of the Labor Force, March 1974,* Washington, D.C.: 1975.)

*Includes the U.S. Bureau of Census categories of craftsmen, foremen, operatives, transportation operatives, non-farm laborers, farm laborers, and service workers.

than do blue-collar husbands. The higher the husband's income, the greater his relative power in the family.

Women whose husbands have professional or managerial jobs are less likely to work outside the home. When they do work, they most frequently find professional or managerial jobs themselves, although some of them take clerical or sales jobs. Economic necessity does not force these women to work as it does women with working-class husbands. They have more choices to make, i.e., to decide whether their children require them at home or whether they would prefer to have a career. When these women stay home, they often find housework to be unfulfilling, especially since they usually have the educational credentials to be doing more stimulating work. They may devote extra hours to housework, doing their own sewing or baking, or put time into voluntary organizations and community activities. These activities, however, do not have the status in American culture that professional activities have. They do not give middle-class women a material basis for resisting demands their husbands may make for their wives to leave them free of housework or childcare responsibilities.

Many younger middle-class housewives provided support for the women's liberation movement. Since middle-class housewives are economically dependent on their husbands, they are especially susceptible to sexist demands. Furthermore, when they decide to work they often find that they cannot obtain jobs commensurate with the years of education they have obtained. A major thrust of the women's movement has been to open professional and managerial positions to women on a basis equal to that of men.

When middle-class women obtain desirable professional or managerial jobs, they naturally experience less on-the-job oppression than working-class women who have lower-paying, less-interesting, and lower-status jobs. The oppression they do experience, however, comes more because of their sex than their class. They tend to compare their position with that of men who have similar educational training and career experience. The grating discrimination, in the daily life of managerial and professional women, in favor of men in similar positions with whom they come into daily contact, may well be greater than the differences in treatment between men and women workers in the same factory. This is true because men and women factory workers are generally treated so poorly, not because the position of women is so good in the working class.

The difference between middle- and working-class women may be getting greater as more and more working-class women work. Middle-class husbands experience less brutalization on the job, and probably have fewer frustrations to take out on wives than do working-class men. Indeed, the fact that the life of a middle-class housewife is not as oppressive as working-class jobs explains why many middle-class women choose not to work even when the opportunity is available to them. For working-class women, however, earning an income frees them from approaching poverty. Working and financial independence thus bring about a considerable improvement in the condition of working-class women.

Quite different from either middle- or working-class women are the women of the capitalist class. There is a sexual division of labor within this class. Rather few upper-class women work as managers of corporations (but when they do it is in top positions). Most involve themselves primarily in various volunteer "civic work" projects, organizing charitable functions and running the social activities of the capitalist class. These activities play a key role in maintaining the social cohesiveness of the class. Others amuse themselves as international "jet setters." These women in good measure set the social and cultural standards for the rest of the population. They are presented as models to admire and emulate. In all their activities they are on the top, surrounded by servants, employees, and sycophants.

These women are freed from the drudgery of housework and child care by their familial wealth. They have maids and cooks and live-in child care to relieve them of these responsibilities. With the development of modern contraceptives, they are able to enjoy relatively free sexual lives without running the risk of an illegitimate pregnancy. While in the past upper-class men were quite concerned about their wives' sexual infidelities, the new norms seems to be that affairs are all right so long as no public scandals are generated.

Upper-class women have privileged lifestyles and are essentially free from oppression by even the men of their own social class. They obtain good educations and can easily find well-paid employment if they so desire through family and personal connections. They generally have access to inherited wealth and can obtain lucrative alimony payments if they leave their husbands. Although a sexual division of labor exists in the upper class, these women cannot really be said to be the victims of either sexist or class oppression.

CLASS AND POLITICAL DIVISIONS

The differing class positions of women in American society give rise to different political attitudes and affiliations. Women do not vote in a bloc; rather they divide along essentially the same social lines as men do. Even on issues of special importance to women, such as the Equal Rights Amendment or abortion legislation, women differ in their opinions as much as men do. Women are in the forefront of movements both for and against these feminist issues. And women are active on both sides of political disputes that do not directly involve women *as women* but are of interest to them as members of other groups.

The women who are most involved in the feminist movement are generally college educated, young, and employed in professional or managerial jobs. Feminism is also strong among students in larger colleges and universities, who are preparing for middle-class careers. Antifeminism is most common among middle-aged, middle-class housewives who are eager to protect their traditional rights as wives to support from their husbands. Attitudes on feminist issues are closely correlated to attitudes on other issues. Women who are generally liberal in their political views tend to support feminism, while conservative women support antifeminist movements.

Working-class women are less likely to join either feminist or antifeminist movements. When they are active, it is most likely to be as part of their labor union or political party, where they struggle to maintain equal rights as women as well as to improve their situation as workers. As more and more women become integrated into the labor force, one can expect to see this pattern of political involvement become more common. Women develop a feminist consciousness and organization to assure that they are treated equally with men. Once they have been fully integrated in the labor market, further improvement in their position requires uniting with men who share their economic interests. Working-class women in clerical, factory, or service jobs need much more than equality with men in similar jobs if they are to improve their lot.

Here we see the final similarity between racism and sexism. Both serve to divide members of the working classes. Antidiscriminatory movements, when successful, serve both to eliminate the special oppression of the groups that suffer discrimination and to encourage members of oppressed classes to unite in struggle against their more general class oppression. The oppression of women in contemporary capitalist societies is an outcome of the need of the capitalist system for a compliant and low-paid labor force (both inside and outside the home). For this to be altered, changes have to be made in the basic economic system.

Women in politics.

Summary

Sexism is similar to racism in that it is used to justify paying a certain category of workers wages that are less than those paid to other workers and to channel some workers into especially menial labor. The consequences of sexism are different, however, because most women live together with men in intimate family relationships. Women are distributed throughout the class system, and women in different classes have different interests and politics.

The division of labor between the sexes has changed as a consequence of economic changes during different historical periods. In primitive societies, the division of labor was largely conditioned by the necessity for women to give birth to and raise large numbers of children. With industrial capitalism a pattern developed where men worked in factories and women remained home as housewives, performing the tasks necessary to support their husbands and bring up another generation of workers. Improvements in household technology, lower death and birth rates, a shorter working day, and technological changes in the workplace have combined to reverse this trend. The proportion of women in the labor force has steadily increased since the 1890s and should reach approximate parity with men by about the year 2000.

Photos by Neil Benson

Integration into the labor force has meant that women are becoming increasingly independent of their husbands. They have, however, become more dependent on capitalist employers, who take advantage of sexist attitudes to channel women into certain occupations, especially clerical and service work and low-paying helping professions. Consequently, sexism remains a persistent problem in monopoly capitalist societies.

Review Questions

1. What was the division of labor between men and women in primitive societies?
2. How have technological developments affected housework?
3. When did the role of "housewife" develop?
4. What proportion of the American labor force is made up of women?
5. What effect has women's working had on relationships between husbands and wives?
6. Which occupations are disproportionately filled by women?

7. In which occupations are women underrepresented?

8. What advantages does the sex typing of occupations have for capitalists?

9. How are sexist ideas about masculinity and femininity taught to the general population?

10. Women of which social class are most likely to be employed outside the home?

11. Women of which social class are most likely to be active supporters of the feminist movement?

12. How do women's lives differ according to their social class?

13. How does women's voting behavior compare with that of men?

Suggestions for Further Study

1. Obtain a recent copy of a popular illustrated magazine. Make a note of all photographs of women. Note how many are portrayed as housewives, and how many are portrayed in what kinds of occupational or other settings. What percentage are presented as sexual objects in advertising aimed at men? How many are presented in advertising for cosmetics or clothing for women? Contrast these findings with the photographs of men in the same magazine. Go to a library and find the issue of the same magazine published twenty years previously. Contrast the portrayal of sexual roles during that period.

2. Visit a large department store, government office, or other place of employment that is open to the public. Observe as many male and female employees as possible, and note the type of work they are doing.

3. Read a biography of a woman who achieved fame through an achievement of her own (rather than through marriage or association with a famous person). In what ways was her achievement made more difficult by her sex? Was there any way in which it was facilitated?

4. Join together with a small group of students of your own sex to discuss how sexism has affected your lives. In what ways have you felt constrained by pressures to conform to stereotyped ideas of proper behavior for a person of your sex? In what ways have your relationships with members of the other sex been affected? Have you been afraid to be assertive because it is a "masculine" trait, or to be tender because it is a "feminine" trait? How have your plans for the future been limited by sexual roles? You may wish to write up a summary of your impressions, or get together with a group of members of the other sex to compare notes.

Selected Readings

Altbach, Edith Hoshiro. *From Feminism to Liberation*. Cambridge, Mass.: Schenkman, 1971.

Benston, Margret. "The Political Economy of Women's Liberation." *Monthly Review* 21:4 (Sept. 1969).

Blood, Robert, and Wolfe, Donald. *Husbands and Wives*. Glencoe, Ill.: Free Press, 1960.

Christoffel, Tom, and Kauffer, Katherin. "The Political Economy of Male Chauvinism," in Christoffel, Tom; Finkelhor, David; and Gilbarg, Dan. *Up Against the American Myth*. New York: Holt, 1970.

Dall Costa, Mariarosa. *Women and the Subversion of the Community*. Bristol, G. B.: Falling Wall Press, 1972.

Davies, Margery. "Woman's Place Is at the Typewriter." *Radical America* 8:4 (July–Aug. 1974).

Davies, Margery, and Reich, Michael. "The Relationship Between Sexism and Capitalism," in Edwards, Richard, et al., *The Capitalist System*. Englewood Cliffs, N.J.: Prentice-Hall, 1972.

Deckard, Barbara. *The Women's Movement*. New York: Harper & Row, 1975.

Dixon, Marlene. "Public Ideology and the Class Composition of Women's Liberation (1966–69." *Berkeley Journal of Sociology* 16 (1971).

———. "Why Women's Liberation—2?" in Roberta Salper (ed.). *Female Liberation*. New York: Knopf, 1971.

Duverger, Maurice. *The Political Role of Women*. Paris: UNESCO, 1955.

Engels, Frederick. *The Origins of the Family, Private Property and the State*. New York: International, 1972 (1884).

Firestone, Shulamith. *The Dialectics of Sex*. New York: Bantam, 1971.

Glazer-Malbin, Nona, and Waehner, Helen Youngelson (eds.). *Woman in a Man-Made World*. Chicago: Rand McNally, 1972.

Guettel, Charnie. *Marxism and Feminism*. Toronto: Women's Press, 1974.

Hedges, Janice, and Barnett, Jeanne. "Working Women and the Division of Household Tasks." *Monthly Labor Review* 95:3 (1972), 9–14.

Komarovsky, Mirra. *Blue-Collar Marriage*. New York: Random House, 1964.

———. *The Unemployed Man and His Family*. New York: Dryden, 1940.

Krebs, Juanita. *Sex in the Market Place*. Baltimore: Johns Hopkins U. Press, 1971.

Leacock, Eleanor Burke. Introduction to F. Engels, *The Origins of the Family, Private Property and the State*. New York: International, 1972.

Mitchell, Juliet. *Women's Estate*. New York: Pantheon, 1972.

Morgan, Robin (ed.). *Sisterhood Is Powerful*. New York: Pantheon, 1970.

Radical America. *Woman's Labor* 7:4 and 5 (July–Oct. 1973).

Reich, Wilhelm. "Imposition of Sexual Morality," in Wilhelm Reich. *Sex-Pol.* New York: Vintage, 1972 (1935).

————. *The Sexual Revolution.* New York: Farrar, Straus & Giroux, 1962 (1930).

Rowntree, John and Mary. "More on the Political Economy of Women's Liberation." *Monthly Review* 21:8 (Jan. 1970).

Rowbotham, Sheila. *Women, Resistance and Revolution.* New York: Pantheon, 1973.

Szymanski, Albert. "Male Gain from Sexual Discrimination." *Social Forces* 56:2 (Dec. 1977).

————. "Racism and Sexism as Functional Substitutes." *The Sociological Quarterly* 17:1 (Winter 1976).

————. "The Socialization of Women's Oppression. *Insurgent Sociologist* 6:2 (Winter 1975).

U.S. Department of Labor. *Handbook on Women Workers.* U.S. Department of Labor, 1969.

Vanek, Joann. "Time Spent in Housework." *The Scientific American* 231:5 (Nov. 1974).

Zaretsky, Eli. *Capitalism, the Family and Personal Life.* New York: Harper & Row, 1976.

Chapter 13

Ecology and Population

Ecology is the study of the relationship between societies and their physical environment. It includes the impact of the environment on society, the impact of society on its environment, and their mutual interaction. At low levels of technological development, societies are largely influenced by the environment. Hunting and gathering peoples, for example, are dependent on the bounty of nature. They must go wherever they can find food, water, and other essentials for their survival. With horticultural and agricultural technology, people became less dependent on the vagaries of nature. They planted and cultivated food, assisting nature to produce what they needed when and where they needed it. These peoples were, however, still greatly limited by nature. Over the years, they developed a harmonious relationship with their environment which was stable over many centuries.

DESTRUCTION OF THE ENVIRONMENT

With the growth of industrial technology, the balance between society and nature was upset. People obtained the technological capability to greatly influence the environment. This technology could be used to increase productivity and produce more goods which the people needed. It could also be used to produce useless commodities while destroying the natural environment. Capitalist societies have developed an antagonistic relationship with nature. To a great extent, they are dependent on using up finite, exhaustible resources such as coal and oil.

Capitalist societies have done much harm to the environment. The air, rivers, lakes, oceans, and the land itself are being inundated with chemical wastes and with the superfluous products and garbage of monopoly capitalism. This will come as no surprise to anyone living in the United States in the late twentieth century. We can smell the pollution in the air and see the filth in our rivers. Our newspapers, magazines, and television stations have given much attention to this problem. Even major corporations spend a lot of money on advertising designed to convince us that they are really doing their best to clean up the environment.

What is perhaps less clear is the reasons why this deplorable situation exists. Capitalist propaganda often attempts to blame pollution on the individual consumer. It is the consumer's fault that his automobile pollutes the air and burns too much gasoline, that his beer comes in non-returnable cans, or that there is no natural gas to heat his home. But consumers did not create the automotive industry or the throwaway society. These were sold to them by corporations that wanted to make a profit by selling as much as possible to as many people as possible. Nor are individual consumers responsible for the vast pollution caused by industries themselves.

Rivers and lakes are used as sewers by industry. They are full of the pesticides and detergents manufactured and pushed on us by the corporations. Most of the space in newspapers goes to hawking the products of the corporations and attempting to entice people to spend more of their money. A high proportion of all trees cut goes into the production of newsprint for this purpose. Cars are built to last little beyond the three or four years it takes to pay for them, and as a result about 12 million are junked each year. Like all other goods produced by monopoly capitalism, automobile production is geared not to the production of durable goods that will satisfy human needs but rather to the need to sell as much as possible in order to make as much profit as possible. Thus, in the late 1960s before government regulations forced them to change, General Motors spent $500 million a year on style changes and $300 million a year on advertising, but only $40 million a year to develop cleaner engines.

Capitalist corporations go to great efforts to influence the spending habits of the American public. For example, the powerful automobile companies and their satellites in glass, rubber, steel, concrete, oil, and construction oppose government assistance to public transportation and actively support the ever-expanding super-highway system. Already about 50 percent of the urban area in the United States is given over to use of the automobile. This percentage continues to increase as more and more super-highways are built. As a result the air becomes ever more poisonous. Faced with a lack of reliable public transport and the constant propaganda of the media in favor of private automobiles rather than mass transit, virtually all families come to own at least one car, and to most families two cars become the ideal. Corporate propaganda claims that air pollution is not the fault of industry but the result of individuals choosing to own cars.

The constant propaganda of the media for more and newer goods is a necessary consequence of monopoly capitalism's need to build up sufficient demand for its products and to give its working class sufficient motivation to continue working at meaningless jobs for 40 or more hours a week. The induced demand for products built to break down or become obsolete in a short time results in a great many people going into debt. The condition of being a debtor forces us to work harder to pay our bills. This chains us even more to alienated labor and compensatory, but equally meaningless, consumption. Tremendous resources are utilized in advertising and in designing products that have obsolescence built into them. Advertisements are scientifically designed to play on our weaknesses, desires, and vanities.

THE ENVIRONMENT AND THE PROFIT SYSTEM

The capitalist economic system provides no inherent controls on pollution. Under capitalism, industries must do whatever is most profitable. That is what they are in business for. And it is more profitable to dump waste products in the river than to dispose of them properly. It is more profitable to let industrial smoke pollute the air than to install a filtration device to protect the atmosphere. The only possible advantage is that, once the natural air and water have been destroyed, the capitalists may be motivated to sell us water in bottles and clean air in pressurized containers. Already in Tokyo it is possible to put a coin in a dispenser and get a whiff of pure air when one is about to keel over from the carbon monoxide in the city's air.

Similarly with energy supplies. Capitalists are motivated by the profit system to sell as much electricity, oil, and gas as possible. Only when they have engineered a "crisis" in supplies in order to drive prices up higher do they make even half-hearted attempts to encourage resource conservation. While individual capitalists may enjoy a clean environment as much as anyone else, environmental pollution is inherent in the capitalist economic system and can be eliminated only by placing such severe restraints on the system that it cannot function freely according to market principles. Thus, the capitalists are quite correct when they attack the consumerists and environmentalists as being essentially anti-business. While most consumer and environmental activists are not drawn into these movements by anti-capitalist sentiments, they are inevitably drawn into confrontation with big business because they find that big business is normally on the wrong side of environmental issues.

Careful planning by public agencies is needed in order to develop an industrial system that is able to function in harmony with nature. Such planning must give greater weight to resource conservation and to protection from pollution than to increasing production. This is fundamentally inconsistent with the capitalist mode of production, which is based on production of commodities for profit, and which must constantly expand by creating new products necessary only for corporate profit goals.

POPULATION AND ECONOMIC GROWTH

When capitalists are asked to explain why resources are running out, or why there is pollution, or why there is poverty and deprivation in the midst of plenty, their first answer is frequently "too many people!" With such a response capitalists deflect criticism from themselves and blame problems that their own system has created on the people who are the victims of that system. What is the evidence for their claim? What, in fact, is the link between population growth and economics? This is actually a very complex question, and one that needs to be discussed in detail. The vast preponderance of scientific evidence, however, has made one point clear. The relationship is the reverse of that claimed by capitalism's defenders. It is poverty and deprivation that are the fundamental causes of rapid population growth, not the other way around. The development of a just and prosperous economic system would result in a stable population level. Blaming poverty on people having too many babies is simply another variant of the common elitist argument of blaming the victims for the system that oppresses them.

A look at statistics gathered by the United Nations shows that the amount or density of population in a country has little or nothing to do with its economic status. Nations can be poor or rich with large or small population densities. Some countries, such as Japan, West Germany, the United Kingdom, and Denmark, have high concentrations of population and high gross domestic products per capita. Other countries, such as the United States, Canada, and Australia, have low densities of population and high economic productivity. Similarly, some countries such as India, Bangladesh, and South Korea are highly populated and poor. Others, such as Zaire, Burma, Brazil, and Colombia, have low population densities and low gross domestic products. Population density, *per se*, has little to do with economic productivity in any but the most primitive societies. This is recognized by all serious students of population trends.

What is more controversial is the relationship between the *rate* of population increase and economic development. Here the situation is more complex. United Nations statistics show that poorer countries tend to have a higher rate of population growth than richer countries. A classic United Nations study published in 1963 showed that in countries with the lowest level of economic and social development the average woman of child-bearing age (15 to 49 years) had 2.96 daughters. In countries with the highest level of economic and social development, the average woman had 1.49 daughters. For a society to be stable in population, there should be on the average one daughter for each woman of child-bearing age. Thus, the poorer countries had a higher rate of population growth.

All the statistics comparing poor and rich societies confirm this same general finding: the lower the level of economic development in a society, the higher the rate of population growth is likely to be. But this fact does not tell us anything about the *causal* relationship between economic development and population growth. The fact that two variables are correlated means only that there is some relationship between them. There are three different causal conditions which can account for a correlation between two variables. Variable A may be caused by variable B. Or variable B may be caused by variable A. Or both variables A and B may be caused by some other variable or set of variables.

How can we determine which of these causal hypotheses is valid? In this case, as with most important social science questions, we cannot use the experimental method. We have no power to experimentally manipulate the variables in question, for example, by lowering the birth rate in Bangladesh in order to see if the economy then advances, or by making the United States a poor country in order to see if people then had more children. Since we cannot manipulate the variables experimentally, we must use the historical and comparative methods. This means that we look at the variables in question under a large number of conditions in a variety of countries and at different times. We can then observe how changes in one variable lead to changes in the other. We can also compare different groups within the same country to see how variations in social conditions are related to changes in the birth rate.

Growth Rates and Variables

Fortunately, a great deal of research has been done on this question and we are consequently in a position to draw some well-substantiated conclusions. First of all, if we look at the history of the currently wealthy countries we find a pattern that is generally known as "the demographic transition." When these countries were poor, they had high birth rates and high death rates. Economic development began when these rates were still high. The first change that occurred was a decrease in the death rate (the number of people dying each year out of each 1000 in the population) due to better nutrition and health standards. This led to an increase in the rate of population growth. As people become more affluent and urban, and as they realize that improved health standards mean that more of their children will grow to adulthood, they begin to have fewer children. Thus, the decline in the birth rate took place *after* economic development had started and *after* the death rate had begun to decline. The demographic transition, then, is from a situation of high birth and death rates, to one with a lower death rate, to one with relatively low birth and death rates.

The relatively high rates of population growth in many developing countries today can be taken as showing that they have begun this process. As their economies improve, and as they have access to better public health services, their death rates decline. While we can expect that with further development their birth rates will also decline, this tends to happen somewhat later. During the period of transition, the rate of population growth tends to be high.

If we look at the factors influencing birth rates within countries in more detail, we find that improving social and economic conditions is the key to lowering the birth rate. A number of variables have been shown to lead to lower birth rates:

Health Care.   The availability of better health care lowers birth rates both by making birth control available and by making it possible for families to have fewer children with the assurance that they will grow to adulthood.

Urbanization.   When people move to urban areas, children become an expense rather than an advantage, as they are on a farm. City life also provides more opportunities for people to do other things rather than stay home and raise children.

Income.   In capitalist societies, as families get more income, they can afford to have better health care and to send their children to school, which is often an expensive process. Higher income also frees them from having to have many children to support their family, and especially to support the parents in their old age. For a country to have a reduced birth rate, it is necessary that income be relatively evenly distributed so that even the poorest people have an adequate income. If increased income is concentrated among the wealthier strata, as it is in countries such as the Philippines, Brazil, and Mexico, the birth rate remains high. Countries with no more income overall but with a more equal distribution of income, show declining birth rates (see Rich, 1973 for data). The above relation applies only to the capitalist countries where individual income determines one's education, health care, and social security. In the socialist countries, where everyone is guaranteed a satisfactory income, education, and good social services, birth rates tend to be significantly lower than in capitalist countries at similar levels of economic development.

Women's Liberation.   As more opportunities for paid employment outside the home become available to women, they tend to have fewer children. As women's position in society improves, they tend to delay marriage and to practice contraception more effectively.

Scientific research on population growth rates has provided a clear reply to the misconception that overpopulation is the cause of poverty and underdevelopment. Poor people in capitalist societies have large families because they hope that their children will provide them with help in the struggle for survival. They need to be sure that at least some of their children will grow up to provide them with support in their old age. For these poor people, having many children is a quite rational decision. This contrasts markedly with the situation of more affluent urban families (as it does with all families in socialist countries). In these families, rather than children beginning to work in the fields at around the age of 5 or 6, they must be sent off to school for a long period of years, after which they leave the home and soon begin to support their own children. Although these families are wealthier, they can actually afford fewer children, given the cost of raising each of them in an urban setting.

Population Policy

Population policy is an arena of some political controversy in Third World countries. Some traditional groups in these countries have encouraged high rates of population growth. This is done for economic reasons as well as because of cultural traditions. When the population is large, there is a surplus of workers. This means that wages can be kept low and rents on houses and farmland high. If the ruling group resists technological innovation and industrialization, it is indeed true that increasing the population increases the amount of misery among the poor classes. But this is the case because of the repressive social system, not because overpopulation is placing a strain on natural resources.

The danger in this policy of encouraging overpopulation is that it can lead to unrest and possibly to revolutionary pressures from the poorest class. Thus, the more sophisticated liberal members of the ruling classes may recognize that encouraging population growth is playing with fire. The American foundations and government agencies concerned with this problem have recognized the dangers of rapid population growth and are actively encouraging birth control and population limitation.

Control of population growth is probably a desirable goal. Exploration of other planets in our solar system has shown them to be exceedingly unattractive places to live. As long as the human race is confined to the planet Earth, space is limited. Although the sensationalist claims of "the population explosion" hysterics are grossly exaggerated, any rate of population growth will eventually (in the distant future) result in the earth being uncomfortably filled with people, and it would be more pleasant to stop population growth long before that point is reached. If we are to control population growth, however, we must do so by eliminating poverty. Some progress in this direction can be made under capitalism, especially if it is coupled with strong reformist measures designed to insure that the lowest strata of the population receive at least a small proportion of the economic benefits of industrialization. But, because of the economic contradictions of capitalism, significant poor populations remain in even the wealthiest capitalist countries. The data show, however, that poor countries that have adopted socialist relations of production have achieved rapid economic growth, the elimination of poverty, and declining birth rates.

Summary

While animals and primitive peoples live in harmony with their natural environment, capitalist industrial societies are profoundly destructive to the earth on which we live. The profit system does not provide an incentive for preservation of the environment during industrial production. It does provide an incentive for the production of unnecessary commodities and for the maintenance of wasteful lifestyles. Thus, it is not surprising that destruction of the environment has become a major issue in advanced capitalist countries.

Apologists for capitalism frequently blame environmental destruction, poverty, poor health standards, and other social problems on the people who live in their societies. They claim that there are too many people, or that the population is growing too quickly, so these problems cannot be solved. An examination of the data shows the fallacy of these arguments. There is no correlation between population density and the wealth of nations. Rates of population increase have been shown to decrease whenever the living standards of the population of a country improve. If we wish to control population growth, we must do so by eliminating poverty. To call for ending poverty by controlling population growth is to confuse effect with cause.

Review Questions

1. Why does the profit system encourage industries to pollute the environment?
2. In what ways does capitalism encourage excessive consumption of goods?
3. What relationship is there between population density and economic productivity?
4. What is the causal relationship between economic development and population growth?
5. What are some of the social conditions that have been shown to have an effect on the rate of population increase?
6. How is the distribution of income related to the rate of population growth?

Suggestions for Further Study

1. If there is a Public Interest Research Group organized on your campus, find out about its activities in defense of the environment. Which groups in society tend to be lined up on the opposite side of the issues?
2. Visit your nearest office of a state Department of Environmental Quality. Find out what the major problems are with air and water quality in your area, and the sources of the pollutants. What health problems are caused by this pollution? How much of it can be attributed to industrial pollution or to unnecessary consumption?
3. Make an estimate of the amount of energy you use in a typical week for transportation, home heating, recreation, etc. Include energy used to produce and trans-

port products that you use. How might your energy consumption be less in a
society which was rationally planned to minimize energy consumption?

Selected Readings

Baran, Paul. *The Political Economy of Growth.* New York: Monthly Review, 1957.

Berent, Jerzy. "Causes of Fertility Decline in Eastern Europe and the Soviet Union."
Population Studies 24:1,2 (1970).

Bogue, Donald. *Principles of Demography.* New York: Wiley, 1969.

de Castro, Josue. *The Geography of Hunger.* Boston: Little, Brown, 1952.

Dumont, Rene. *Lands Alive.* New York: Monthly Review, 1965.

Jacoby, Erich. *Agrarian Unrest in South East Asia.* New York: Columbia U. Press,
1949.

Kocher, James E. *Agricultural Development, Equity, and Fertility Decline.* New
York: Population Council, 1973.

Marx, Karl, and Frederick Engels. *Marx and Engels on Malthus.* New York: International, 1954.

Miro, Carmet, and Walter Mertens. "Influences Affecting Fertility in Urban and
Rural Latin America." *Milbank Memorial Fund Quarterly* 46:3 (July 1960).

Moore, Barrington. *Social Origins of Dictatorship and Democracy.* Boston: Beacon,
1966.

Research Triangle Institute. *Social and Economic Correlates of Family Fertility: A
Survey of the Evidence.* Research Triangle Park, N.C., 1971.

Research Triangle Institute. *Social and Economic Correlates of Family Fertility: An
Updated Review of the Evidence* (by Loewenthal, Normal and David, Abraham).
Research Triangle Park, N.C., 1972.

Rich, William. *Smaller Families Through Social and Economic Progress.* Washington,
D.C.: Overseas Development Council, 1973.

Slater, Guiseppi, et. al. *The Earth Belongs to the People: Ecology and Power.* San
Francisco: People's Press, 1970.

Szymanski, Albert. "Economic Development and Population." *Studies in Comparative International Development* 9:2 (Summer 1974), 53–69.

United Nations. *Statistical Yearbook,* 1976.

United Nations. *Population Bulletin* 7, 1963.

U.S. Census Bureau. "Women by Number of Children Ever Born," in *U.S. Census
of Population: 1960 Subject Reports.* Washington, D.C.: Government Printing
Office, 1964.

Weisberg, Barry. *Beyond Repair: The Ecology of Capitalism.* Boston: Beacon, 1971.

Chapter 14

Social Movements and Revolution

The student who has read this far in this book may well be asking the following question: "Even if I accept the fact that much of what I have read so far is true, what can I possibly do about it?" This is a fair question. In the second chapter we argued that radical sociology is based on practice. Of course, all sociologists attempt to gather and test valid information about the world as it exists. But the real test of those ideas, especially if they are radical ideas that criticize existing society, comes when they are used to bring about changes.

Radical sociologists must, therefore, accept the challenge of the question, "What is to be done?" We cannot, however, offer an easy answer. We have no *guru* who promises instant salvation in return for a few prayers, no week-end seminar that promises to totally change your life for a few hundred dollars, no *mantra* that you can mumble under your breath to achieve inner peace. While we have no objection to people seeking to make their private lives tolerable in whatever way they can, our analysis makes us highly skeptical of anyone who promises to solve problems that are rooted in the basic structure of society by treating the individual who is the victim of that society. Social problems of this sort transcend the individual. Thus, our answer to the person who is unhappy with things the way they are but doesn't know what to do about it must be to recall the last words of labor martyr Joe Hill: "Don't mourn. Organize." The first step must be to join together with other people who share your interests and concerns. Only as part of an organized collective effort do you have any real chance of changing society.

Of course, this answer only raises more questions. What group should I join? What should the group do? These are very difficult questions. In the 1960s many radicals thought it was enough to march through the streets with militant slogans and hope that people would see the wisdom of their arguments. And these demonstrations were useful in focusing attention on racial discrimination, the war in Vietnam, and other issues. But the expectations many people had in the 1960s that profound social change could be brought about by a handful of militants shouting slogans, or even by a huge crowd of people parading through Washington, were bound to be disappointed. The radical movement of the 1960s had no adequate analysis of the nature of the society it confronted. In the rush to build a mass movement to confront the urgent issue of Vietnam, expectations were raised beyond any reasonable likelihood of success. This led, inevitably, to disillusionment and withdrawal from political activity.

We should not, however, be overly discouraged by the collapse of the militant social movements of the 1960s. As we study social movements, we learn that it is typical for them to go through periods of intense militance followed by periods of relative inactivity. We can only get an adequate perspective on social movements by studying them objectively and scientifically, just as we study other social phenomena. Only in this way can we obtain reliable knowledge of when movements emerge, of what strategies and tactics they use, and of when they are likely to succeed or fail.

THE NATURE OF SOCIAL MOVEMENTS

Social movements are collective efforts to change societies. Movements arise when societies fail to meet basic human needs. If people's needs were being met, there would be no need for social movements. But unmet needs are not enough to create a social movement. Tremendous oppression and dissatisfaction can exist in a society without generating active movements for change. For a movement to grow, people must feel that there is an alternative to their condition. They must feel that there is at least a reasonable possibility of achieving that alternative. And they must feel that their cause is noble and just, worthy of the time and effort—and even personal risk—which they put into it.

When we consider the tremendous power of the state, and all the institutional advantages held by the ruling class in society, it is a testimony to the human spirit that movements for change arise again and again. Many times these efforts fail, because social conditions were not ready for their success or because of tactical or strategic errors made by their leadership. Failure can cause tremendous suffering and oppression. When the slave revolt led by Spartacus failed in Italy in 71 B.C. the road from Capra to Rome was lined with the crucified bodies of some 6,000 rebellious slaves. When the uprising in Paris in 1871 was crushed, more than 10,000 *communards* were slaughtered by the forces of reaction.

But when social movements succeed, they can bring about tremendous changes in society. Without the English revolutionary movements in the seventeenth century, and the French revolution of 1789, we would not have had modern parliamentary democracies in the Western world. Without the Russian revolution of 1917 or the Chinese revolution of the 1940s Russia and China would not have moved beyond capitalism. Without the suffrage movement, women would not have the vote. Without the civil rights movement, black people would not enjoy the measure of equal rights in American society they have today. Indeed, without the abolitionists they might still be slaves.

Of course, it is very difficult to evaluate the consequences of a social movement, or to do more than speculate about what would have happened had they not existed. While it is hard to know precisely where cause stops and effect begins, we know that social movements are an integral part of the process of social change. People who wish to be more than spectators in the drama of history must join in the movements that are at the cutting edge of change in their time.

Social movements often grow spontaneously, and even the best of leaders may not anticipate developments. Even when a movement has started, it is difficult to predict its course or to know what action to take in order to make it successful. But if we are to be successful in our participation in social movements, we must make every effort to understand the social forces that are behind them. We must try to learn from past experience about what methods have worked, and under what conditions. This chapter is devoted to these questions, with a focus on movements for change in contemporary capitalist society.

TYPES OF SOCIAL MOVEMENTS

There are two basic ways of classifying social movements. One is in terms of the groups or classes they serve and who support them. The other is in terms of the methods they use in advancing the goals of these groups or classes. *Leftist* movements aim to advance the interests of those on the bottom of society. Their struggle is for social equality. The specific classes they represent vary according to the class nature of the society. Thus, in a capitalist society, the left, whenever it is supported by more than a few intellectuals, is based in the working class. Leftists may also be based among groups that have been oppressed because of their racial or ethnic background, or their sex. *Rightist* movements defend the interests of those who are on the top of society. The usual role of these movements is to resist changes proposed by leftist movements, and in so doing to defend the system of inequality.

Of course, there is a whole range of movements from right to left, with some movements representing positions more or less in the middle. Often, these middle-of-the-road movements are supported by the middle classes, who wish to see some changes towards a more egalitarian society but don't want to go too far.

In terms of the methods used, movements can be categorized as *reformist* or *revolutionary*. Reformist movements seek to make limited social changes without upsetting the whole order of society. They seek to make changes gradually and peacefully. Revolutionary movements believe that only a profound change in the basic structure of society will suffice to advance the interests of their supporters. They seek to bring about a total transformation in a short time. Of course, a movement may change from reformist to revolutionary, or vice versa, depending on its appraisal of the situation that it faces. Within any large social movement there are usually revolutionary and reformist tendencies that struggle for control of the movement itself.

How Movements Change

Most movements begin as reformist movements. This is because they emerge in response to a particular problem that is experienced by one group of people. Thus, a movement may emerge among workers at a particular plant against oppressive working conditions and benefits there. Movements may grow among women or members of a minority group to resist some particular discrimination that they suffer as members of an oppressed group. Or a specific injustice such as American intervention in Vietnam may stimulate a movement among certain sectors of society.

These movements are limited both in their geographical spread and in their ideological or political sophistication. They begin as struggles against specific grievances. In many cases, they are successful in reaching their goal. The ruling class, or its representatives with whom they must deal, may decide that the best strategy is to give in to the limited demands made by the movement. As long as the ruling class is able to do this, without compromising its own essential interests, it is impossible for more radical movements to grow.

When, however, conditions are such that the rulers of society cannot accede to the demands raised by limited, moderate social movements, these movements tend to become more radical. They learn that the specific problem that concerned them cannot be solved without making basic changes in the capitalist system itself. They learn that in order to make such basic changes they must join in struggle with other people who are also oppressed by capitalism—with other people who share a class position with them. Thus, under certain conditions, limited movements dealing with specific evils of the system tend to develop into class movements demanding the abolition of the capitalist system and the establishment of an egalitarian and democratic society with dignity for all.

This escalation in the ideologies of movements is usually paralleled by a similar escalation in their tactics. While peaceful petition and protest campaigns are enough to pursue the limited demands of a reformist movement, the powers that be are unwilling to grant more revolutionary demands in response to these methods. As the frustrations of the members grows with the failure of the authorities to grant their

Photo by Neil Benson

A confrontation between police and demonstrators.

demands, they tend to adopt more militant tactics, which provoke more severe repression from the authorities, which can further outrage the revolutionaries and further polarize the situation.

Unless some outside event intervenes to cut off this cycle of confrontation, it continues until one side or the other is defeated. If the authorities are well organized and in firm control of their armed forces, it is usually possible for them to defeat armed revolutionary movements. If those in power are clever, they are likely to make concessions towards the less militant, reformist demands of the movement. By repressing the more radical leadership, and reaching a compromise with the reformers, they are able to avoid revolutionary turmoil while making significant but limited concessions. Thus, the threat of revolution often helps the reformers.

The most frequent course of development for leftist movements in advanced capitalist societies seems to be to go from reformism to revolutionary strategy, and then to retreat back to reformism once the revolution has failed. This pattern was followed by the social democratic and Communist parties of Europe, and similar trends have been followed by the black, student, and women's movements in the United States.

Of course, there are times in history when the revolutionary forces succeed in overthrowing the authorities. While successful social revolutions are relatively infrequent, they are earth-shaking in their consequences. Socialist revolutions in Russia, China, and Cuba, for example, have radically transformed these societies by making fundamental changes in the basic relations of production. These successful revolutions take place when social conditions are ripe. Not even the most dedicated and well-led revolutionary organization can bring about radical change if the masses of people in a society are not ready for it, and if the armed forces of repression have not been weakened either by defeat in war or by internal decadence and decay. Revolutionary groups may facilitate the process by initiating actions that serve as a catalyst for mass uprisings. Or, they may simply be in a position to provide leadership once a more or less spontaneous mass movement has overthrown a repressive regime.

In Russia, for example, revolutionaries were unable to do much more than underground propaganda and organizational work until the tsarist government was fatally weakened by its insistence in pursuing a losing war with Germany. The collapse of this regime occurred as a consequence of spontaneous uprisings while most revolutionary leaders were still in exile. Only after nine months of an ineffective liberal government, which insisted on pursuing the war effort, were the Communists able to take power. In China, the Communists built their armed forces while they were allied with their conservative enemies in a war against the Japanese invaders. In Yugoslavia, Communists came into power because they were the only effective resistance against the German invaders. Cuba is the leading example of a country where the collapse of the ruling class came about as a consequence of internal decadence and decay without being facilitated by defeat in a war.

In the United States and in Western Europe, the authorities have so far been successful in repressing revolutionary movements. In so doing, they have made concessions to the reformers that have greatly improved life in those societies. Reforms such as the eight-hour day, social security, unemployment insurance, medicare, and universal public education came about in good part in response to radical movements. While these reforms undercut some of the most urgent pressures for revolution, they have done so by relieving some of the symptoms of capitalism, not by curing its basic structural contradictions. Tremendous inequalities remain in these societies and provide the motivation for continued pressures for more fundamental social change.

The person who may wish to consider joining a social movement is faced with a serious decision. He or she may be convinced of the need for a revolutionary change in society or may be motivated by the need to solve a more limited societal problem such as environmental pollution, unemployment, militarism, or racial or sexual discrimination. The motivation may be even more localized, a response to abuses by the particular employer that he or she works for or to problems in a particular community or on a college campus. Regardless of the motivation, however, anyone joining a movement will be well advised to think carefully about the likelihood of success. Similarly, once one is involved in a movement, it is necessary to help guide that movement towards strategies and tactics that are likely to be effective under the social conditions existing at the time. This requires an appraisal of a number of social conditions, which are discussed in the next section of this chapter.

CONDITIONS FOR THE SUCCESS OF SOCIAL MOVEMENTS

There are six major social conditions that determine the probability of success of social movements. If all of these conditions are favorable, revolutionary movements can succeed. Reformist movements, however, can often succeed in accomplishing more limited goals if these conditions are only partially present. Two of the conditions must be present before a movement can begin. These preconditions are social inequality and widespread feelings of frustration. Two are necessary for the ideological growth of the movement. These are a decline in the legitimacy of the system and the development of an effective radical ideology or counterconsciousness. And two are necessary for the final success of the movement. These are an effective organization and strategy of the group leading the movement and an ineffective response from the ruling class. We will consider each of these conditions in turn.

Inequality

Social inequality is a necessary source of pressures for social change. Social movements are called into being because inequality is social in origin, i.e., when it is a consequence of social organization. Primitive societies had little power over nature and as a result starvation and other miseries were frequent. But this was no cause for social movements to emerge since the problems were not a result of social oppression.

Poverty, in and of itself, does not result in the development of social movements. Poor peasants in Vietnam or Cuba may have a lower material standard of living than poor whites or blacks in the United States. But this is due to the low level of technological development in these societies, not to exploitation by a wealthy class that monopolizes the fruits of a highly productive economy. Thus, there is no force producing egalitarian social movements in these societies as there is among poor blacks in the United States whose poverty is an artificial social product.

Similarly, middle-class American women live under material conditions that are much more privileged than those of the vast majority of the world's population. There is, however, no reasonable justification for them to be treated as inferior to men with similar educational and social backgrounds or denied equal employment opportunities or access to credit. The humiliation they suffer because of sexist social practices is translated into a social movement because there is no objective material reason why their needs cannot be met except that found in the social structure of society.

What is important is not how poor people are, but how big the gap is between what they have and what they believe they could or should have. Thus, there may be more pressures for change in a relatively wealthy society with a wide range of inequality than in a poor society where everyone suffers from a common poverty.

Frustration

Objective inequality is not sufficient to create social movements. Mere awareness of inequality is not enough to motivate people to go to the trouble of trying to change things. The energy for change comes from the emotions. It comes from feelings of frustration that arise when people's needs are not met. If people were computers that could be programmed to do anything their masters wanted, there would be no pressure for change, even if some computers were treated much worse than others. But people have physical and emotional needs that cannot be met in a class society which gives power and wealth to some at the expense of others.

Frustration of physical needs such as the need for food and shelter can give rise to social movements in a society where the powerful are well fed and housed. In the French Revolution, for example, the force that first drove the masses to the streets was the lack of bread. Sustained social movements, however, require more than mere physical frustration as a motivation. Sustained movements come about because of frustration of people's nonmaterial, emotional drives, especially the drive for dignity. People do not imperil their own or others' lives in a revolutionary movement for unimpressive reasons; nor do they generally risk their lives simply in order to eat. A revolutionary must feel in his or her bones the truth of the maxim that "It is better to die on your feet than to live on your knees." Frustration of material drives generally leads only to pressures for reform. It is frustration of psychological drives that is the motive force for revolution. Revolutionaries are people who feel so degraded by society that they are willing to risk their own lives in an attempt to reestablish dignity for their brothers and sisters in oppression.

Poverty and degradation are permanent features of class societies. These societies have survived as long as they have because they provide escape mechanisms for people. Such mechanisms enable people to relieve some of their frustrations, although they do not resolve the underlying cause. Some of these mechanisms include Messianic religions, consciousness-contracting drugs, alcohol, patriotic movements, escapist movies and television programs, racism, and sexism. A male worker who is frustrated at work may stop off at a bar and get drunk, then come home and take out his remaining frustrations on his wife and children. Or he may take out his hostilities on some racial or ethnic minority that has been used as a scapegoat in rightist propaganda.

Social movements that seek to change oppressive social conditions must, therefore, compete with a whole range of opiates which class societies offer to ameliorate people's frustrations. For movements to be successful, they must show people that

Marching on a picket line is a traditional tactic for raising issues and seeking support.

Photo by Neil Benson

the true cause of their problems lies in the defects of society. The must offer a viable alternative. They must also offer short-term satisfactions, such as comradeship and emotional support, to sustain people during the period of struggle before the movement's ends are achieved. Thus, while frustration is a necessary cause of social movements, it is not sufficient to create effective social movements.

Decline in Legitimacy

Before the energies produced by the inequities of class society can be realized in a social movement, the legitimacy of class society must be undermined. People must lose faith in established authority and its ways of doing things. They must lose faith in the ideologies or rationales that the dominant groups use to justify the current state of affairs.

Reformist movements emerge when people question the legitimacy of only a limited part of the system. They feel that the society is basically good, but that there are limited defects that need to be changed. Often they are enthusiastic about pressuring for change because they believe it will not be difficult to persuade those in power to accept the changes they want. If their appraisal of the situation is correct, their needs will be satisfied by the system. If it is incorrect, they may come to question the legitimacy of the system as a whole when it fails to respond to their demands. In this case, it is essential that they recognize that change would be possible under a different system. Otherwise, they may become resigned and disillusioned, not satisfied with the system but not believing that an alternative is possible. Only when they see the possibility of radical change to create a new system are they ready to support a revolutionary movement.

The ruling class and its supporters have many mechanisms for shoring up people's support for the system. A basic method is to make people feel they are inadequate to question the superior knowledge and wisdom of those in authority. Deference for authority is rooted in the character structure of the masses through the family, schools, media, religion, military training, and the structure of jobs. People are constantly taught to follow orders, accept one's lot in life, and do what they are told. They are conditioned to feel that they are incapable of self-determination, for any number of reasons. Blacks are taught that they are inferior to whites, women that they are inferior to men, workers that they are inferior to managers, students that they are inferior to teachers, voters that they are inferior to politicians, soldiers that they are inferior to officers, etc. Indeed, it is on such conditioning that class society is built. Unless the majority of people have respect for authority and are convinced of their own inadequacy, class society cannot function.

Just as class society generates the inequality and frustration that are the motive force for social movements, so it generates the conditions that lead to the decline in the legitimacy of the system. This is part of the contradictory nature of capitalist and other class societies: the more they develop, the more the contradictions within them become acute. In addition to all the factors associated with class contradictions and economic crises (discussed in Chapters 4 and 5) this happens because of processes such as the following:

1. Advances in scientific knowledge are needed to help the system to grow, but this scientific knowledge tends to undermine belief in traditional religious faiths and other conventional doctrines that support the system.
2. Increased education is needed to prepare people to work in the system, but it also may give some people intellectual tools which enable them to see the weaknesses of the system.
3. Rapid changes in the economic institutions are caused by the growth of the system, but these give people the feeling that change is in the nature of things and that nothing is sacred.
4. Governmental institutions that were adequate to deal with the problem of early capitalism can no longer deal with its mature problems, yet they cannot be changed without giving up the traditional authority they have developed.

5. As people achieve the goals offered by the system, they discover that these goals
    are not as desirable as they seemed. This would appear to be the source of
    large-scale disaffection from advanced monopoly capitalist society, which claims
    its reason for being is its ability to deliver material goods. As more and more of
    the working class attain a relatively high material standard of living (where none
    of their material drives are frustrated), the hollowness of their aspirations for ma-
    terial affluence becomes increasingly apparent. The appeal of working for ever
    more material goods is undermined and replaced by an increasing consciousness
    that the goal of life ought to be the satisfaction of the *non*-material drives, such as
    the drives for meaningful work, community, dignity, and love.

It is not only the decline of the authority of the dominant institutions such as the
church, the state, the presidency or the monarchy, and the boss that is critical but
also the decline in the legitimacy of the traditional safety-valve institutions of the society. The possibility of political radicalization increases as faith in Messianic religion,
drugs, and reformist political parties dwindles. The decline of the legitimacy of
these safety-valve institutions means that the energies previously tied up in these
activities is released for mobilization by radical political movements.

Alternative Ideology

It is not enough that people are turned off; they must also get turned on. It takes
more than the belief that the present order of things is bad or even that things could
be different. The masses of the oppressed must come to believe that things *should*
and *ought* to be different, and further, they must be convinced that they can have an
effect in bringing about the necessary change. Unless people feel they can have an effect they will turn to nonpolitical alternatives such as drugs, fads, or religion, rather
than to political activities that they are convinced could not make a difference. Thus,
one way in which dominant groups retard the development of movements for change
is by encouraging political cynicism, that is, the feelings that all politicians are corrupt,
socialism would be as bad as capitalism, that it makes no difference who the leaders
are or what the system is, and that it is not worth the trouble to change the political
system. The defeatism encouraged by the system serves the same purpose. The belief
that any attempt to change the existing order would be crushed or that the existing
order is so powerful that no act of resistance to it could hope to succeed results naturally in inaction, as well as bitterness. Cynicism and defeatism are major obstacles for
any potentially massive revolutionary movement to overcome.

A popular ideology explains the sources of popular oppression as products of the
socially unnecessary existing institutional arrangements, outlines an alternative form
of social organization where social relationships would be based on fraternity and
equality, and moreover, instructs in the way to overthrow the existing system of

Common social aspirations are symbolized in this wall painting.

social relationships and establish a new one (including advice on necessary strategies, tactics, and organizational forms). An effective revolutionary ideology serves as a vocabulary by which to articulate the frustrations of the people and to make alternative ways of living real for them. Such ideologies, once formulated by intellectuals or revolutionary organizations, can spread very rapidly, serving as a catalyst in awakening the energies of people alienated from the system but who had not previously been convinced that anything could be done about it. Thus, virtually all successful revolutionary movements of recent times began with a few intellectuals, or a small organization of committed cadre, and caught on very rapidly because they brought to the masses of the oppressed a message that they wanted to hear—a message that accurately reflected their social situations and provided them with a realistic hope for liberation.

Marx, Engels, Lenin, Mao Tse-tung, Ho Chi Minh, "Che" Guevara, and the majority of revolutionary leaders were middle-class intellectuals who developed or became converts to revolutionary analyses while students in universities. As students, they made the decision to dedicate their lives to bringing the revolutionary message to the oppressed. Many succeeded marvelously, but only because the theories they articulated fit well with the situations of those they addressed, and only because the strategies, tactics, and organizational forms suggested by the ideologies worked. Exactly why it is that significant numbers of upwardly mobile students from middle-class backgrounds defect to revolutionary causes in times of crises is not fully understood. Probably some combination of sympathy for human suffering, intellectual understanding, their own oppression as students or anticipated oppression in their careers, and personal rejection of their own families results in the defections that occur. Whatever the motives, revolutionary movements without such defecting intellectuals would probably be impossible, since they almost always play the central leadership role in successful or near-successful movements against capitalism. Just as capitalism generates the preconditions of movements dedicated to destroying it and further damages the legitimacy of its institutions, it likewise produces the leaders and the ideology of working people's movements committed to revolution.

Intellectuals are only one source of anticapitalist ideology. By creating the conditions that greatly facilitate intercommunication among people in similar oppressive conditions, capitalism facilitates the development of a common consciousness among many people. The more people in a similar oppressive situation communicate with one another, the more they are likely to develop a common understanding of the sources of their oppression and an alternative vision of a different mode of life. Moreover, they are more likely to feel their strength through coming to understand the importance of the work they do and the power of their numbers in potentially changing the system. Thus, capitalism, by building larger and larger factories, by eliminating most of the independent petty bourgeoisie, by creating working-class living districts, and by constructing modern communication and transportation facilities, encourages more and more communication among people in the same class situation, who thereby tend to develop a class consciousness and an understanding of their power.

The belief that things could be different is affected by the rate of mobility in a society. The more upward mobility, the more people realize that they are not inherently inferior, and the higher the probability that the existing justifications that claim that the producing classes must necessarily be subordinate to the ruling classes is undermined. The belief in the natural inferiority of the producing class is eroded not only for the individuals who are upwardly mobile but for those who observe this upward mobility in others as well.

The belief that things should and must be different increases when people lose confidence in the possibilities of their own individual advancement, or perhaps more crucially, in the individual advancement of their children (since oppressed people so often live vicariously through their children). The less that people who are not convinced of their own innate inferiority feel they can get ahead as individuals, the more likely they are to turn to political solutions to answer the compulsion of their frustrations. That is, the more likely they are to adopt ideologies that claim that the social order should and can be different from what it is.

Long-term improvement in economic and social conditions tends to create the general feeling that improvement is natural and an expectation that things can and should continue to get better. A sharp reversal in the long-term improvement in social and economic conditions has the effect of giving people the idea that things *must* be different, i.e., that the current system is the obstacle to the continued improvement of their lot.

Very frequently, the first segment of the oppressed population to become radicalized is not the most oppressed, but rather the relatively less oppressed. During the earlier stages of the development of a radical movement, it is usually students, teachers, skilled and highly skilled workers who first become involved. During this stage, the more oppressed strata remain politically apathetic or conservative and hostile to radicalism. However, as a radical movement grows, it increasingly involves the more oppressed strata of the working classes and peasantry. Once mobilized, the greater frustration and deprivation of these groups drives them to become more radical than the relatively more privileged groups that had earlier been the left wing. When a movement is on the decline, this may work in reverse. The more oppressed, who during the peak of a movement had been the most militant and leftist, may become demobilized before the more skilled and professional groups. These latter groups thus can return to the left of the movement.

The more educated strata of the oppressed have a greater access to news, history, political economy, and the workings of the state, as well as generally a propensity to communicate with one another more explicitly about political issues. The feeling that the present order is not immutable is encouraged in the intermediate groups by their own life experiences of mobility, while the downtrodden's sense of futility is often reinforced by their own life failures. These factors lead the relatively less oppressed to develop the feeling that not only can and should things be different but that they can have an effect on changing things, much sooner than the less literate, more isolated, and terrorized sections of the population.

It would appear that as long as frustration stemming from class society is present, a group is potentially revolutionary no matter how much better off it might be than some other oppressed group. Whether or not an oppressed group will be radical cannot be predicted by how oppressed it is. The extent of oppression determines only how militant and leftist the potential radicalism of a strata is. Whether or not a group is actually radical is a result of the decline of legitimacy and the availability of a revolutionary ideology.

Organization, Strategy, and Tactics

It is not enough that a socially oppressed group becomes conscious of its situation and develops a desire and understanding of how to make things different. In order to have a reasonable chance at success, it must have access to an effective organization, strategy, and tactics. By *tactics*, we mean the actual techniques used by a political movement to gain power; by *strategy*, the way these techniques are put together in order to attempt to win; by *organization*, the internal structure of coordination among the members of the movement.

Social movements use a wide variety of organizational structures. Some are tightly disciplined and have the full commitment of their members. Others are more loosely organized, with decisions being made in mass meetings and with members free to decide when they will or will not go along with the will of the majority. Others consist of localized collectives without any central leadership at all. A tightly organized and disciplined group is more capable of operating under highly repressive conditions; indeed it may function secretly in a society that prohibits leftist social movements. These movements have been successful in seizing power in a number of countries, such as Russia and China, largely because they had disciplined cadres ready to assume leadership during periods of social conflict and disorganization. The test of practice shows that this form of organization has been quite effective since it was first perfected in the Russian revolutionary movement.

This does not mean, however, that a tightly disciplined Leninist form of organization is the most appropriate under all conditions. At the early stages of a movement, before a mass base has been developed, it is often more effective to build a loose political organization that can reach out to large numbers of people whose commitment to the cause of the movement is not yet deep. Once a movement has developed into a serious mass movement, it may well turn to Leninist forms of organization if reformist politics prove ineffective.

Critics of Leninist forms of organization have expressed concern that these forms tend towards authoritarianism since they may concentrate power in the hands of small groups of leaders. They argue that any excesses of power of the Soviet bureaucracy during the Stalin years in the Soviet Union show the danger of a highly disciplined and centralized movement assuming state power. On the other hand, these critics have not been able to develop any other form of organization that can successfully make and consolidate an actual socialist revolution. Consequently, Leninist models of organization are most frequently supported by activists who feel that revolutionary change is necessary, while decentralized forms tend to be used more frequently by reformist groups. Of course, in many movements both forms of organization exist alongside each other and play complementary or competing roles.

Just as activists have differed greatly on questions of organization, they have differed on questions of the best tactics and strategies to be used. There are a tremendous variety of tactics available to movements. These range from the most peaceful and innocuous of tactics such as circulating petitions, writing letters to Congresspeople, and running candidates in elections, to more assertive nonviolent tactics like mass demonstrations, sit-ins, strikes, and boycotts, to violent strategies and tactics such as armed insurrections, guerrilla warfare, bombings and assassinations, and military coups after infiltrating the armed forces.

The choice of tactics depends on larger strategic considerations, i.e., on an ap-

Photo by Neil Benson

A demonstration to save a free public hospital.

praisal of what combination of approaches is likely to be effective given the social conditions in a society at a particular point in time. This depends on the changing consciousness and condition of the masses, and on the condition of the state apparatus. There is no one strategy that is appropriate under all conditions. Generally speaking, less militant means are appropriate at the early stages of a movement when the main goal is to raise people's consciousness about the nature and causes of their problems. Only after people's consciousness has been raised, and after attempts at peaceful reform have failed, are the masses of people likely to feel the need for militant revolutionary measures.

Even the most dedicated revolutionary must accept the fact that often nothing can be done to bring about a revolution at a particular point in time. There is little or nothing that can be done about the basic conditions of class inequality in a society, and not too much that can be done to delegitimize the existing regime. Revolutionaries have the greatest impact in developing alternative ideologies to those of the state, and in choosing organizational forms, strategies, and tactics. It is here that the decision making of revolutionary groups can make a difference. There are some situations where, because the conditions for a successful revolution are not present, even optimal organizational forms, strategies, and tactics would be bound to fail. There are other situations where even the most inept organizational forms, strategies, and tactics decided on by revolutionaries could succeed, because all the other conditions are so ripe for revolution that it would happen in spite of the effort of the revolutionaries. But most of the time in capitalist societies, the organizational forms, strategies, and tactics adopted by revolutionaries do make a difference. There have been revolutionary attempts that probably failed because of the decisions of the revolutionaries (Germany, 1918; Hungary, 1919; France, 1944 and perhaps, 1968) and those that have succeeded because of such decisions (Russia, 1917; Cuba, 1959; China, 1949). It should be noted that almost every successful revolutionary movement in the twentieth century has been guided by Marxist-Leninist ideas on organization, strategy, and tactics. This, combined with the fact that virtually all oppositional movements in capitalist countries during this same time period have gravitated toward Marxism-Leninism (the black movement in the United States, the student movement everywhere, the IWW, the anarchist working-class movements that developed into the Communist parties of Europe), gives great support to the Marxist-Leninist claim that they have developed a *science* of revolution.

Response of the Privileged

All the preconditions for revolution and the conditions of consciousness could be ripe and the revolutionary movement could have the most effective organizational forms and strategy, yet if the ruling class makes the proper response it can usually prevent a successful revolution. Normally, only if the ruling class makes mistakes will a revolutionary movement succeed. If a ruling class has faith in itself and what it stands for, and the historical and sociological sense of how to respond to the revolutionary challenge, it is usually able to win. But when because of loss at war, the disaffection of its youth, widespread corruption, severe internal divisions, or simple loss of will, a ruling class loses confidence in itself, it is highly unlikely that it could get itself together enough to meet the challenge from below. Instead, a challenge to a disunited and weak ruling class is met by greater disunity and widespread willingness to make significant concessions, for example, as in czarist Russia when the ruling class was split into pro- and anti-czarist camps.

Even if a ruling class is together, it may still fail to turn back the thrust from below unless it adopts the proper strategy. The ruling class has essentially two basic strategies open to it: repression and manipulation-cooption. It can choose to follow a hard line of putting down demonstrations with force, jailing, executing, or driving into exile the leaders, banning oppositional organizations, etc. At times, this is the most effective response. The ruling class can also follow the opposite strategy of making nonessential concessions with a lot of publicity to make the oppressed class *think* significant gains are being made, giving great rewards (of money, prestige, or position) to the leaders of oppositional organizations, granting concessions now with the intention of withdrawing them as soon as things quiet down, changing the personnel in power as well as the official ideology without changing the substance of power, etc. At times, such a course is the most effective strategy. Just as is the case with the strategic options open to the revolutionaries there is no rule of thumb here. The wise ruling class must learn from its successes and failures informed by history and social science. However, it is frequently best to follow a mixed policy that attempts to buy off those leaders who are for sale and grant impressive-sounding concessions to the masses, while at the same time repressing the more militant and principled leadership. This strategy is designed to split the masses from their more radical leaders, thereby destroying the power of the opposition. This was the strategy followed by the U.S. ruling class in the face of an increasingly radical challenge from the black movement in the 1960s. The heads of some reformist organizations were given government positions, and some highly publicized but nonsubstantial concessions were made in the form of formal integration and poverty programs, while the militant leadership of the Black Panthers and other such revolutionary organizations were assassinated, jailed, framed on conspiracy charges, or driven into exile. The net result of this effort was the separation of black people from their more radical leadership and their gratitude to the more reformist leaders who have come to administer the various ruling-class handouts.

LOOKING TOWARD THE FUTURE

The progressive movements in the United States are at a low ebb, following a peak of radical enthusiasm in the late 1960s. This is not surprising. As we noted earlier, social movements occur in cycles, frequently characterized by a more or less spontaneous breakthrough on their up-swing. A revolutionary movement usually peaks with an attempt to come to power. If it fails, demoralization often sets in and deflates the energy of both the cadre and their supporters. This may lead to the gradual withering away of the revolutionary organization, or its decay into a tiny, ineffective, sectarian group.

A peak in a movement can also be reached because of poor decisions by the leadership. The leadership may attempt to seize power when there is no realistic opportunity for doing so. Or they may "sell out," making concessions to the authorities unnecessarily, under conditions when revolution is possible. An organization out of touch with the consciousness of its base can get too far ahead or too far behind the masses of the oppressed and lose their confidence and support. People will thus turn away from the organization and perhaps away from political solutions altogether, in favor of drugs, religion, or other forms of escapism.

Often, because of their enthusiasm, radical leaders exaggerate their own support and underestimate the capability of the state to repress them or to co-opt their supporters. This certainly occurred during the 1960s when leaders such as Rennie Davis organized unrealistic attempts to radically transform state policies by marching on Washington and "stopping the government." This was not much more rational than his later belief that flying saucers would descend to greet his "perfect master" at the Houston astrodome. When a movement sets unrealistic goals, it is easy for the state to repress it. However, it must be noted that often conditions are such that even the most rationally and carefully chosen tactics cannot succeed.

Once a movement goes on the defensive and begins losing support, the decline often accelerates and more and more supporters become demoralized, lose the sense that they can change things and that things could be different, and drift away. There is, however, a natural bottoming out to this phase of decline. The underlying structural contradictions that gave rise to the movements are still present. Reformist organizations continue to try to deal with these problems, and their activists may become increasingly radicalized. A new generation emerges, bringing new enthusiasm not corrupted by the cynicism and defeatism of their older brothers and sisters. Perhaps because of a new crisis in society, the example of a successful revolution somewhere else, disillusionment with drugs and religion, or because of the inspiration of a new set of young leaders, popular consciousness again becomes more and more optimistic about the hopes and possibilities of social transformation. Optimism feeds on itself just as pessimism did. People feel stronger and stronger and the possibilities for radical transformation look more and more real.

Even the most superficial observer today can recognize that the conditions for revolution are not now fully developed in American society. However, the ability of social scientists—or of revolutionaries—to predict the future of social movements is not impressive. During the 1950s everyone commented on the apathy and complacency of American youth. While some radicals expected that the working class would become radicalized, no one—radical or conservative—predicted the emergence of student radicalism in the 1960s. No one predicted the growth of the civil rights movement and revolutionary militancy among blacks. Leaders in other countries have been similarly unable to predict the course of events. Even that most insightful and effective revolutionary leader, V. I. Lenin, wrote in January, 1917, that he did not expect to see a revolution in Russia in his lifetime. Yet, within two months, a spontaneous uprising of the people had overthrown the centuries-old tsarist regime. Revolutionary waves often break out spontaneously with little or no instigation by organized movements.

While we would be foolish to claim that we can do better than others have in the past in predicting the future of the progressive movement in our country, we can at least point out that the fact that the movement in the late 1970s is at a low ebb does not mean that it will not renew itself in the 1980s. Let us examine the state of each of the six conditions for the success of a movement in the United States today. Of course, we recognize that our appraisal may become rapidly out of date as conditions change.

Inequality

Serious inequality remains a persistent problem in American society. The degree of inequality has not changed significantly since the 1930s. Under the capitalist mode of production, we can expect this condition to remain as a constant force creating dissatisfaction and potential pressures for change.

Frustration

Much of the frustration of the 1960s was caused by rising expectations. People expected things to get better, and were promised improvement by politicians. Frustration among minorities and women was also great because they expected equal treatment with white men. Today, these sources of frustration are declining. People have been told by their leaders and by the media that they should not expect things to get better because of the energy crisis, pollution, etc. Racial and sexual inequality are declining. However, new sources of frustration are emerging, in part because of the decline of the United States as a world power, persistent economic stagnation, and the growth of a college-educated class that cannot find suitable employment. A sudden collapse in the economy might greatly increase levels of frustration; however, given the level of our knowledge of economic cycles we cannot predict accurately whether or not this is likely to happen.

Decline in Legitimacy

Belief in the legitimacy of the system is significantly lower than it was in the 1940s and 1950s. To a great extent this is a result of Vietnam and Watergate, as well as of the continuing inability of the government to resolve economic problems such as inflation and unemployment. Major corporations, such as the oil monopolies, are widely distrusted. Bourgeois political leaders are aware of this decline in legitimacy, and have placed great emphasis on restoring "confidence in government." Corporate leaders have increased their efforts to propagandize for the "free enterprise" system. The increase in crime, especially mass looting as happened during the 1977 blackout in New York City, reveals that rejection of the system is widespread, particularly among the most oppressed groups in the society, and is ready to be expressed when an opportunity presents itself.

Alternative Ideologies

The United States is unique among advanced capitalist nations in the weakness of ideologies that present an alternative to the capitalist system. Experience in other countries shows that alternative ideologies do not develop spontaneously among the people. Rather, they must be developed and systematically brought to the people by organized political parties. The immediate prospect for progressive change is greater in Western Europe than in the United States today, because the socialist and Communist parties of those nations have systematically educated the masses in alternative ideologies.

Effective Organization, Strategy, and Tactics

The United States lacks an effective revolutionary socialist party with a mass base among the working class. It also lacks a mass reformist social-democratic party, although the liberal wing of the Democratic Party espouses many of the same reforms that have been favored by the social-democratic parties of Europe. This lack is due to peculiarities of American history, such as the open frontier, the racial and ethnic divisions within the working class, the high standard of living of U.S. workers, and the long period of American dominance in the world system. These factors made it possible for the ruling class to divide and destroy militant working-class parties, while offering sufficient reforms to the masses of workers to cut their feelings of frustration and urgency in demanding change.

There is every reason to anticipate that the period of American exceptionalism will end as the United States loses its dominance in the world, as racial, ethnic, and sexual divisions among the working class are lessened, and as the contradictions inherent in the capitalist economy continue to develop. Some radicals believe that the Democratic Party will be captured by leftist elements and converted into a social-democratic party. Others believe that a new party based on the labor movement and the working class will be organized. There are also a number of small Marxist-Leninist parties and organizations that are attempting to build a base in the working class.

Given the lack of a mass socialist organization, many activists in the 1970s have focused their efforts on movements that are more limited in their goals. These movements deal with the problems of specific groups, such as women, blacks, Puerto Ricans, farm workers, etc. Or they deal with specific problems, such as environmental pollution, nuclear power plants, high military spending, or the need to support activists who are suffering torture in countries such as Chile and Iran. Or they focus on problems in specific communities, working on things such as food co-operatives, bookstores, health clinics, etc. Each of these specific movements can play a useful role, both in helping to ameliorate specific problems and in building consciousness and organization. However, if the analysis presented in this book is correct, the problems that they deal with cannot be resolved until these specific movements become part of a broader movement designed to change the fundamental production relationships in society.

Response of the Privileged

The American upper class and state apparatus are fairly well organized, in comparison to many other ruling groups in the world, and are reasonably skillful in combining repression with co-optation in responding to movements for change. There are differences within the ruling class along regional, interest, and ideological lines, but the ruling class remains united in its fundamental determination to defend the capitalist system. It retains the allegiance of large sectors of the professional and managerial class which profit from the existing system.

The Vietnam war and black ghetto riots of the 1960s showed, however, that there are limits to the extent to which the ruling class can count on its armed forces to repress revolutionary movements either in this country or in the empire. The American army was near a state of collapse in Vietnam, with soldiers committing open acts of mutiny and even killing officers who insisted on ordering them into battle. In this country the police and military succeeded in repressing the ghetto and youth riots. However, it is not proven how effective they would be against an uprising of white workers.

CONCLUSIONS

Given the low level of organizational and ideological development in the United States, there is no one "correct" political strategy that can be guaranteed to be successful. Priority must be given to developing an alternative ideology that is capable of generating enthusiasm among the masses of the people, to spreading consciousness of this ideology among the people, and to building organizational forms that will be capable of effective leadership. Some people believe a strong Leninist party is needed so that revolutionaries will be prepared to seize power if the system collapses due to a crisis. Others believe that at this time, at least, the best that can be done is to press for reforms in the hope of building consciousness and commitment while educating people in the eventual need for more fundamental changes. There is no reason why these two kinds of activities cannot go on simultaneously, with the relative successes and failures of such activities eventually determining which is most effective. The conditions for revolutionary change are much more favorable in many other countries around the world than they are in the United States, and readers in those countries will naturally want to make their own estimation of them.

We recognize that many readers will not share our political convictions and will choose to avoid involvement in radical movements. However, the vast majority of our readers, whether or not they are able to pursue middle-class careers, will find their lives shaped by the contradictions of the capitalist society in which they must earn their living. Attempts to find individualistic solutions to these problems must eventually prove ineffective. We can only hope that as people's consciousness of this fact grows, so too will their commitment to joining together to work for a solution.

Summary

Social movements develop when large numbers of people join together in efforts to change social conditions that are oppressive to their real or perceived human needs. Leftist movements advance the interests of those on the bottom of class societies, while rightist movements defend the interests of those on top. Reformist movements seek to make limited changes within the framework of existing society, while revolutionary movements work toward profound changes in social structure. Most movements begin with limited goals and become more revolutionary if they discover that their needs cannot be met within the limitations of existing society.

Movements emerge when conditions of social inequality are felt as frustrating by a large class of people, when the legitimacy of the existing system is undermined, and when an effective radical ideology wins support among the people. They are most successful when they build an effective organization, and when the response from the ruling class is ineffective. Movements can succeed only when the contradictions of the existing system have created social conditions that facilitate their growth and weaken the ability of the power structure to resist them. Under some conditions only limited reformist movements can succeed in attracting a mass following, while at other times revolutionary movements can make profound changes in social relationships.

At the present time in the United States, social inequality, frustration, and disillusionment with the system are relatively high. Alternative ideologies are not well diffused among the people, however; nor are radical forces well organized. The state retains considerable effectiveness in repressing radical movements and co-opting reformers. These conditions may well change as the position of the United States in the world system continues to decline and the inherent contradictions of its capitalist productive system continue to develop.

Review Questions

1. What are some of the reasons for the collapse of many of the radical movements of the 1960s?

2. What are some of the changes in societies that have been brought about by social movements?

3. Why do reformist movements often develop into revolutionary movements, then sometimes return to reformism?

4. How have authorities in the United States and Western Europe dealt with revolutionary workers' movements?

5. What are the six conditions for the success of social movements?

6. What is the role of intellectuals in social movements?

7. Why do social movements sometimes break out after a long period of improvement in social and economic conditions?

8. Which segments of an oppressed population are often the first to become active in social movements?

9. Under what conditions is a tightly organized and disciplined social movement likely to be necessary for success?

10. What is the difference between strategy and tactics?

11. What are some of the errors that leaders of social movements can make?

12. What strategy have leaders of the Western European socialist and Communist parties adopted in recent years?

13. What are the major weaknesses of progressive forces in the United States?

Suggestions for Further Study

1. Attend at least one public meeting or event organized by a social movement in your area. Observe what kinds of people are present, in terms of their social background and group affiliations. Determine as much as you can of the ideology of the movement, of its own conception of the problems of society that it is trying to confront, and the solutions it offers. What strategies and tactics does the movement use in furthering its goals? How is it organized? What would be your appraisal of the likelihood of success given social conditions in your area as best as you know them? You may find out a great deal more if you interview some of the active members of the movement.

2. Many areas of the country have a rich history of active social movements, even if these movements are not active today. Question some people who have lived in your community for many years in an attempt to find individuals who were active in these movements. For example, perhaps you can find someone who was active in the labor movement in the 1930s, in the civil rights movement in the 1950s or 1960s, or in the movement against the Vietnam war in the late 1960s. Interview at least one such person, finding out as much as you can about the history of the movement. How do they appraise its effectiveness today?

3. Choose one social movement that particularly interests you. Read as much of the published literature on this movement as you can. Which of the six conditions for the success of social movements facilitated its success? Which made its efforts more difficult? What is the present state of the movement?

Selected Readings

Brenan, Gerald. *The Spanish Labyrinth*. Cambridge, G.B.: Cambridge U. Press, 1960 (1943).

Brinton, Crane. *The Anatomy of Revolution*. New York: Vintage, 1963 (1938).

Caute, David. *The Left in Europe Since 1789*. New York: McGraw-Hill, 1966.

Chakotin, Sergei. *The Rape of the Masses*. New York: Alliance, 1940.

Chorley, Katherine. *Armies and the Art of Revolution*. Boston: Beacon, 1973 (1943).

Dubofsky, Melvyn. *We Shall be All*. Chicago: Quadrangle, 1969.

Fanon, Frantz. *The Wretched of the Earth*. New York: Grove, 1966.

Foster, William Z. *History of the Communist Party of the U.S.A*. Westport, Conn.: Greenwood, 1969 (1952).

Giap, Vo Nguyen. *People's War, People's Army*. New York: Praeger, 1962.

Gorz, Andre. *Strategy for Labor*. Boston: Beacon, 1968.

Gramsci, Antonio. *The Modern Prince and Other Essays*. New York: International, 1959.

Guevara, Ernesto "Che." *Guerilla Warfare*. New York: Monthly Review, 1961.

Hicks, John. *The Populist Revolt*. Lincoln: U. of Nebraska Press, 1961 (1931).

Hinton, William. *Fanshen*. New York: Random House, 1966.

Hobsbawm, Eric. *Primitive Rebels*. New York: Norton, 1965.

Lanternari, Victorio. *The Religions of the Oppressed*. New York: Knopf, 1963.

Laslett, John M., and Lipset, Seymour Martin. *Failure of a Dream?* Garden City, N.Y.: Doubleday, 1974.

Lefebvre, Georges. *The Coming of the French Revolution*. Princeton, N.J.: Princeton U. Press, 1947.

Lenin, V. I. *Selected Works*. Moscow: Foreign Languages Publishing House, 1967. See especially *What Is to be Done; The State and Revolution; Left-Wing Communism: An Infantile Disorder*.

Lipset, Seymour Martin. *Agrarian Socialism: the Cooperative Commonwealth Federation in Saskatchewan*. Berkeley: U. of California Press, 1967 (1950).

Mao Tse-Tung. *Selected Works in Four Volumes*. Peking: Foreign Languages Publishing House, 1961–1967; See especially "Analysis of Classes in Chinese Society," "Report on Investigation of the Peasant Movement in Hunan," "On Practice," "On Contradiction," "The Chinese Revolution and the Chinese Communist Party," "On Protracted War," "On New Democracy," and "Rectify the Party's Style of Work."

Marx, Karl, and Engels, Frederick. *The Communist Manifesto* in *Selected Works in One Volume*. Moscow: Foreign Languages, 1958 (1848).

Minh, Ho Chi. *On Revolution*. Edited by Bernard Fall. New York: New American Library, 1967.

Moore, Barrington. *Social Origins of Dictatorship and Democracy*. Boston: Beacon, 1967.

Neuberg, A. *Armed Insurrection*. New York, St. Martin's, 1970.

Pike, Douglas. *Viet Cong*. Cambridge, Mass.: MIT Press, 1966.

Pollack, Norman. *The Populist Response to Industrial America*. Cambridge, Mass.: Harvard U. Press, 1962.

Rude, George. *The Crowd in History*. New York: Wiley, 1964.

Selznick, Philip. *The Organizational Weapon*. New York: McGraw-Hill, 1952.

Stalin, Joseph. *The Foundations of Leninism*, in Bruce Franklin (ed.), *The Essential Stalin*. Garden City, N.Y.: Anchor Books, 1972 (1924).

Trotsky, Leon. *The History of the Russian Revolution*. Ann Arbor: U. of Michigan Press, 1957 (1932).

Weinstein, James. *The Decline of Socialism in America*. New York: Monthly Review, 1967.

Wolf, Eric. *Peasant Wars of the 20th Century*. New York: Harper & Row, 1970.

Index